P9-APL-400

macromedia®
dreamweaver® mx
training from the source

khristine annwn page

macromedia®
PRESS

Macromedia Dreamweaver MX: Training from the Source

Published by Macromedia Press, in association with Peachpit Press, a division of Pearson Education.

Macromedia Press
1249 Eighth Street
Berkeley, CA 94710
510/524-2178
510/524-2221 (fax)
Find us on the World Wide Web at:
http://www.peachpit.com
http://www.macromedia.com

Copyright © 2003 by Macromedia, Inc.

All rights reserved. No part of this book may be reproduced or transmitted in any form or by any means, electronic, mechanical, photocopying, recording, or otherwise, without the prior written permission of Macromedia, Inc.

Notice of Liability
The information in this book and on the CD-ROM is distributed on an "as is" basis, without warranty. While every precaution has been taken in the preparation of the book and the CD-ROM, neither Macromedia, Inc., its licensors, nor Macromedia Press shall have any liability to any person or entity with respect to liability, loss, or damage caused or alleged to be caused directly or indirectly by the instructions contained in this book or by the computer software and hardware products described herein.

Trademarks
Macromedia is a registered trademark of Macromedia, Inc. Other product names mentioned within this publication may be trademarks or registered trademarks of other companies.

Printed and bound in the United States of America

ISBN 0-201-79929-4

9 8 7 6 5

CREDITS

Author
Khristine Annwn Page

Production Coordinator
Myrna Vladic

Compositors
Rick Gordon, Emerald Valley Graphics
Debbie Roberti, Espresso Graphics

Editors
Kari Brooks, Wendy Sharp

Indexer
Emily Glossbrenner

Technical Review
Angela Drury, Macromedia
Corona Rivera, Macromedia

ACKNOWLEDGMENTS

Thanks to the many people who have helped and made possible much of the work on this book and the "Lights of the Coast" Web site, the profiled Web sites and the people who created them, and the authors of Dreamweaver extensions.

In particular, I'd like to express my gratitude to all of my family and friends for their patience, support, and encouragement during the writing of 'the book'. Many thanks and Blessings to Mary, Rick, and Richard Page for just about everything; to Wendy Sharp and Kari Brooks for your patience, direction, and ability to keep everything on track; to Laura Tempest Schmidt for keeping me sane; to Keith Schmidt for driving me crazy; to Bryon Kennedy for all your help, love, and great work on the Web site; and to the Fates. :)

DEDICATION

For both of my grandmothers

table of contents

introduction

Macromedia's Dreamweaver MX combines visual layout tools with text-based HTML editing features for the creation, management, and maintenance of Web sites. It gives beginners immediate access to the tools needed for creating Web pages, while allowing experienced developers who are familiar with hand-coding to work directly with the code when needed. This flexible program makes advanced techniques accessible and easy to use. The integration of powerful design, code, and reference features provides a wealth of benefits to both beginners and advanced users.

This book is intended to familiarize you with the Dreamweaver development environment and focuses on equipping you with the skills needed to lay out and design Web pages. Because it is geared toward beginner and intermediate users who may have little or no previous experience with Dreamweaver, coverage of advanced application building and dynamic Web site creation with the use of databases, server behaviors, and Web applications is outside the scope of this book. These features require knowledge and understanding of dynamic design concepts, and of the languages used to create these sites including ASP, JSP, ColdFusion and more. For those who are interested in learning about the code, Lesson 12 will get you started in the coding environment, demonstrating how to work with Dreamweaver's coding tools and pointing you to resources within the program that will enable you to learn more.

This Macromedia training course steps you through the projects in each lesson, presents the major features and tools in Dreamweaver MX, and guides you toward developing the skills you need to create Web sites. This curriculum should take approximately 21 hours to complete and includes the following lessons:

Lesson 1: Dreamweaver MX Basics
Lesson 2: Working with Graphics
Lesson 3: Creating Links
Lesson 4: Elements of Page Design
Lesson 5: Adding User Interactivity

The project site that you will be working on throughout the book, "Lights of the Coast," explores the history, technology, and culture of lighthouses. This is just one example of the kinds of Web sites that you can create with Dreamweaver. You can see the actual "Lights of the Coast" Web site online at http://www.northwindstudios.com/lighthouse.

Additional examples of Web sites that can be created with Dreamweaver are provided at the end of many of the lessons. There you will have the opportunity to see how the concepts are used in other real-world examples and use materials from those sites to complete a suggested activity for more practice with the skills you have learned in the respective lesson.

Each lesson begins by outlining the major focus of the lesson and introducing new features. Learning objectives and the approximate time needed to complete all the exercises are also listed at the beginning of each lesson. The projects are divided into short exercises that explain the importance of each skill you learn. Every lesson will build on the concepts and techniques used in the previous lessons.

This training course also features the following elements:

Tips: Alternative ways to perform tasks and suggestions to consider when applying the skills you are learning.

Notes: Additional background information to expand your knowledge, as well as advanced techniques you can explore in order to further develop your skills.

Boldface terms: New vocabulary that is introduced and emphasized in each lesson.

Blue text: Text that you will need to type.

Menu commands and keyboard shortcuts: There are often multiple ways to perform the same task in Dreamweaver. The different options will be pointed out in each lesson. Menu commands are shown with angle brackets between the menu names and commands: Menu › Command › Subcommand. Keyboard shortcuts are shown with a plus sign between the names of keys to indicate that you should press the keys simultaneously; for example, Shift+Tab means that you should press the Shift and Tab keys at the same time.

Appendixes: Appendix A contains a table with special characters, regular expressions, and their meanings for use with Dreamweaver's Find and Replace feature, covered in Lesson 14. Appendixes B and C provide shortcuts for Dreamweaver commands for use on Macintosh and Windows systems, respectively.

CD-ROM: The files you will need to complete the projects for each lesson are located in the DWMX_project folder on the enclosed CD. Inside the project folder are subfolders titled with the name of the lesson—Lesson_01_Text, for example—that contain the subfolders and files necessary to perform the tasks in the respective lesson. Which subfolders are included will depend on the projects in the lesson. Common subfolders include *Completed*, which contains the completed files for each lesson so you can compare your work and see the end result of the project; *Images*, which contains all the images necessary for the lesson; and *Text*, which includes text documents you will need to import into Dreamweaver. The files you will use for each of the projects are listed at the beginning of each lesson.

For additional practice with the skills you will learn in each lesson, try recreating the starting files that have been provided for you in the lesson files.

MACROMEDIA TRAINING FROM THE SOURCE

The Macromedia Training from the Source and Advanced Training from the Source series are developed in association with Macromedia, and reviewed by the product support teams. Ideal for active learners, the books in the Training from the Source series offer hands-on instruction designed to provide you with a solid grounding in the program's fundamentals.

The instructions in this book are designed for Web designers, Web developers, and others interested in creating Web pages. This course assumes you are a beginner with Dreamweaver but are familiar with the basic methods of giving commands on a Macintosh or Windows computer, such as choosing items from menus, opening and saving files, and so on. For more information on those basic tasks, see the documentation provided with your computer.

Finally, the instructions in this book assume that you already have Dreamweaver MX installed on a Macintosh or Windows computer, and that your computer meets the system requirements listed on page 4-5. This minimum configuration will allow you to run Dreamweaver MX and open the training files included on the enclosed CD. If you do not own Dreamweaver MX, a demo version is included on the CD. You will be able to complete the lessons with the trial version of the software, but the demo version will function for only 30 days, after which the program will no longer launch without a serial number. Follow the instructions in the ReadMe file to install the demo version of the software.

Welcome to Macromedia Training from the Source. We hope you enjoy the course.

WHAT YOU WILL LEARN

You will develop the skills you need to create and maintain your own Web sites as you work through these lessons.

By the end of this course, you will be able to:

- Format text in different sizes, color, and styles
- Use HTML styles to speed up your text-formatting process
- Import and clean up text from text files, Word documents, and spreadsheets
- Insert graphics and control their appearance
- Create and manage internal and external links throughout your site
- Learn how to make changes directly within the HTML code
- Place text and graphics within tables to achieve more control over the layout
- Make use of image rollovers and other interactive elements
- Use the Site window to manage your files and folders
- Develop library items in order to use the same elements quickly and repeatedly
- Create templates to set the look and feel of a site
- Make your pages accessible and redirect visitors according to the browser version they are using
- Incorporate different types of files such as Flash Objects and Flash Text
- Insert a background graphic or change the background colors of your pages
- Specify text attributes using cascading style sheets to gain more control over the appearance of text
- Use the extensive Find and Replace feature to make changes in single documents or throughout the entire site
- Create forms to collect information from visitors
- Test and run reports on your Web pages to verify their compatibility with multiple types of browsers
- Customize and extend Dreamweaver's capabilities to suit your needs

MINIMUM SYSTEM REQUIREMENTS: MACINTOSH

- Power Mac G3 or better
- Mac OS 9.1 or higher, or Mac OS X 10.1 or higher
- Netscape Navigator or Internet Explorer 4.0 or later
- 96MB of RAM (128MB recommended)
- 275MB available disk space
- 256-color monitor capable of 800×600 resolution (1024×768, millions of colors recommended; thousands of colors required for OS X)

NOTE *Dreamweaver MX requires Apple Macintosh Runtime for Java (MRJ) 2.2.5 or greater. To download and install the current version of MRJ, see the ReadMe file on the CD-ROM. If you have Macintosh OS X, you already have at least the minimum version of Java that Dreamweaver requires.*

Macintosh memory issues: Symptoms of Dreamweaver running on low memory include images turning a light, solid gray with diagonal lines forming an X across the area occupied by the image. If this occurs, try the following:

- Check the minimum system requirements listed earlier in this section.
- Close other applications.
- Allocate more memory. In many cases, applications cannot work properly if they don't have enough memory allocated to them. When a software product is shipped, it defaults to a specific memory setting. Sometimes, this default memory allocation is too low for a user's specific use, and the amount of allocated memory needs to be increased.

To increase the amount of memory allocated to Dreamweaver, quit Dreamweaver. Navigate to the folder containing the Dreamweaver application. Click once on the Dreamweaver application icon to select it. Choose File > Get Info > Memory. (You can also use the keyboard shortcut Command+I to open the Get Info dialog box for Dreamweaver, and then select Memory in the Show pop-up menu.) In the Preferred Size text box, increase the numeric value. Apple recommends that you increase the preferred size in increments of ten. Users may also set the Minimum Size to match the Preferred Size. This will insure that Dreamweaver allocates all the memory you've specified when launched. If there is not enough memory available, a warning may occur and Dreamweaver won't launch. Close the Get Info dialog box and relaunch Dreamweaver. To check the amount of memory you've allocated to Dreamweaver, choose About This Computer from the Apple Menu. About This Computer will show you the amount of memory being used by an open application (including the operating system).

MINIMUM SYSTEM REQUIREMENTS: WINDOWS

- Intel Pentium II processor or equivalent 300+ MHz
- Windows 98, 2000, NT, ME, or XP
- Microsoft Data Access Components (MDAC) 2.6 or later
- Netscape Navigator or Internet Explorer 4.0 or later
- 96MB of available RAM (128MB recommended)
- 275MB available disk space
- 256-color monitor capable of 800×600 resolution (1024×768, millions of colors recommended)

dreamweaver mx basics

Dreamweaver MX is an HTML editor that gives users visual design and editing capabilities combined with the ability to work directly with code. Dreamweaver helps speed production time for your Web sites and provides tools for the management and maintenance of those sites.

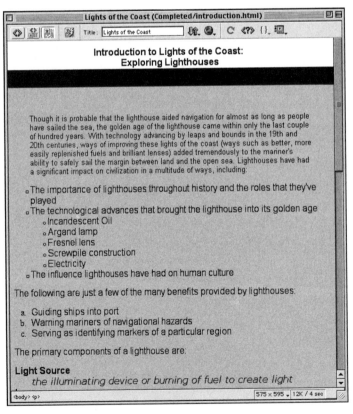

In this lesson, you'll learn how to format text, test your pages, and use HTML styles while creating the introduction page for the "Lights of the Coast" project Web site.

In this lesson, you'll learn the basics of HTML layout and production in Dreamweaver MX, and you'll become familiar with the program's interface and tools. You will begin to use the main site-management features by setting up a local site for the pages that you create.

This lesson teaches you how to import text in different file formats, as well as how to work with text and document settings to create a simple Web page and test your work in different browsers—a vital part of creating accessible Web sites.

You can find an example of the completed lesson, introduction.html, in the Completed folder inside the Lesson_01_Text folder on the CD-ROM.

WHAT YOU WILL LEARN

In this lesson, you will:

- Identify the tools and become familiar with the Dreamweaver interface
- Set up a new local site and specify preview browsers
- Create, save, and title a new document
- Specify a background image and default text colors
- Place text on a page
- Position and format text
- Use the Assets panel to save colors and apply them to text
- Create and apply HTML styles
- Create and modify Flash text

APPROXIMATE TIME

This lesson should take about two hours to complete.

LESSON FILES

Media Files:
Lesson_01_Text/Images/background.gif

Starting Files:
Lesson_01_Text/Text/introduction.txt

Completed Project:
Lesson_01_Text/Completed/introduction.html

EXPLORING THE TOOLS

1) Open Dreamweaver MX.

Before jumping into the creation of any Web pages, you need to become familiar with the variety of tools and panels in Dreamweaver that will enable you to effectively produce a Web site. If this is your first time opening Dreamweaver, you will see a Welcome window that provides information for users who are new to Dreamweaver, as well as a rundown of the new features for those who are already familiar with the program. Buttons on the bar at the bottom of this window allow you to navigate through the program information. If you want to close this window and view it another time, you can always access it from Help > Welcome. Also visible when you open Dreamweaver will be a new document window—this is where your design and coding work will be done. You may also see panels for adding or changing text and objects, working with site files and more. The visible panels might include the Insert bar, the Property inspector, the Site window, and the Answers panel.

You will see that the majority of Dreamweaver's panels are grouped according to their functions within panel groups. These panel groups include Design, Code, Application Building, Files, and Answers. Panel groups let you quickly hide or access your most frequently used panels. You can access all of the panels within these groups, as well as others, from the Window menu.

If you have opened Dreamweaver before, the panels will be placed exactly where they were the last time you quit the program. In the Window menu, a checkmark next to an item indicates that the panel or toolbar is open and visible. There may be instances in which a panel is hidden beneath another panel or the document window. To display a hidden panel, choose it from the Window menu again. If the panel you choose is in a panel group that is not currently visible, both the panel and the panel group containing that chosen panel will appear.

NOTE *If a panel is selected but cannot be seen, choose Window > Arrange Panels to reset all open panels to their default positions. The Insert bar will move to the top left corner of the screen, the Property inspector will move to the bottom of the screen, and all other open panels will move to the right of the screen. For Windows users only, Dreamweaver MX introduces a new workspace that integrates all Dreamweaver-related windows and panels into one window. Windows users can switch back to floating windows and panels by choosing Edit > Preferences, selecting the General category, and clicking the Change Workspace button. The Workspace Setup dialog box will open; there you can select the desired workspace option. The Dreamweaver MX Workspace is the integrated workspace. The Dreamweaver 4 Workspace uses the floating windows and panels. Click OK to close the Workspace Setup dialog box, and click OK to close the Preferences dialog box. You must restart Dreamweaver in order for any changes to the workspace settings to take effect. The Dreamweaver MX Workspace is the recommended workspace. The integrated workspace is not available in the Macintosh version.*

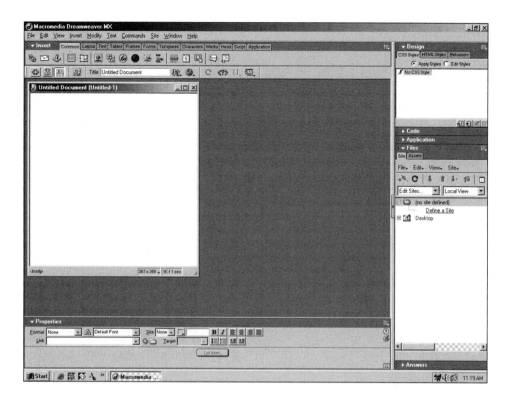

2) Move the pointer over the document window. Rest the pointer over a button to see its name.

The majority of your work will take place within the document window, where you can insert, modify, and delete the wide variety of elements that make up your Web page. As you work, the document window displays an approximation of the way your page should appear in a browser. By default, this page will initially be called Untitled Document, as you can see on the document title bar. The name of the file will be also be shown on the title bar, displayed in parenthesis after the title of the document. The name of the document is also shown in the Title text field on the document toolbar. On the Macintosh, the toolbar is part of the document window. In Windows, the toolbar is a separate panel that you can move if necessary; it is located just above the document window.

There are three viewing modes in Dreamweaver: Design View, Code View and Split Design and Code. The buttons for these modes are located on the left side of the document toolbar. At this point, the viewing mode you are using should be Design View. The button will highlight to indicate that Dreamweaver is displaying the page in that viewing mode. You will work with the Code View and Split View in Lesson 12. If the document window is shown split into two panes with code in one, you will need to select the Design View icon located on the document toolbar.

9

In the bottom left corner of the document window is the Tag Selector. The Tag Selector always starts from the **<body>** tag, hierarchically displaying HTML tags that apply to the currently selected element.

TIP *You can use the Tag Selector to select and navigate through the elements in your page by using the HTML tags that correspond with those elements. This tool allows you to move quickly through the hierarchy of code on the page, to see what element you are working with, and to select other elements easily. Getting used to working with the Tag Selector will be particularly helpful when you begin using tables in Lesson 4.*

You'll become familiar with the many buttons and customizable options in the document window as you work through the lessons in this book.

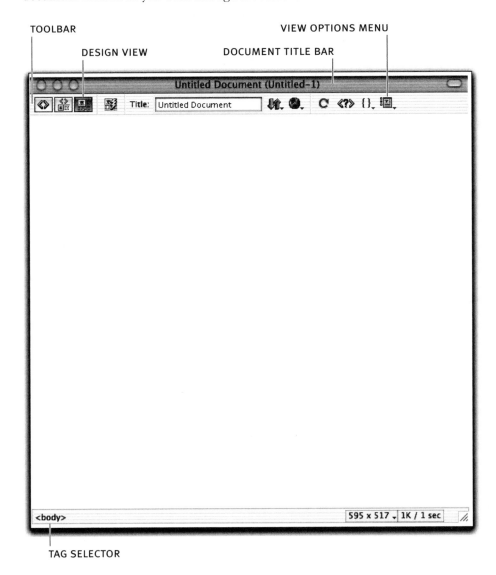

TOOLBAR

DESIGN VIEW

VIEW OPTIONS MENU

DOCUMENT TITLE BAR

TAG SELECTOR

3) Move the pointer over the Insert bar. Rest the pointer over a button to see its name.

The Insert bar contains many of the objects or elements that you can add to your page, including images, tables, special characters, forms, and frames. The elements you can insert are arranged in groups according to their type. The groups include Common, Frames, Forms, Layout, Characters, and more. You can select a group by clicking the corresponding tab. A number of special characters, for example, are in the Characters group while common elements such as an image or table are in the Common group. You can also access these objects and elements through the Insert menu.

NOTE *Throughout this book, the words "object" and "element" are used interchangeably. Where possible, "object" has been used when referring to the button, and "element" has been used for the item once it appears within the document window.*

To insert an element, you can drag the object's icon from the Insert bar to the location you would like it to appear in the document window. You can also place the insertion point in your document where the element should appear, and then click the object's icon in the panel. When you click the icon, the element appears in the document at the insertion point.

NOTE *Depending upon the object you select, a dialog box may appear, giving you options for the element's properties and placement. For certain objects, such as tables and images, you can bypass the dialog boxes and insert a placeholder element instead by holding down the Option key (Macintosh) or Alt key (Windows). Using a placeholder may be useful if you are working on pages for which photographs or artwork are forthcoming. Dreamweaver MX now includes a button, located on the Common tab of the Insert bar, specifically for the creation of placeholder images.*

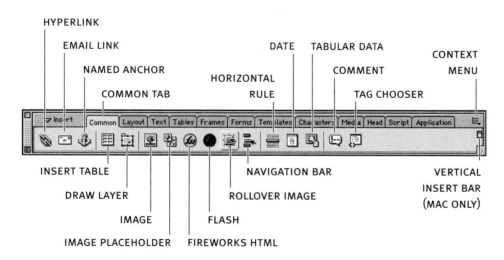

On the Macintosh, you can also view the Insert bar in a vertical orientation by clicking the Vertical Insert Bar icon located in the lower right corner of the panel. When viewing the vertical panel, access object groups by clicking the black arrow, which indicates the objects pop-up menu, located at the top right corner of the panel. The vertical orientation will place the objects in different locations and slightly change the groups of objects from what they were on the horizontal Insert bar. This option is not available in Windows.

4) Move the pointer over the Property inspector. Rest the pointer over a button to see its name.

You will use the Property inspector to view and modify the attributes of selected text, images, tables, and other elements on your page. The Property inspector is contextual—the attributes that it makes available will change depending on what is selected in the document window. To reduce or expand the Property inspector, click the expander arrow in the bottom right corner of the panel. If the Property inspector is reduced, there may be additional properties that are not visible until you expand the panel.

WORKING WITH PANELS

As you saw when you first opened Dreamweaver at the beginning of this lesson, most of the panels you will use while creating Web pages are **docked**—combined in tabbed windows—within panel groups. Docking maximizes your screen area while giving you quick access to the panels you need. Each panel group can be expanded to display all the panels it contains, or reduced to show simply the name of the group. Once you become familiar with the Dreamweaver panels and tools, you can customize the interface in order to make the program work with your specific needs by rearranging panels and reordering panel groups.

1) Click the arrow on the Design panel group to make it expand. If the Design panel group is not visible, choose Window > HTML Styles.

If the Design panel group is visible but reduced, choosing Window > HTML Styles is another way to expand the group, because the Design panel group contains the HTML Styles panel. You will work with the HTML Styles panel later in this lesson to set text styles.

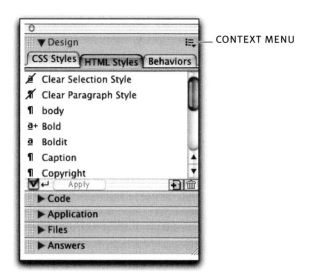

CONTEXT MENU

2) Click the context menu located on the upper right of the Design panel group and choose Group HTML Styles With from the drop-down menu. Choose New Panel Group from the bottom of the menu.

The HTML Styles panel is now in a separate panel group that is called HTML Styles. You will no longer see a tab in this panel group because it contains only one panel.

You can rearrange panels as needed in Dreamweaver by choosing a different panel group for a panel to be placed in or by defining new panel groups as you just did. You cannot undock a panel by dragging its tab out of a set of docked panels. You must use the context menu to create a new panel group if you need to use a panel separately from other panels.

NOTE *You can rename panel groups by clicking the context menu and choosing Rename Panel Group. The Rename Panel Group dialog box will appear; here you can define a new panel group name.*

3) In the HTML Styles panel group, click the context menu and choose Group HTML Styles With from the drop-down menu. Choose the Design panel group from the list.

Notice that the HTML Styles panel is placed back into the Design panel group on the right side. Whenever you group a panel with a panel group that already exists, the panel that you are placing into the group will appear to the right of the existing panel tabs. If you want to change the order of panel tabs within a panel group, you will need to create new panel groups for the other panels and then group those panels with the desired panel group again until you achieve the desired order.

NOTE *The lessons in this book assume that you are using the default configuration of panels in Dreamweaver MX, with no changes to the order or names of panels and panel groups except for what you have done in this exercise.*

4) Rest the pointer over the dots to the left of the Design panel group arrow. When the pointer turns into a hand (Macintosh) or a crosshair with arrows (Windows), click and drag the Design panel group out of the window and release it.

You have now separated the entire Design panel group from the window of panel groups.

5) Rest the pointer over the dots to the left of the Design panel group arrow. When the pointer turns into a hand (Macintosh) or a crosshair with arrows (Windows), click and drag the Design panel group back to the top of the panel groups window and release it when you see the gray line above the Code panel group.

The Design panel group is now back in the same window as the other panel groups. You can rearrange the order of panel groups by using the dots to move any of the groups above or below the other groups. When you drag a panel group back into the window, you will see the thick gray line appear between the existing panel groups. That gray line indicates where the panel group you are moving will be placed. Depending on the preferences set for appearance on your computer, this line may be a different color.

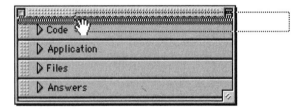

At times you may be unable to find a particular panel. Changes in screen resolution can be one cause of this problem. If you are missing a panel and can't bring it up by choosing it from the Window menu, you might need to choose Window > Arrange Panels to snap panels to the sides of your screen.

NOTE *Windows users have three additional options in the integrated workspace: Cascade, Tile Horizontally, and Tile Vertically. If you have more than one document window open at a time, Cascade will cause those windows to float, stacked on top of the other, within the document window portion of the integrated workspace. Tile Horizontally will cause the document windows to appear stacked horizontally. Tile Vertically will cause the document windows to appear side by side vertically. These options can be accessed from the Window menu.*

DEVELOPING YOUR SITE STRUCTURE

Spending the time to develop a thorough outline or flowchart will help you to develop your ideas, obtain a better understanding of the scope of your project, and save you time and resources down the road. A good Web site should be intuitive and create a positive, unique user experience. The creation of an effective Web site starts with defining and summarizing the reason and need for the site. Ask yourself or your client who the site is for, why it is needed, and what purpose it will serve. What do you want to express through your site, and how will you communicate that? What impressions do you want to make, and what do you want the visitors of your site to come away with?

Knowing your audience is vital. Who will your visitors be? Defining a general user profile will help you to effectively reach your target audience. Once you know who that audience is, you will need to consider what technologies they are likely to have. What kinds of plug-ins, browsers, and operating systems will the majority of your visitors be using? The types of equipment used by your visitors is important to consider in order to create a Web site that will be accessible to your intended audience. For example, you wouldn't want to create a site that uses elements that are only supported by the most recent and up-to-date browsers if most of your audience is using older machines that can't even run those browsers.

Web sites depend a great deal on structure and file management; a Web site with a poor structure can be confusing to navigate, hard to use, and difficult to maintain. In order to make a site that is clear, communicative, and easy for visitors to use, you will need to plan out the structure and hierarchy of files and folders within your site completely before you begin to build any HTML documents.

Identifying and collecting site assets is an important part of the preparation to design and produce a Web site. You will need to gather all the content, such as text, graphics, and multimedia elements that will be used on the site.

For the lessons in this book, all the work described in this section has already been done. You are ready to begin working on the project site "Lights of the Coast."

DEFINING A LOCAL SITE

The first step in creating a Web site—before you begin to create any individual pages—is to designate or create the folder that will contain everything within the site. This process is called defining a local site. The designated folder, known as the **local root folder**, will set the boundaries of the local site that resides on your hard disk and will mirror the remote site, which is the actual site on the Web server that your visitors will access. Defining a local site enables you to maintain the same folder hierarchy between the local and remote versions, which is crucial to creating and maintaining a functional site.

The creation of a local site, comprised of the local root folder within which you set up the structure of the site's files and folders, will prevent your site from accessing any files outside of the local root folder. Files on your hard disk that are outside of the local root folder will not be available to the remote server. Many Dreamweaver features, such as the potential to update all references to a file that has been moved to a different location in the site, will require the definition of a local site in order to function fully. The locations and links to all files contained in your site will be relative to the root folder. You should always create and work within local sites. If you don't, you may have problems with links, paths, and file management. (Dreamweaver's tools for these features are covered in later lessons in this book.)

The development of your site will occur in the local site on your hard disk, where you will build and initially test your pages.

1) Copy the DWMX_project folder from the CD-ROM to your hard disk.

The DWMX_project folder will be the root folder of your local site. This folder contains all the files and folders for "Lights of the Coast," the project site you will create as you work through lessons in this book. When you begin work on other sites, you will need to create individual root folders for each of those sites.

The name of a root folder can be the name of the respective site or any name you choose. If you create multiple sites, it will be helpful to use names that can be distinguished easily from one another. The name of the root folder is simply for file management purposes and will not be visible to the visitors of the site.

NOTE *You should save your local root folder in a location on your hard disk that is outside of the Dreamweaver application folder. If you ever need to reinstall Dreamweaver, your work would be lost if you saved it inside the Dreamweaver application folder.*

2) In Dreamweaver, choose Site > New Site. Choose the Basic tab in the Site Definition dialog box.

The Site Definition dialog box opens with two tabs, Basic and Advanced, which allow you to choose how you would like to go through the process of defining a site. The Basic version, which is shown by default when you open the dialog box, walks you step-by-step through the process. The Advanced version gives you a number of additional options and settings to configure, and it does not include the explanatory text descriptions you will see in the Basic View.

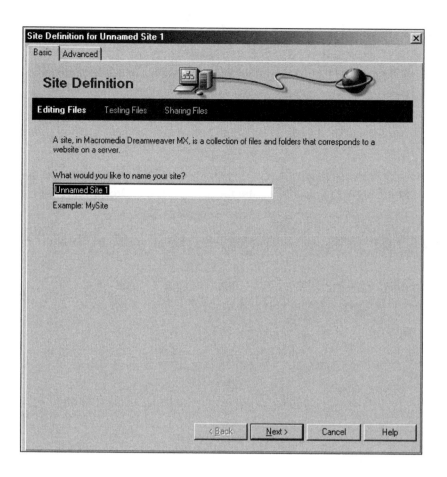

NOTE *If you have never defined a site in Dreamweaver, the Site window (if it is open) will display a folder indicating there is no site defined. For Windows users, this folder is also shown in the local files pane on the right side of the Site window along with a link to Define a Site. Clicking the Define a Site link will open to the Basic tab of the Site Definition dialog box.*

3) Dreamweaver poses the question, "What would you like to name your site?" Type Lights of the Coast in the Site Name text field, and then click Next.

"Lights of the Coast" is the name of the project site you are creating in this lesson. When you create your own sites, the names that you assign can be anything that identifies them. Clear and specific site names allow you to immediately tell sites apart by name, making it easier to manage multiple sites. The site name is for your reference only and will not be visible to users of your site.

NOTE *This section of the Basic setup corresponds to the Site Name text field of the Local Info category in the Advanced View.*

4) Dreamweaver asks, "Do you want to work with a server technology such as ColdFusion, ASP.NET, ASP, JSP, or PHP?" Click the radio button for the option "No, I do not want to use a server technology." Click Next to advance to the next section.

Since you will be creating pages for a static site in this book's lessons, you should select the No option. You can edit the site definition at any time by choosing Site > Edit Sites....

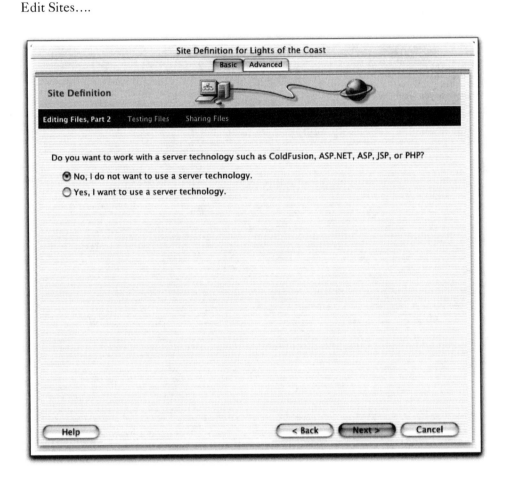

NOTE *This section of the Basic setup corresponds to the Testing Server category in the Advanced View, which gives you additional options that are involved with creating dynamic sites, such as choosing the server model that will be used on your remote server.*

5) At the top of this section Dreamweaver asks, "How do you want to work with your files during development?" Click the radio button for the option "Edit local copies on my machine, then upload to server when ready (recommended)."

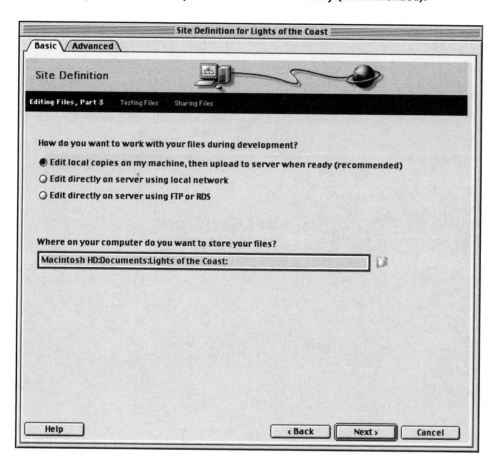

In this book's lessons, you will be working with files on your machine. You do not need to have access to a server.

6) Also in this section Dreamweaver asks, "Where on your computer do you want to store your files?" Click the folder icon to the right of the text field and browse to find the DWMX_project folder.

The DWMX_project folder is the folder that you copied from the CD-ROM to your hard disk in step 1.

For Macintosh: Select the DWMX_project folder and click Choose.

For Windows: Select the DWMX_project folder and click Open. Then click Select to choose the DWMX_project folder as your root folder. The text "Select:DWMX_project" will appear in the lower left corner of the dialog box to indicate that the DWMX_project folder will be selected.

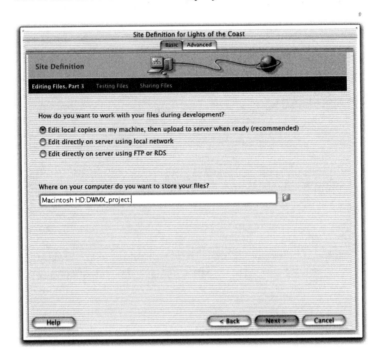

The pathname to the root folder, DWMX_project, is displayed in the text field and is relative to your hard disk. This text field allows you to specify the folder on your hard disk within which all of the files for the site are stored. This folder is the equivalent of the root folder on the remote site. Dreamweaver will use this local root folder to determine the paths for documents, images, and links in your site. You will learn about paths and links in Lesson 3.

By default, the text field initially contained the path to a folder called Lights of the Coast. Using that default would have created a new folder on your hard disk called Lights of the Coast, which would usually be placed in the Documents folder on the Macintosh or in the My Documents folder on the C drive in Windows. That folder would have become your local root folder. In this case, however, you shouldn't create a new folder because you need to choose the DWMX_project folder (that already exists and contains many files which you will need to work with in this book's lessons) as your local root folder.

When you are creating your own sites, if you do not already have a folder you may find it useful to allow Dreamweaver to automatically create one for you, based on the name your chose for your site.

NOTE *This section of the Basic setup corresponds to the Local Root Folder text field of the Local Info category in the Advanced View. The Advanced site definition view also allows you to select Refresh Local File List Automatically. This option is checked by default, causing Dreamweaver to update the site list whenever you add a new file to the site folder. If you uncheck this option, you will need to refresh the local files manually whenever you make changes such as adding or deleting files. Enable Cache is another option in the Advanced View, and it too is checked by default. Enable Cache allocates memory to store frequently used site data, improving the speed of linking and site-management tasks. Although you usually will want to leave this option selected, keep in mind that re-creating the cache can slow operations on very large sites.*

7) Click Next to advance to the next section. Choose None from the drop-down menu below the question "How do you connect to your remote server?"
For the lessons in this book, you will be working on a local site only. You do not need access to a remote server.

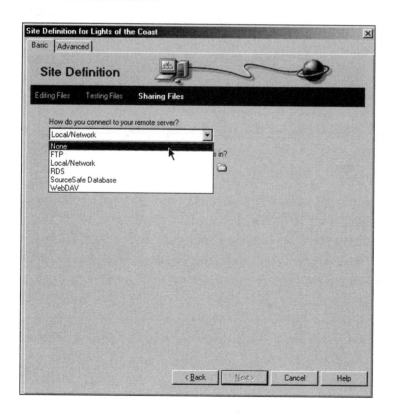

NOTE *This section of the Basic setup corresponds to the Remote Info category in the Advanced View, which gives you additional options that are involved in transferring files to a remote server.*

8) Click Next to advance to the next section. Review the information about the site you have just defined and click the Done button at the bottom of the dialog box.

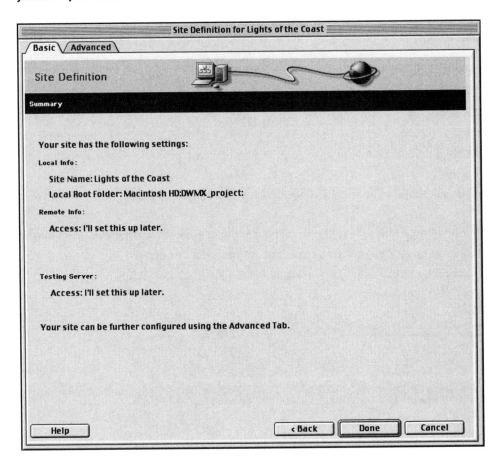

Since you chose the No options for the Application Server and Remote Info sections, Dreamweaver displays "Access: I'll set this up later." for both. When you click Done, Dreamweaver may display a dialog box to let you know that the site cache will be created. Click OK and Dreamweaver will scan the files in your DWMX_project folder in order to create the cache and display the Site window when it is done.

The Site window will open (Macintosh) or the Site panel will become active (Windows) and display the DWMX_project folder within the right pane of the window in the Local Files column. Macintosh users can close the Site window.

SPECIFYING PREVIEW BROWSERS

As you develop Web pages, you will need to continually test how your work appears in different browsers, such as Netscape and Internet Explorer. What you see in the Dreamweaver document window is only an approximation of how the pages will look. Every browser has differences in how it displays Web pages, and while some of these discrepancies are slight, the differences can sometimes be very significant. You'll notice differences even between different versions of the same browser. The more you test your site in multiple browsers and operating systems, and make changes accordingly, the more certain you can be that visitors to the site will see your pages as you intended them to look. The Preferences in Dreamweaver enable you to specify which browsers you want to use to preview the pages in your site. To speed up the process you can define a primary and a secondary browser and use a keyboard shortcut for each.

1) Choose File > Preview in Browser > Edit Browser List.

The Preferences dialog box opens to display the Preview in Browser preferences. Dreamweaver may automatically list one or more of the browsers that are on your computer.

When you click a browser name in the browser list, the check boxes below the list will show whether it is the primary or secondary browser. If you have more than two browsers, it will leave both boxes unchecked to show that it is neither.

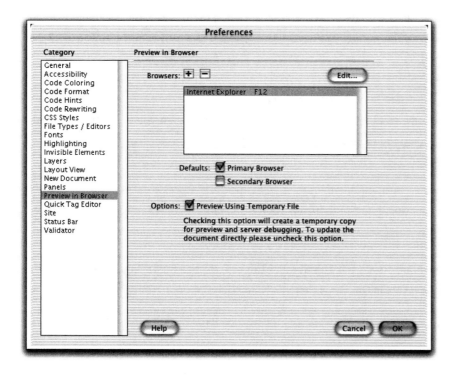

TIP *Alternatively, you can choose Edit > Preferences and select Preview in Browser in the Category list, located on the left side of the dialog box, to open the same Preview in Browser Preferences dialog box. You can also use the keyboard command Command+U (Macintosh) or Ctrl+U (Windows) to open the Preferences dialog box. If you are using Macintosh OS X, you can also access the Preferences by choosing Dreamweaver > Preferences.*

2) Click the plus sign (+) button to add another browser to the list.

When the dialog box appears, browse your hard disk to find and choose a browser application. Check the Primary Browser check box if you want to launch this browser by pressing Command+F12 (Macintosh) or Control+F12 (Windows) when you preview your pages. Check the Secondary Browser check box if you want to preview your documents in this browser by pressing Control+F12. (You'll be previewing the pages you develop while completing the lessons in this book often, so using these shortcuts will save you time.)

To remove a browser from the list, select the browser name in the list and click the minus (–) button.

To change a browser choice, select the browser name in the list. Then click Edit and locate a different browser.

3) Leave the Preview Using Temporary File option checked. Click OK when you are done adding browsers.

The Preview Using Temporary File option is checked by default. Leave this option checked so that Dreamweaver will create a temporary file to use when previewing pages in a browser.

CREATING AND SAVING A NEW PAGE

While Dreamweaver opens a new, untitled document when you open the program, you will often need to create subsequent new pages. Whenever you create a new page, the first thing you should do is save your document.

If you have an untitled document that Dreamweaver opened automatically, you can close that document without saving it by selecting the document and choosing File > Close.

1) Choose File > New. Click the General tab and choose Basic Page in the category list. Choose HTML in the Basic Page list and click the Create button.

TIP *You can use the keyboard commands Command+N (Macintosh) or Ctrl+N (Windows) to open the same New Document dialog box.*

The New Document dialog box opens with two tabs: General and Templates. The options to create a new HTML (Hypertext Markup Language) page are in the General View. For this exercise, you are creating a new HTML page from the Basic category.

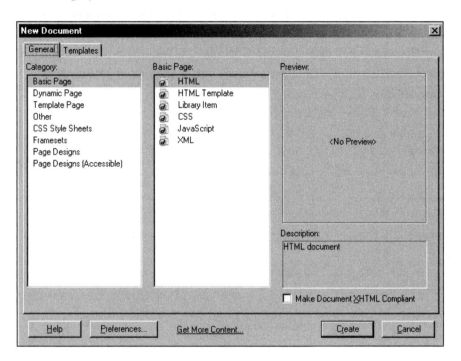

NOTE *By default, the new untitled document, which opens each time you start Dreamweaver, is a standard HTML document. You can change what kind of document it is by clicking the Preferences button at the bottom of the dialog box. The New Document preferences will open, which allows you to set the default document type as well as the extension and encoding.*

The New Document dialog box also gives you additional options for creating a variety of page types including HTML, XML, and dynamic pages using scripts such as ASP and ColdFusion. You can access specific page types by choosing from the list of categories that includes templates, CSS styles, framesets, and pre-designed sample HTML pages. You will not be using any of these additional page types at this time, but you should be aware of them.

NOTE *At the bottom of the New Document dialog box is an option to Make Document XHTML Compliant. By nature HTML is limited, particularly in that new features are generally not backwards compatible and there are a wide number compatibility issues for cross-platform use. XHTML (Extensible Hypertext Markup Language) extends the capabilities of HTML by reforming HTML as an XML (Extensible Markup Language) language. The advantages to using XHTML include both backward and forward compatibility, operability on alternate Web access devices such as cell phones or hand-held computers, and the potential for extensibility. You should leave this option unchecked for the exercises in this book.*

2) Choose File > Save and locate the folder Lesson_01_Text where you will save this file. Type introduction.html in the File Name text field at the bottom of the Save As dialog box, and then click Save.

Don't wait until you have text or graphics on the page to save—save your pages as soon as you open new documents. Provided that your file is saved first, when you import graphics or other media, all the paths that reference where those elements are located in your site will be made properly. If you have not saved your document, a file:// pathname will be used that describes the location of the element you are inserting relative to your hard disk. If you try to insert an object without first saving the document, Dreamweaver will warn you that it needs to use a file:// pathname for the element.

TIP *You can use the keyboard commands Command+S (Macintosh) or Ctrl+S (Windows) to save your document. Always remember to save often so you won't lose a lot of work if your computer crashes for any reason.*

You can use either extension: .html or .htm. Dreamweaver adds the extension .html (Macintosh) or .htm (Windows) to the filename automatically when you save. You can see which extension is set as the default by choosing Edit > Preferences and selecting the New Document category. The default extension is displayed in a text field, although it is grayed-out. Both extensions can be used on either Macintosh or Windows; however, they are not interchangeable—introduction.htm is not the same as introduction.html. You could save a file as either introduction.html or as introduction.htm because the extensions represent the same kind of file. You can also have both introduction.html and introduction.htm on the same server because they are recognized as two separate files. It is usually easier to stick with one or the other so you are able to make the correct links. Linking to introduction.html will not work if your file is really named introduction.htm. Links and paths will be covered more in Lesson 3.

You can change this extension in the document-type XML file.

TIP *For Windows users, if your system is set to automatically add the appropriate extension after you save, do not include the .htm in the File name text field.*

For Macintosh users, the .html extension will appear in the Save As dialog box.

Throughout this book, the extension .html is used in the examples and materials included on the CD-ROM. If you are using Windows, you will be prompted to save your files as .htm instead. You can use whichever extension you prefer.

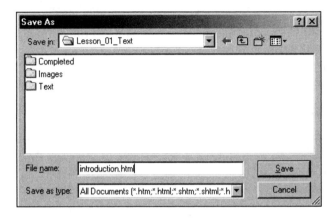

Naming your files for use on a Web server is a little different from naming your files for use on your hard disk. First, you need to know what operating system the server will be using—the most common systems are Unix, Windows NT, and Macintosh. The naming structure is different on each of these platforms. Unix, for example, is case-sensitive, which means that myfile.htm does not equal MYFILE.HTM. Using all lowercase names for your files will make naming files simpler and help you maintain consistency. You should only use alpha characters (A–Z) and numbers (0–9) to name your files. Here are other important conventions to follow:

- Don't ever use spaces in filenames. Use the underscore or hyphen characters to simulate a space if you need to separate words. Problems can arise due to the fact that browsers substitute %20 for spaces.

- Do not use any special characters such as %, *, >, or /.

- Avoid beginning your filenames with numbers.

TIP *Keep folder and filenames as short as possible. Remember that the folder name becomes part of the URL you type to get to the page. You should follow the naming guidelines in this section for folders as well as files.*

GIVING YOUR PAGE A TITLE

Every HTML document you create needs to have a title. The title is used primarily for document identification. It is displayed in a browser's title bar, indicates the content of a page, and appears as the bookmark name. You should choose a short, informative phrase that describes the document's purpose. Get into the habit of adding a title to each page you create before you add text or graphics to the page. If you forget, Dreamweaver titles the file Untitled Document.

Type Lights of the Coast into the Title text field on the document toolbar. Press Return (Macintosh) or Enter (Windows), or click in the introduction.html document.
If you don't see the document toolbar with the Title text field, choose View > Toolbars > Document. The Title text field will initially display Untitled Document—you are now replacing that placeholder title with a title for the introduction page of the project site.

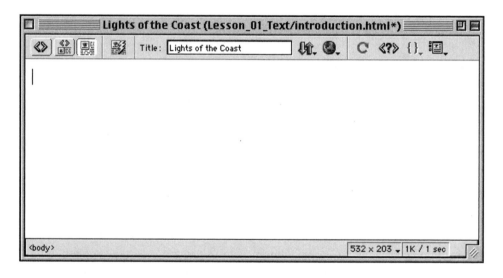

NOTE *Dreamweaver gives you several reminders if you haven't titled your page. Look at the document title bar, which displays the title and the filename. If you see "Untitled Document (filename.html)", you haven't titled your document. You'll also see "Untitled Document" in the Title text field on the document toolbar.*

28

SPECIFYING A BACKGROUND COLOR

In Dreamweaver, you can change the background color of a page easily by using a palette of colors known as the Web-safe color palette. This palette is a collection of 216 colors that appear the same in browsers on both Macintosh and Windows. In this exercise, you will access that palette from the Page Properties dialog box to change the background color for introduction.html.

1) Choose Modify > Page Properties.

TIP *You can use the keyboard commands Command+J (Macintosh) or Ctrl+J (Windows) to open the Page Properties dialog box.*

The Page Properties dialog box appears. There are no defaults displayed in this dialog box, even though white is the default background color for the document window in Dreamweaver. If you do not define a background color, the page will use the browser default when a visitor views the page.

Page Properties		
Title: Lights of the Coast		OK
Background Image:	Browse...	Apply
Background:		Cancel
Text:	Visited Links:	
Links:	Active Links:	
Left Margin:	Margin Width:	
Top Margin:	Margin Height:	
Document Encoding: Western (Latin1)	Reload	
Tracing Image:	Browse...	
Image Transparency:	100%	
	Transparent Opaque	
Document Folder: Macintosh HD:DWMX_project:Lesson_01_Text:		
Site Folder: Macintosh HD:DWMX_project:		Help

2) Click the color box for Background option. A color palette pops up, and the pointer changes automatically to an eyedropper. In the color palette, move the eyedropper over a color swatch.

Notice that the hexadecimal equivalents for the colors are displayed at the top of the color palette as you roll over the swatches. In HTML, colors are defined in hexadecimal code using RGB—red, green, and blue. Hexadecimal is a base-16 numbering system that uses 0 through 9 and A through F. In the six-digit code used in HTML to describe color, the first two digits represent red, the second two digits represent green, and the last two digits represent blue. For example, #00FF00 will have no red, a bright green, and no blue; #000000 has no red, no green, and no blue—it is black.

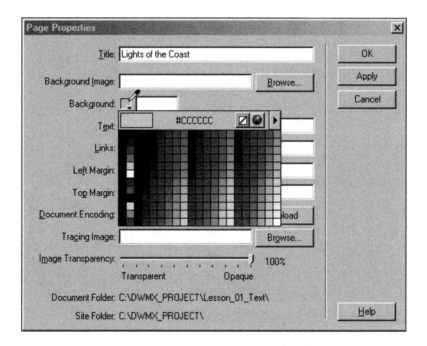

TIP *You can also move the eyedropper over the document window and choose a color from items there such as text and images.*

3) Click the pale tan swatch that displays the hexadecimal code #CCCC99.

The pale tan color #CCCC99 is now selected as the background color for your page. You can also type the hexadecimal code directly into the text field to change the color.

4) Click Apply to view the color change in your document.

Clicking Apply allows you to view your changes without closing the Page Properties dialog box. If you just want to close the dialog box, clicking OK will close it and apply the change automatically.

N O T E *For more colors, click the arrow located in the top right corner of the color pop-up window and choose a color palette from the pop-up menu. Keep in mind that other palettes may not contain cross-platform, Web-safe colors.*

USING A BACKGROUND GRAPHIC

In this exercise, you'll add a background graphic to the introduction.html document. A background graphic is generally a small graphic that tiles on your page by repeating itself to the extent of the width and height of the browser window. You can define both a background color and a background graphic for your pages. On slow connections or in slow browsers, you may see the background color displayed first—a good reason to set a background color even if you plan on using a background image. Once the background graphic has loaded, it remains onscreen, overriding the background color.

1) Choose Modify > Page Properties.

The Page Properties dialog box appears.

2) Click the Browse button next to Background Image text field. Choose the bkg_inside_tan.gif graphic in the Images folder in the Lesson_01_Text folder and click OK to close the Page Properties dialog box.

Your changes are applied to the document, and you will see the background image tiling in the document window. The bkg_inside_tan.gif image tiles across the page, creating horizontal bands of white, black, and tan.

If you wanted to delete a background graphic, you would need to open the Page Properties dialog box and delete the filename in the Background text field. For this lesson, however, you should leave the background image in the document.

NOTE *If you have not saved your file when you created the document, the entire pathname of the graphic relative to your hard disk is displayed in the text field. When you save your file, the pathname changes to the location of the graphic relative to your local root folder. It is always best, however, to save your file before importing any graphics—even background images. You will learn more about pathnames in Lessons 2 and 3.*

SPECIFYING THE DEFAULT FONT COLOR

When you change the background color or add a background graphic, you might also need to change the color of the text that is displayed. Black text won't display on a black background, for example. When choosing a color scheme for your document, try to select combinations of colors that work well together and have enough contrast between them. Colors that are too similar to each other can be very hard to view, as can complementary colors, especially on a computer screen. In the following steps, you'll change the default font color in the introduction.html document.

1) Choose Modify > Page Properties.
The Page Properties dialog box appears.

2) Click the color box for the Text option.
A color palette like the one you used to change the background color pops up.

3) Select the dark reddish-black color with the hexadecimal code #330000 and click OK.

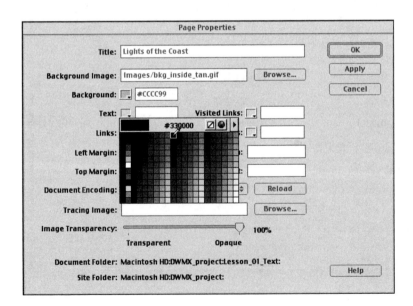

You can either type the hexadecimal color code into the text field, or you can click to select the color from the swatches. After you click OK, the Page Properties dialog box closes, and you return to your document.

PLACING TEXT ON A PAGE

You can add text to introduction.html by typing it directly on the page.

1) In the document window, type Introduction to Lights of the Coast: Exploring Lighthouses.

The first heading for the introduction.html page appears in the document window as you type it.

2) From the Format drop-down menu on the Property inspector, choose Heading 4.

You have tagged the text as a level-4 heading.

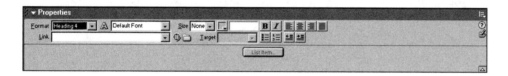

HTML has six levels of headings, numbered 1 through 6. Heading 1 has the largest font size.

Headings are displayed in larger or bolder fonts than normal body text. Tagging a paragraph as a heading automatically generates a space below the heading. You cannot control this spacing.

NOTE *In many documents, the first heading on the page is identical in content to the title. In multiple-part documents, the text of the first heading should be related information, such as a chapter title. The title you set earlier for the entire page should identify the document in a wider context (including both the book title and the chapter title, for example).*

3) Press Return (Macintosh) or Enter (Windows).

You have just created another line below "Introduction to Lights of the Coast: Exploring Lighthouses" that, by default, is tagged as a paragraph. The paragraph format is generally used for regular body text.

4) Save the file.

Whenever you modify your document, notice the asterisk (*) that Dreamweaver inserts near the filename at the top of the document window. This asterisk indicates that the file has been modified but not yet saved. The asterisk disappears once you save the document. Be sure to save your documents often in order to prevent the loss of work.

IMPORTING TEXT

You can add text to a page by copying and pasting from an existing document. If the text is from an application that supports drag-and-drop copying (Microsoft Word for the Macintosh, for example), you can open both Dreamweaver and that application and then copy and paste or select and drag the text into Dreamweaver.

Dreamweaver can also open files created in word-processing or page-layout applications, provided that those files were saved as ASCII text files. For example, Dreamweaver can open a Microsoft Word document if you save the file in Microsoft Word as text (.txt) or if you choose File > Save as Web Page in Microsoft Word to create an HTML version of the document. Text files (.txt files) always open in a new window using the Code View in Dreamweaver. After you open a text file in Dreamweaver, you can copy and paste the text you need into another file.

Simple document formatting, such as paragraphs and line breaks, can be retained, but you need to understand what differences exist between the ASCII format on Macintosh and Windows platforms. Files created in Windows use an invisible control character called a line feed to indicate a new line within the text. Macintosh computers do not use the line-feed character. If you open a Windows text file in SimpleText on a Macintosh, you'll see a small rectangle at the beginning of each new paragraph, indicating the line-feed character. If you open a Macintosh text file in Windows, all the paragraphs merge because of the missing line-feed character.

You can change your preferences to match the file format of text files you receive and want to open in Dreamweaver.

1) Choose Edit > Preferences to display the Preferences dialog box and select Code Format in the Category list. Then, from the Line Break Type drop-down menu, choose CR LF (Windows).

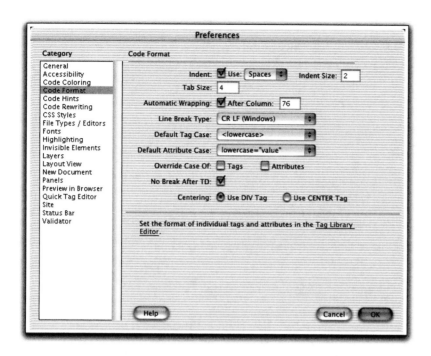

In the Line Break Type menu, your choices are CR LF (Windows), CR (Macintosh), and LF (Unix). If you are using a Macintosh, change this setting to CR LF (Windows). If you are working in Windows, make sure the CR LF (Windows) setting is selected.

2) Click OK.

The Preferences dialog box closes.

3) Use Dreamweaver to open Lesson_01_Text/Text/introduction.txt, and then select and copy all the text. In the introduction.html file, position the insertion point below the "Introduction to Lights of the Coast: Exploring Lighthouses" heading and paste the text to insert it.

You can use the Edit menu to copy and paste the text (choose Edit > Copy and/or Edit > Paste), or you can use the familiar keyboard commands: Command+C (Macintosh) or Control+C (Windows) to copy, and Command+V (Macintosh) or Control+V (Windows) to paste.

Once you have pasted the text, you may need to add additional returns as necessary between the heading you typed earlier and new text to prevent the black bar from obscuring any text.

4) Save the file.

You can close the introduction.txt file. Leave introduction.html open for the next exercise.

NOTE *In the Windows Dreamweaver MX Workspace, the document window is displayed with a tab at the bottom. If you have more than one document open, you can switch to a different document by clicking the corresponding tab. Right-clicking the tab will give you the option to close the file. These options are not available on the Macintosh.*

CREATING A LINE BREAK

If you want to create a new line, with no space between it and the previous line of text (a single line break in the text), you need to insert a line break. This technique is useful for an address line, for example, when you want a new line for each line in the address without the extra spacing that paragraphs create.

In introduction.html, position the insertion point in the heading, just before "Exploring." Then press Shift+Return (Macintosh) or Shift+Enter (Windows).

The text after the insertion point moves to the next line. A line break, not a new paragraph, has been created so no additional spacing appears between the two lines.

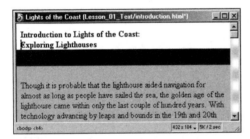

CENTERING AND INDENTING TEXT

The alignment options available to you are default (no alignment), Align Left, Align Center, Align Right, and Justify. Default is the same as left.

1) In introduction.html, position the insertion point in the heading "Introduction to Lights of the Coast." Click the Align Center button in the Property inspector.

The heading is centered. Since you inserted a line break between "Lights of the Coast:" and "Exploring," both lines of text are now centered. Text that is separated by line breaks is still a part of the same paragraph block, so any paragraph formatting that you apply, such as headings or alignments, will affect everything contained within the paragraph.

NOTE *If you use two line breaks, you can simulate the appearance of a new paragraph. However, since you are not actually creating a new paragraph, you may have difficulty when you try to apply formatting styles to text that has two line breaks instead of a single paragraph return.*

In addition to aligning text, you can also indent paragraph blocks. To do this, you will want to use the Text Indent and Text Outdent buttons on the Property inspector.

2) Select the first body paragraph of introduction.html; then click Text Indent in the Property inspector.

TEXT OUTDENT   TEXT INDENT

TIP *You can also choose Text > Indent to indent the selected text.*

The paragraph is now indented. Indents can be used to set off certain portions of text from the standard body text. When you use Text Indent, the text is indented at both the left and right margins of the page. You cannot control the amount of indentation because it is determined by the browser and can differ from browser to browser.

To remove an indent, click the Text Outdent button in the Property inspector or choose Text > Outdent.

NOTE *If you try to indent one paragraph and nearby paragraphs become indented as well, check to see whether you are using paragraph breaks or double breaks. Place the pointer at the beginning of the paragraph you want to indent. Then press Delete (Macintosh) or Backspace (Windows) until you reach the end of the preceding paragraph and press Return (Macintosh) or Enter (Windows) to create a paragraph break.*

MAKING LISTS

Dreamweaver creates two basic types of lists: ordered and unordered. An **ordered list** consists of list items that are ordered numerically or alphabetically. You have the option of using Arabic or Roman numerals or uppercase or lowercase letters. An **unordered list** is often called a bulleted list because each list item has a bullet in front of it. The bullet symbol Dreamweaver displays by default can be changed to a disc, a circle, or a square.

In this exercise, you'll make two lists: one ordered and one unordered. Then you'll revise the list styles by using the List Properties dialog box.

1) In introduction.html, select the text starting with "Guiding ships into port" and ending with "Serving as identifying markers of a particular region." Click the Ordered List button in the Property inspector.

The selected text is indented and numbered.

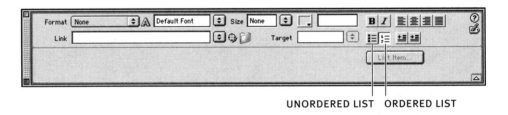

UNORDERED LIST   ORDERED LIST

TIP *You can also choose Text > List > Ordered List to change the selected text to an ordered list format.*

You can change the numbering scheme of ordered lists by modifying the list's properties. You'll do this in the next step.

2) Click any line in the list. Then click the List Item button in the Property inspector.

TIP *With the cursor in the list, you can choose Text > List > Properties to open the same List Properties dialog box.*

Select only one line in the list. If you select the whole list, the List Item button is dimmed and not available for you to use. If the List Item button is not visible, click the expander arrow in the bottom right corner of the Property inspector.

The List Properties dialog box opens.

The ordered list type is known as a Numbered List in the List Type drop-down menu.

3) From the Style drop-down menu, choose Alphabet Small (a,b,c). Then click OK.

NOTE *Alphabet Small is an option in the Style drop-down menu only if you clicked the Ordered List icon. If you clicked the Unordered List icon, you would need to change the List Type drop-down menu to Numbered List before choosing the style.*

All items in the list are alphabetized.

NOTE *The List Item area at the bottom of this dialog box contains a New Style drop-down menu that you can use to change the look of a single item or several items in a list, instead of changing the organization and look of the whole list. Also available in this area is the Reset Count To text field, which will allow you to change the count of the list beginning with the line the insertion point is placed in.*

Creating and modifying an unordered list is a similar process. You'll try it in the following steps.

4) Select the following three lines of text: "The importance of lighthouses throughout history and the roles that they've played," "The technological advances that brought the lighthouse into its golden age," and "The influence lighthouses have had on human culture." Click the Unordered List button in the Property inspector.

TIP *You can also choose Text > List > Unordered List to format the selected text as an unordered list.*

The selected text is indented and bulleted.

You can change the default bullet symbol of unordered lists by modifying the list's properties, just as you did with the ordered list.

The unordered list type is known as a Bulleted List in the List Type drop-down menu.

5) Click any line in the list and choose Text > List > Properties.
The List Properties dialog box opens.

6) From the Style drop-down menu, choose Square. Then click OK.
All items in the list now use the square bullet symbol.

NOTE *The color of numbers and bullets used in ordered or unordered lists will be the color you set as the document default for text color in the Page Properties dialog box.*

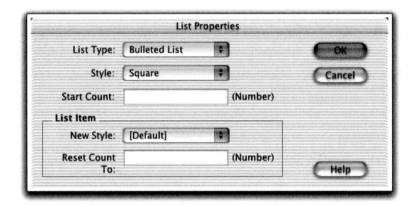

MAKING DEFINITION LISTS

A **definition list** consists of a series of terms and their definitions. The word or term to be defined is left aligned; the definition is indented and placed on the next line. For this type of list to work, a term and its definition must be separate paragraphs—they cannot use line breaks.

1) In introduction.html, select the text starting with "Light Source" and ending with "associated with the operation and maintenance of lighthouses." Choose Text > List > Definition List.
The terms are now at the left margin, and their indented definitions are on succeeding lines.

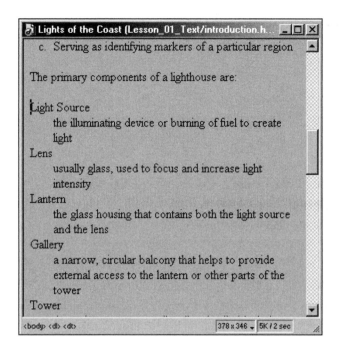

2) Save the file and preview it in the browser.

Now that you have put work into creating and formatting all these lists, it is a good time to save your document.

NESTING LISTS

You can create **nested lists**, which are lists within lists. You can also change the type of lists that are nested. You can have an ordered list within a definition list, for example. By default, bullets are displayed as filled circles, open circles, and squares (in that order) as you nest lists. Dreamweaver calls the bullet types bullet, circle, and square. The corresponding HTML terminology is disc, circle, and square.

Some browsers display open square bullets. Netscape 4.7 for the Macintosh displays open squares, for example, but Internet Explorer 5.0 for the Macintosh displays filled squares. In Windows, the squares are filled.

1) In introduction.html, add a new item to the first list by placing the insertion point at the end of the line "The technological advances that brought the lighthouse into its golden age" and pressing Return (Macintosh) or Enter (Windows).

This step adds another item after that line, at the same level.

2) To nest the item you are about to create, click the Text Indent button in the Property inspector. Type Incandescent oil vapor lamp.

The item indents to the next level.

NOTE *If you want to delete a nested list, position the insertion point within the nested item, but do not select it. Click the Text Outdent button in the Property inspector, and then delete the nested text.*

3) Type the following items on separate lines in the nested list: Argand lamp, Fresnel lens, Screwpile construction, **and** Electricity.

Just as when you indent text, you cannot control or adjust the spacing of outdented text, lists, or nested lists.

CHARACTER FORMATTING

You can apply a variety of formatting options to the text you create in Dreamweaver in order to emphasize certain points, words, or phrases. Options to set include bold, italic, and underline.

1) In introduction.html, select the words "Light Source" in the definition list you created in the preceding section.

You will apply bold formatting to the selected text.

2) Click the Bold button in the Property inspector.

You can also choose Text > Style > Bold to apply the bold format to the selected text. The keyboard shortcuts are Command+B (Macintosh) and Ctrl+B (Windows).

You can apply italic formatting in the same way.

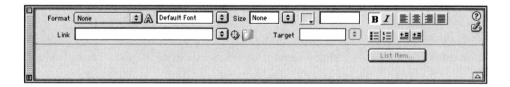

TIP *Be careful of using the underline formatting on your Web pages. One of the ways a link is designated on a Web page is with an underline. Using the underline style for text other than links could potentially confuse your visitors.*

REPEATING A COMMAND

Many times, you repeat the most recent formatting you did on another paragraph or other selected text. The Repeat command reduces that task to a simple keystroke. The first two items listed in the Edit menu are the Undo and Repeat commands. You'll want to remember their keyboard shortcuts:

Undo: Command+Z (Macintosh) and Ctrl+Z (Windows)

Repeat: Command+Y (Macintosh) and Ctrl+Y (Windows)

1) In introduction.html, select the word "Lens" in the definition list. Press Command+Y (Macintosh) or Ctrl+Y (Windows).
Because you used the Bold command most recently, it is applied to the selected text.

2) Repeat the bold formatting on the other terms in the definition list.
You can also access the Undo and Redo commands through the history panel: Window > Others > History.

CHANGING THE FONT

To make your page more interesting and easier to read, you may want to change the font used to display the text. Although a great deal of information is available concerning how type is used for print, not all of that knowledge translates to the Web. You have to consider the fact that users are free to change the screen size or to change the font size and color of the text. The way type flows on a page can change from user to user. The most dramatic difference occurs between font sizes on a Macintosh and in Windows. Macintosh computers display text approximately 25 percent smaller than the same text on Windows computers.

If you are accustomed to laying out or developing print media (such as a magazine or brochure), you might be frustrated by the lack of typographic control, such as line and letter spacing, in HTML. You also can't control widows (a single word on a line) in Web text, and you can't control line spacing in paragraphs.

TIP *Generally, sans-serif fonts are easier to read on a computer screen than serif fonts.*

You can change the font for the entire page or for selected text on the page, as you will see in the following exercise.

1) In introduction.html, select the text "Introduction to Lights of the Coast: Exploring Lighthouses." From the Property inspector's Font drop-down menu, choose Arial, Helvetica, sans-serif.

NOTE *A number of formatting options can be applied in the document window if you use Control-click (Macintosh) or right-click (Windows) to access the context menu.*

The font you choose must be installed on the user's computer in order for that user to see your page as you designed it. Do not make the assumption that all fonts are loaded on everyone's computer. The combinations of fonts will instruct the browser to change the displayed text to another font, depending on the fonts installed on your computer. If the first choice in the font list is not available, the browser attempts to use the second choice and then the third. If none of the fonts in the list are available on the user's computer, the text is displayed in the browser's default font.

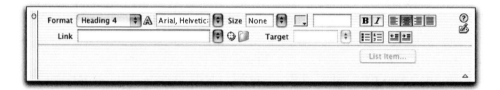

The font combinations (such as Arial, Helvetica, sans-serif) are useful, but they may not always include the specific fonts you want to use. You can change the font combination by choosing Edit Font List from the Property inspector's Font drop-down menu or by choosing Text > Font > Edit Font List to display the Edit Font List dialog box.

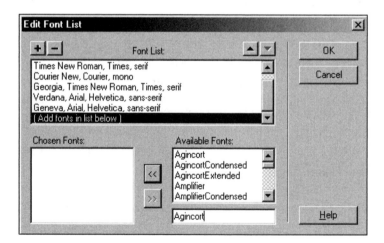

Select a font combination, and then choose among the following options:

- To add or remove fonts: Select the font, and then click the directional buttons between the Chosen Fonts list and the Available Fonts list.

- To add or remove a font combination: Click the plus sign (+) or minus sign (−) button in the top left corner of the dialog box.

- To add a font that is not installed on your system: Type the font name in the text field below the Available Fonts list and click the directional arrow to add it to the combination. Adding a font that is not installed on your system is useful, for example, for specifying a Windows-only font when you are authoring on a Macintosh.
- To move a font combination up or down in the list: Click the directional arrow buttons in the top right corner of the dialog box.

Close the Edit Font List dialog box.

2) Select the remainder of the text on the page. From the Property inspector's Font drop-down menu, choose Arial, Helvetica, sans-serif.
You have selected and formatted all text below the title with the same font.

3) Save the file and preview it in the browser.
The text will now display with the fonts you selected in your browser depending on what fonts you have installed on your computer.

TIP *You can remove font settings and return the type to its default setting by first selecting the text that uses the font you want to remove. In the Property inspector, choose Default Font from the Font drop-down menu or choose Text > Font > Default Font.*

CHANGING THE FONT SIZE
In HTML, the options for changing the font size on the page are limited. You will have more control when you begin to use cascading style sheets (CSS), which are covered in Lesson 11.

Select the first indented paragraph near the top of the page. From the Property inspector's Size drop-down menu, choose –1.
You'll notice that the sizes are listed as 1 through 7, +1 through +7, and –1 through –7. Selecting just the number (1 is smallest, 7 is largest) sets the absolute size. Picking a plus or minus number chooses the font size relative to the base size of the font. The number +1, for example, makes the font size one size larger than the base size.

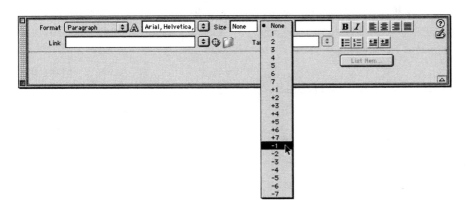

The default base size for text in a browser is 3. If you choose +3 for the font size, you are effectively changing the size to 6 (3 + 3). The largest size for the font is 7, and the smallest is 1. Any font size larger than 7 displays as 7; for example, if you set the font size to +6, 3 + 6 is larger than 7 but the font will still only be displayed as 7.

Using relative sizes gives you more control over the appearance of size relative to all the text on your page; it is generally more accessible for users than absolute sizes.

TIP *You can also choose Text > Size, Text > Size Increase, or Text > Size Decrease to affect the size from the submenus.*

CHANGING THE FONT COLOR

You can easily change the color of your text in Dreamweaver.

1) Select the text "Introduction to Lights of the Coast: Exploring Lighthouses."
Click the Text Color Picker button in the Property inspector.

The Web-safe color palette appears.

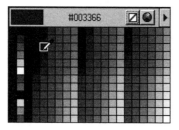

2) Choose a dark blue color (#003366).

The Color Picker window closes automatically after you click a color, and Dreamweaver applies the color immediately. You can also access the color picker by choosing Text > Color, which gives you access to several Color Picker windows.

SAVING COLORS AS FAVORITES

All colors used in your site are located in the Assets panel. To ensure that the colors you use are consistent across your site, you can save commonly used colors in the Assets panel as Favorites.

1) Click the arrow to the left of the Files panel group.

The Files panel group opens and gives you access to the Assets panel.

If the Files panel group is not open, you can choose Window > Assets. If the Files panel group is already open, and the Assets panel is displayed, you can skip this step.

2) In the Assets panel, click the Colors icon in the left column and click the Site radio button for Colors at the top of the panel.

You will see the colors that you have already used within the "Lights of the Coast" project site.

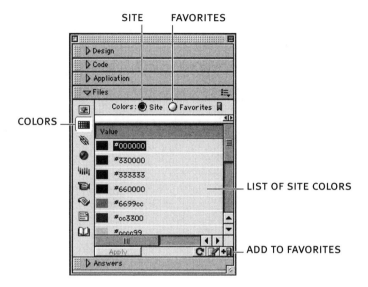

3) Select #330000 from the list of site colors on the Assets panel. Click the Add to Favorites button in the bottom right corner of the Assets panel.

Dreamweaver will display a dialog box informing you that the color has been added to your favorites. You will need to click the Favorites radio button for Colors at the top of the Assets panel in order to see the dark red color of your page header listed in your favorites.

47

CREATING HTML STYLES

As you design your Web pages, you will want to use font changes to make your pages more interesting. You can easily change the font, including its size and color, but if you want to use the same color, the same font, and the same size for all your pages, you would have to remember the settings from page to page and selection to selection. HTML styles save the text and paragraph formatting from selected text, making it easy for you to apply that style to other paragraphs in your document or to any document in your site. Using HTML styles can make the formatting throughout your documents more consistent, greatly speed up the process of formatting text, and give you the ability to share your styles with other members of your design team. If you change or delete an HTML style, text originally formatted with that style does not change.

NOTE *To apply formatting that updates your pages, you will need to use cascading style sheets, which are covered in Lesson 11.*

The following exercises demonstrate using HTML styles on a page. You will format some text, define several HTML styles, and then apply those formatting styles to other portions of the document.

1) Select the text "The Lighthouse of Alexandria." Apply bold formatting to the text. In the Assets panel's Site list, select the dark blue #003366 and click Apply at the bottom of the Assets panel.

The remaining lighthouse names in this section of notable lighthouses need the same formatting. You'll use an HTML style for this purpose.

2) With "The Lighthouse of Alexandria" selected, choose Window > HTML Styles.

The HTML Styles panel opens.

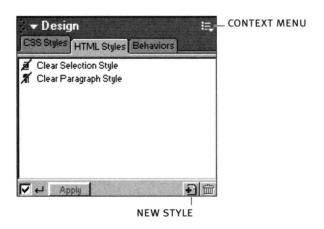

3) Click the New Style button at the bottom of the panel.

TIP *You can also choose New from the context drop-down menu to add a New Style.*

The Define HTML Style dialog box appears.

The Define HTML Style dialog box lets you make any necessary changes in the format of the styles. Since you had "The Lighthouse of Alexandria" selected, all of the formatting you applied to that text is reflected in this dialog box.

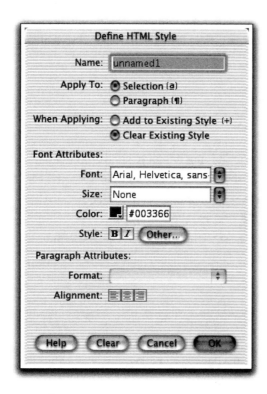

NOTE *Any changes you make in the Define HTML Style dialog box are not applied to the original text. If you want to make changes in the original text, you need to apply the style directly to that text.*

4) Type Lighthouse in the Name text field. In the Apply To list, choose Selection. Then click OK.

The dialog box closes, and your new style appears in the HTML style panel.

5) Select the text "(Egypt)", apply italic formatting, and make the color #333333. Make a new HTML style for this selection, naming the style Place. Click OK.

Notice the icon that resembles an underlined "a" appears next to this new style. This icon indicates a selection style.

6) Select the text "the illuminating device or burning of fuel to create light" in the definition list. Change the font to Verdana, the style to italic, and the text color to #333300. Make a new HTML style for this text, naming the style Definition. In the Apply To list, select paragraph and click OK to close the dialog box.

Notice the paragraph icon (¶) that appears next to this new style. This icon indicates a paragraph style.

APPLYING HTML STYLES

Now that you have several HTML styles defined, it's time to try applying them. Applying a style to a selection means you have to highlight all the appropriate text before applying the style. Applying a style to a paragraph means you have to place the insertion point within the paragraph—you don't have to select each word in the paragraph.

1) With the HTML Styles panel open, select the text "usually glass, used to focus and increase light intensity."

In this case, the style to be applied is a paragraph syle, so you can either select the text entirely or simply place the insertion point within the text. Each line within a list is treated as a separate paragraph.

2) Click Definition in the HTML Styles panel.

The style is applied to the paragraph.

NOTE *To edit an HTML Style, make sure that no text is selected in the document window. Control-click (Macintosh) or right-click (Windows) on a style name in the panel and choose Edit from the drop-down menu. (Alternatively, you can double-click a style name to open the Define HTML Style dialog box.) If you make a change, such as Font Attributes, and click OK, any new selections created with the style (or selections to which you apply the style) reflect the change you made. The change you make in a style does not affect the text that already has that formatting applied. If you want current text to reflect the new formatting, you have to reapply the style.*

3) Apply the Definition style to the remaining definitions in the list.

The style is applied to the rest of the definitions.

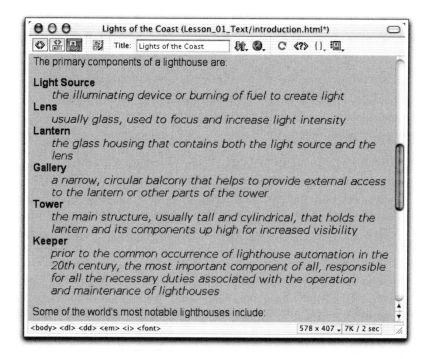

NOTE *Deleting a style can be a little tricky. First, you must make sure that no text is selected in the document and that the Auto Apply check box in the bottom left corner of the HTML Styles panel is not checked. Then you have to select the style you want to delete and click the trashcan icon in the bottom right corner of the panel. If you forget to turn off the Auto Apply option and have any text selected, you might see that text on the page change to the HTML style you selected to delete. You can clear the text formatting by selecting the formatted text and selecting Clear Paragraph Style or Clear Selection Style in the HTML Styles panel. All formatting will be removed, regardless of whether it was applied with an HTML style or through the Property inspector. If you are clearing a paragraph style, you can place the insertion point anywhere in the paragraph—you don't have to select the whole paragraph.*

4) Select the text "(U.S.A.)" just after "Cape Hatteras." In the HTML Styles panel, click Place.

This time you are applying a selection style, so make sure you highlight all the text that should be styled. After you click Place, the style is applied to the selected text.

5) Apply the Place style to the rest of the locations listed in the Notable Lighthouses of the World section.

The HTML styles you create can be used in other projects or shared with other users. When you create an HTML style, a file named Styles.xml is saved in a folder named Library. You can copy the Styles.xml file and move it to other site folders or share it with coworkers.

6) Apply the Lighthouse style to the rest of the lighthouse names listed in the Notable Lighthouses of the World section.

You have applied to your document a variety of HTML styles that can help you save time and maintain consistency throughout your site.

ADDING SPECIAL CHARACTERS

When you work in Dreamweaver, you sometimes need characters and other information that you cannot access directly from the keyboard. These special characters have specific HTML codes or alternative keyboard commands that may be difficult to remember.

1) Click the Characters tab on the Insert bar.

The Insert bar displays some of the most commonly used special characters.

COPYRIGHT CHARACTER

2) From the Insert bar, drag the copyright character to the bottom of the page. To the right of the copyright character that is inserted, type 2002, Lights of the Coast.

> **TIP** *You can also click to place the insertion point where you'd like the copyright symbol to appear in the document—in this case, at the bottom of the page. Then click the copyright symbol, and it will be placed at the insertion point.*

While the Character tab of the Insert bar gives you quick access to many of the most common characters, it doesn't provide an all-encompassing list.

NOTE *If the character you want to use isn't available in the Insert bar, you can still select it by clicking the Other Character button or choosing Insert > Special Characters > Other. When the Insert Other Character dialog box opens, click the character you want to use, and then click OK.*

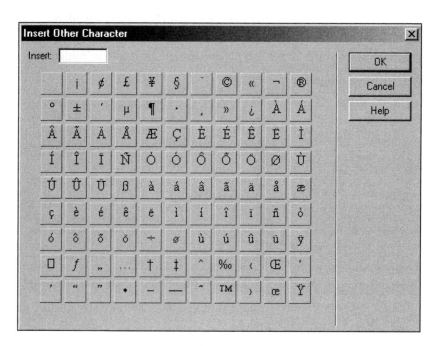

ADDING HORIZONTAL RULES

A **horizontal rule** is a line that goes across the page and provides a visual division between sections of your content. In this exercise, you will add a horizontal rule above the copyright information.

1) From the Common tab on the Insert bar, click the Insert Horizontal Rule button and drag a horizontal rule to the bottom of the document, just to the left of the copyright information.

If the Insert bar is not visible, choose Window > Insert. You can also click in the document and choose Insert > Horizontal Rule. Once you insert the horizontal rule, it will be selected in the document window. It will be placed just above the copyright information, which will drop down to a line below the horizontal rule.

2) With the horizontal rule still selected, type 70 in the W (width) text field on the Property inspector. Choose % from the drop-down menu to the right of the value you just typed.

The horizontal rule extends across 70 percent of the browser window regardless of the browser width. The rule is displayed as a thin bar on the page.

NOTE *Choose pixels from the menu to specify an absolute width. If you choose this option, the rule is not resized when users resize the browser window.*

3) Deselect Shading. Type 1 in the H (height) text field.
Deselecting the Shading check box displays a solid bar. The horizontal rule is 1 pixel high.

You can also choose to align the bar horizontally by choosing left, center, or right from the Align drop-down menu. The default alignment for horizontal rules is centered.

4) Save the file and preview it in the browser.
Notice how the horizontal rule appears. You can make changes by selecting it and modifying the properties in the Property inspector.

ADDING A DATE AUTOMATICALLY
Sometimes you may need to keep track of the date you last modified a page on your site. Dreamweaver lets you place a date and time on your pages to track this information. Dreamweaver can update the date and time automatically every time you save, so you don't have to do it manually.

In the following exercise, you'll add a date.

NOTE *This date is not a dynamic date that changes according to the date and/or time a user accesses the page. This date simply tells your users when your pages have been updated.*

1) Place the insertion point where you want the date to appear.
This information is usually displayed at the bottom of a page.

54

2) Click Date in the Common tab of the Insert bar to place the current date on the page.

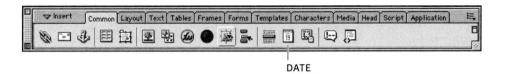

DATE

TIP *You can also choose Insert > Date to open the Insert Date dialog box.*

The Insert Date dialog box opens.

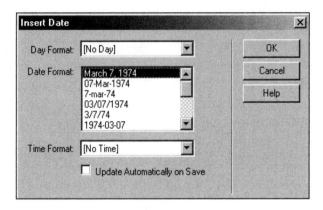

3) From the Day Format drop-down menu, choose the Thursday option. From the Date Format drop-down menu, choose March 7, 1974. From the Time Format drop-down menu, choose 10:18 PM on Macintosh OS 9 and Windows, or 9:18 PM on Macintosh OS X. Check the Update Automatically on Save check box to update the date on your page each time you save your document. Click OK.

The current day, date, and time are displayed. This information will change every time you save the document. Thursday is used as an example in the Insert Date dialog box of how the day will appear in your document. The date and time are also examples.

NOTE *You can change the date format if it is updated automatically. Click the date in your document. Then, in the Property inspector, click Edit Date Format. The Edit Date Format dialog box opens. This dialog box is the same as the Insert Date dialog box and is where you will make any necessary changes. Make the appropriate changes, and then click OK. Your changes are applied to the document.*

ADDING FLASH TEXT

When you add a heading to your page, your options are to use text and format it as a heading tag, or to create a graphic and insert it into the page. Text formatted as a heading will load quickly because it is text, but your font and size choices are limited. Using graphics as headings solves the font-choice problem, but you may not have access to a graphics program or just not enough time to create the graphic you need.

Flash text provides the best of both these options. You can use any font you choose and create the text within Dreamweaver. The text you create is saved as a small Flash file (.swf).

1) Position the insertion point in front of the text "Some of the world's most notable lighthouses include:". On the Media tab of the Insert bar, click the Flash Text button.

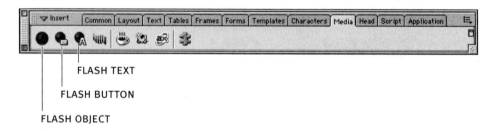

FLASH TEXT

FLASH BUTTON

FLASH OBJECT

Make sure that you don't click the Flash Button or Flash Object button.

The Insert Flash Text dialog box appears.

2) Make the following changes.

- From the Font drop-down menu, choose Comic Sans MS. (If Comic Sans MS is not available on your machine, choose another font.)

- In the Size text field, type **22**.

- From the Color drop-down menu, choose a dark red color.

- From the Rollover drop-down menu, choose a blue color.

- In the Text window, type **Some of the world's most notable lighthouses include:**.

- For Bg Color, type **#CCCC99**, or use the eyedropper and click the background in the document window.

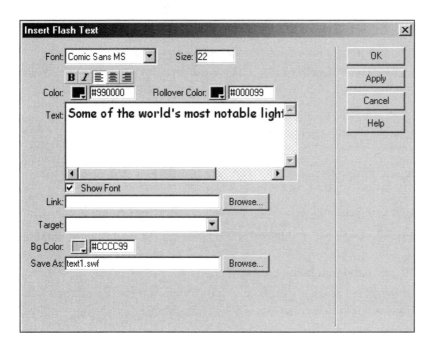

3) In the Save As text field, type notable.swf, and then click OK.

The Insert Flash Text dialog box closes.

4) In the Property inspector, click Play to start the Flash animation.

This step enables you to view the animation within Dreamweaver as it would appear in a browser.

5) In the document window, place the pointer over the Flash text.

The text changes to the rollover color you chose.

6) In the Property inspector, click Stop.

The Flash text no longer changes when you roll over it in Dreamweaver. To preview it, you must either click Play again or preview the document in a browser.

7) In the document window, select the Flash text and resize it by dragging one of the handles.

It doesn't matter what size you make the Flash text. Because the text is Flash text and not normal body text or a bitmap graphic, you can resize it directly in the document window.

NOTE *Resizing graphics (discussed in Lesson 2) within Dreamweaver is not recommended. But you can resize the Flash text image that you create because it is a vector graphic. Vector graphics are scalable; bitmap graphics (such as GIFs and JPEGs) are not.*

Because the Flash text is a vector graphic, you can increase or decrease the image size without concern about loss of image quality.

TIP *Hold down the Shift key to constrain the proportions while you resize the Flash text.*

You can now delete the text "Some of the world's most notable lighthouses include:" that appears after the Flash text you just inserted.

8) Save the file and preview it in the browser.

The text will roll over to the color you chose as it did when you previewed the Flash file in Dreamweaver. At this point, the text does not actually link to any page, although it acts like a link. You'll work with links in Lesson 3.

MODIFYING FLASH TEXT

Changing Flash text objects within Dreamweaver is easy.

NOTE *Although creating and working with Flash text is quick and easy, you should always consider whether your audience is likely to have the correct plug-ins before adding it to your site.*

1) In the document window, double-click the Flash text.

If you can't select the text, first click Stop in the Property inspector.

The Insert Flash Text dialog box opens.

2) Change the options to your liking, and then click Apply to see the results of your changes. When you finish, click OK to close the Insert Flash Text dialog box.

The edited Flash text is placed on the page, and the .swf file has been updated.

WHAT YOU HAVE LEARNED

In this lesson, you have:

- Familiarized yourself with Dreamweaver's Insert bar; the Property inspector; the document window; and other tools, windows, and panels (pages 8–14)

- Prepared to create a Web site, set up a local site, and defined the local root folder (pages 15–22)

- Specified preview browsers and used the keyboard shortcuts throughout the lesson to test your page (pages 23–24)

- Created a new page, saved the document with proper naming conventions, and gave the page a title (pages 24–28)

- Specified a background color and default font color (pages 29–33)

- Learned how to import text in different ways (pages 33–36)

- Positioned text by using paragraphs, breaks, and alignments (pages 36–37)

- Created three list types and modified their properties (pages 38–42)

- Applied text formatting of style, size, and color by using the Property inspector (pages 42–47)

- Customized font combinations and settings (pages 43–47)

- Automated the process of formatting text by creating and applying HTML styles (pages 48–52)

- Added special characters to the page (pages 52–53)

- Added a date to the page and set it to update every time the page is saved (pages 54–55)

- Created and edited Flash text (pages 56–58)

working with graphics

LESSON 2

Graphics play a significant part in capturing the attention of your audience and effectively communicating the intended message of your Web site. In this lesson, you will create Web pages that incorporate graphics, text, and Flash. In the process, you'll learn about different graphic file formats, how to control their appearances in an HTML document, and how to combine them with text.

The features in Dreamweaver MX give you a great deal of control over the graphics used in your site. You are able to modify image properties quickly within Dreamweaver, as well as immediately open images within an external image editor. The Assets panel

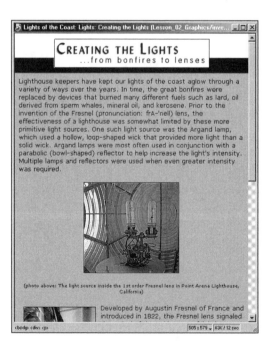

In this lesson, you'll create a page like this one while you learn to incorporate graphics with text on your Web pages.

simplifies the management of graphics by enabling you to create catalogs of all the images used in your site or of images that you need to have available.

If you would like to view the final result of this lesson, open invent_lens.html in the Completed folder within the Lesson_02_Graphics folder.

WHAT YOU WILL LEARN

In this lesson, you will:

- Identify graphics formats and explore their differences
- Insert graphics into a page
- Modify the properties of your images
- Give your images names and **`<alt>`** tags
- Change the positioning of graphics on a page
- Align text with an image
- Wrap text around an image
- Use the Assets panel to manage graphics
- Insert buttons and animations from Macromedia Flash

APPROXIMATE TIME

This lesson should take about one hour to complete.

LESSON FILES

Media Files:

Lesson_02_Graphics/Images/bkg_inside_tan.gif
Lesson_02_Graphics/Images/invlens_header.gif
Lesson_02_Graphics/Images/ptarena_lens.jpg
Lesson_02_Graphics/Images/ptarena_outlens.jpg
Lesson_02_Graphics/Images/ptarena_belowlight.jpg
Lesson_02_Graphics/Images/lens_demoY.swf
Lesson_02_Graphics/Images/ptarena_prism.jpg

Starting Files:

Lesson_02_Graphics/Text/invent.txt
Lesson_02_Graphics/Text/lens_demo.txt

Completed Project:

Lesson_02_Graphics/Completed/invent_lens.html
Lesson_02_Graphics/Completed/lens_demo.html

PLACING GRAPHICS ON THE PAGE

The most common and widely supported graphic formats on the Web are GIF (Graphic Interchange Format) and JPEG (Joint Photographic Experts Group). When deciding whether to save a graphic as a GIF or a JPEG, aim for the highest image quality and the lowest possible file size.

As a general rule, you should use GIF if the artwork has large areas of solid, flat colors and little or no blending of colors. GIF works well with text, vector graphics, images with a limited number of colors and very small image dimensions. GIF images can be saved, at maximum, using 8-bit color mode in which only 256 colors can be represented. GIF files tend to load faster, have more optimization options, and support transparency and animation.

You should usually choose JPEG for photographic images or images with a large tonal range. The JPEG format handles blending of colors very well and can produce much higher quality photographic images at a fraction of the size of a GIF. JPEG saves the image in 24-bit mode, retaining all the colors and using a lossy form of compression in which redundant data is lost. The lower the quality of a JPEG, the more information is lost about the image through this discard of data.

In this book, all the images you will be working with have already been saved for use on the Web as GIFs and JPEGs. You will not need to save or optimize any graphics.

1) Create a new file and save it as invent_lens.html in the DWMX_project/Lesson_02_Graphics folder. Type Lights of the Coast: Lights: Creating the Lights as the document title.

In this step, you are specifying the basic document settings you learned in Lesson 1. The document you are creating in this lesson is part of the Lights section of the Lights of the Coast project Web site. To indicate the location of the page to viewers, you are giving the page a title that starts with the name of the site, gives the name of the section the document is in, and finally gives the name of the document itself. This naming method makes it very clear what page will be shown in the browser and where this page is located within the site.

2) In Modify › Page Properties, change the background color to #CCCC99. Type #000000 into the text color field on the Page Properties dialog box to set the text color to black. Choose images/bkg_inside_tan.gif from the Lesson_02_Graphics/Images folder as the background image and click OK to close the Page Properties dialog box.

It is best to apply these general document settings before you begin laying out your pages. You can always modify them later, but it helps to see the document with the colors and settings that it will be using.

62

3) Place the insertion point in the first line of the document. Click the Image button on the Common tab of the Insert bar.

The Select Image Source dialog box opens which will allow you to insert a graphic into the page. An alternative method is to choose Insert > Image.

IMAGE

TIP *Select Preview Images to see a thumbnail of the image that you will choose. The button will change to Hide Preview. Images are displayed in the Select Image Source dialog box along with their dimensions, file size, and approximate download time. On Macintosh OS X, there is no Select Preview Images button; you will see the preview in the right pane of the Select Image Source dialog box once you have selected an image.*

4) Locate the file Lesson_02_Graphics/Images/invlens_header.gif.

The document filename invent_lens.html appears below the Data Sources button and above the Relative To menu. The Data Sources button is used for dynamic sites in which a document executes on an application server. You will not need to use Data Sources in this book because you are not creating a dynamic, data-driven site. The Relative To menu, which should already be set to Document by default, lets you choose how Dreamweaver references images: with document-relative or site root-relative references. In **document-relative referencing**, Dreamweaver constructs the path to the image based on the relative location of your HTML document to the graphics file. **Site root-relative referencing** constructs the path to the image based on the relative location of your HTML document to your site root.

Generally, you should use document-relative links and paths. If you have an extremely large site or plan to move pages frequently, you might want to use site root-relative referencing.

NOTE *Until you save your file, Dreamweaver has no way to make these kinds of references, so it will substitute a pathname based on the location of the image on your hard disk instead of a valid link. These paths will not work on a remote site. You should always save your document before you insert graphics. If you don't, Dreamweaver displays an alert box and then fixes the path when you do save the Dreamweaver file. If the image you select in the Select Image Source dialog box is outside of your local site, Dreamweaver will also display this alert beneath the Relative To menu: Chosen file is not under site root.*

5) Click Open (Macintosh OS 9), Choose (Macintosh OS X) or OK (Windows).

The image appears in the document window.

> **NOTE** *This image was saved as a GIF in order to maintain crisp lines for the text. As a JPEG, the same image would show JPEG **artifacts** (small, blocky squares where redundant data is discarded, which are more common in areas of solid, flat color) in the white background if saved to approximate the small file size of the GIF. If the image were to be saved as a higher quality JPEG in order to achieve the same image quality as the GIF, it would have a much larger file size. In this case, GIF was the best option.*

RESIZING AND REFRESHING GRAPHICS

When you import a graphic, the width and height of the image are shown in the Property inspector and placed into the code automatically, giving the browser the information it needs to define the layout of the page. This important option can make a difference in the speed of loading your graphics. You can change these numbers in Dreamweaver.

1) In invent_lens.html, click the invlens_header.gif image to select it. In the Property inspector, change the width to 220 pixels and the height to 38 pixels.

You are using the width and height tags to make this graphic appear in smaller dimensions without making the actual graphic file smaller. Notice that the file size of the selected image that is displayed in the Property inspector does not change.

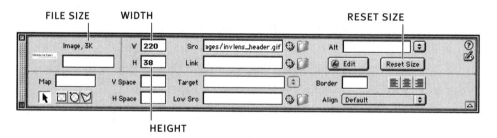

FILE SIZE   WIDTH   RESET SIZE

HEIGHT

2) Click one of the selection handles—the black squares—on the border. Drag to resize the image and make it larger than the original size.

The width and height specifications update automatically. Notice that the new dimensions you have set are displayed in bold. This bold formatting is an indicator that the graphic has been resized. At times, you may resize a graphic accidentally, and the bold numbers will clue you to that change. You can also change the size by changing the numbers in the Width and Height text fields.

TIP *Hold down the Shift key while you drag the image's selection handles to constrain the proportions of the image.*

Notice that when you scaled the image larger, the image quality diminished. Images display in browsers at screen resolution, which is 72 dpi. This resolution is not high enough to display an image with a specified size larger than the actual size of the graphic. You could scale the image smaller, and it will look OK, but you won't have changed the file size, so the graphic will take just as long to download. When you adjust the size of an image within Dreamweaver, you are only changing the size at which it displays in the browser—you are not resizing the actual graphic itself. Always adjust the image size in your image-editing software (such as Macromedia Fireworks or Adobe Photoshop) to ensure that you have the smallest file size possible.

TIP *The Property inspector for images features an Edit button in the top half and right side of the panel. This option provides a quick way to open and modify your images in an external image editor. To choose your preferred editor, choose Edit > Preferences and select File Types/Editors in the Category list of the Preferences dialog box. You can use this dialog box to assign different editors according to the file extensions. Production with Dreamweaver MX, Flash, and Fireworks can be integrated through what is known as* **roundtrip editing***, a feature that causes file updates to be transferred between the programs.*

3) In the Property inspector, click Reset Size on the right side of the panel.
The image resets to the original size of the graphic. Notice that the width and height numbers revert to plain text, indicating that the image is set at the original size.

NOTE *When using very large images, or images which are located on other servers, you can provide a visual clue to viewers by using a low source image. By defining a low source, you are choosing a lower quality image that will appear first. The higher-quality image will appear in its place when the download is complete. When an image is selected, the Property inspector provides a Low Src text field for defining a low source image. Click the Browse for File folder icon next to the field to choose an image.*

POSITIONING GRAPHICS

When you place an image directly in the body of a document, you have a limited number of options for positioning it. The following exercise is a method of creating an alignment that uses **<div>** tags. These tags are essentially containers that specify the alignment of everything between the tags. You will learn about other ways to align images later in this lesson and also in Lesson 4.

65

1) In invent_lens.html, click the invlens_header.gif image to select it. In the Property inspector, click the Align Center button.

If you don't see the Align Center button, click the expander arrow in the bottom right corner. The image becomes centered on the page.

ALIGN CENTER   EXPANDER ARROW

TIP *The Align Center button is not the same as the Align drop-down menu that you will see below the three alignment buttons.*

2) Insert a paragraph break after the page-title graphic by clicking off of the image and pressing Return or Enter. Import the text from invent.txt, select all the text and click the Align Left button in the Property inspector to set the alignment to the left.

You can copy and paste the text from invent.txt into the invent_lens.html document just like you did in Lesson 1.

When you work with multiple elements, you must put them in separate paragraphs to give them different alignments. You cannot center part of a paragraph and align the rest left. When you insert text directly below an image, for example, you need to use a regular paragraph break (press Return on a Macintosh or Enter in Windows) between the image and the text. If you use a single line break (by pressing Shift+Return on the Macintosh or Shift+Enter in Windows) between them, any alignment you apply affects both the image and the text, because they would be considered part of the same paragraph block.

3) Set the following text options using the Property inspector for all the text: font should be Verdana, size should be –1.

You can save this file and preview it in the browser.

ADDING A BORDER AROUND AN IMAGE

At times, you need to set an image apart from the background to make it stand out. One way to create this effect is to place a border around the image. A border can draw attention to an image, and it can continue a stylistic look throughout a site. At times, a border can also indicate a link.

In invent_lens.html, click the invlens_header.gif image to select it. Then, in the Border text field of the Property inspector, type 1.

Dreamweaver adds a 1-pixel border around the image.

You can set the width of the border to any number you want. The border color will be the same as the default text color that was specified in Page Properties dialog box.

NOTE *When you start assigning links to images in Lesson 3, the border color will be the same as the default link color specified in Page Properties. You can also affect the border color of an image by putting font-color tags around the image tag in the code. You will work with the code in Lesson 12.*

ASSIGNING NAMES AND <Alt> TAGS TO IMAGES

Names and **<alt>** tags are important, although largely invisible, parts of your Web pages. It is generally a good practice to assign names and **<alt>** tags, because they help both you and the users of your site. The functions of these elements are described in the following exercise.

1) Select the invlens_header.gif image and type header in the image name text field on the Property inspector.

The image name text field is not labeled on the Property inspector. It is located in the upper left corner, directly under the size of the image.

IMAGE NAME

The name you assign to the image is an internal name, used mainly for functions such as Behaviors (covered in Lesson 5). Although naming your images is not essential, doing so is good practice. You should keep image names short, enter them in lowercase, and avoid using spaces or special characters.

2) Type Creating The Lights...from bonfires to lenses in the Alt text field.

The Alt option lets you specify text that will be displayed if users have graphics disabled, if their browsers are not capable of displaying graphics, or if a particular image fails to load. In this case, the text you have typed is the same text shown in the image.

You must add **\<alt\>** tags to any graphics that are critical for site navigation. Adding **\<alt\>** tags to other images is also useful, because if users have graphics disabled or are using a text-only browser, they will be able to see some of the information they are missing. Additionally, people with vision disabilities use a reader that voices the **\<alt\>** tags along with the text on a Web page. Further, **\<alt\>** text is displayed briefly in Internet Explorer when the user moves the pointer over the graphic.

INSERTING AN IMAGE FROM THE ASSETS PANEL

You may find it difficult to manage all your images, especially if you are working on a large site. The Assets panel provides a way for you to keep track of those images. Before you begin the following exercise, make sure that the Assets panel is open. It is in the Files panel group. If the Files panel group is not visible, choose Window > Assets.

1) Open the Files panel group. On the Macintosh, the Assets panel is the only panel in the Files panel group, so you will not see the Assets tab. In Windows, you will need to select the Assets panel from the Files panel group. Click the Images button located at the top of the column of buttons on the left side of the Assets panel (or the Files panel group if you are on the Macintosh).

The other buttons represent different types of assets that may be available to your site, including colors, which you used in Lesson 1.

You can work with the Assets panel in two ways: view it with the Site list, which gives you a complete list of the images in your site; or view it with the Favorites list, which allows you to add images.

TIP *You can also open the Assets panel by choosing Window > Assets. On the Macintosh, the Files panel group contains only the Assets panel, so you will not see the Assets tab even though you have actually opened the Assets panel.*

2) Click the Site button at the top of the Assets panel.

All images within the site are shown in the Site Assets window. The images appear in this window automatically, whether or not they are used in any document. It may take a few seconds for the panel to create a catalog of the image assets available for your site. If you haven't created a site cache for this site, the Assets panel prompts you to do so; the Assets list cannot be created without a site cache.

If you add a new asset to your site, it might not appear in the Assets panel immediately. To update the panel to match all the images in your site, you need to refresh the site catalog. To do so, click the Refresh Site List button in the bottom right corner of the Assets panel.

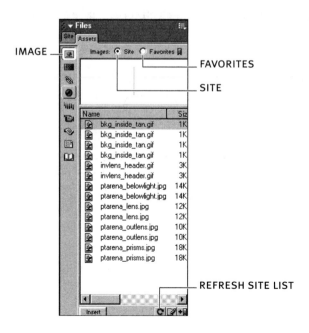

69

3) Insert a paragraph break after the first paragraph by pressing Return (Macintosh) or Enter (Windows). Find the ptarena_lens.jpg graphic in the Assets panel that is located in the Lesson_02_Graphics/Images folder and drag it to the document between the first and second paragraphs.

You may see multiple copies of the same images in the Assets panel. This is due to duplicates of lesson files that are contained in the Completed folders for each lesson, and the fact that you will be using certain files many times throughout the course of this book. On your own sites, you probably will not have this situation, unless you duplicate files in each folder.

TIP *Alternatively, you can place the insertion point in the document, select the image in the Assets panel, and click the Insert button.*

The image appears in the document window.

NOTE *This photographic image was saved as a JPEG. The same image would appear posterized if saved as a GIF image, because all of the different shades would be mapped to only a few colors. In this case, JPEG was the best option.*

4) Select the image you just inserted. In the image-name text field of the Property inspector, type lightsource. In the Alt text box, type Point Arena Light Source Photo. Define a border of 1 pixel.

Giving names and **<alt>** tags to your images as you insert them will save you time and make it easier to work with them in Code View later, if necessary.

5) Center the ptarena_lens.jpg image. Create a line break after the image and type the following: (photo above: The light source inside the 1st order Fresnel lens in Point Arena Lighthouse, California).

Providing captions for your images will help viewers understand them in the proper context. The caption will be centered, because it is considered to be in the same paragraph block as the image above.

6) Use the Property inspector to apply the following text formatting to the text: the font should be Verdana, the size should be –2, and the color should be #333333.

In this case, you are fading the text and making it smaller in order to subtly differentiate it from the body text of the document.

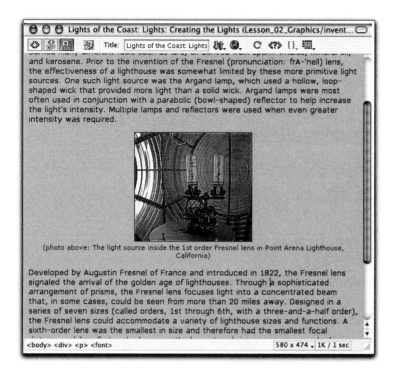

Lights of the Coast: Lights: Creating the Lights (Lesson_02_Graphics/invent...

Title: Lights of the Coast: Lights

and kerosene. Prior to the invention of the Fresnel (pronunciation: frA-'nell) lens, the effectiveness of a lighthouse was somewhat limited by these more primitive light sources. One such light source was the Argand lamp, which used a hollow, loop-shaped wick that provided more light than a solid wick. Argand lamps were most often used in conjunction with a parabolic (bowl-shaped) reflector to help increase the light's intensity. Multiple lamps and reflectors were used when even greater intensity was required.

(photo above: The light source inside the 1st order Fresnel lens in Point Arena Lighthouse, California)

Developed by Augustin Fresnel of France and introduced in 1822, the Fresnel lens signaled the arrival of the golden age of lighthouses. Through a sophisticated arrangement of prisms, the Fresnel lens focuses light into a concentrated beam that, in some cases, could be seen from more than 20 miles away. Designed in a series of seven sizes (called orders, 1st through 6th, with a three-and-a-half order), the Fresnel lens could accommodate a variety of lighthouse sizes and functions. A sixth-order lens was the smallest in size and therefore had the smallest focal

`<body> <div> <p> <font>`   580 x 474 ▾ 1K / 1 sec

MANAGING IMAGES WITH THE FAVORITES LIST

Placing images that you use repeatedly in a Favorites list can be a time-saver. You can add any image contained within the site to your Favorites list. This list will be empty when you start using Dreamweaver. In the following exercise, you will add an image from the Site category to your Favorites list and then organize that list.

1) In invent_lens.html, select ptarena_outlens.jpg in the Site list and click the Add to Favorites button , located in the bottom right corner of the Assets panel.

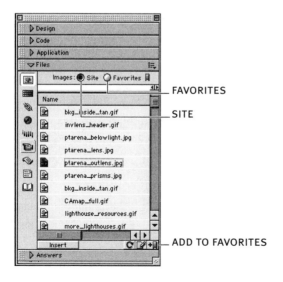

A dialog box appears to let you know that the selected assets have been added to this site's Favorites list. Choose OK to acknowledge the message and close the dialog box.

TIP *You can use an alternative method to add an image to the Favorites list. First, in Site View, select the image you want to use. From the options drop-down menu in the top right corner of the Files panel group, choose Add to Favorites. Yet another method is to make an image in your document window a favorite. To do this, Control-click (Macintosh) or right-click (Windows) the image and choose Add to Image Favorites from the context menu that appears. This context menu contains a wide variety of options and also works for other elements such as text and Flash objects.*

2) From the Images options at the top of the Assets panel, select the Favorites radio button.

The Assets panel now displays the list of favorites, and the image you added in the previous step is in the list.

As you begin to manage your images through the Assets panel, you probably will need to remove as well as add images. When an image is selected in the Favorites list, the Add to Favorites button becomes the Remove from Favorites button. Clicking Remove from Favorites causes the selected image to disappear from the list.

3) Click the icon for New Favorites Folder at the bottom of the panel and type Fresnel **in the folder-name text field.**

You can organize your images in folders to make them easy to locate.

TIP *You can also select New Favorites Folder by clicking the arrow at the top right of the panel to access the drop-down menu.*

NEW FAVORITES FOLDER

4) Drag the ptarena_outlens image into the Fresnel folder.

You can click the small arrow (Macintosh) or plus sign (+) button (Windows) to see the contents of the folder and click again on the arrow (Macintosh) or minus sign (–) button to collapse the folder.

Images in Favorites are listed by their nicknames (with no extensions such as .jpg or .gif), which Dreamweaver assigns automatically based on the image's filenames. You can change these nicknames—in the Favorites list only—by clicking the name, pausing, and clicking again. Don't double-click. Double-clicking an image in either the Site list or the Favorites list will cause the image to be opened in a graphical editor if one is defined, such as Adobe Photoshop or Macromedia Fireworks.

A border appears around the text field, and the name is highlighted. Start typing to replace the highlighted text.

NOTE *If you need to delete a folder that you created in the Favorites list, select the folder and then click Remove from Favorites at the bottom of the Assets panel.*

WRAPPING TEXT AROUND IMAGES

Layout options in HTML include wrapping text around images. The following exercise demonstrates how to create a text wrap. You can use the same procedure to align images with other elements, such as other images.

1) In invent_lens.html, place the insertion point at the beginning of the second paragraph. Insert ptarena_outlens.jpg.

The image is placed in the document and appears in the default position, with the first line of the text starting at the baseline of the image.

2) Select the ptarena_outlens.jpg graphic and choose Left from the Align drop-down menu in the Property inspector.

ALIGN MENU

The image is aligned left. The text on the right wraps to the bottom of the ptarena_outlens.jpg graphic and then returns to the left margin of the window. By changing the Align attribute, can wrap multiple lines of text around the image. When you choose Left or Right from the Align menu, Dreamweaver places an image-anchor symbol at the point where the image was inserted. If necessary, you can move this anchor to a new location. The anchor needs to be at the beginning of the text for the text wrap to work properly. This symbol indicates where the HTML tag for the image is in relation to the text. If you don't see the symbol, choose View > Visual Aids > Invisible Elements. A check next to this command indicates that the option is selected. The symbol will not be visible in the browser.

NOTE *The Align menu contains several options for images, including Top and Text Top. If the list is confusing to you, remember that text can wrap only on the left or the right side of an image, so the only options you can choose are Left and Right. The other options are for placement of a single line of text next to a graphic.*

3) Give the ptarena_outlens.jpg image a border of 1 pixel. Save the file and preview it in the browser.

Keep in mind that whenever you select an alignment option other than Browser Default, you are applying an alignment to an image. When this happens, the image is offset slightly from the original position. You cannot control or get rid of this offset.

74

The amount of offset varies from browser to browser but usually is only a couple of pixels and not noticeable. The offset may be a problem, however, if you are trying to align images in tables. In that case, you need to use other methods to control the placement of your images.

The amount of text that wraps around the image will depend on the size at which the text displays in the browser window, the amount of text, and how big the browser window has been opened. When you resize the window (whether in Dreamweaver or a browser), the way the text wraps around the image will change. Keep in mind also that what you see in the Dreamweaver document window is only an approximation of what will be seen in the browser.

NOTE *When you first insert an image, the contents of your document that come after the image may be pushed downward. When you use the Align Left option, those contents might not always pop into place when you are using tables (you will learn to use tables in Lesson 4). This may cause the document to look as if there is extra space. If that happens, simply click outside of the outermost table, in the body of the document.*

ADJUSTING THE SPACE AROUND AN IMAGE

When you wrap text around graphics, you'll probably want to adjust the space around the image, as well. You can add vertical space (V Space) and horizontal space (H Space).

1) In invent_lens.html, click the ptarena_outlens.jpg image to select it.

Right now, the text is very close to the edge of this graphic. The page would look better and the text would be easier to read if space was added around the image.

2) In the Property inspector, type 10 in the H Space text field.

V SPACE

H SPACE

This setting creates 10 pixels of space on the left and right sides of the image. You cannot add space on only one side.

3) Type 6 in the V Space text field.

This setting creates 6 pixels of space at the top and bottom of the image. You cannot add space on only one side.

INSERTING AN IMAGE PLACEHOLDER

You have the option to insert an image placeholder if you do not have the final image. A placeholder can be inserted and used to approximate how the final graphic will appear on the page in combination with text, tables, or other elements.

1) Place the insertion point on a new line after the second paragraph of body text. Click the Image Placeholder button on the Common tab of the Insert bar.

The Image Placeholder dialog box appears.

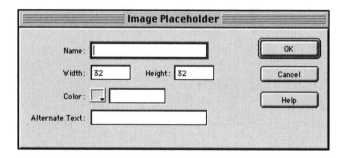

2) In the name text field, type belowlight. Set the width to 250 and the height to 195. Click the color box and use the swatches to pick black; then type below the light source in the Alt text field. Click OK.

The image placeholder appears in the document window. It is black and displays the image name and the dimensions.

Image placeholders will display as broken images when you preview in a browser. To fix this, you will need to replace the image placeholder with the intended image as described in the next exercise.

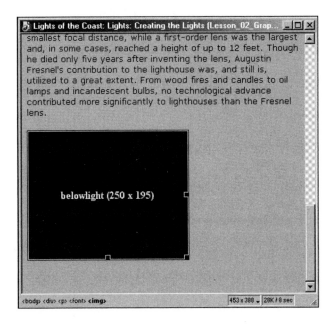

NOTE *The default width and height for an image placeholder is 32×32 pixels.*

REPLACING AN IMAGE PLACEHOLDER

Once you have created the final graphic or received the necessary image from your client, you will need to replace the image placeholder you used to approximate the graphic.

1) Double-click the image placeholder in the document window.

The Select Image Source dialog box opens.

2) Choose ptarena_belowlight.jpg from the Lesson_02_Graphics/Images folder.

The image replaces the placeholder in the document window. The name and alt text that were assigned to the image placeholder are now applied to the image.

ALIGNING AN IMAGE RELATIVE TO A SINGLE LINE OF TEXT

Many times, you'll want to control the placement of an image in relation to a single line of text that appears near it. You can change the relative location of the image to the text by using alignment options. The seven options discussed in the following exercise work well for aligning a single line of text near a graphic.

TIP *The options used in this exercise don't work for wrapping multiple lines around a graphic. To wrap multiple lines, you will need to choose either the Left or Right alignment options, as demonstrated in the Wrapping Text Around Images exercise.*

1) Position the insertion point to the right of the belowlight graphic and type Point Arena, California. **Select the text and change the font to Verdana, the size to –2, and the color to #333333.**

Initially, the text is aligned with the bottom of the graphic, and it is too close to the graphic.

2) Select the belowlight graphic, and add a 1-pixel border to it. In the Property inspector, type 10 **in the H Space text box.**

The graphic and text move apart, and a thin border appears around the image.

3) From the Align drop-down menu, choose Absolute Middle.

This option aligns the baseline of the text with the middle of the image.

The other options are as follows:

- **Baseline**: Aligns the bottom of the image with the baseline, or bottom line, on which the text sits. This option normally is the browser default.

- **Top**: Aligns the image with the top of the tallest item in the line. That item may be text or a larger image.

- **Middle**: Aligns the baseline of the text with the middle of the image.

- **Bottom:** Aligns the same way as Baseline.

- **Text Top**: Does what you would expect Top should do, which is to align the image with the top of the tallest text in the line. (This option usually, but not always, is the same as Top.)

- **Absolute Middle**: Aligns the middle of the image with the middle of the text line or the largest item in the line.

- **Absolute Bottom**: Aligns the bottom of the image with the lowest point of the text line.

4) Save the file and preview it in the browser.

You can also use these options to position images relative to other images; you're not limited to using text.

ADDING FLASH BUTTONS

You can achieve special effects by using Flash objects. Because Flash graphics are vector-based, their file sizes are very small, which helps them load quickly in the user's browser.

Flash buttons have several states, depending on the position of the pointer and whether the mouse button has been clicked. The first state is the appearance of the button when the pointer is not on it. The second state is when the pointer is on the button but the mouse button has not been clicked. The third state is when the pointer is on the button and the mouse button has been clicked. You can create and maintain Flash buttons in Dreamweaver from a set of available button styles.

1) In invent_lens.html, position the insertion point on a new line under the belowlight graphic in the document window.

You'll insert a Flash button here to take the user back to the main page of the site.

2) In the Insert bar, select the Media tab and click the Flash Button icon.

FLASH BUTTON

The Insert Flash Button dialog box opens.

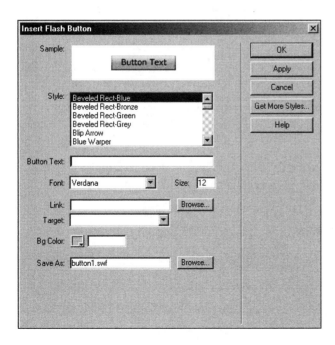

3) In the Style list, scroll down and select Glass-Silver. In the Button Text text field, type Main. Choose Verdana (or another font if Verdana is not available) from the Font menu. In the Size text box, type 12.

You can edit these settings later, if necessary. The next exercise will show you how.

4) For Bg Color, click the color box. Then, using the eyedropper pointer, click anywhere on the background of the document window.

The background-color code #CCCC99 appears in the Bg color text field.

5) In the Save As text box, type main-button.swf. Then click OK at the top right of the dialog box.

The Insert Flash Button dialog box closes and a button with the specifications you set will appear in the document. Since you just inserted the button it is selected.

You should always name your Flash buttons. If you don't, Dreamweaver automatically assigns them a name.

6) With the button still selected, click the Play button in the Property inspector.

The button is in its original state, and the selection handles disappear.

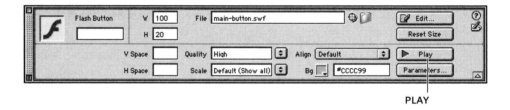

PLAY

7) In the document window, move the pointer over the Main button. Then click the button.

The button changes to its rollover state when the pointer is moved over it. The button changes to its clicked state when clicked.

8) Click Stop in the Property inspector. Save the file and preview it in the browser.

The button changes states just as it did in Dreamweaver, depending on the pointer position and mouse click.

MODIFYING FLASH BUTTONS

You can change many of the button attributes.

1) In the document window, double-click the Flash button you created.

The Insert Flash Button dialog box opens.

NOTE *If the dialog box does not open when you double-click a Flash button, make sure you click Stop in the Property inspector.*

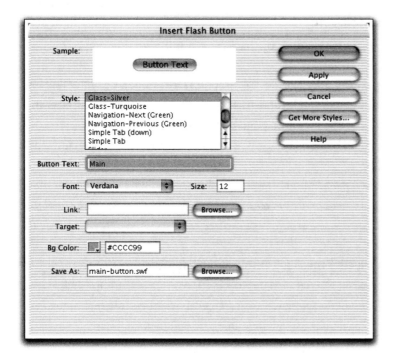

2) Make changes in the Flash button settings. Set the options however you want.

Change the font to Arial, for example.

3) Click Apply to see the changes. Click OK when you finish.

You can add your own template buttons by using Flash to create them outside Dreamweaver.

ADDING FLASH ANIMATIONS

You can add Flash animations to your document as easily as you can add an image, provided that the animation already exists. You cannot create animations directly within Dreamweaver.

1) Create a new document and save it as lens_demo.html in the Lesson_02_Graphics folder. Use Modify > Page Properties to set the title as Lights of the Coast: Lights: Refraction. **Set the background graphic as bkg_inside_tan.gif from the Lesson_02_Graphics/Images folder. Set the background color as #CCCC99, and set the default text color as #000000. Click OK.**

You have saved the document and set the background and page title properties.

2) Open lens-demo.txt from the Lesson_02_Graphics/Text folder. Copy the text and paste it into the lens_demo.html document. Add an extra paragraph break after the first paragraph and place the insertion point on the new line.

Be sure to use a paragraph break and not a line break. You need a new paragraph block.

NOTE *You may need to add additional paragraph breaks between the two lines of header information at the top of the document and the first paragraph to prevent the black bar of the background from obscuring the text in the first paragraph.*

3) In the Assets panel, click the Flash button in the left column.

The Flash assets appear in the panel. The Site and Favorites lists for Flash assets work the same way as they do for image assets. You can use the same techniques to manage and organize Flash files as you do to manage and organize images.

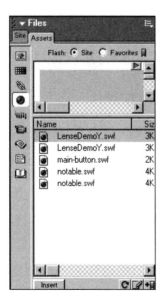

TIP *You can also insert a Flash animation by clicking the Flash icon on the Media tab of the Insert bar.*

4) In the Site list, select LenseDemoY.swf; then click Insert.

The Flash animation is placed on the page.

5) In the Property inspector, make sure the boxes for Loop and Autoplay are checked. Click Play to view the animation in Dreamweaver.

To view animation files in Dreamweaver, you must click Play. Click Stop when you are done testing.

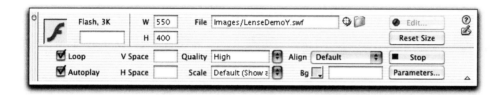

TIP *You can resize animations by dragging their selection handles. Hold down the Shift key to constrain the proportions.*

6) Save the file and preview it in the browser.

Autoplay causes the Flash animation to begin playing as soon as the page is loaded into the browser. The animation plays repeatedly because you chose Loop in the Property inspector.

NOTE *Always be sure to select a .swf file when you insert a Flash animation. Do not insert .fla or .swt files, because they do not show up in a browser.*

INSERTING AN ACCESSIBLE IMAGE

It is important to create sites that are accessible to people with disabilities. Dreamweaver's accessibility tools make it easier for Web developers to comply with accessibility standards such as Section 508 of the Rehabilitation Act. You'll learn more about accessibility in Lesson 7.

1) Choose Edit > Preferences.

The Preferences dialog box opens.

2) From the Category list, choose Accessibility. In the list of objects displayed on the right, check the box for images. Click OK to close the Preferences dialog box.

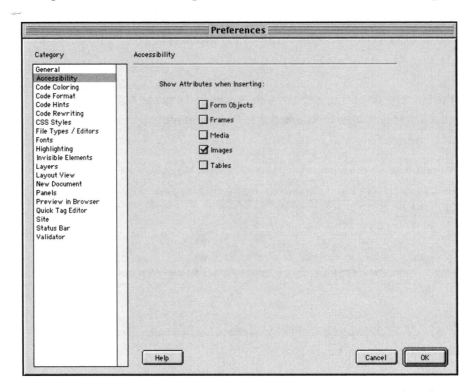

Dreamweaver's image accessibility authoring options are now enabled.

If you wish to turn off this feature at a later point, you can uncheck the box for images in the accessibility preferences.

3) Create a new paragraph between the caption for the Flash animation and the caption for the Prism image that you will insert in the following step. Click the Image button on the Common tab of the Insert bar.
The Select Image Source dialog box opens.

4) Choose ptarena_prisms.jpg from the Lesson_02_Graphics/Images folder and click OK.
The Image Tag Accessibility Attributes dialog box opens, which will prompt you to enter Alternate Text and a Long Description.

5) In the Alternate Text field, type Prisms. Leave the Long Description field as is and click OK.

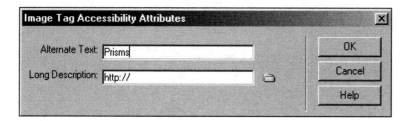

The Alt text field on the Property inspector displays "Prisms."

Long descriptions are not displayed on the Property inspector. Since you did not define a long description for this image, no tag has been created for it. A long description is usually text-based content that serves as a substitute for its respective image. The long description is used by those who are not able to view the displayed image and are using an alternative method of accessing the page, such as a screen reader. It is meant to be longer and more definitive than the Alt text. For full accessibility, you should create long descriptions whenever the Alt text does not adequately and completely serve to stand in for the visual element.

NOTE *You can set a default folder for your images in the Local Info category of the Advanced tab on the Site Definition dialog box. If you choose a folder, Dreamweaver will open the Select Image Source dialog box to the directory you choose. You will not be limited to that folder; it simply becomes the default.*

6) Choose Edit > Preferences. In the Accessibility category, uncheck the box for images. Click OK to close the Preferences dialog box.
The accessibility option for images is turned off.

ON YOUR OWN: SOLAR EVENTS

The Solar Events Web site, a resource of the Sun-Earth Connection Education Forum, promotes learning about sun science. Events geared toward schools, classrooms, museums, and community groups include Sun-Earth Day and Solar Week.

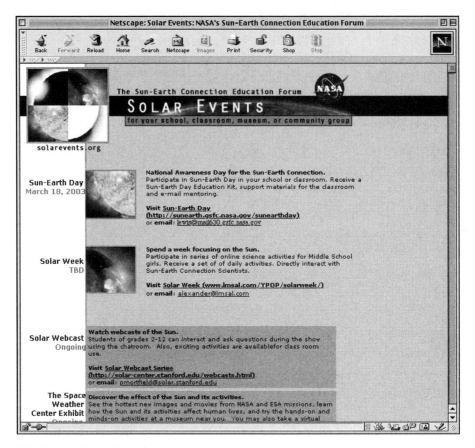

http://www.solarevents.org/

Credits: Web Site © UC Regents, The Center for Science Education @ Space Sciences Laboratory, UC Berkeley

The Web site was designed by Ideum and produced using Dreamweaver for a wide variety of tasks. Images for the site were placed into the HTML file in the same way that you have placed images into the project files in this lesson.

In this bonus activity, you will recreate just a portion of the Solar Event page on your own. The files you will need for this exercise are located in the Bonus/Lesson_02 folder. Start by creating a new page and using the images in the Bonus/Lesson_02/ Images folder to insert a background graphic, header graphic, and an additional image. You can view the final file in the Bonus/Lesson_02/Completed folder.

TIP *All four margin text fields should all be set to 0 in the Page Properties dialog box.*

WHAT YOU HAVE LEARNED

In this lesson, you have:

- Placed JPEG and GIF images on the page (pages 62–64)

- Resized images and reset them to their original dimensions (pages 64–65)

- Positioned images (pages 65–66)

- Added a border around an image (pages 66–67)

- Assigned names and **<alt>** tags to images (pages 67–68)

- Used the Assets panel to manage images in the site (pages 68–73)

- Wrapped text around images (pages 74–75)

- Adjusted the space around images (page 75)

- Inserted an image placeholder (pages 76–77)

- Aligned images relative to text (pages 77–78)

- Added and modified Flash buttons (pages 79–81)

- Added Flash animations (pages 82–83)

- Inserted images with accessibility options (pages 83–86)

creating links

The power of HTML comes from its capability to connect regions of text and images with other documents. The browser may highlight these regions (usually with color or underlines) to indicate that they are **hypertext links**—links that are not required to be sequential or linear, often called hyperlinks or links. A **link** in HTML has two parts: the name (or URL—Uniform Resource Locator) of the file to which you want to link; and the text or graphic that serves as the clickable area, called the **hotspot**, on the page. When the user points to the hotspot and clicks it, the browser uses the path of the link

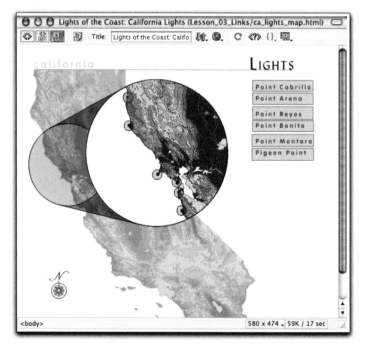

In this project, you will create text and graphic links to pages within this site as well as to other Web sites.

to jump to the linked document. In some browsers, the path of the link is displayed in the status area of the browser window (bottom left part of the window) when the pointer is positioned over the link.

In this lesson, you will create text and image links on a Web page, add hotspots to an image to make it an image map, and link to named anchors within a page.

To see an example of the finished pages, open Lesson_03_Links/Completed/ intro.html for the text and graphic links, profiles.html for the named anchors, and ca_lights_map.html for the image map.

WHAT YOU WILL LEARN

In this lesson, you will:

- Specify link colors according to the link type

- Create text and graphic links

- Create email links automatically and manually

- Use anchors to jump to different parts of the page

- Create image maps to provide multiple links in the same image

APPROXIMATE TIME

This lesson should take about one hour to complete.

LESSON FILES

Media Files:

Lesson_03_Links/Images/light_resources.gif
Lesson_03_Links/Images/more_lights.gif
Lesson_03_Links/Images/CAmap_full.gif

Starting Files:

Lesson_03_Links/intro.html
Lesson_03_Links/profiles.html
Lesson_03_Links/ca_lights_map.html

Completed Project:

Lesson_03_Links/Completed/intro.html
Lesson_03_Links/Completed/profiles.html
Lesson_03_Links/Completed/ca_lights_map.html

SPECIFYING LINK COLORS

You can specify the default color of text links on your page in order to be consistent with the set of colors you have chosen to use in your document. The colors you select should contrast, but not clash, with the background so the links can be read clearly. The link color should also stand out from the regular body text in the document, enabling viewers to spot the links easily. Browsers will display the colors you set for links—unless the option to override a page's colors is checked in the user's browser preferences. You will use the same dialog box to choose these colors that you used when selecting the default text color in Lesson 1.

1) Open the intro.html document, located in the Lesson_03_Links folder. Choose Modify > Page Properties to open the Page Properties dialog box.

In this dialog box, you can define colors for three link types:

Links: The initial color a user sees before clicking the link. The standard default browser color for a link is blue.

Visited Links: The color that a link changes to if a user clicks the link. The standard default browser color for a visited link is purple.

Active Links: The color to which a link turns if a user holds down the mouse button after clicking the link. The standard default browser color for an active link is red. Some pages use the same color for Active Links as they do for Links.

2) Use the text fields next to the color boxes to select the colors for your links by typing in #660000 for the Links color, #CC3300 for the Active Link color, and #333333 for the Visited Links color.

When you know the hexadecimal values of your colors, you can enter the numbers directly in these text fields. Dreamweaver automatically fills in the color box with the matching color swatch. On the other hand, if you choose a color swatch from the palette, Dreamweaver automatically fills in the text field with the hexadecimal value. You can click the color box to bring up the palette, as you did in Lesson 1, and the hexadecimal value will be displayed at the top of the palette as you rollover the color swatches.

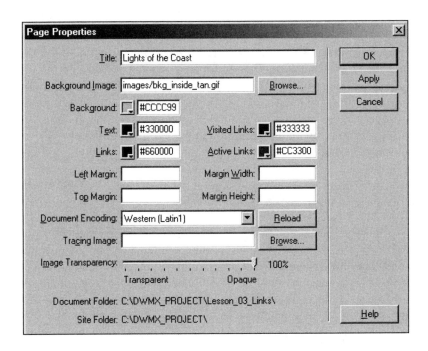

NOTE *The number sign (#), also known as a pound sign, indicates that what follows is hexadecimal code and not a named color (like black, white, red, etc.). While Dreamweaver will accept a value without the number sign, it is best to include it. When you use the color box to select a swatch, you'll notice that the number sign is included.*

3) Click OK to close the Page Properties dialog box and return to your document. Save the intro.html file.

The default link colors for your page are now the colors you specified. You will see the colors after you begin to create links. Keep this document, intro.html, open. It contains all the text and graphics you will need to create links in the following exercises.

INSERTING EMAIL LINKS

Providing a linked email address makes it easy for your visitors to contact you from a Web page. You should always include some method of contact that allows visitors to correspond or interact with someone in your organization.

1) Click at the beginning of the sentence "Some of the world's most notable lighthouses include:" and press Return (Macintosh) or Enter (Windows) to create a blank paragraph below the definition of Keeper. Place the cursor on the new paragraph line that was created.

You will insert an email link here, below the definition list for lighthouse components.

91

EMAIL LINK

2) Click the Email Link button in the Insert bar, or choose Insert > Email Link.

The Insert Email Link dialog box appears, displaying options for text and email.

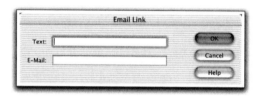

NOTE *The Insert bar is open by default. If it is not visible, choose Window > Insert to open the panel or Window > Arrange Panels to reset the panels to their default positions.*

3) In the Text text field, type Suggest more lighthouse terms. In the Email text field, type your email address. Then click OK.

The text appears on the page as a link. The Property inspector shows the email address in the Link text field when you place the insertion point within the link.

4) At the bottom of the document, select the text "Lights of the Coast" that is located to the right of the © symbol.

If you select text that is already on the page and then open the Insert Email Link dialog box, the selected text appears in the Text text field.

Contact information commonly appears at the bottom of a page, often near copyright information.

5) In the Link text field of the Property inspector, type mailto: immediately followed by your email address. Make sure you type the colon and that you do not leave a space between the colon and your email address.

You have entered an email link manually.

CREATING HYPERTEXT LINKS

Hypertext links can take the user to another document within the current Web site or to a page on another Web site. They can direct the user to other HTML files, images and other media, and downloadable files. The following exercise shows you how to link to a document within the current site.

1) In the intro.html document window, select the word "History" in the first line of the bullet list near the top of the page.

You will create a link for this word.

2) In the Property inspector, click the folder icon to the right of the Link text field.

The Select File dialog box opens.

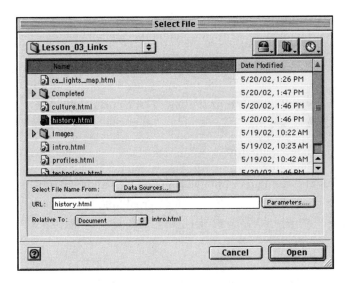

3) Select the history.html file in the Lesson_03_Links folder, and click Open (Macintosh OS 9), Choose (Macintosh OS X) or OK (Windows).

The filename history.html appears in the Link text field, and the text you selected in the document is marked as a link. The link is underlined and appears in the color you chose for your links in the first exercise of this lesson.

NOTE *You can override the page's default link color for individual links by placing the font-color tags inside the link tags. You may have to move the tags manually in Code View. You will work with Code View in Lesson 12.*

This link is an example of a document-relative path, which is the best option to use for local links in most Web sites. A **document-relative path** omits the part of the absolute URL that is the same for the current document and the linked document, leaving only the portion of the path that differs. A path to a file in the same folder, for example, would be expressed as name_of_file.html.

4) Repeat steps 1 through 3 to link the word "Technological" in the next line of the bulleted list to technology.html, and the word "culture" in the last line of the bulleted list to culture.html.

When you know the names of the files, you can type them directly in the Link text field.

TIP *If you need to use the same links multiple times, you can save time by choosing recently used links from the drop-down menu to the right of the Link text field on the Property inspector.*

5) Save the file and preview it in the browser.

The three links you just created should take you to the corresponding pages. Always test your links to be sure they go to the correct locations!

TIP *You can preview your document in the browser by pressing the F12 key to open the primary browser that you defined in Lesson 1.*

CREATING GRAPHIC LINKS

You can also use images to link to documents within your site, as well as to sites other than your own. This exercise shows you how to create an external link. You can use the same techniques you used in the preceding exercise to link images to files on your site.

1) Below the list of notable lighthouses in the intro.html document, click the Lighthouse Resources graphic to select it. Type links.html in the Property inspector's Link text field.

This link is a relative path, just like the text links you created to history.html, technology.html. and culture.html in the previous exercise. You can use graphics to provide links just as easily as text.

2) Below the graphic you just linked, click the More Lighthouses graphic to select it, and type http://www.pbs.org/legendarylighthouses/index.html in the Property inspector's Link text field. You must type the complete URL.

This link is an absolute path. An **absolute path** provides the complete URL of the linked document. You must use an absolute path to link to a document that is located in a Web site other than your own, or to anything that is outside of the root folder.

TIP *If a URL is long or complex, you can go to that site in your browser, copy the URL, and then paste it into the Link text field.*

3) Save the file, and preview it in the browser.

Notice that when you roll over the graphics at the bottom of the page, you see the hand indicating that they are linked. The link locations will appear in the browser's status bar as you roll over the links.

NOTE *When you attach a link to an image, if you have not specified the image border in the Property inspector, Dreamweaver applies a default border of 0 pixels. If you do define a border, the color will be the same as your page's default link color. You can change the color of the border for individual images by placing font-color tags around the image tag and inside the link tags in the code. You'll work with code in Lesson 12.*

TARGETING LINKS

When you link to a page, the linked page usually replaces the current browser page. At times, however, you may want to display the new browser page in a different window. If you link to a site outside your site, for example, you lead users out of your pages. If users haven't bookmarked your URL, they might not remember how to return to your site. When an outside link opens a new browser window, the original page remains in the first window.

1) In the intro.html document, select the More Lighthouses graphic. From the Property inspector's Target menu, choose _blank.

In Dreamweaver, you change where the linked page is to be displayed by using targets. Targets other than _blank are used with frames. You will learn about frames in Lesson 9. The additional targets are as follows:

- **_blank**: Loads the linked document into a new, unnamed browser window.
- **_parent**: Loads the linked document into the parent frameset or window of the frame that contains the link.

- **_self**: Loads the linked document into the same frame or window as the link. This target is the same as the default, so you usually don't have to specify it.

- **_top**: Loads the linked document into the full browser window, thereby removing all frames.

2) Save the file and preview it in the browser.

When you click the bottom graphic, the linked page opens in a new browser window. You can close this file.

NOTE *Use caution when opening new browser windows. New windows impose extra RAM requirements on the user's computer as each window is opened. Besides taxing a machine's memory resources, multiple windows may annoy or confuse your visitors.*

INSERTING AND LINKING TO NAMED ANCHORS

When a document is long or has many sections, you may need to create a series of links that will jump the user to specific places in the document. This technique eliminates the need for the viewer to scroll through the document. A **named anchor** marks the place in the page to which a link jumps. In this exercise, you will insert a named anchor.

1) Open profiles.html from the Lesson_03_Links folder. Choose Modify › Page Properties to open the Page Properties dialog box. Set the same colors for links and visited links that you used for the intro.html document in this lesson's first exercise.

Recall the links color's hexadecimal value was #660000 and the visited-links value was #333333.

This file contains a large amount of text that requires the visitor to scroll to see the entire document.

2) Position the insertion point before the text "Name: Pigeon Point Light" at the bottom of the document. Click the Named Anchor button on the Common tab of the Insert bar.

The Insert Named Anchor dialog box opens.

TIP *You can also insert a named anchor by choosing Insert > Named Anchor.*

3) Type pigeon in the Anchor Name text field; then click OK.

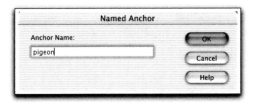

Don't use spaces, punctuation, or special characters (such as copyright symbols, number signs, etc.) in the name. Each anchor name must be unique. There should never be more than one anchor with the same name in the same document—the browser will not be able to jump the user to the correct anchor.

A yellow icon appears on the page to represent the anchor. The icon may be selected when it first appears on the page—selected anchor icons are blue. This icon is an invisible element that will not appear in the browser.

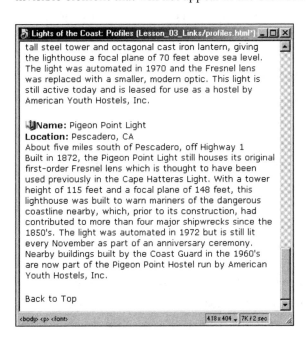

TIP *If you can't see the named anchor icon, make sure that the Invisible Elements option is turned on by choosing View > Visual Aids > Invisible Elements. When you insert a named anchor, a dialog box opens to warn you that you will not be able to see the anchor unless the Invisible Elements option is turned on. Named anchors must also be checked in the Invisible Elements category of the Preferences. You can check this by choosing Edit > Preferences and selecting the Invisible Elements category. The Named Anchor box should be checked.*

4) Select the text "Pigeon Point" from the list of lighthouses at the top of the document.

This text will act as a navigational element by jumping the user to the corresponding section of the page. You will make this text a link that references the named anchor you created near the bottom of this page in the preceding steps.

5) Type #pigeon in the Link text field of the Property inspector.

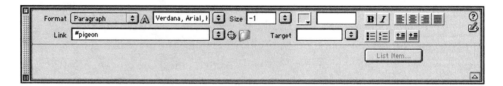

The number sign (#) is required to tell the browser that this link is internal (will remain on the original page). Make sure that the name you type after the number sign is exactly the same as the anchor name. You should follow the naming guidelines from Lesson 1 when you name your anchors, because they are case-sensitive. For example, if you name your anchor "pigeon" and then type **#Pigeon** in the Link text field, your link might not work consistently in all browsers.

Pigeon Point is now linked to the Pigeon Point profile section near the bottom of the page. Now you will repeat the process for Point Cabrillo.

6) Add another anchor before the "Name: Point Cabrillo" text and name the anchor cabrillo.

You have created a second anchor.

TIP *If the anchor is inserted in the wrong place, you can drag it to a new position.*

7) Select the words "Point Cabrillo" in the list of lighthouses at the top of the document. Drag the Point to File icon (located next to the Link text field in the Property inspector) to the cabrillo anchor you just made. Release the mouse button when the pointer is directly over the anchor.

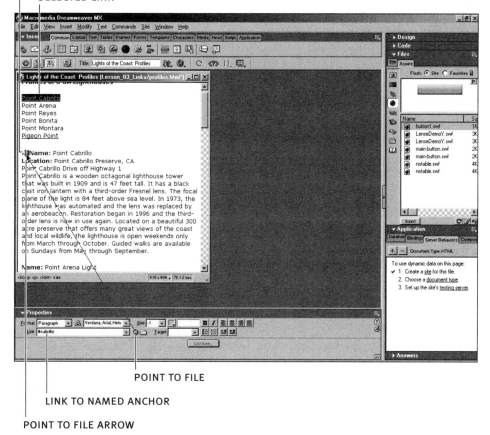

NAMED ANCHOR

SELECTED LINK

POINT TO FILE

LINK TO NAMED ANCHOR

POINT TO FILE ARROW

The link is made. Using the Point to File icon to create links may help prevent typing errors.

NOTE *You can also use the Point to File icon to link to other files in your site if the Site window is open. With the text or graphic selected that you want to link, click the Point to File icon and drag it over the Site window. The Site Window will come to the front if it is behind the document window or other panels, and you can continue to drag the mouse until you have the pointer directly over the file you wish to link to.*

8) Insert anchors and links for the remaining navigational headings and the corresponding sections of the document. For the anchor names, type arena, reyes, bonita, and montara for their respective lighthouses.

You can edit the names of any anchors you create by clicking the anchor. The Property inspector will change to show that a named anchor is selected. You can change the name in the Property inspector's Name text field.

9) Insert an anchor at the very top of the page in front of the text "Profiles of 6 CA Lighthouses" and name it top. Select "Back to Top" at the bottom of the page and link it to #top.

In long documents, it is common practice to include links at the end of every section to a named anchor at the top of the page or to a navigational table of contents. This common anchor is usually called **#top**. When you use anchors in this way, users don't need to scroll back up to the top of the page if they want to continue using those links to jump to other sections. Any number of links on the page can reference the same anchor.

10) Save the file and preview it in the browser.

The navigational terms at the top of the page will now link to their corresponding sections. You can close the profiles.html file.

CREATING IMAGE MAPS

In this exercise, you will continue to use named anchors and learn how to link to a particular section in another document.

You've experienced how easy it is to make an image link to a page. The user can click the image to go to that linked page. You can also divide the image into several links by using an **image map** to place individual hotspots on the image. These hotspots are not limited to rectangles; they can have other shapes. In the following exercise, you will add a rectangular hotspot and a circular hotspot.

The example you will use to create an image map in this exercise happens to be a map of California. Conceptually, image maps work quite well when applied to geographical maps; however, you can apply an image map to any image regardless of what that image is.

1) Open ca_lights_map.html from the Lesson_03_Links folder. Select the map graphic.

This large image is a geographical map that shows the locations of six California lighthouses and lists the names of each to the right of the map. The graphic needs to be divided into 12 hotspots: six spots for the locations and six for the names.

2) In the Property inspector, type californiamap in the Map text field.

Don't use spaces or special characters in the name. You can have several image maps on one page, but each map on that page must be uniquely named. If you fail to name your maps, Dreamweaver will create automatic, sequential names for each (Map1, Map2, Map3, etc.). The generic name of Map1, however, does not indicate anything in particular about the image map or graphic that it is applied to. On the other hand,

the name you are using in this exercise, californiamap, suggests that the image map
has something to do with California. By creating your own names in the Map text
field, you will tie the names with specific meaning to the image maps. Short, concise,
and specific names will serve you best.

MAP TEXT FIELD   EXPANDER ARROW

TIP *If you don't see the Map text field, click the expander arrow in the bottom right corner
of the Property inspector.*

3) Select the Rectangular Hotspot tool below the map name in the Property inspector. Click and drag around the words "Point Cabrillo" and "Point Arena."

A translucent blue-green area with handles appears around the names on that
portion of the image, and the Property inspector displays the hotspot properties.
Dreamweaver automatically places a null link (#) in the Property inspector's Link
text field. Do not delete this character—it serves as a placeholder link to indicate
that the area is clickable.

NULL LINK

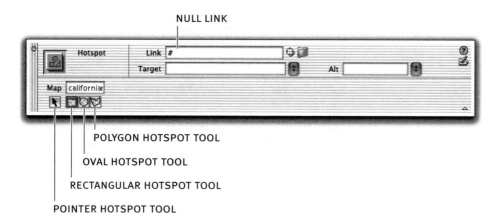

POLYGON HOTSPOT TOOL

OVAL HOTSPOT TOOL

RECTANGULAR HOTSPOT TOOL

POINTER HOTSPOT TOOL

NOTE *When you create one or more image maps, a map icon will appear, usually at the
bottom of the document. The map icon looks very similar to the named anchor icon, and it is
visible only in Dreamweaver—it will not appear in the browser. You can turn the visibility of
these kinds of items on and off through the View > Visual Aids menu. This book assumes that
you leave the visual aid visibility at default.*

4) Select the Pointer Hotspot tool below the Map text field on the Property inspector. Resize the hotspot you created in step 3 by dragging a handle until the hotspot encompasses only the name "Point Cabrillo."

The hotspots you create are easy to edit—you can resize, move, or delete them at any time. To move the hotspot, position the pointer inside the hotspot and drag. To delete the hotspot, select it and press Delete (Macintosh) or Backspace (Windows).

5) In the Property inspector, type Point Cabrillo in the Alt text field.

The hotspot **<alt>** text serves a similar purpose as **<alt>** text for an image; it gives an indication of where this hotspot will link to.

6) Type profiles.html#cabrillo in the Property inspector's Hotspot Link text field.

Be sure to replace the original number sign (#) in the Link text field with the link you have typed in.

In the previous exercise, you created a named anchor in the Point Cabrillo section of the profiles.html file. Now you are making this region of the California map graphic point directly to the Point Cabrillo section, instead of linking to the top of the page as it would if you had made the link profiles.html. The use of anchors to link to specific portions of other pages helps your site to be more functional, directing your viewers to what they are looking for immediately and reducing the amount of time they have to spend scrolling through long documents. The more functional and easy to use your site is, the more likely it is that you will have new and repeat visitors.

7) In the Property inspector, select the Oval Hotspot tool. In the ca_lights_map.html document, drag a circle around the topmost target-style circular dot located on the detail of the California.

You have created a circular hotspot around Point Cabrillo. You adjust the placement of the circular hotspot by using the Pointer Hotspot tool to move it or by using the arrow keys to move it once it has been selected.

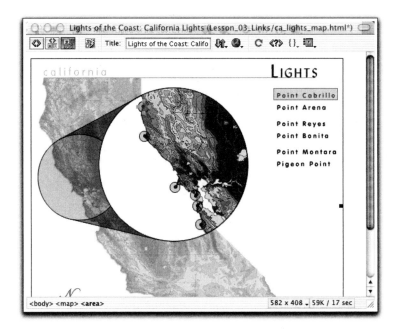

NOTE *If two or more hotspots overlap each other, the first one you created will take precedence over any subsequent hotspots that overlap it.*

8) Type Point Cabrillo into the Alt text field on the Property inspector. In the Link text field, replace the number sign (#) with http://www.pointcabrillo.org and choose _blank from the Target pop-up menu to have the link open in a new browser window.

You have directed the circular region to open the link in a new, unnamed browser window. You must have the hotspot on the image selected in order to modify the link, target, or alt text for the hotspot.

TIP *You can also use the Polygon Hotspot tool to click multiple points around any area with a more complicated shape for which you want to create a hotspot. When you use the Polygon tool, each click creates a point. A line connects each subsequent point to the preceding point. As you click, you'll see the translucent hotspot area begin to form. You can continue clicking until you have the shape you want. You do not need to "close" the shape by clicking back on the original point. The more points that a polygon shape uses to define the hotspots the more code is necessary in the document to describe those areas.*

103

When you finish working with the image map, you can click outside the hotspot to another area of the image. Clicking outside the image map resets the Property inspector to display image properties.

9) Use the Rectangular Hotspot tool to create clickable areas for the five remaining lighthouse names, displayed to the right of the map. Apply the following attributes for each lighthouse:

For Point Arena: Alt text—**Point Arena**; link—profiles.html#arena

For Point Reyes: Alt text—**Point Reyes**; link—profiles.html#reyes

For Point Bonita: Alt text—**Point Bonita**; link—profiles.html#bonita

For Point Montara: Alt text—**Point Montara**; link—profiles.html#montara

For Pigeon Point: Alt text—**Pigeon Point**; link—profiles.html#pigeon

Remember to replace the original number signs (#) in the link text fields with the links given above. If you leave the original number sign in, the link will not work. You must however, include the number signs that are in the above links themselves.

Each lighthouse name now links to the corresponding section of the profiles.html document.

TIP *You can hold down the Shift key while using the Rectangular Hotspot tool to constrain the proportions to a square.*

10) Save the file and preview it in the browser.
Test the links on the image map you have created.

NOTE *If you copy an image map and paste it into another document, Dreamweaver retains the links and hotspots.*

WHAT YOU HAVE LEARNED

In this lesson, you have:

- Specified the default colors of links, visited links, and active links to match the colors of graphics used in the page (pages 90–91)
- Created email links automatically using the Insert bar and manually using the Property inspector's Link text field (pages 91–92)
- Created text and graphic links to pages within the site as well as to other sites (pages 93–95)
- Targeted a link to open in a new window (pages 95–96)
- Inserted named anchors for each section of a document and linked the corresponding titles of those sections to each named anchor (pages 96–100)
- Created image maps with multiple hotspots of different shapes and sizes, learned how to edit the hotspots, and specified their links (pages 100–104)

elements of page design

LESSON 4

A good way to build quick and basic Web pages is to place content such as text and images directly on a page as you did in the first three lessons of this book. It is a simple and straightforward way of presenting information; however, it is a method with very limited options. You can wrap text around an image; align text or images to the left, center, or right of a page; and create indented blocks of text—but you can't do much more.

One means to gain more control over the placement of elements on your pages is to use **tables**. Tables in HTML allow you to present information in an organized manner; they contain rows and columns where you can place content in **cells**. Cells can then be merged to create larger cells. The arrangement of content within tables enables you to

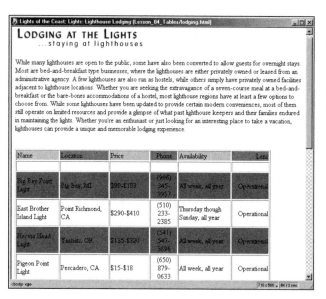

In this lesson's exercises, you will create tables to hold text and graphics and learn how to lay out your pages with consideration for the constraints of your users' viewable area.

construct pages with a greater degree of design precision. Using tables, you can place objects in specific locations on a page and create more complex visual arrangements. In this lesson, you will create several different pages. You will use combinations of tables to develop layouts that are far more compelling visually than the same information would be without the use of tables to display the content.

If you would like to view the final result of this lesson, open foghorns.html, lodging.html, lights.html, and lighthouse.html files in the Completed folder within the Lesson_04_Tables folder.

WHAT YOU WILL LEARN

In this lesson, you will:

- Learn how to create tables to control the layout of your pages
- Modify the table properties, including border, background, spacing, color, alignment, and size
- Import tabular data from spreadsheets
- Modify a table by adjusting rows and columns
- Sort a table
- Export a table
- Determine the optimal size of your layout
- Import a tracing image
- Create accessible tables

APPROXIMATE TIME

This lesson should take about two hours to complete.

LESSON FILES

Media Files:
Lesson_04_Tables/Images/…(all files)

Starting Files:
Lesson_04_Tables/Text/…(all files)

Completed Project:
Lesson_04_Tables/Completed/foghorns.html
Lesson_04_Tables/Completed/lodging.html
Lesson_04_Tables/Completed/lighthouse.html
Lesson_04_Tables/Completed/lights.html
Lesson_04_Tables/Completed/lens_stats.html

CREATING A TABLE IN LAYOUT VIEW

Dreamweaver MX provides two options for creating tables: layout view and standard view. Layout view works much like a page-layout program in which you can draw boxes on the page and then fill the boxes with text or graphics. You can resize the boxes, and you can place the boxes anywhere on the page.

In this exercise, you will begin to create a page in the "Lights of the Coast" project site using layout view. You will learn about standard view, and how to create tables using that method, later on in this lesson.

NOTE *In layout view, the exact numeric values of cell widths and heights, as well as the placement of those cells, will be somewhat different from the examples shown here. Use the examples as guides for the general layout of your page.*

1) Create a new HTML document and save it as foghorns.html in the Lesson_04_Tables folder. Title the document Lights of the Coast: Technology: Sound and set the background color of the page to white.

The page you are creating is a part of the Technology section of the "Lights of the Coast" project site. The page title you have typed will indicate this to the visitors of the site.

You will use layout view to create a table in this document in the following steps.

2) From the Insert bar, select the Layout tab and click Layout View.

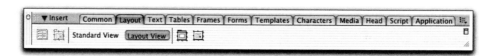

You have switched to layout view, in which you can easily place elements on the page. You may see the info box titled "Getting Started in Layout View," which briefly describes the main tools: the layout cell and the layout table. You can click OK to close this dialog box.

NOTE *There is a check box for "Don't show me this message again." If you leave this box unchecked, the next time you restart Dreamweaver you will see this dialog box again if you switch to layout view.*

A light gray bar, with the text "Layout View" centered on it, appears just below the document window toolbar (Macintosh) or the document title bar (Windows), appearing to be within the document itself. This bar will not be visible in the browser as it is used only in Dreamweaver to indicate that you are working in layout view.

TIP *You can also choose View > Table View > Layout View to switch to layout view. You can also use the keyboard shortcut Command+F6 (Macintosh) or Ctrl+F6 (Windows) to switch to layout view.*

3) Click the Draw Layout Cell icon in the Layout area of the Insert bar.

The pointer changes to a plus sign (+) when you move the pointer into the document window.

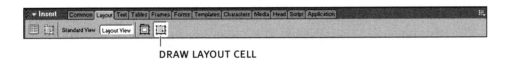

DRAW LAYOUT CELL

A layout cell lets you draw a boxed area, called a cell, anywhere on the page. All content in a table will always be contained within a cell. Every table has one or more cells. A cell is the area created by the intersection of a row and a column. In layout view, you don't need to worry about the number or arrangement of rows and columns when creating your table—Dreamweaver creates and manages the rows and columns for you automatically when you designate the location of the cells on your page.

4) Place the pointer in the center of the page; then click and drag to draw the cell.

A layout table is drawn automatically to contain the cell. The layout table is drawn as wide as the document window, but you can resize the table to any size you need. The cell is outlined in blue to distinguish it from the table, which appears outlined in green. A solid blue line indicates that the insertion point is within the cell, while a dotted blue line indicates that the insertion point is not in the cell. All parts of the table other than the cell are shown in gray. The thin white lines indicate the rows and columns Dreamweaver creates in order to construct a table when you draw layout cells. When you move the pointer over the border of the cell, it turns red to indicate which cell you are over.

NOTE *By default, layout tables appear with a tab at the top. The tab makes it easier to identify the table; it contains column numbers and a column menu. The tab causes the table to drop down from the top of the page; this extra space will not be visible in the browser, however. To remove the tab from the table, choose View > Table View > Show Layout Table Tabs. A checkmark next to an option in the menu indicates that option is enabled.*

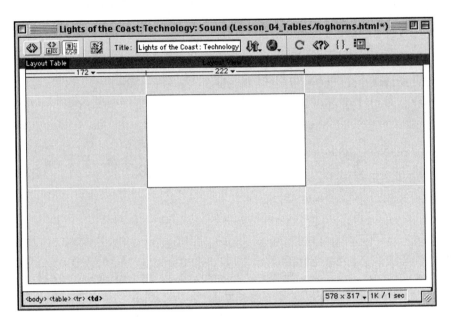

5) Insert the foghorn_title.gif graphic from the Lesson_04_Tables/Images folder into the layout cell you just drew.

TIP *From the Site portion of the Image Assets panel, you can just select and drag the graphic from the Assets panel into the cell on the page.*

You have inserted an image as you did in Lesson 2. The cell will expand to fit the graphic if it was smaller than the size of the graphic. The new size is displayed in parentheses at the top of the window.

NOTE *If you get the accessibility options when you insert the foghorn_title.gif, you should go to Edit > Preferences and select the accessibility category. Uncheck all of the boxes and click OK to turn the accessible images option off.*

MODIFYING TABLE LAYOUT

As you design your pages in layout view, you will want to move, resize, or add new cells to add content. A layout cell cannot overlap other cells and cannot be moved outside the layout table.

1) In the foghorns.html document, select the cell by moving the pointer over the border and clicking as it turns red.

The cell border turns blue and handles appear, which you can drag to resize the cell.

TIP *You can also Command-click (Macintosh) or Ctrl-click (Windows) within a cell to display the resize handles.*

2) Drag the cell border to resize the cell, fitting it closely around the graphic. The cell should be the same size as the graphic.

In the table tab, the size listed in the parentheses replaces the old size display. If the cell you initially created was smaller than the size of the graphic, then the cell will have enlarged automatically to fit around the image exactly and you will not need to resize it. If the cell you created was larger than the graphic, then you must resize the cell to make sure that the borders of the layout cell line up flush with the edges of the image.

3) Drag the top border of the cell to move the cell to the top and center of the page.

If you moved the cell to the right or left to center it, notice that the column numbers in the surrounding layout table change to display the new size.

NOTE *Sometimes the old and new column numbers remain onscreen, showing conflicting widths for the same column. If this happens, you need to choose Make Cell Widths Consistent from the column-header menu. The column-header menu is a drop-down menu that you can access from the arrow next to the number displaying the width of the column. If only one number is displayed, this option is grayed out.*

4) Use the arrow keys to move the cell to the left.

The arrow keys move the cell one pixel at a time. Hold down the Shift key to move the cell 10 pixels at a time. Leave some space in the column between this cell and the side of the table. The column to the left of the cell containing the image should be 40 pixels wide.

5) Below the top cell, draw three more cells in a single column down the middle of the page, with a little space between them.

Your page should look similar to the example shown here. Don't be concerned about the sizes of the columns listed at the top of the page; they will vary according to the exact placement of your layout cells. You will adjust their positions later in this lesson.

When you draw a cell on the page, white guides appear to help you place other cells that you want to align with the first cell. Use the horizontal guides to align the tops of the cells.

TIP *To draw multiple cells without clicking Draw Layout Cell more than once, hold down Command (Macintosh) or Ctrl (Windows) as you draw the first cell. You can continue to draw new cells until you release the modifier key.*

6) Of the three cells you just created, expand the topmost cell so it's as wide as the cell that contains the foghorn_title.gif graphic. Open foghorn.txt from the Lesson_04_Tables/Text folder. Copy the first paragraph and paste it into the first cell below the foghorn_title.gif graphic.

The cell will expand if necessary to fit the content.

7) Move both of the remaining cells to the far left, aligned with the left edges of the cells above. Draw one more cell to the right of those two cells. Copy the remaining text from the foghorn.txt file and paste it into the new column.

You will adjust the size of this cell later in this lesson. Your page should look similar to the example shown here. Remember that the exact sizes of the columns are not important at this point. The bottom left cell may expand downward when you insert the text into the new column. If that happens, just select the empty cell and use the handle on the bottom of the cell to change the size of the cell approximately back to what it was.

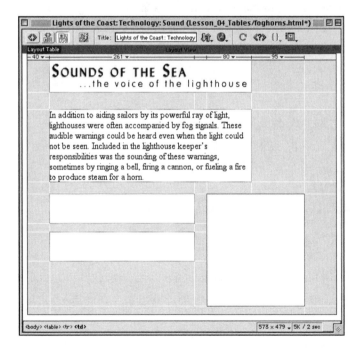

8) Create a third cell below the two cells at the left. Insert fogsignal.jpg into the topmost of the three cells and insert foghorn.jpg into the bottom cell. Create a fourth cell below the cell containing the foghorn.jpg image.

113

If the graphics are too large, the cell sizes will enlarge horizontally or vertically as necessary to fit the graphics. If the graphics are too small, you should resize the cells to fit closely around the graphics, as you did with the foghorn_title.gif image.

9) In the empty cell between the two foghorn images you inserted in the previous step, type the following caption: Image above: Fog signal converted to diaphone at Point Montara, CA. Photograph post-1912, courtesy of Point Montara Light. **Format the text as Verdana, –1. Adjust the size of the middle cell so it is the same width as the cells containing the two foghorn images.**

You will adjust the formatting of this cell in the following exercise.

10) In the empty cell below the foghorn.jpg image type the following caption: Image above: Compressor foghorns at Point Montara, CA. Photograph 1970, courtesy of Point Montara Light. **Format the text as Verdana, –1. Adjust the size of the bottom cell so it is the same width as the cells containing the two foghorn images.**

Providing captions helps viewers understand the significance of each image.

11) Click the border of the cell to the right of the foghorn images that contains the two paragraphs of text to select it. Use one of the selection handles on the blue border to drag the left side of the cell to the left, toward the foghorn images, to enlarge the cell. Leave only a small space between it and the cells containing the foghorn images.

You want to enlarge the cell, not move it. Your page should now look similar to the example shown here.

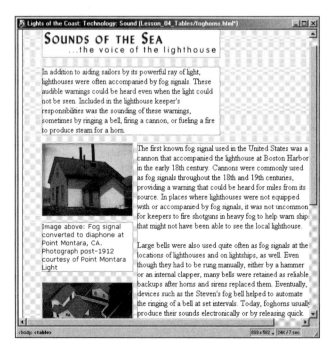

CELL FORMATTING

You can change several options for each cell. You can add background colors to each cell or to the entire table.

You can also control the alignment of objects within each cell of a table horizontally and vertically. The default HTML setting for horizontal alignment in a cell is left. The default HTML setting for vertical alignment in a cell is center. When you draw a cell in layout view, Dreamweaver changes the vertical alignment to top, but you can change that option easily.

1) In the foghorns.html document, select the cell in which you added the caption for the fogsignal.jpg image. Type the code #FFCC99 into the Bg color text field in the Property inspector. Set the background of the cell for the second caption to the same color.

The color of the cell changes to the color you selected. Be sure to select the cell so you can see the selection handles, as opposed to placing the insertion point inside the cell.

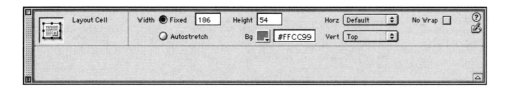

N O T E   *To change the background color of the entire table, select the table by clicking the green table border or any of the gray areas of the table. Click the Bg color box and choose a color for the table.*

2) Choose Center from the Horz drop-down menu in the Property inspector for the cells of both captions.

This step changes the alignment of the text in the cell to center.

3) Change the Vert setting to Middle for the cells of both captions.

This step centers the text vertically in the cell.

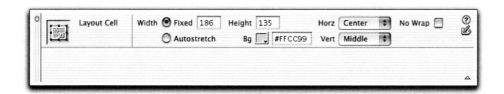

115

LAYOUT WIDTH AND SPACER IMAGES

In layout view, you can control the width of tables in two ways: by setting a fixed, width, which is the default; or by using Autostretch, which causes the cells to change width depending on the width of the browser. In this exercise, you will apply Autostretch and learn about spacer images.

1) In the foghorns.html document, select the top text cell just below the foghorn_title.gif graphic. Click Autostretch in the Property inspector.

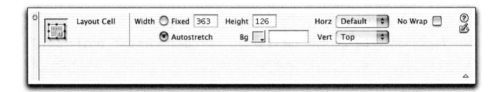

The Choose Spacer Image dialog box appears if a spacer image is not associated with your site.

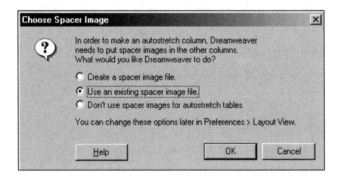

If the dialog box appears, choose Use an Existing Spacer Image File click OK and locate spacer.gif in the Lesson_04_Tables/Images folder. The spacer file location will be saved in your preferences. Choose Edit > Preferences > Layout View to change or remove the spacer image.

NOTE *The dialog box includes an option to create a spacer-image file. If you are working on a site for which there is not an existing spacer image that you have created, you should choose this option and click OK to navigate to the directory where you want Dreamweaver to save the spacer image. The Images folder is the best place.*

The Autostretch column is displayed in the table tab as a zigzagged line. Dreamweaver inserts spacer images to control the layout of the fixed-width columns when you

116

select Autostretch. A spacer image controls the spacing in the layout but is not visible in the browser window.

TIP *You can also click a column header's drop-down menu and choose Make Column Autostretch in order to apply the Autostretch option.*

2) Save and view the page in the browser, then change the width of the browser.

Notice that the column stretches as you change the width. When you select a column to Autostretch, you cause all cells in that column to Autostretch. Use the white guides on the page to determine whether another cell is within the column you've selected.

If you choose not to use spacer images, columns change size or even disappear if they do not hold content. You can insert and remove spacer images yourself or let Dreamweaver add them automatically when it creates an Autostretch column. To insert and remove these images yourself, choose one of the following options from the column-header menu:

- **Add Spacer Image**: The spacer image is inserted into the column. You will not see the spacer image, but the column might shift slightly.

- **Remove Spacer Image**: The spacer image is removed, and the column might shift.

- **Remove All Spacer Images**: Your whole layout might shift slightly—or dramatically, depending on your content. If you do not have content in some columns, they might disappear.

117

The column-header menu is contextual and will change depending on which column you select. All three options above will not be available in all columns.

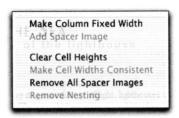

You've completed a page by using layout view. Next, you'll work in standard view to create tables. You can close the foghorns.html document.

CREATING A TABLE IN STANDARD VIEW

When you created the table in the previous exercise, Dreamweaver did the majority of the work for you. In layout view however, because Dreamweaver is doing the work, you lose a certain amount of control over how the table is defined. In standard view you must do that work yourself. The advantage of using standard view is more precise and specific control over how the tables are constructed. Additionally, some Dreamweaver features such as layers (covered in Lesson 15) do not function in layout view—you must use standard view.

Although layout view is an easy way to design your pages, you will often need to view your page in standard view, which shows you the HTML table structure. You can create tables yourself in this view or view the table Dreamweaver created when you drew a table in layout view.

If the information you want to present is structured in rows and columns, using a standard table is easier than drawing the rows and columns yourself. Often, you will have more control of your table in standard view.

1) Open a new document. Save the file as lodging.html, title the page Lights of the Coast: Lights: Lighthouse Lodging, and make the document background color white. Insert the lodging_header.gif from the Lesson_04_Tables/Images folder at the top of the page.
The page you are creating is a part of the Lights section of the "Lights of the Coast" project site. The page title you have typed will indicate this to the visitors of the site.

You'll use this document in the following exercises to learn more about creating tables and working with their contents.

2) Click Standard View in the Layout tab on the Insert bar.

When you create tables in standard view, you'll see the table borders and all the cells of the tables. The layout icons in the Insert bar should be grayed out.

TIP *You can also choose View > Table View > Standard View to switch to standard view. You can also switch to standard view from layout view by using the keyboard shortcut Shift+ Command+F6 (Macintosh) or Shift+Ctrl+F6 (Windows).*

3) Open the lodging_introduction.txt file from the Lesson_04_Tables/Text folder. Copy the text, and then paste it into your page in a new paragraph after the lodging header. Format the text as Verdana, –1.
Your table will follow this text.

4) Place the insertion point in a new paragraph after the text and click the Common tab in the Insert bar. Then click the Insert Table button.

TIP *You can also use the Table button on the Tables tab of the Insert bar to insert a table.*

The Insert Table dialog box opens.

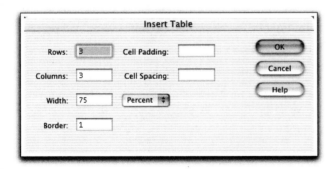

The Insert Table dialog box contains these options:

- **Rows**: The number of table rows. The Dreamweaver default is 3.
- **Columns**: The number of columns. The Dreamweaver default is 3.
- **Width**: The width of the table in pixels or as a percentage of the browser window. Tables specified in pixels are better for precise layout of text and images. Tables specified in percentages are a good choice when the proportions of the columns are more important than their actual widths. The Dreamweaver default is 75 percent.
- **Border**: The width of the table border. The Dreamweaver default is 1.
- **Cell Padding**: The amount of spacing between the cell content and the cell walls. If you leave this option blank, cell padding defaults to 1 pixel. If you don't want cell padding, be sure to type **0** in the text field. The Dreamweaver default is blank.
- **Cell Spacing**: The amount of spacing between table cells, not including the border. If you leave this option blank, cell spacing defaults to 1 pixel. If you don't want cell spacing, be sure to type **0** in the text field. The Dreamweaver default is blank.

TIP *You can choose Insert > Table to open the Insert Table dialog box. You can also use the keyboard shortcut Option+Command+T (Macintosh) or Ctrl+Alt+T (Windows) to open the Insert Table dialog box.*

5) Type 2 for Rows and 6 for Columns. Change the Width to 600 pixels, set the Border to 1, and leave the Cell Padding and Cell Spacing text fields blank. Then click OK to close the dialog box.

The table appears on your page with a gray border, showing the two rows and six columns.

6) Type Name in the first cell of the first row, and then press Tab to move to the next cell. Type Location and press Tab. Type Price and press Tab. Type Phone and press Tab. Type Availability, press Tab, and type Lens.

You can use the Tab key or the arrow keys to move between cells. Tab is the quickest method to jump to the next cell to the right or down to the next leftmost cell if you are at the end of a row. If you move to a cell that already has content in it, that content is selected when you use Tab.

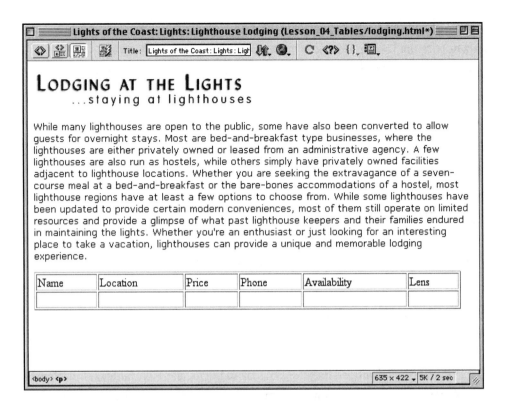

7) Click after the table; then press Return (Macintosh) or Enter (Windows).

The insertion point is in a new paragraph. The columns of your table may shift slightly, changing their widths.

You could continue to enter the remaining text for the table. In the next exercise, however, you will use another method to fill the table.

IMPORTING DATA FROM SPREADSHEETS

If you have text in a spreadsheet or even in a Microsoft Word table, you can insert it into Dreamweaver easily. You need to save or export the text from Microsoft Word as a tab- or comma-delimited file in order to make it compatible with Dreamweaver. You can also use tab- or comma-delimited files that have been exported from other programs such as Microsoft Excel. In this exercise, the text file has already been exported for you.

1) In the lodging.html document, choose Insert > Table Objects > Import Tabular Data or click the Tabular Data icon on the Common tab of the Insert bar.

The Import Table Data (Macintosh) or Insert Tabular Data (Windows) dialog box opens.

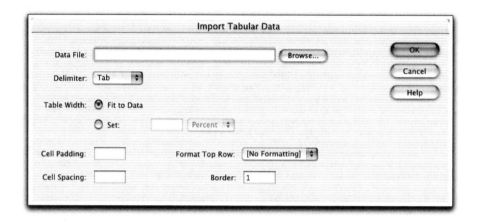

2) Click Browse and choose lodging_data.txt in the Lesson_04_Tables/Text folder. Then choose Tab from the Delimiter menu. For Table Width, choose Set, type 600 in the text field, and choose Pixels from the drop-down menu. Leave both Cell Padding and Cell Spacing blank. Format Top Row should be set to (No Formatting) by default, and Border should be 1. Click OK.

A table is built for you according to the options you just selected, and the data from the tab-delimited lodging.txt file that you are importing has been inserted into that new table.

COPYING AND PASTING TABLE CELLS

You now have two tables—the first table contains titles for each column, and the second table contains the data. Now you want to combine the two tables. You can copy and paste multiple table cells at the same time, preserving the cell's formatting, or you can copy and paste only the contents of the cell.

Cells can be pasted at an insertion point or in place of a selection in an existing table. If you want to paste multiple table cells, the contents of the Clipboard must exactly match the structure of the table or the selection in the table that the pasted cells will replace. You can copy one cell and paste it to replace a selected cell, but you cannot copy two cells and paste them to replace a single cell. The number and orientation of the cells that you copy must match the number and orientation of the cells you plan to replace.

1) In the lodging.html document, select all the cells in the second table by clicking the top left cell and dragging across the cells to the bottom right cell.

The selected cells are displayed with black borders. Selecting the cells in this manner selects the cells themselves, not the entire table. You will see black outlines around each cell.

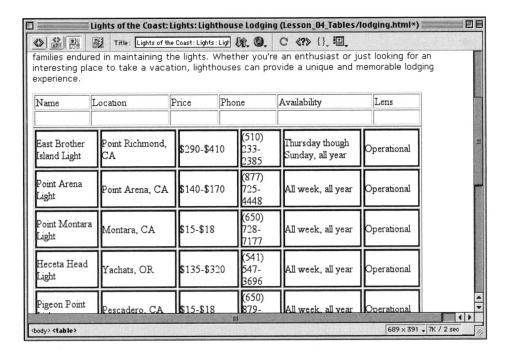

2) Choose Edit > Copy or press Command+C (Macintosh) or Ctrl+C (Windows).

To be cut or copied, the selected cells must form a rectangle.

3) Click once inside the first cell of the second row in the top table.

This empty cell is where the copied cells will be pasted.

4) Choose Edit > Paste or press Command+V (Macintosh) or Ctrl+V (Windows).

All the cells from the second table are inserted into the first table. Click outside the table to deselect the cells.

Name	Location	Price	Phone	Availability	Lens
East Brother Island Light	Point Richmond, CA	$290-$410	(510) 233-2385	Thursday though Sunday, all year	Operational
Point Arena Light	Point Arena, CA	$140-$170	(877) 725-4448	All week, all year	Operational
Point Montara Light	Montara, CA	$15-$18	(650) 728-7177	All week, all year	Operational
Heceta Head Light	Yachats, OR	$135-$320	(541) 547-3696	All week, all year	Operational
Pigeon Point Light	Pescadero, CA	$15-$18	(650) 879-0633	All week, all year	Operational
Saugerties Light	Saugerties, NY	$160	(845) 247-0656	All week, all year	Operational
Big Bay Point			(906)		

NOTE *If you are pasting entire rows or columns, the rows or columns are added to the table. If you are pasting an individual cell, the contents of the selected cell are replaced if the Clipboard contents match the structure of the selected cell. If you are pasting outside a table, the rows, columns, or cells are used to define a new table.*

If you need to remove the contents of cells but leave the cells themselves intact, select one or more cells but not an entire row or column. Then choose Edit > Clear or press Delete. If you need to remove an entire row, drag across all the cells in the row to select it, and press Delete. The row and all its contents will be deleted.

SELECTING A TABLE

Now that all the content from the second table is in the first table, you no longer need the second table. To delete it, you need to select the table first. Dreamweaver provides several methods for selecting a table. You will find that some methods are easier to use than others, depending on the complexity of the table structure.

1) In the lodging.html document, select the second table by positioning the pointer anywhere inside the table, and then selecting the `<table>` tag in the Tag Selector on the bottom left corner of the document window.

TIP *You can also select a table by clicking the top left corner of the table or anywhere on the right or bottom edge. The pointer turns into a hand (Macintosh) or a cross (Windows) when you are close to the edge. Wait until you see the pointer before you click. Another way to select a table is to click inside the table and choose Modify > Table > Select Table.*

Selection handles appear around the table when it is selected. When the table is selected, you cannot see the black borders around any of the cells; you see only one black border around the entire table.

Lights of the Coast: Lights: Lighthouse Lodgin (Lesson_04_Tables/lodging.html*)

Title: Lights: Lighthouse Lodgir

Light	Leonard, OR	$15-$18	728-7177	All week, all year	Operational
Heceta Head Light	Yachats, OR	$135-$320	(541) 547-3696	All week, all year	Operational
Pigeon Point Light	Pescadero, CA	$15-$18	(650) 879-0633	All week, all year	Operational
Saugerties Light	Saugerties, NY	$160	(845) 247-0656	All week, all year	Operational
Big Bay Point Light	Big Bay, MI	$99-$183	(906) 345-9957	All week, all year	Operational
Sand Hills Light	Ahmeek, MI	$125-$185	(906) 337-1744	All week, all year	Not Operational
Two Harbors Light	Two Harbors, MN	$99-$115	(888) 832-5606	All week, May through October	Operational
Selkirk Light	Pulaski, NY	$125-$150	(315) 298-6688	All week, all year	Operational
Rose Island Light	Newport, RI	$120-$185	(401) 847-4242	All week, all year	Operational
West Point Light	Prince Edward Island, Canada	$75-$130 (Canadian)	(800) 764-6854	All week, May through September	Operational

`<body> <table>` 618 x 407 9K / 3 sec

NOTE *In addition to the* **<table>** *tag, you will also see the* **<tr>** *and* **<td>** *tags in the Tag Selector. The tag* **<tr>** *represents the table row. The tag* **<td>** *represents the table data, otherwise known as a cell. Selecting a* **<td>** *tag will select the corresponding cell, and allow you to make changes to the cell in the Property inspector.*

2) With the table selected, press Delete (Macintosh) or Backspace (Windows) to remove the second table.

The second table is gone.

TIP *When the pointer is inside a cell, the keyboard shortcut Command+A (Macintosh) or Ctrl+A (Windows) will select the cell. Using the keyboard shortcut a second time will select the entire table.*

125

SELECTING AND MODIFYING TABLE ELEMENTS

You can easily select a row, a column, or all the cells in the table. Earlier in this lesson you selected **contiguous cells**—that is, cells that adjoin or touch one another. You can also select noncontiguous cells—those that do not touch—in a table and modify the properties of those cells. You cannot copy or paste noncontiguous cells. The following steps demonstrate various selection methods.

1) In the lodging.html document, select the noncontiguous cells in the top row of the remaining table by holding down Command (Macintosh) or Ctrl (Windows) and clicking the first cell, which contains the text "Name." Continue to hold down the Command or Ctrl key and click the cell containing the text "Price" and also the cell containing the text "Availability."

All three noncontiguous cells are selected, as shown by the black borders around the individual cells.

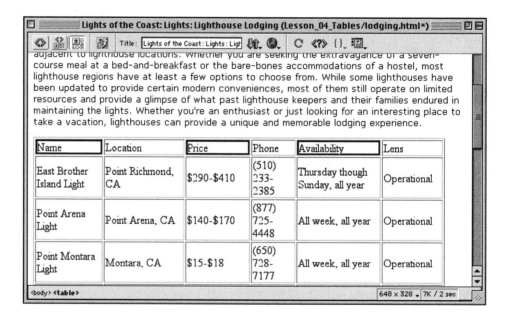

2) Use the Property inspector to change the background color of the selected cells to #CCCCFF.

You can change the background color of single cells, multiple cells, or the entire table, depending on what you have selected. In this step, you change multiple cells at the same time.

You may need to click outside of the table in order for the change to be applied.

126

3) Select the noncontiguous "Location," "Phone," and "Lens" cells; change their background colors to #9999CC.

You can also apply a background image to single cells, multiple cells at once, or entire tables. The background-image option is also available in the Property inspector, right above the background-color option.

4) Click inside the "Point Arena" row and position the pointer at the left end of the row, just on the table border. Click when the selection arrow appears; then change the background color to #6699CC.

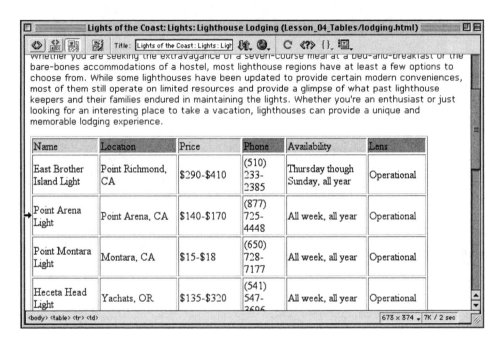

You may need to roll the pointer up and down the left border of the table in order to get the selection arrow to appear. This selection arrow is a quick way to select a single row or column in a table. When you click the border, all cells in the table become selected and are displayed with black outlines.

5) Continue to change the color of other rows in the table to match the example.

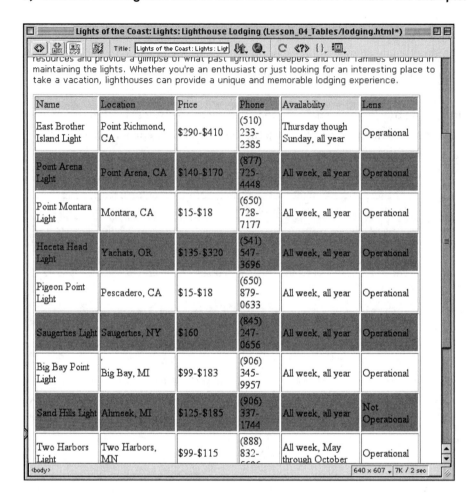

The rows now alternate between white and blue.

6) Select the "Phone" column by positioning the pointer at the top of the column. Click when the selection arrow appears.

You have selected the entire column.

7) In the Property inspector, change the horizontal alignment to Center. Leave the vertical alignment as Default.

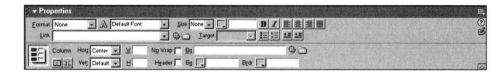

In standard view, the default setting for horizontal alignment does the same thing as the left setting—it aligns the contents of the selected cells to the left. The default setting for vertical alignment does the same thing as the middle setting—it aligns the contents of the selected cells to the middle.

8) Select the Lens column by clicking the top cell; then hold down the Shift key and click the bottom cell.

The entire column is selected.

9) In the Property inspector, change the horizontal alignment to Right.

The lower half of the Property inspector contains the following cell attributes:

- **Merge**: Combines two or more selected cells into one cell.

- **Split**: Divides a single cell into multiple cells.

- **Horz**: Sets the horizontal alignment of the cell's contents to the browser default (usually left for regular cells and center for header cells) or to left, right, or center.

- **Vert**: Sets the vertical alignment of the cell's contents to the browser's default (usually middle) or to top, middle, bottom, or baseline.

- **W** and **H**: Sets the width and height of selected cells in pixels. To use percentages, follow the value with a percent sign (%).

- **No Wrap**: Prevents word wrapping; cells expand in width to accommodate all data. Normally, cells expand horizontally to accommodate the longest word and then expand vertically.

- **Header**: Formats each cell as a table header. The contents of table header cells are bold and centered by default.

- **Bg (top)**: Sets the background image for the cells.

- **Bg (bottom)**: Sets the background color for the cells. Background color appears inside the cells only—that is, it does not flow over cell spacing or table borders. If your cell spacing and cell padding are not set to 0, gaps appear between the colored areas even if the border is set to 0.

- **Brdr**: Sets the border color for the cells.

You may need to click the expander arrow on the right side of the Property inspector if you do not see these options. You will work with some of these options in the following exercises.

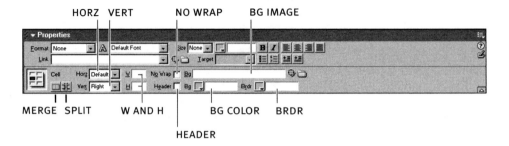

SORTING A TABLE

You can perform a simple table sort by sorting on the contents of a single column. You can also perform a more complicated sort by sorting on the contents of two columns. You cannot sort tables that contain merged cells. The following exercise demonstrates sorting.

1) In the lodging.html document, select the table and then choose Commands > Sort Table.

The Sort Table dialog box opens.

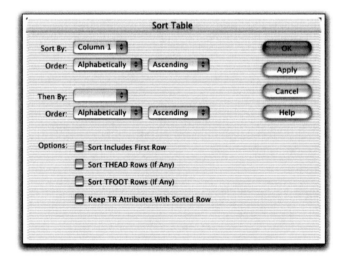

All the default settings will work for this exercise. The first row in the table contains the column headers; you don't want to sort them. (Note that not including the first row is the default option because the check box is initially unchecked.)

2) Set the following options.

Sort By: Select the column to sort. For this exercise, select the first column.

Order: Specify whether you want to sort the column alphabetically or numerically. For this exercise, select Alphabetically. This option is important when the contents of a column are numerical. An alphabetical sort applied to a list of one- and two-digit numbers results in an alphanumeric sort (such as 1, 10, 2, 20, 3, 30) rather than a straight numeric sort (such as 1, 2, 3, 10, 20, 30). Choose Ascending (A to Z or low to high) or Descending for the sort order.

Then By: For this exercise, leave this blank. Then By lets you choose to perform a secondary sort on a different column. The sort methods in the menu are the same as the methods that are available in Sort By.

Sort Includes First Row: Choose this option to include the first row in the sort. If the first row is a heading that shouldn't be moved (as it is in this exercise), leave this check box unchecked. For this exercise, leave this unchecked.

Keep TR Attributes with Sorted Row: If you changed any attributes for a row, you can retain that attribute in the row by choosing this option. Suppose that you sort a table with a color in the first row. After sorting, the data in the first row moves to the second row. If Keep TR Attributes with Sort Row is selected, the color moves with the data to the second row. If this option is not selected, the color remains in the first row. For this exercise, leave this unchecked.

3) Click Apply or OK.

The table is now sorted alphabetically using the data in the first column, but the row headers remain in the first row. Save your document.

MODIFYING A TABLE

After you create a table, you may find it is too large or too small, or you may need to add columns and rows. You can adjust these table properties easily.

1) In the lodging.html document, move the pointer over the vertical table border on the right side of the table. When the pointer changes to a two-headed arrow, drag the column border slightly to the right.

You may have to move the pointer up and down over the border to get this tool to appear.

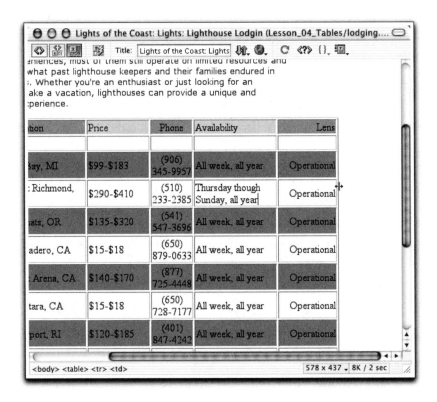

You have enlarged the table. You can see the new width by selecting the table and looking at the number in the Width text field in the Property inspector. Use caution when dragging border of a table to change its size. Whenever you drag table borders in this way, Dreamweaver automatically assigns and updates widths. Sometimes, this width may not be what you want. In that case, click the Clear Column Widths and Clear Row Heights buttons in the Property inspector.

2) Click the right cell of the last row of the table (the bottom right cell) and press the Tab key.

If the pointer is in the last cell of a table, pressing the Tab key will cause the insertion point to be place in the leftmost cell of a new row.

3) In the left cell of the row you just inserted, click and drag to the right to select all the cells in the row. Click the Merge Cells button in the Property inspector.

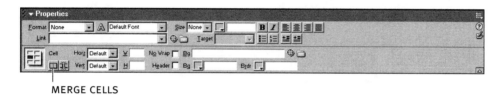

MERGE CELLS

The six cells now form one long cell that spans six columns. The attributes of the first cell, such as color and alignment, are applied to the merged cell.

NOTE *You can split cells in the same manner by clicking the Split Cell button in the Property inspector or by choosing Modify > Table > Split Cell. This method returns the number of cells to the original number if you merged them, or it can split a cell into any number of rows or columns.*

You can merge any number of cells in one column or any number of cells in one row. You can also merge cells in multiple rows and columns, but the cells to be merged must form a rectangle. You cannot merge cells to create an "L" shape.

TIP *To merge cells, you can also choose Modify > Table > Merge Cells. The keyboard shortcuts for merging rows are Option+Command+M (Macintosh) or Ctrl+Alt+M (Windows). Pressing just the M key on the Macintosh will also merge the selected cells.*

4) In the cell you have just merged, type © 2002, Lights of the Coast.

Merging cells gives you many more options for layout. You can merge any number of cells as long as they make up a rectangular selection.

NOTE *If you need to delete a row, click the row and then choose Modify > Table > Delete Row. You can also Control-click (Macintosh) or right-click (Windows) on the table and choose Table > Delete Row from the context menu.*

5) Click the last row of the table and choose Modify > Table > Insert Rows or Columns. In the Insert Rows or Columns dialog box that appears, choose Rows from the Insert options, type 1 in the Number of Rows text field, and choose Above the Selection in the Where options.

The Insert Rows or Columns dialog box allows you to specify whether to insert before or after the current row. When you use this dialog box, you have control over where the new rows or columns are placed, and you can insert any number of rows or columns.

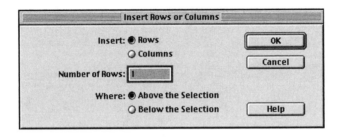

NOTE *If you choose Modify > Table > Insert Row, the new row is inserted above the current row by default. You can also Control-click (Macintosh) or right-click (Windows) the row above and choose Table > Insert Rows or Columns from the context menu.*

This new row you have inserted acts as a spacer between the copyright and the information about the lighthouses above it. Giving each section or block of information on your page a little space helps the viewer to differentiate between the text on the page—it is difficult to read information when there is a lot of text that all runs together.

EXPORTING A TABLE

The HTML code defining the table you create in Dreamweaver has all the tags required to display that table in a browser. If you need to extract the table information to place in a database, a spreadsheet, or a word-processing or page-layout application, you can't just copy and paste the text. All you'll get is the text with no row and column formatting. But you can export the table and save the file as a tab-delimited file that most word-processing and spreadsheet applications can read.

1) In the lodging.html document, select the table.

You can be in layout view or standard view. You will export this table from Dreamweaver into a new file.

2) Choose File > Export > Table.

The Export Table dialog box opens.

3) From the Delimiter drop-down menu, choose Tab.

Most word processing and spreadsheet applications can read both comma- and tab-delimited tables. When you choose File > Export > Table, Tab is selected by default. Your choices of delimiter values for the table data are Tab, Space, Comma, Semicolon, and Colon. If you are not sure which option to use, choose Tab.

4) From the Line Breaks drop-down menu, choose line breaks for the operating system you are using: Macintosh, Windows, or Unix.

Line breaks are the characters inserted at the end of each line. You dealt with them in Lesson 1 when you imported text. When choosing which type of line breaks to use, select the the operating system for which you are exporting the file. You may need to choose an operating system other than your own if the file will be used on a different platform.

5) Click Export. In the dialog box that opens, name the exported file export_lodging.txt and save it in the Lesson_04_Tables folder.

The entire table is exported to a new file with the name you chose. The file you created is an ASCII text file.

You can save and close the lodging.html document.

USING IMAGES IN TABLES

You can also use Standard View to create tables containing images. Tables are often used to construct the layout of a page with multiple images or to reassemble an image that has been sliced. An image may be sliced into several smaller images in order for it to be **optimized** for the Web (the process of optimizing includes decreasing the file size of the image while maintaining the highest possible image quality). The resulting pieces need to be aligned with each other by using a table.

In this exercise, you will create a table that will be used on pages throughout the "Lights of the Coast" project site.

135

1) Create a new HTML page, save it as lighthouse.html and title it Lights of the Coast.

This page will contain a number of tables.

2) Create a new table with the following settings: 5 rows, 3 columns, 617 pixels wide, 0 Cell Padding, 0 Cell Spacing, and 0 Border.

The table you create should look like this example.

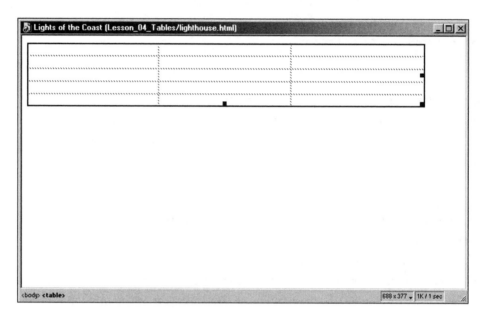

3) Select all five cells in the first column and merge them. In the second row, select and merge the two cells in the second and third columns. In the fourth row, select and merge the two cells in the second and third columns. In the fifth row, select and merge the two cells in the second and third columns.

Your table should now look like this.

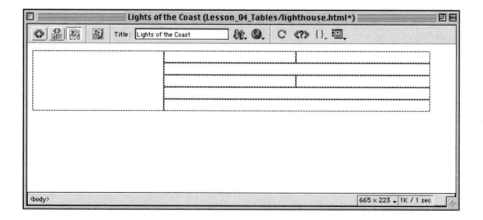

136

4) Place the insertion point in the first column and use the Vert drop-down menu on the Property inspector to change the vertical setting of the cell to "Top." Insert into the cell the nav_lighthouse.jpg from the Lesson_04_Tables/Images folder.

The image of the lighthouse you just inserted will now stay at the top of this column, regardless of how tall the table eventually becomes.

5) Place the insertion point in the second column of the first row. Insert nav_titlebar.gif from the Images folder.

When you insert images into cells in Dreamweaver, the empty cells have a tendency to collapse, and look as if they are no longer there. They are actually still there, but they have just been squished together. In these cases, you may need to use the arrow keys to navigate through your tables, as you will do in the following step.

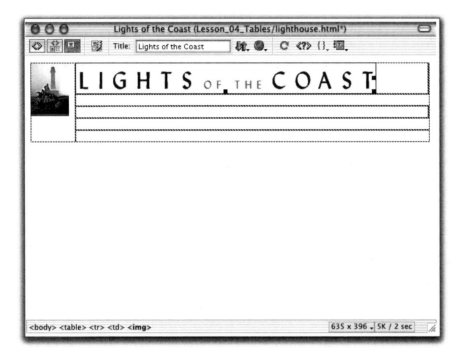

6) Select the title bar image "Lights of the Coast" and press the right arrow key once to move off the image.

The insertion point is now in the cell that contains the nav_titlebar.gif image and it is directly to the right of the image.

7) Press the right arrow key once more to move to the next column.

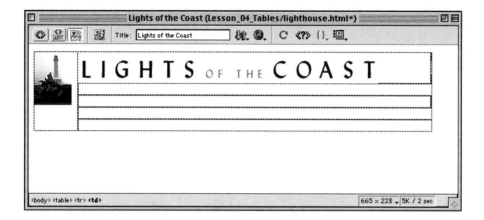

The insertion point is now in the third column of the first row. If the columns have collapsed completely, it may be difficult to see the blinking pointer between the dotted lines indicating the boundaries of the cells.

TIP *Once the pointer is in the correct cell, typing a small amount of text will cause the cell to expand. This may help you to see the columns more clearly. If you use this method, it is very important to be sure that you delete the text, or replace it with the appropriate text or image(s). Extra characters can cause problems in some tables, particularly if you've calculated the table size solely for specific images.*

Refrain from dragging the borders of the table and resizing it in order to see columns that have collapsed. Resizing your table will change its dimensions by adding height tags and width tags. The dimensions defined by those tags could create problems, such as causing the images to not line up flush with each other. If height or width tags are created, you can select the table and click the clear row heights and clear column widths buttons on the Property inspector. You may need to redefine the width of the table after clearing column widths.

CLEAR COLUMN WIDTHS

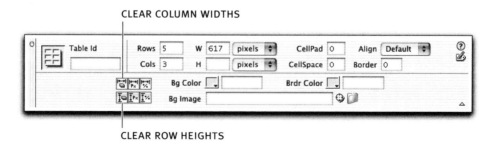

CLEAR ROW HEIGHTS

8) Press the down arrow key once to move the insertion point into the third row. With the insertion point in this location, click the image icon on the Insert bar and choose nav_rightspace.gif from the Images folder to insert the image into the cell.

You only needed to use the down arrow key once to get to the third row because you are in the second column; the second row doesn't have a second column since the two cells in that row were merged.

The nav_rightspace.gif image will appear in the cell and cause the columns of the table to reappear.

9) Place the insertion point in the second row. Insert into the cell the nav_topline.gif from the Images folder. Place the insertion point in the fourth row. Insert into the cell the nav_botline2.gif from the Images folder. Click outside of the table.

When you click outside the table, Dreamweaver causes the table to refresh, and the cell containing the nav_botline2.gif image now fits exactly around the edges of the image. This image and the nav_rightspace.gif image you inserted in the previous step are holding the spaces necessary to create the final look of this page. Tables often need images to force them to hold the dimensions you want. Without an image to hold that space, your columns may shift around as they did when you created the lighthouse lodging information table.

NESTING TABLES

A **nested** table is one that is placed within the cell of another table. Nested tables are used for a variety of purposes. In the earlier days of the Web, nesting tables was usually considered a bad practice because of the problems it caused (including sometimes crashing a viewer's browser). These days, however, browsers are capable of a great deal more. Nested tables are commonly used to create pages that would otherwise have to use one incredibly complicated table or not be able to use the intended design at all. Nesting tables allows you to create more complex layouts and keep each of your tables as simple as possible. The more complex a single table is, the harder it is to create and the more likely it will be to break.

1) In the lighthouse.html document, click outside of the table and press Return (Macintosh) or Enter (Windows) several times. Create a new table with the following settings: 3 rows, 1 column, 93 pixels wide, 0 Cell Padding, 0 Cell Spacing, and 0 Border.

It is often easier to put together the table you plan to nest by creating it outside the larger table, because you will be able to clearly see the borders of the smaller table while you are inserting the necessary images and content.

2) Place the insertion point in the first row, and then click the image icon on the Insert bar to insert nav_main.gif into the cell. In the second row, insert nav_introduction.gif. In the third row, insert nav_credits.gif.

Your small table should now look like the following example.

As you insert images, if your tables contain images that line up flush with one another as they do in this small table, you may not be able to see the dotted lines separating the individual cells.

NOTE *As you work with tables, keep in mind that the dotted lines, which Dreamweaver uses to indicate the cell and table borders, each take up 1 pixel of space. Those extra pixels of space created by the dotted lines do not exist when the document is seen in a browser. However, those pixels of space may cause tables viewed within Dreamweaver to look larger than they really are. For example, in a document you might have two tables. The first table may have five columns and the second table may have only one column. The first table would appear in Dreamweaver to be 4 pixels wider than the first, even though if you were to view the page in a browser both tables would be the same width. You can always turn off table borders by choosing View > Visual Aids > Table borders. On the other hand, table borders are generally very useful and it can be very difficult to work with tables when you have them turned off.*

3) Select and copy the small table with the main, introduction, and credits images you just created. In the table at the top of the page, place the insertion point in the third column of the first row and use Edit > Paste to insert into the cell the table you just copied.

The smaller table is now nested into the cell in the third column of the first row of the first table. In this exercise, you have nested a table in order to simplify the layout of the large table. You can now delete the original small table at the bottom of the page.

TIP *You can use Edit > Cut instead of Edit > Copy to copy and delete the small table at the same time.*

Try to avoid nesting tables more than four or five levels deep. Keep in mind that older browsers—particularly versions of Netscape—may have difficulty displaying too many levels of nested tables (sometimes due to the increased memory required to display those nested tables). In order to determine whether the nested tables you create will work correctly for your visitors, you need to test your pages in a variety of browsers on different platforms.

Don't get in the habit of creating extraneous nested tables. Nesting is a good technique that can be used to achieve cohesive, advanced layouts, but it should be done in a carefully considered and purposeful manner. If you find yourself nesting many levels of tables, you should probably rethink your layout. A simpler layout means less code is created, making it more likely that the page will download quickly, and there will be less potential for problems. If you end up with an improper display in a browser, multiple levels of nested tables can also make it more difficult to find the cause of those errors in the code.

4) Click at the bottom of the page outside the existing table and press Return (Macintosh) or Enter (Windows) several times. Create a new table with 1 row, 5 columns, 465 pixels wide, 0 Cell Padding, 0 Cell Spacing, and 0 Border.
You are creating a second table to nest inside the larger table.

5) In the first column, insert nav_history.gif. Select the nav_history.gif image, and press the right arrow key twice to move off of the image and into the second column. In the second column, insert nav_technology.gif. Select the nav_technology.gif image, and press the right arrow key twice to move off of the image and into the third column. In the third column, insert nav_lights.gif. Select the nav_lights.gif image, and press the right arrow key twice to move off of the image and into the fourth column. In the fourth column, insert nav_resources.gif. Select the nav_resources.gif image, and press the right arrow key twice to move off of the image and into the fifth column. In the fifth column, insert nav_culture.gif.
All images are located in the Images folder.

Your table should now look like the following example.

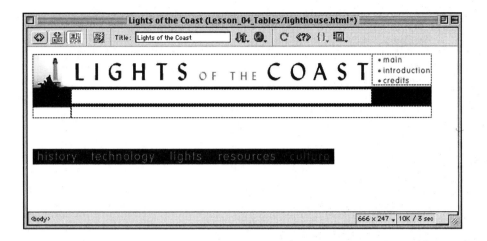

6) Select and copy the small table with the five images you just inserted. Place the insertion point in the second column of the third row of the table at the top of the page and use Edit > Paste to insert the table you just copied into the cell.

The table is now nested into the cell in the second column of the second row of the first table. You can now delete the smaller table at the bottom of your document.

In this exercise, you have nested tables that have content of fixed widths—that content is the images you have placed in the table cells. In the last table you created, the combination of the widths of the five images equals the width of that table. In a table such as this, if you were to replace one or more of those images with text typed directly into the cells (HTML text as opposed to a graphic), there would no longer be an object of a fixed width in those cells. You could define the widths of all five cells, but that often will not hold the cells to their defined dimensions. One technique to force cells to hold their dimensions is to create an additional row at the top of the table with spacer images in each cell. You would set the height of the spacer images in each cell to 1 pixel and set the width of each spacer image to the desired measurement. The combined widths of all five spacer images should equal the width of the table itself. Graphic programs such as Adobe ImageReady and Macromedia Fireworks often use spacer images in this manner when generating HTML for tables according to how an image has been sliced.

143

OUTLINING A TABLE

You can create borders for your tables by entering a number value into the border text field on the Property inspector as you did at the beginning of this lesson. However, table borders created using the border attribute will display inconsistently in different browsers, particularly across different platforms. To get around this, you can nest tables to create a border or outline that will be consistent and compatible with the various browsers and platforms. This technique will provide you with a greater degree of control over how the outline of the table will appear.

1) In the lighthouse.html document, click at the bottom of the document and press Return (Macintosh) or Enter (Windows) several times. Create a new table with 1 row and 1 column. Make it 558 pixels wide. Cell padding should be set to 1, Cell Spacing should be set to 0, and the Border should be set to 0.

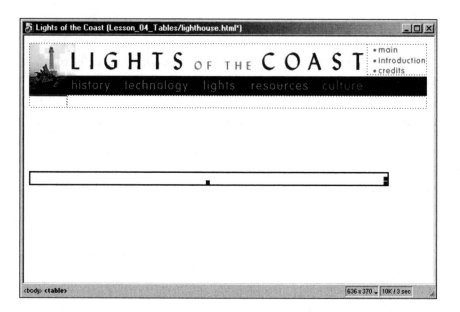

This is the first, outer table. The cell padding defines the width of table outline that you are creating.

TIP *You can set a higher value for cell padding to increase the width of the table outline.*

2) Place the insertion point into the single cell. Use the Property inspector to set the background color of the cell to black (#000000).

The background color of this cell will be the color of the table outline.

3) With the insertion point still in the same cell, click the Table icon on the Common tab of the Insert bar. Set the options as follows: 1 row, 1 column, 100 percent width, Cell Padding of 6, Cell Spacing of 0, and a Border of 0.

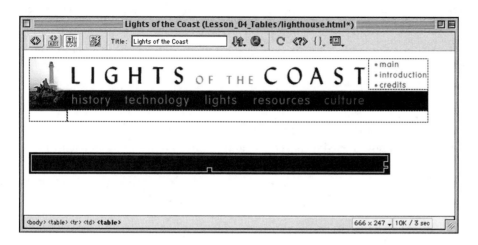

A table is now nested inside the first table. The nested table will expand to 100 percent of the available space for content in the cell—556 pixels. The first table is 558 pixels, but since it has a cell-padding value of 1, a single pixel space is created on all sides of the cell (top, bottom, left, and right). Therefore, the available space inside that cell is 2 pixels less that the total width of the table. The single pixel of space around the cell will create the outline effect.

NOTE *Although you could set the size of the inside table to a fixed width, using 100 percent will do the same thing while giving you the advantage of increased flexibility. For example, if you use a fixed width for the nested table and decide to change the size of the outside table, you will also have to change the size of the nested table. However, if you use 100 percent for the width of the nested table, it will always be displayed at the correct size—regardless of any changes you make to the outside table.*

4) Click to place the insertion point into the single cell of the nested table you just created. Use the Property inspector to set the background color of the cell to white (#FFFFFF).

The background of the nested table is now white, and you can see the outline effect created by the 1-pixel cell padding of the outer table.

145

5) Select and copy the outside table. Place the insertion point in the right cell of the bottom row of the table at the top of the page, select Top from the Vert menu on the Property inspector and paste the copied table into the cell.

By selecting and copying the outside table, you copied everything within that table; that includes the nested table. The outlined table is now nested inside the first table and creates the effect of a page dropping down from the top bar. At this point, you have three levels of nested tables.

The original outlined table at the bottom of the page is no longer necessary so you should delete it.

Your page should now look similar to the example shown here.

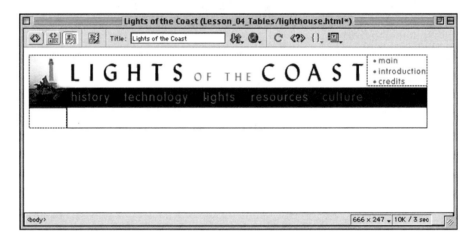

6) Choose Modify > Page Properties, select bkg_inside_tan.gif for the background image, set all four margin options (Left Margin, Margin Width, Top Margin, Margin Height) to 0 and click OK. Save the file and preview it in the browser.

Inserting the background image shows you how the outlined table works with other elements on the page to create a unified look in the design. Setting the margins of the page to zero makes the table line up flush with the top and left sides of the browser, as well as with the background image, which was created for a page with zero margins. The outlined table will expand downward as you insert content into it.

Experiment with tables on your own pages to create effects that work with your designs.

146

DESIGNING FOR COMPUTER SCREENS

In the print world, a designer creates pages to be viewed in final form at a fixed size. The paper stock, printing quality, and size are all controlled. A Web designer, on the other hand, has to account for a greater number of possibilities. You have to consider not only the variety of browsers users might have, but also the size and resolution of their monitors. The kinds of screens on which users are viewing Web pages have increased and will continue to do so. It is now possible to view Web pages on a cell phone or on palm-type PDAs.

If you have only text on a page, the text reflows within the page based on the size of the browser window. As a Web designer, you then have no control of the look of the page. The user can maximize the window, making long, hard-to-read lines. If you want to control the flow of the text on the page, you can place your text within a table to limit line length for text in a cell.

When you design with fixed table widths, you may want to design to the lowest common denominator of monitor sizes that your audience will be using. If you think most of your users have 13-inch monitors, you should use that size. Remember that the browser takes up some room to the left and right of the screen, even if the user maximizes the window. There is no set rule for the amount of room a browser uses, so you should allow for the browser. For 13-inch monitors, for example, make the maximum table size 600 pixels. To determine the maximum table size, refer to the following chart.

Resolution (in pixels)	Device
160×160	Palm-type device
240×320	Pocket PC
544×372	Web TV
640×240	Windows CE
640×480	13-inch monitor
800×600	15- to 17-inch monitor
1024×768	17- to 19-inch monitor
1200×1024	21-inch monitor

NOTE *The visitor's need to be able to print Web pages is important to consider. It is particularly important to make your pages printable, or provide printer-friendly versions, for pages with a great deal of text or pages that viewers will be likely to need to print. The dimension for a printable page is 535 pixels.*

USING WINDOW SIZE TO CHECK LAYOUT

You can check your layout directly within Dreamweaver to determine what your page will look like on different sized screens using the Window Size drop-down menu.

NOTE *This menu is only available in Design View. You will work with other document views in Lesson 12.*

At the bottom of the lighthouse.html document window, click the black arrow next to the box displaying the window size. Choose 760×420 (800×600 Maximized).
The document window will reset to 760×420.

WINDOW SIZE

NOTE *You can also add your own size presets to the list by choosing Edit Sizes at the bottom of the drop-down menu.*

You can save and close the lighthouse.html document.

USING A TRACING IMAGE

At times, you may be given pages that someone else has designed in a graphics program such as Macromedia FreeHand, Adobe Photoshop, or QuarkXPress. If you can convert the page to a JPEG, GIF, or PNG graphic, you can import that image into Dreamweaver and use it as a guide, or **tracing image**, to re-create the HTML page.

The tracing image is visible only inside Dreamweaver. It is not embedded in the HTML code and will not be displayed in the browser. The tracing image will appear behind everything on your page in Dreamweaver. While you're using a tracing image, the background color or background image of your page is hidden, but that background color or image will display when you look at the page in a browser.

1) Create a new document and save it as lights.html in the Lesson_04_Tables folder. Title the page Lights of the Coast: Lights.

In this exercise, you'll insert a tracing image into this document.

2) Choose View > Tracing Image > Load.

The Select Image Source dialog box opens.

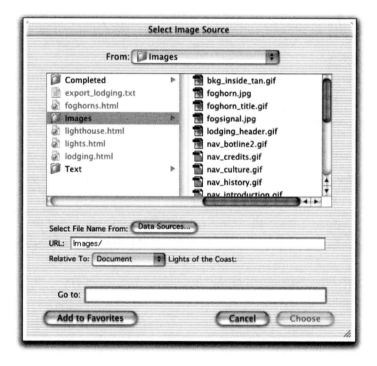

3) Choose the file table_trace.jpg, located in Lesson_04_Tables/Images; then click Open (Macintosh OS 9), Choose (Macintosh OS X), or OK (Windows).

The Page Properties dialog box opens.

4) To see your image on the page, click Apply. Drag the Image Transparency slider to the left to lighten the image to 50 percent. Click Apply to see the change.

You want to be able to see the image but not be distracted by it.

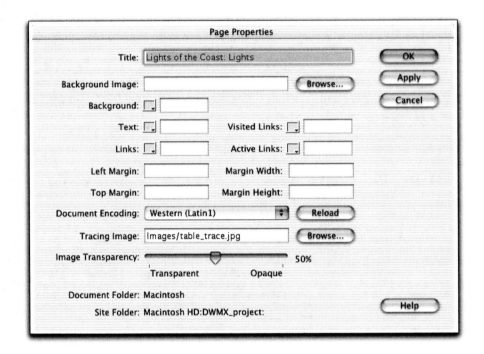

5) Set the Left Margin, Top Margin, Margin Width and Margin Height all to 0. Then click OK to close the Page Properties dialog box.

Dreamweaver simulates the margin between the edge of the browser window and the items in the page. If you change this margin in the Page Properties dialog box, Dreamweaver will use the margin options you specify to place the tracing image. The default margin (used if the margin text field is left blank) may vary depending on the browser, but it is approximately 7 pixels.

NOTE *You can change the position of a tracing image by choosing View > Tracing Image > Adjust Position and specifying the x- and y-coordinate values. You can also move the tracing image one pixel at a time by using the arrow keys while the Adjust Position dialog box is open. To move the image five pixels at a time, press Shift and an arrow key. When you move the tracing image into the space reserved for the margin, as defined in the Page Properties dialog box, the coordinate values will appear to be negative numbers. Choosing View > Tracing Image > Reset Position returns the tracing image to the top left corner of the document window with margin space (0,0). Choosing View > Tracing Image > Align with Selection aligns the tracing image with the selected element. The top left corner of the tracing image will be aligned with the top left corner of the selected element.*

6) Type Creating the Lights...from bonfires to lenses **at the top of the page.**

Notice how the text is displayed with the tracing image behind it. A tracing image can be your guide while you lay out a page. The use of a tracing image reinforces how it is helpful to have a clear and thought-out plan for how your page will appear ahead of time.

You can save and close the lights.html document.

INSERTING ACCESSIBLE TABLES

It is important to continually consider how accessible your pages will be to your visitors. You can use the Insert Accessible Table feature to have Dreamweaver prompt you for the kinds of information needed to create accessible content as you insert tables. The goal of creating accessible pages is to develop content that is functional for the widest possible audience, including those with disabilities. You will learn more about accessibility in Lesson 7.

1) Create a new document and save it as lens_stats.html. Title the page Lights of the Coast: Technology: Lenses: Stats**. Place the text from lens_stats_intro.txt into the page and create a new paragraph line below the text.**

You will insert an accessible table here in the following steps.

2) Choose Edit > Preferences and choose Accessibility from the Category list.

Options for accessibility will display on the right side of the dialog box.

3) Click the check box next to Tables at the bottom of the list and click OK.

The dialog box closes, and you return to your document.

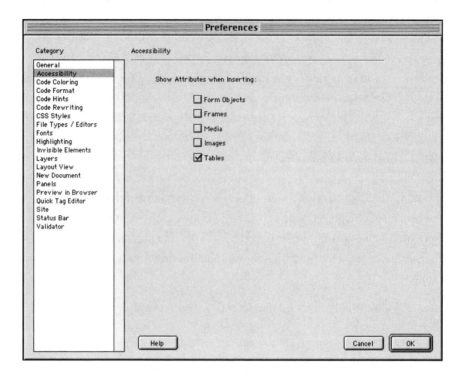

4) Click the Table icon on the Common tab of the Insert bar. Set the table options as follows: 2 rows, 3 columns, Cell Padding of 3, Cell Spacing of 0, Border of 1, and width of 500 pixels.

The Accessibility Options for Tables dialog box opens. You now have a number of new options and settings to choose from.

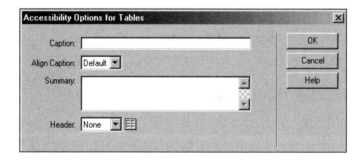

152

5) Type Lens Stats in the Caption text field and choose Top for the Align Caption option.

The caption feature will cause a table caption to appear in the browser after you complete the table settings in the following steps. Captions can be aligned to either the top or bottom of a table. If you leave this option blank, no caption will be inserted.

6) Type This table lists each Fresnel lens order and their approximate diameters and heights in the Summary text field.

A table summary should provide a concise and descriptive, but fairly brief, synopsis of the material contained within the table. It should indicate what the content of the table is. Table summaries are contained within the code and will not be visible in the browser window.

7) Choose Row from the Header drop-down menu and click OK to insert the table.

The Header attribute does not display in the browser window. It is used primarily by screen readers, assistant programs for the blind or visually impaired. This option will apply scope tags to each cell of the top row of the table. The scope tags will make any information that you place in the cells of that top row act as identifiers for each of the cells in their respective columns. For example, if you type **Order** in the top cell of the first column, the remaining cells in that column would be prefaced verbally by the word "Order" when read aloud by a screen reader in order to indicate the content of those cells.

NOTE *The Column option on the Header drop-down menu works in the same way: It places the scope tags in the cells of the leftmost table column so you can enter header information in those cells to indicate the content of their respective rows.*

8) From left to right, starting with the cell in the first column of the first row, type Order Classification **in the first cell, type** Approximate Diameter (in inches) **in second cell, and in the third cell type** Approximate Height (in feet)**. Use the Vert drop-down menu on the Property inspector to align each of the three cells to Top.**

These terms will now act as identifiers for the cells in their respective columns.

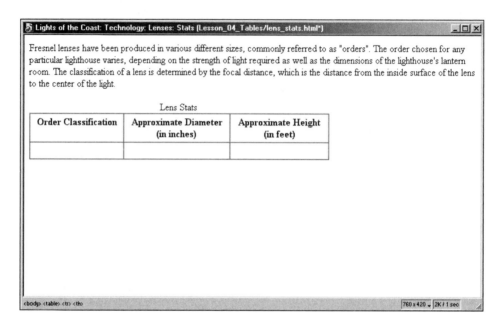

9) Place the insertion point in a new paragraph below the existing table. Click the Tabular Data icon on the Common tab of the Insert bar to bring up the Import Tabular Data dialog box.

You will import the tabular data for lens stats into a new table in order to import the information.

10) Click Browse and choose lens_stats.txt in the Lesson_04_Tables/Text folder. Then choose Tab from the Delimiter menu. For Table Width, choose Set; then type 500 **in the text field and choose Pixels from the drop-down menu. Set the Cell Padding to 3 and Cell Spacing to 0. Format Top Row should be set to (No Formatting) by default, and Border should be 1. Click OK.**

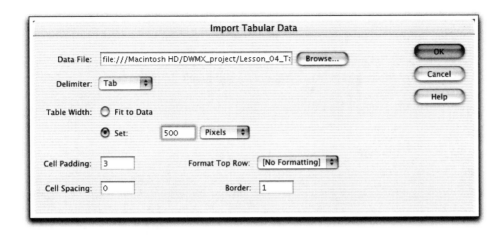

A table is inserted containing the data from the tab-delimited lens_stats.txt file. The settings for this new table match the settings for the table you inserted with the accessibility options earlier in this exercise.

11) Select all the cells in the second table by clicking in the bottom right cell and dragging across the cells to the top left cell; then choose Edit > Copy.

All of the cells in the table are selected as indicated by their black borders. To be cut or copied, the selected cells must form a rectangle.

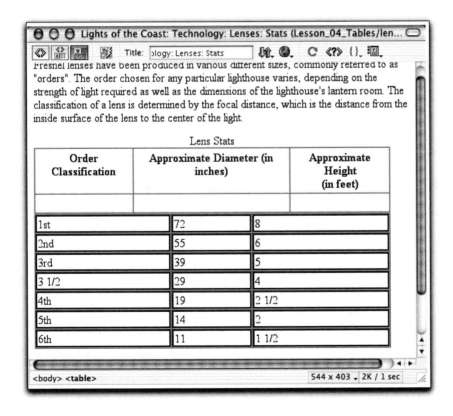

12) Click the first cell of the second row in the top table and choose Edit › Paste. Delete the bottom table. Save the file and preview it in your browser.

This cell is where the copied cells will be pasted. All the cells from the second table are inserted into the first table. You can delete the blank, bottom row.

You can see in the browser how this page will appear to many visitors. For those visitors who are using a screen reader to access the information in your page, this table will be read as follows:

"Caption: Lens Stats
Summary: This table lists each Fresnel lens order and their approximate diameters and heights.
Order Classification: First; Approximate Diameter in inches: 72; Approximate Height in feet: 8
Order Classification: Second; Approximate Diameter in inches: 55; Approximate Height in feet: 6"

The screen reader would continue to read the remaining content in the table in the same manner.

13) Choose Edit › Preferences and uncheck the box for Tables in the list of accessible objects.

The remaining lessons in this book will use the basic table option without accessibility attributes. You can choose to enable Dreamweaver's accessibility features at any time through these preferences.

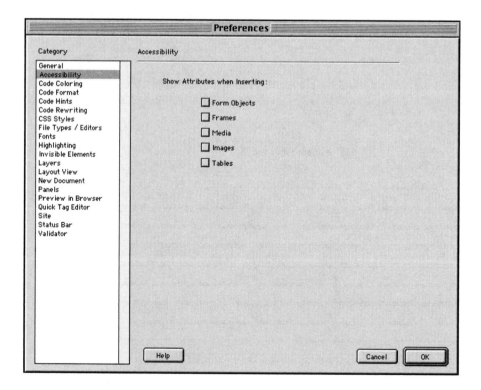

N O T E *The accessible tables feature will not apply accessibility attributes to tables that already exist on your pages. For those tables, you would have to enter the appropriate tags into the code.*

You can close this file.

ON YOUR OWN: EXHIBIT BASED TEACHING PARTNERSHIPS (EBTP)

The Exploratorium is a museum of science, art, and human perception located in San Francisco, CA. The Exhibit Based Teaching Partnerships (EBTP) Web site was designed by Ideum for the Exploratorium's Exhibit Services. This site is not publicly available; it is intended for partner museums. The EBTP site contains a range of information about the groups of Exploratorium exhibits that rotate to a variety of international museums, as well as other aspects of the program. It consists of images, video, maintenance manuals, and more.

N O T E *The EBTP site is a password-protected, members-only Web site. The Exploratorium Exhibit Services Web site is the parent site.*

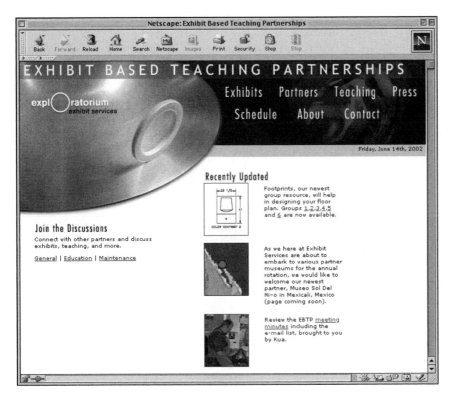

http://www.exploratorium.edu/exhibit_services/
Credits: © Exploratorium, www.exploratorium.edu

"Dreamweaver gives us excellent control over tables, which are essential for complex layouts. We frequently create complex tables to allow for optimization of graphics and inclusion of "rollovers." Having the ability to easily modify tables makes our work much easier."—Jim Spadaccini, Ideum

In this bonus activity, you will recreate the main page of the EBTP Web site on your own. The files you will need for this exercise are located in the Bonus/Lesson_04 folder. This page is made up of tables nested inside other tables. Start by examining the Completed file in-depth. Begin your page by creating a new page and using the final file as a guide for creating the tables. You can view the final file in the Bonus/Lesson_04/Completed folder.

TIP *Deconstructing the completed file will help you understand how the tables were created. Make a backup copy of the file and try unnesting tables to see how they are constructed.*

WHAT YOU HAVE LEARNED

In this lesson, you have:

- Used tables to lay out your pages (in Layout View) (pages 108–118)

- Modified the table properties (including border, background, spacing, color, alignment, and size) (pages 111–129)

- Created a standard table (in Standard View) (pages 118–120)

- Imported tabular data from an external document as a Dreamweaver table (pages 121–122)

- Sorted the information in a table (pages 130–131)

- Modified a table by adding and merging rows and columns to adjust the layout (pages 132–134)

- Exported a Dreamweaver table to an ASCII text file that other applications can read (pages 134–135)

- Created a table in which you inserted a variety of images (pages 135–139)

- Learned to nest tables by placing one table inside the cell of another table (pages 140–143)

- Used the technique of nesting tables to create an outline around a table (pages 144–146)

- Learned how the variety of screen sizes and screen resolutions can affect how you determine your page layout (pages 147–148)

- Imported a tracing image that you used as a guide for your layout (pages 149–151)

- Used attributes to make content within a table accessible to a wider audience, including those with disabilities (pages 151–158)

adding user interactivity

LESSON 5

In this lesson, you will use Dreamweaver behaviors to create rollovers, new browser windows, and menus. A **behavior** combines a user event (such as moving the pointer over a graphic button in the browser) with an action or series of actions that take place as result of that event. Behaviors are prewritten JavaScript codes that you can easily incorporate into your Web site. You can use behaviors to add interactivity to your pages, enabling your users to change or control the information they see.

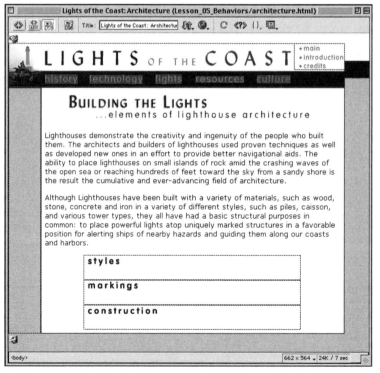

In this project, you will create rollovers with images that are already on the page and learn how to make more than one image on the page change at the same time.

You can specify more than one event to trigger a behavior and more than one action for each event. Dreamweaver includes several predefined behavior actions. If you are proficient with JavaScript, you can add your own behaviors. You can also download new behaviors from the Dreamweaver Exchange Web site, http://www.macromedia.com/exchange/dreamweaver/, by choosing Help > Dreamweaver Exchange. If you have an Internet connection, your primary browser will open, and you will be taken directly to the Web site. You will need to become a member of Macromedia.com in order to download extensions—membership is free. You will learn more about extending Dreamweaver in Lesson 17.

To see examples of the finished pages: open Lesson_05_Behaviors/Completed/local_history.html for the basic rollover; open Lesson_05_Behaviors/Completed/architecture.html for the multiple rollovers, Popup message, status-bar message and Pop-Up menu; open Lesson_05_Behaviors/Completed/Check_browser/markings_tables.html for the browser redirect; and open Lesson_05_Behaviors/Completed/light_sources.html for the new browser window.

WHAT YOU WILL LEARN

In this lesson, you will:

- Create rollovers
- Add user interactivity to your pages by using behaviors
- Add multiple behaviors to one user action
- Add behaviors to image maps
- Create a status-bar message
- Redirect users based on the version of their browser
- Open a new browser window
- Create a pop-up menu

LESSON FILES

Media Files:

Lesson_05_Behaviors/Images/…(all files)

Starting Files:

Lesson_05_Behaviors/acetylene.html

Lesson_05_Behaviors/architecture.html

Lesson_05_Behaviors/fuel.html

Lesson_05_Behaviors/light_sources.html

Lesson_05_Behaviors/lime.html

Lesson_05_Behaviors/location.html

Lesson_05_Behaviors/markings_layers.html

Lesson_05_Behaviors/markings_tables.html

Lesson_05_Behaviors/oxyhydrogen.html

Lesson_05_Behaviors/photovoltaics.html

Lesson_05_Behaviors/Text/…(all files)

Completed Project:

Lesson_05_Behaviors/Completed/…(all files)

INSERTING A ROLLOVER IMAGE

One of the most common uses of JavaScript on Web pages is to create a **rollover**—an image that changes when the user moves the pointer over it. You can create rollovers in Dreamweaver without ever looking at the HTML or JavaScript code. A rollover is a simple behavior that is included in the Common Insert bar. When you use this method, Dreamweaver creates the behavior behind the scenes.

1) Create a new document and save it as local_history.html in the Lesson_05_ Behaviors folder. Title the page Lights of the Coast: History: Locations **and set the background color of the page to white.**

In the following steps, you will create a rollover on this page.

2) Click in the document window to place the insertion point at the top of the page. In the Insert bar, click the Rollover Image button.

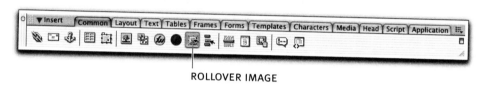

ROLLOVER IMAGE

The Insert Rollover Image dialog box opens.

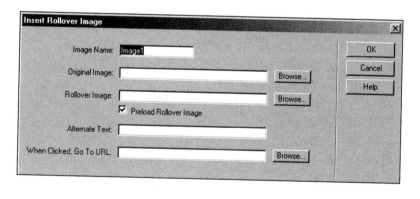

Dreamweaver steps you through the process of creating rollovers in this dialog box. If you haven't initially placed your images on the page, you might prefer this method, because it enables you to insert an image and define it as a rollover at the same time. In the next exercise, you will create rollovers for images that have already been placed on the page.

TIP *Alternatively, you can choose Insert > Interactive Images > Rollover Image to insert a rollover image using the same dialog box.*

3) In the Image Name text box, type local for the image name.

The dialog box provides a text field in which you can name the image. If you don't name your rollover images, Dreamweaver assigns generic names automatically in a numeric order: Image1, Image2, etc.... It will be more helpful to you in creating your Web pages if you make it a standard practice to give all rollovers specific and meaningful names that clearly indicate what they are for. When naming your images, don't use spaces or any special characters.

4) Click the Browse button next to the Original Image text field and find local_off.gif in the Lesson_05_Behaviors/Images folder.

This image will appear on the page before the user rolls over it.

5) Click the Browse button next to the Rollover Image text field and find the rollover image local_on.gif in the Lesson_05_Behaviors/Images folder.

When this page is viewed in a browser, the visitor will initially see the local_off.gif image. The local_on.gif image will replace the local_off.gif image when the user rolls over local_off.gif in the browser window.

TIP *When creating your graphics, make each image with the same dimensions. If you don't, the second rollover image will be resized to the size of the first image. Resizing distorts the second image.*

6) Type Locations in the Alternate Text text field. Click the Browse button next to the When Clicked, Go To URL text field and find the file location.html in the Lesson_05_Behaviors folder. Leave the Preload Rollover Image box checked. Then click OK.

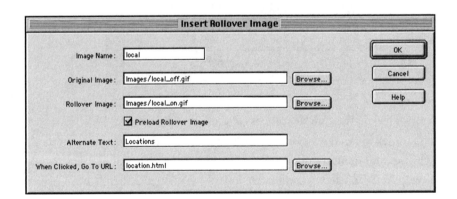

The rollover now links to the file you chose. The URL you chose in the When Clicked, Go To URL text field now appears in the Link text field on the Property inspector when the image is selected.

NOTE *If you leave the text field blank, Dreamweaver fills it with a number sign (#), otherwise known as a **null link**, in the Link text field of the Property inspector. The number sign tells the browser to display the pointing-hand when the user rolls over the graphic. The number sign will also cause the browser to stay on the same page if the rollover is clicked in the browser. You can replace the number sign with a link value in order to go to a different page or URL, but do not leave the Link text field in the Property inspector empty, because doing so will remove the JavaScript that creates the rollover.*

When the rollover image is selected, the resulting behavior will appear in the Behaviors panel, which you'll use in the next exercise.

7) Save your file and test it in the browser.
You can close this file.

TIP *When creating your graphics, make the file sizes as small as possible. Remember that with rollovers, you are displaying not one but two images for the same button. The file size of a rollover like the one you inserted in this exercise is doubled because there are two images to download.*

ADDING BEHAVIORS

This exercise demonstrates creating rollovers from graphics that have already been placed on the page. The result is the same as the last lesson—an image will swap to show a different image when the user rolls over it. In this exercise, however, you are using a different method to insert rollovers for images that are already on the page. You will insert the behavior for the rollover using the Behaviors panel. When you are creating your own Web pages, if you have already placed your original images on a page you should use this method. If you haven't, you can use the method from the previous exercise to set both the original image and the rollover image in one step.

1) Open the architecture.html from the Lesson_05_Behaviors folder.
The file contains a number of tables and graphics that have already been placed for you, using the techniques you have learned in Lessons 1 through 4.

2) In the Property inspector, use the image-name text field to name the three images near the bottom of the page as follows: styles_off.gif should be named styles, markings_off.gif should be named markings, and construction_off.gif should be named construction.

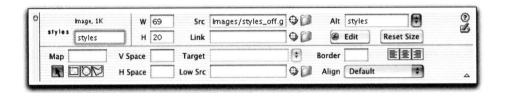

Naming the images to match their content or their function is a good method. This naming practice helps to clearly indicate what images are associated with the chosen names.

3) Select the Styles image. Open the Design panel group and click the Behaviors tab.
The Behaviors panel opens.

ACTIONS MENU

> **TIP** *You can also choose Window > Behaviors to open the Behaviors panel.*

4) Click the plus sign (+) button on the Behaviors panel and choose Swap Image from the Actions drop-down menu.
The Swap Image dialog box opens. The Swap Image behavior is what creates the rollover effect you used in the previous exercise: it swaps a new image in to replace the original image that the visitor rolled over.

An **action** is what happens as a result of user interaction. When you select an action, Dreamweaver adds that action to the list in the Behaviors panel. The Actions drop-down menu displays or disables actions depending on what element you have selected in the document window.

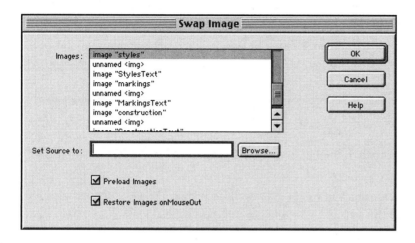

NOTE *Dreamweaver also adds an appropriate event (or events) for that action automatically. The **event** is what causes the action to occur. An event could be the user rolling over an image or clicking a button, for example. For rollovers, Dreamweaver uses **onMouseOver** events by default. You will learn to change the events later in this lesson.*

5) In the Images list, make sure that the styles image is selected.

The image will be listed as "styles." This is the name you defined in step 2 for the image that you selected and added an action for in the Behaviors panel in step 4. By selecting the image in the list you are designating that when the user rolls over it, the image will be replaced with the rollover image. You will choose the rollover image in the next step.

NOTE *If you were to choose a different image from this list, that image would be replaced with the rollover image when the user rolls over the styles image. You will do this in the next exercise.*

Keep in mind that if you don't name your images, they all appear with the name, "unnamed <img>" in this dialog box. This is why it is so important to name your images properly; it is very hard to work with behaviors if the images are not clearly and logically named. In a list full of unnamed images, it can be difficult to distinguish which images you are working with.

6) Click the Browse button next to the Set Source To text field and find styles_on.gif in the Images folder to use for the rollover image.

Set Source To defines what the rollover image will be. This is the same as choosing the rollover in the previous exercise. Generally, the original appearance of an image is known as the "off" state, and the instance of the rollover when the user moves the pointer over the image and the image changes is known as the "on" state. Images used for the "on" states often look like a button has been pressed or a word has been highlighted to indicate to the visitor that the object is an active or linked element.

All the rollover graphics you will use for this exercise are in the Images folder, and the names of the rollover-image files have the suffix _on.

7) Click Open (Macintosh OS 9), Choose (Macintosh OS X) or OK (Windows) to pick the image.

After choosing the image, you will be returned to the Swap Image dialog box. An asterisk appears at the end of the image name in the Images list to indicate that an alternative image has been assigned to it for the rollover.

8) Make sure that the Preload Images and Restore Images onMouseOut check boxes are checked. Then click OK.

The Preload Images option is checked by default and is highly recommended. Loading the images that will swap to replace the originals along with the rest of the page when it is first called up by the browser will make your rollovers happen quickly. This setting eliminates any lag caused by the download occurring at the time the user rolls over the image.

The Restore Images onMouseOut option is also checked by default and is recommended. This option makes your swapped images revert to the original images when the user rolls off them. You will notice that Dreamweaver lists this option as a separate action in the Behaviors panel.

9) Repeat steps 3 through 8 for the Markings and Construction buttons, using markings_on.gif and construction_on.gif for the rollover images that you define in the Set Source to text field.

If you ever need to delete a behavior, you can select the object in the document window that contains the behavior, select the action in the Behaviors panel that you want to delete, and then click the minus sign (–) button at the top of the Behaviors panel, or press Delete (Macintosh) or Backspace (Windows).

Since you have not yet defined pages for these rollovers to link to, they will display javascript:; in the Link text field when selected. Do not delete this text, it is necessary for the rollovers to function since there is no link defined yet.

10) Save your file and test the rollovers in your browser.

The images change when you roll over them.

The next exercise demonstrates assigning two swap images to the same user event.

SWAPPING MULTIPLE IMAGES WITH ONE EVENT

You can also have several images swap from their original images to their rollover images at the same time as a result of the same event. You might want two images to swap out, each from their original image to the rollover image, when the user rolls over one button, for example.

In this exercise, you will apply a behavior to the Styles graphic, which will cause the spacer image to swap to an image with the Styles caption as the user rolls over the Styles button. At the same time, the Styles button will change from its original image to the rollover you defined in the previous exercise. For the additional rollover to occur using the same event, you will edit the existing Swap Image action and define the additional image swap in the following exercise.

1) In the architecture.html document, select the Styles button, and then double-click the existing Swap Image action in the Behaviors panel.

Make sure you double-click the Swap Image action, not the Swap Image Restore action.

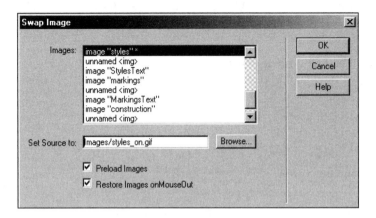

The Swap Image dialog box opens.

2) In the Swap Image dialog box, select the image named StylesText. Click the Browse button to the right of the Set Source to text field and choose the styles_text_on.gif image from the Lesson_05_Behaviors/Images folder.

The StylesText image is the blank image underneath the styles graphic, and it has already been named for you. In this step you are selecting that blank image in the Swap Image dialog box so you can replace it with the styles caption image that will display more information to the viewer.

Look at the Images list in the Swap Image dialog box. Images with an asterisk at the end of the name have been assigned a rollover image. The styles image, for example, has an asterisk next to it because you defined a rollover for that image in the last exercise. Now the StylesText image will also have an asterisk next to it, because you have assigned a rollover for that image in this step. Checking this list is a quick way to verify which images will swap from their original images to rollover images.

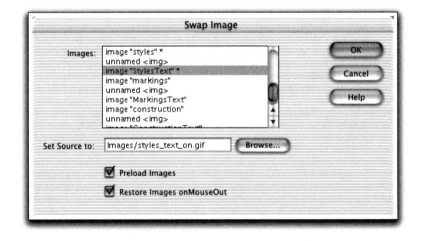

3) Click OK to close the Swap Image dialog box. Then repeat the same process of steps 1 and 2 for the remaining buttons, Markings and Construction.

The blank images are already named for you: MarkingsTextOff and ConstructionTextOff. The images to swap are indicated by the _on suffix. They are located in the Architecture images folder. Swapping multiple images can be useful for giving the user additional information, but keep in mind that too many extra image swaps on one action can slow a browser down.

4) Save your file again and test it in the browser.

When you move your pointer over each button, the button image should change, and the corresponding description text image should also change. When you move away from the button, both the button and the description text graphic should return to the original images.

ADDING BEHAVIORS TO IMAGE MAPS

Moving the pointer over any portion of a standard rollover image will call up the JavaScript and cause the image swap to happen. There may be times, however, when you want the rollover to occur only when the user rolls over a certain part of the image. In such cases, you can use image maps to define those hotspot areas.

1) In architecture.html, use the image-name text field on the Property inspector to name all of the navigational images that are located in a row near the top of the page: nav_history.gif should be named history, nav_technology.gif should be named technology, nav_lights.gif should be named lights, nav_resources.gif should be named resources, and nav_culture.gif should be named culture.

If you were to create standard rollovers for these navigational images, the areas between each of the words would cause the swap image to occur. By using image maps to define the hotspots on the images, you can control when the rollover happens.

2) Draw an image map closely around the word history on the nav_history.gif image.

The image map makes only the word history on the nav_history.gif image clickable.

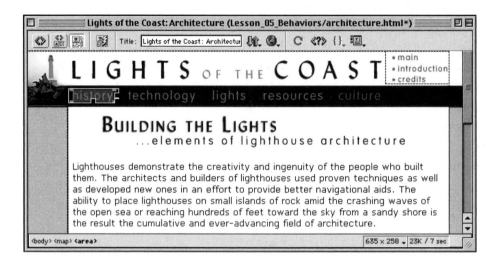

3) Select the cursor tool on the Property inspector and click the image map you just created to select it. Click the plus sign (+) button on the Behaviors panel and choose Swap Image from the Actions drop-down menu.

You are applying a swap image behavior to an image map. The behavior will not apply to any area of the image surrounding the image map.

4) In the Images list, make sure the history image is selected. Click the Browse button next to the Set Source To text field, and find nav_history_on.gif in the Images folder. Click Open (Macintosh OS 9), Choose (Macintosh OS X) or OK (Windows) to pick the image and return to the Swap Image dialog box.

You have now selected the image that will replace the nav_history.gif image when you roll over the hotspot in a browser. The entire image will be replaced, even though the clickable area is only on a certain portion of the original image.

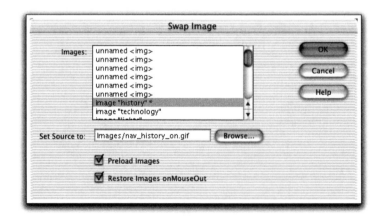

5) Make sure the Preload Images and Restore Images onMouseOut check boxes are checked. Then click OK.

The dialog box closes, and you return to the document window. Whenever the image map on the nav_history.gif image is selected, you will be able to see the Swap Image listed in the Behaviors panel. If you have the image selected but do not have the image map selected, you will not see the swap image listed in the behaviors panel.

6) Repeat steps 2 through 5 for the technology, lights, resources, and culture images. Save the file and test your work in the browser.

The images to use for the swaps are indicated by the _on suffix. Using image maps in combination with behaviors can give you a significant amount of additional control over your images, actions, and events.

Your document should now show the image maps created closely around the navigation word like the example shown here.

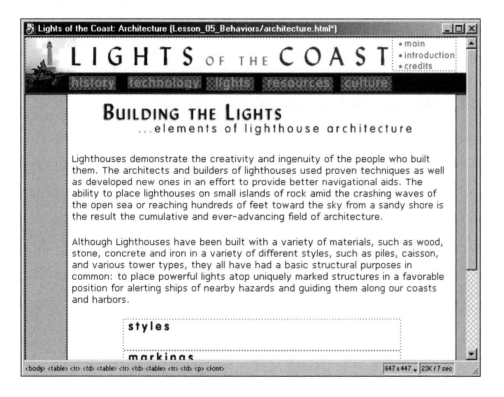

EDITING ACTIONS AND EVENTS

You can edit actions and events in several ways: You can change the event to which an action corresponds, you can attach several actions to a single event, and you can change the order in which those actions occur. For example, Swap Image is the action, and OnMouseOver is the event that corresponds to the rollover behavior. In this exercise you will add an action for a pop-up message and select a corresponding event.

1) In the architecture.html document, select the Markings button. Click the plus sign (+) button in the Behaviors panel and choose Popup Message from the Actions drop-down menu.

The Popup Message dialog box opens, displaying a text field in which you can type your message.

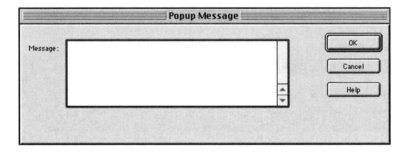

2) Type How unique markings differentiate lighthouses and click OK.

The Popup Message action and the corresponding event appear in the Behaviors panel.

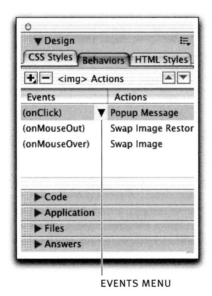

EVENTS MENU

174

3) Select the event in the Behaviors panel, and choose Show Events For > 4.0 and Later Browsers from the Events drop-down menu to the right of the event. Then choose (onMouseOut) from the same Events drop-down menu.

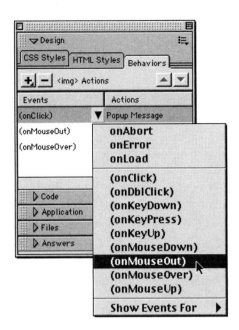

The events in the drop-down menu might differ depending on the action and the browser type you choose. The Events menu appears only when you select an action and event combination in the list. You can choose what browser type to display events for by making a choice from the Show Events For menu at the bottom of the Events menu.

NOTE *The Events pop-up menu is divided into two sections. In the top portion, Dreamweaver displays events that can be attached to objects directly. The bottom section shows, in parentheses, events that need an anchor placed around the object. If you insert a Rollover Image (either by choosing Insert > Interactive Images > Rollover Image, or by choosing Insert Rollover Image from the Insert bar) as you did in the first exercise of this lesson, Dreamweaver adds the anchor for you by inserting a number sign (#) into the Link text field of the Property inspector. If you are not using a rollover, you need to add a null link, using a number sign (#), or a working link in the Property inspector yourself.*

4) Click the up-arrow button in the Behaviors panel to move the Popup Message behavior to the top of the list.

The browser will perform the actions in the order in which they appear in this list. The up arrow moves the action up in the list; the down arrow moves the action down in the list. Use these buttons to change the order in which actions are executed.

5) Save and preview the page in the browser.

Use care when adding the Popup Message behavior to your pages. Like pop-up windows, these messages can quickly annoy your visitors when overused.

Leave this file open to use in the next exercise.

CREATING A STATUS-BAR MESSAGE

A status-bar message can give users extra information about where links will lead them. This message, which appears in the status bar at the bottom of the browser window, replaces the default display of the URL or path to the linked page.

1) In the architecture.html document, select the Styles image. Click the plus sign (+) button in the Behaviors panel and choose Set Text > Set Text of Status Bar from the Actions drop-down menu.

The Set Text of Status Bar dialog box opens, displaying a text field in which you can type your message.

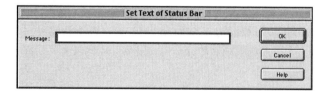

2) Type Architectural styles used in lighthouses and click OK.

If you use status-bar messages, a concise description of the linked material will help your users navigate your pages.

3) Save the file and test it in the browser.

When you move your pointer over the Styles button, you will see the message you created displayed in the status bar at the bottom of the browser window. You can close the architecture.html file.

CHECKING THE BROWSER

Not all browsers support items such as layers and animations. With the Check Browser action, you can detect what browsers are being used by the visitors to your Web site and redirect users to another page if you want to provide advanced features that won't display correctly in other browsers. If, for example, your page contains layers (covered in Lesson 15) or animations (covered in Lesson 16), you could create a static page without the layers or animations and then redirect users with 4.0 browsers to the animation page. Users with older browsers or with JavaScript turned off would remain on the static page.

This exercise uses a page built with tables and a similar page built with layers. You will add a Check Browser behavior and redirect the users with 4.0 browsers to the page that uses layers.

1) Open the markings_tables.html file in the Lesson_05_Behaviors/ folder.

This file was created with tables and thus will display properly in most browsers. This page was created using the techniques you have learned up to this point.

2) Select the <body> tag by clicking <body> in the Tag Selector (in the bottom left corner of the document window).

You are attaching the action to the **<body>** tag to redirect a user before the page loads. You should see **<body>** displayed in the title bar of the Behaviors panel, indicating that the **<body>** tag is selected.

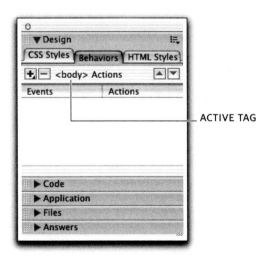

ACTIVE TAG

177

3) Click the plus sign (+) button in the Behaviors panel and choose Check Browser from the Actions drop-down menu.

The Check Browser dialog box opens.

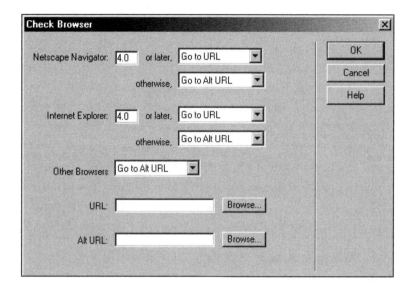

4) For both Netscape 4.0 and Explorer 4.0 or later, choose Go to URL from the appropriate drop-down menu. For both Netscape and Explorer Otherwise, choose Stay on This Page. For Other Browsers, choose Stay on This Page.

When you use the Check Browser behavior, you need to redirect the users who have the latest browsers to another page. If you tried to use this behavior to redirect users with older browsers to another page, it would not work for anyone who uses a browser that does not support JavaScript or who simply turned off JavaScript. If you want to redirect only those users who have older browsers, you need to use a meta tag refresh instead. Meta tags are covered in Lesson 12.

NOTE *To redirect all users to a different page, regardless of their browser version, you should use a meta tag refresh by choosing Insert > Head Tags > Refresh or clicking the Insert Refresh button in the Head category of the Insert bar. In the dialog box, type the URL which you want users redirected to in the Go to URL text field. If you want users to remain on the page for a certain length of time before the browser loads the page that you are redirecting them to, type the time in seconds into the Delay text field. The Refresh This Document option will reload this page in the browser.*

5) Click the Browse button next to the URL text field and locate the markings_layers.html file in the Lesson_05_Behaviors/ folder.

This file is the page to which users of the latest browsers will be redirected. The markings_layers.html file was created using layers, which you will learn about in Lesson 15.

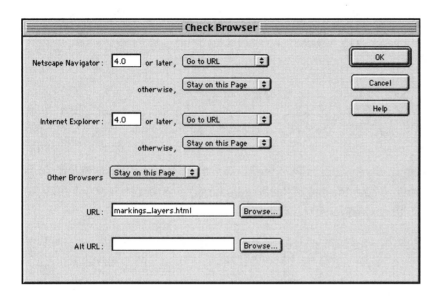

6) Click OK to insert the JavaScript into your page.

The **onLoad** event appears with the corresponding Check Browser action in the Behaviors panel.

7) Save the file and test the page in your browser.

If you have a 4.0 or later browser, you may briefly see the markings_tables.html page before the browser redirects you to the page with layers, marking_layers.html. If you do not have a 4.0 or later browser, you will remain on the static page. You can close this file.

TIP *Many Web designers test their pages in multiple versions of Netscape and Explorer. It is a good idea to have multiple versions on your computer for this reason. You also want to check your pages in both Macintosh and Windows. More information on using Dreamweaver to test your site can be found in Lesson 7.*

OPENING A NEW BROWSER WINDOW

This exercise demonstrates how to open a new browser window when the page loads, which can be used for displaying an advertisement, definition terms, or a wide variety of other information. You could open a browser window by using the _blank target along with a standard link, but you wouldn't have any control over the attributes of that new window. On the other hand, the Open Browser Window behavior lets you control the size along with a number of attributes of the new browser window such as scroll bars and menu bars.

TIP *Although the Open Browser Window option is easy to add, think it through before using it on a Web page. Make sure that the extra window is necessary. Users are often irritated with new windows that continually pop up as they browse the Web.*

1) Open the light_sources.html file in the Lesson_05_Behaviors folder. Select the bolded word "lime" near the end of the first paragraph and place a null link (#) into the Link text field on the Property inspector.

You need to use the null link because this page should stay in the main browser window while another window is opened. The null link enables you to attach the Open Browser Window behavior in the next step.

2) Place the insertion point in the word "lime" and click the plus sign (+) button in the Behaviors panel to add a new behavior, and then select Open Browser Window in the list.

The Open Browser Window dialog box opens. You placed the insertion point in the word "lime" because it needs to be deselected in order for the Open Browser Window option to be available to you in the menu.

Open Browser Window

URL to Display: [_____] [Browse...]   [OK]
                                                     [Cancel]
Window Width: [____] Window Height: [____]   [Help]
Attributes: ☐ Navigation Toolbar   ☐ Menu Bar
            ☐ Location Toolbar   ☐ Scrollbars as Needed
            ☐ Status Bar   ☐ Resize Handles
Window Name: [_____]

3) Click the Browse button and locate the lime.html file.

This file is the page that will load in the new window.

4) Type 350 for the window width and 100 for the window height. Then click OK.

The width and height are chosen based on the size of the content in the new window.
If you are simply displaying a banner ad, you should set the size of the new window
to the width and height of that ad image. If the content has more elements, you should
adjust the size of the window accordingly. You can also set a number of window
attributes as needed. The additional attributes for new windows are as follows:

- **Navigation Toolbar**: The row of browser buttons that includes Back, Forward,
  Home, and Reload. Leave this box unchecked for this exercise.

- **Location Toolbar**: The row of browser options that includes the location field.
  Leave this box unchecked for this exercise.

- **Status Bar**: The area at the bottom of the browser window in which messages
  (such as the load time remaining and the URLs associated with links) appear.
  Leave this box unchecked for this exercise.

- **Menu Bar**: The area of the browser window (Windows) or desktop (Macintosh)
  where menus such as File, Edit, View, Go, and Help appear. You should set this
  option if you want users to be able to navigate from the new window. If you do
  not set this option, users can only close or minimize the window (Windows) or
  close the window or quit the application (Macintosh) from the new window.
  Leave this box unchecked for this exercise.

- **Scrollbars As Needed**: Specifies that scroll bars should appear if the content extends beyond the visible area. Scroll bars do not appear if you do not set this option. If the Resize Handles option is also turned off, users have no way of seeing content that extends beyond the original size of the window. If this is the case, you need to make sure the window is sized appropriately for the content of the page. If the window is too small or too large and has no scroll bars, it will be very frustrating for users. Leave this box unchecked for this exercise.

- **Resize Handles**: Specifies that users should be able to resize the window, either by dragging the bottom right corner of the window or by clicking the Maximize button (Windows) or size box (Macintosh) in the top right corner. If you do not set this option, the resize controls are unavailable and the user cannot drag the bottom right corner of the window. Leave this box unchecked for this exercise.

- **Window Name**: The name of the new window. You should name the new window if you want to target it with links or control it with JavaScript. Leave this text field blank for this exercise.

5) Save your file and test your page in the browser. Repeat steps 2 through 4 for the rest of the bolded terms on the page.

A new window opens with definitions for terms that appear in the light_sources.html document when you follow the link applied to the term.

The pages to use for the remaining terms are oxyhydrogen.html, fuel.html, acetylene.html, and photovoltaics.html.

CREATING A POP-UP MENU

You can integrate JavaScript Pop-Up menus with your navigation in order to give your visitors a list of choices. Dreamweaver's Pop-Up Menu script works in both Netscape (versions 4 and up) and Explorer (versions 4 and up).

NOTE *This script does not work in Opera, an alternative browser that displays these pop-up menus with no background color. When creating a Web site, you should test your pages in the browsers your visitors are most likely to use. It is a good idea to provide alternatives for visitors who use browsers that may not properly display your site. Remember that there are a lot of different browsers available, but it is very difficult—if not impossible—to create a site that works perfectly in each and every one. Try instead to create sites that will work best in the target browsers (those which your audience is most likely to use) and provide alternative ways to access content. A good and commonly used alternative for the example used in this exercise is to provide text links to the main navigational items at the bottom of your pages. You will learn more about testing your site in Lesson 7.*

1) In the architecture.html document, click the image map on the history image to select it.

You can verify that the image map has been selected by looking for the blue selection handles that appear around the defined area of the image map. When it is selected, you should see two actions listed in the Behaviors panel from when you created a rollover for this image earlier in this lesson.

2) Click the plus sign (+) button in the Behaviors panel and choose Show Pop-Up Menu from the Actions drop-down menu.

The Show Pop-Up Menu dialog box appears with the Contents tab active. You will use this portion of the dialog box to define the choices you want to present your visitor with.

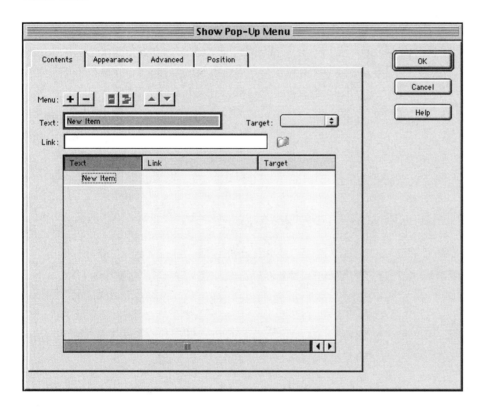

3) In the Text text field, replace the default text "New Item" by typing Location. Click the folder icon next to the Link text field, browse for location.html, and select it.

The Location item is added to the list of menu items. For this item, you are selecting the location.html document that you created at the beginning of this lesson.

4) Click the Menu plus sign (+) button to add a new item. Replace the default text "New Item" by typing Light Sources. Click the folder icon next to the Link text field, browse for light_sources.html, and select it. Add a third item to the list, name it Local History, and link it to markings_local_history.html. Add a fourth item to the list, name it Markings, and link it to markings_layers.html.

The names of menu items and the corresponding pages to which they link can be edited by selecting an item in the list and using the Text and Link text fields to make changes.

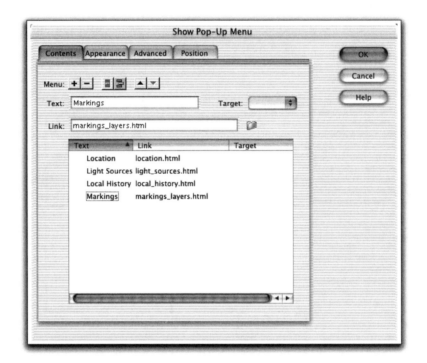

TIP *To delete an item, select it in the list of menu items and click the Menu minus sign (–) button.*

5) Select Light Sources in the list of menu items. Click the Menu up-arrow button to move the Light Sources item to the top of the list. Select Locations in the list and click the Menu down-arrow button to move it to the bottom of the list.

The order of menu items can be rearranged easily with the Menu arrow buttons.

N O T E *You can create subcategories of menu items by selecting the item you want to make a subcategory and clicking the indent item button. Use the outdent item button to move an item to a higher category level.*

6) Click the Appearance tab on the Show Pop-up Menu dialog box. Select Vertical Menu from the orientation drop-down menu. Select the font set beginning with Verdana from the Font drop-down menu and enter 9 in the Size text field. There should be no bold or italic, and the alignment should be left.

T I P *Shorter and more concise menu options help to keep your design clean and easy to use.*

Here you are matching the text options for the Pop-Up menu to the styles used in the "Lights of the Coast" project site.

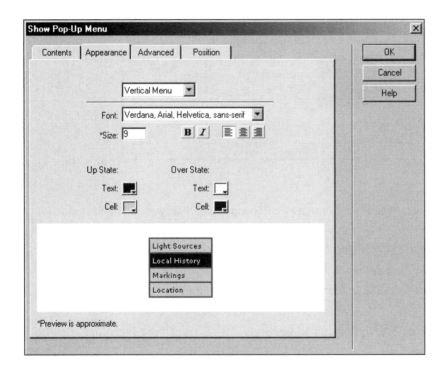

N O T E *If you have less than four choices in your menu list, Dreamweaver will repeat the last entry until there are four choices in the preview shown in this dialog box—this is for display purposes only and will not happen in your document.*

7) Use the color boxes to set the following: Up State Text #999999 (gray), Up State Cell #000000 (black), Over State Text #FFCC66 (yellow), Over State Cell #000000 (black).

These options enable you to set the look of the Pop-Up menu to match the style of the navigational images as closely as possible.

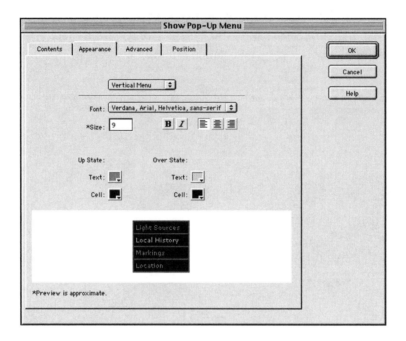

8) Click the Advanced tab on the Show Pop-Up Menu dialog box. The drop-down menus for Cell Width and Cell Height should be set to Automatic. Set the following: Cell Padding 3, Cell Spacing 0, Text Indent 0, Menu Delay 1000. Check the box for Show Borders, and set the border to 0. Set the Border color to #666666 (gray), the Shadow color to #333333 (dark gray), and the Highlight color to #FFFFFF.

Leaving the box for Show Borders checked while setting the border to a size of 0 turns off the outside borders but leaves thin lines separating the individual menu items from each other.

The menu delay controls how long it takes for the menu to disappear after the visitor rolls off of it.

186

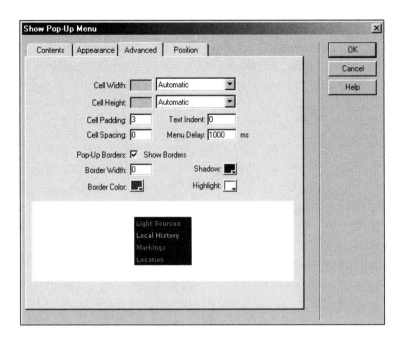

9) Click the Position tab on the Show Pop-Up Menu dialog box. Click the second Menu Position button from the left. Type an X value of 5 and a Y value of 26. Make sure the Hide Menu on MouseOut Event box is checked. Click OK.

In addition to the X and Y axis, you can also use the four general placement buttons on this portion of the Show Pop-Up Menu dialog box in order to position your menu on the page.

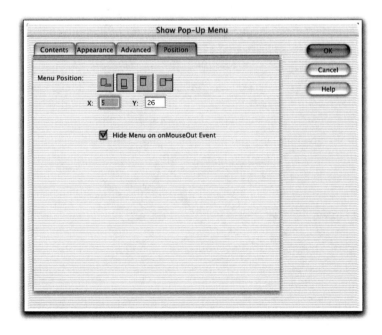

ADDING USER INTERACTIVITY

10) Save the file and preview it in your browser.

Test your menus as much as is possible. When you roll over the history navigation image you will see the Pop-Up menu that you created in this exercise appear below the word "history." The settings that you applied for appearance and position make the menu look integrated with the rest of the navigation.

NOTE *In order to insert the Pop-Up menu, Dreamweaver creates an external JavaScript file with the .js extension. Usually named mm_menu.js, this file is necessary for the pop-up menu to function. It is, however, a fairly large file (in this case, approximately 28KB), so you will need to judge if the addition of scripts such as this are of a size that your visitors can download quickly and easily.*

ON YOUR OWN: AT HOME ASTRONOMY

The At Home Astronomy Web site was designed by Ideum for The Center for Science Education @ Space Sciences Laboratory, UC Berkeley. The site contains a mix of activities and science experiments geared toward families.

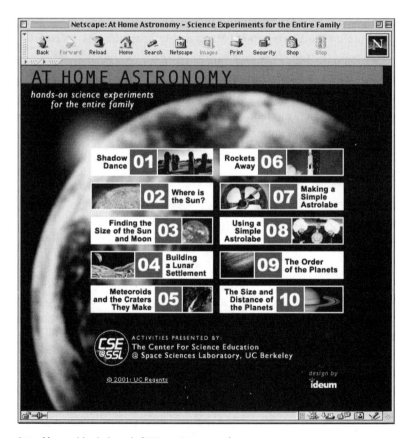

http://cse.ssl.berkeley.edu/AtHomeAstronomy/
Credits: Web Site © UC Regents, The Center for Science Education @ Space Sciences Laboratory, UC Berkeley

"The built-in behaviors save us a lot of time, since we don't have to hand code it all. Also, we know the scripts will work with all the major browsers from 4.0 versions on. This saves us even more time in evaluating and testing JavaScripts."—Jim Spadaccini, Ideum

In this bonus activity, you will apply behaviors to the navigational graphics on the main page of the At Home Astronomy Web site on your own. The files you will need for this exercise are located in the Bonus/Lesson_05 folder. Examine the Completed file before you get started. See how it was constructed and what graphics the Behaviors are applied to. Start with the astronomy.html file that has been created for you using the same techniques that you used to insert tables in Lesson 4 and images in Lesson 2. The title, number, and image graphics for each of the 10 science experiments should cause their respective numbers to roll over to the on state. You can view the final file in the Bonus/Lesson_05/Completed folder.

TIP *Select the "one" graphic and name it* **one**. *Name the text graphic just to the left and name the image graphic just to the right. Click the plus sign (+) button on the Behaviors panel and select the Swap Image behavior. The "one" image will be selected in the Swap Image dialog box. Browse and select one_on.gif for the rollover source. Select the image to the left of the "one" graphic and apply the Swap Image, selecting the "one" image in the Swap Image dialog box and selecting one_on.gif for the rollover source.*

For more practice, try recreating the astronomy.html file from scratch using the one in the Bonus/Lesson_05/Completed folder as a guide.

WHAT YOU HAVE LEARNED

In this lesson, you have:

- Created basic rollovers (pages 163–169)
- Learned how to make multiple images on the page change when the user rolls over one by adding multiple behaviors to one user action (pages 169–173)
- Learned how to edit the behaviors by choosing different events and adding actions while creating a pop-up message (pages 174–176)
- Created a status-bar message to give your viewers more information about a link when they roll over it (pages 176–177)
- Used the Check Browser behavior to redirect users to different pages based on the browser version they are using (pages 177–179)
- Used a behavior to make a new browser window open when the page loads (page 180)
- Created a JavaScript pop-up menu with multiple menu items (pages 182–188)

managing your site

LESSON 6

Site management is a vital part of Web development. The Site window provides extensive management tools that enable you to easily update and control your Web site. You can use the Site window to maintain both your local and remote sites. You can use it to view your site as a list of files, as well as a site map that displays a graphical representation of your Web site's hierarchy. Site maintenance, including moving, adding, and deleting files and folders, is best done in the Site window because Dreamweaver can keep track of your site and update your files accordingly.

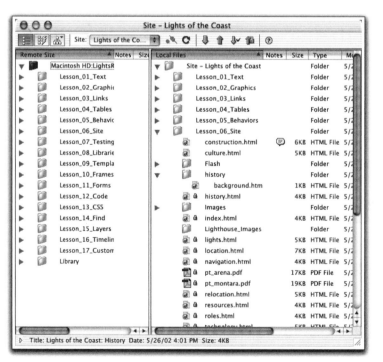

In this lesson, you'll be working with the Site window to manage files and connect to a remote site.

WHAT YOU WILL LEARN

In this lesson, you will:

- Learn about the purposes and uses of the Site window

- Perform site-management functions within the Site window

- Customize the Site window

- Create a site map and use it to manage your files

- Understand the difference between a local site and a remote site

- Set up a connection to a remote site

- Copy files to and from a remote site

APPROXIMATE TIME

This lesson should take about one hour to complete.

LESSON FILES

Media Files:
Lesson_06_Sites/Images/…(all files)

Starting Files:
Lesson_06_Sites/…(all files)

USING THE SITE WINDOW

The Site window displays the file and folder structure of your site. You can use the Site window to add, delete, rename, and move files and folders. By doing all of your file maintenance within the Site window, you ensure that the paths which direct Dreamweaver and the browser to links, images, and other elements will stay correct. These paths will remain correct because Dreamweaver will be able to track your changes and update your files based on those changes. Conversely, if you make file or folder changes in the Finder (Macintosh), in My Computer (Windows) or in Windows Explorer File Manager (Windows), Dreamweaver doesn't recognize the changes and cannot keep the paths correct.

Macintosh users should choose Site > Open Site to open the Site window. Select your site, Lights of the Coast, in the list. Windows users should open the Files panel group, select the Site tab, verify that the site Lights of the Coast is selected in the left drop-down menu and click the Expand button on the Site toolbar.

On the Macintosh, the Site window opens as a new window containing a toolbar with site maintenance related functions. The Site menu allows you to easily switch to any site that you have defined.

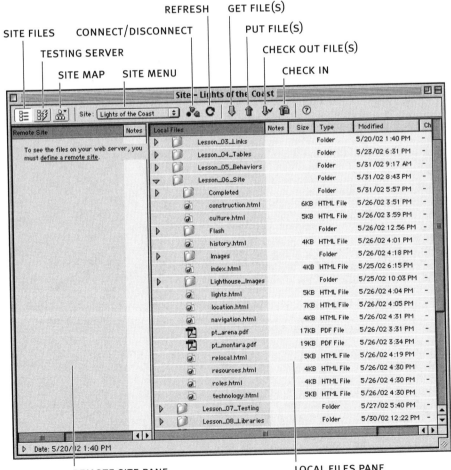

In Windows, the default setting shows the Site window collapsed into a panel in the Files panel group, with only your local files available. The Site panel contains the site toolbar as well as menu options with functions specifically for site maintenance. The Site drop-down menu allows you to switch to any site that you have defined. The right drop-down menu at the top of the panel allows you to switch between Local View, Remote View, Testing Server, and Map View. The Site panel will initially look like the following figure, before you click the Expand button.

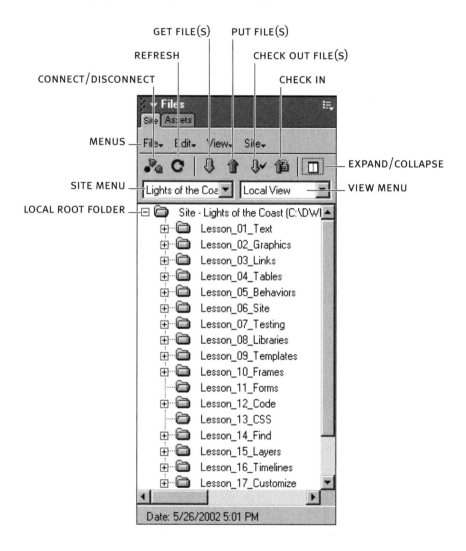

After Windows users click the Expand button, the Site panel will expand into its own window as shown here. The rest of this lesson assumes that Windows users are working with the Site window in its expanded view.

SITE FILES

TESTING SERVER

SITE MAP

REMOTE SITE PANE   LOCAL FILES PANE

Your local files appear in the right pane of the Site window (the Local Files pane). This is the default for the Macintosh. Windows users must click the Expand button to see the Site window in this manner. Once the Site window is expanded, you can collapse it back to the Site panel in the Files panel group by clicking the Expand/ Collapse button again. The local files consist of everything within the root folder, DWMX_project, which you defined in Lesson 1. In this window, that root folder is listed by the name you gave to the site in Lesson 1: Site—Lights of the Coast.

At this point you will see help text displayed in the left pane of the Site window (the Remote Site pane). This help text lets you know that in order to see the files that exist on your Web server listed in this pane, you need to define a remote site.

NOTE *You will define a remote site later in this lesson. Clicking "define a remote site" will open the Site Definition dialog box to the Remote Info category of the Advanced tab. When you connect to the remote site, the remote files appear in the left pane.*

The main Site window tools are located on the toolbar:

- Three buttons on the far left let you pick how you want to view the remote pane: Site Files, Testing Server, or Site Map. The active view is highlighted, and the default is Site Files.

- The Site drop-down menu lists all the sites that you have defined. To open a particular site, simply select the desired site from the menu. For this lesson, you should have Lights of the Coast selected.

- Connect/Disconnect connects to or disconnects from the remote site. If you have not yet defined a remote site, clicking this button will open the Site Definition dialog box. By default, Dreamweaver disconnects the remote site if it has been idle for more than 30 minutes.

TIP *If you need to change the time limit you should choose Edit > Preferences, select the Site category, and change the number listed in the Minutes Idle text field for FTP Connection.*

- Refresh does what you would expect, which is that it refreshes the local and remote directory lists. Any changes that had been made to the file lists will be shown after a refresh. If you have made changes to your site outside of Dreamweaver, in the Finder (Macintosh) or Windows Explorer (Windows), then you may need to refresh your Local Files in order to see the changes.

- Get File(s) copies the selected files from the remote site to your local site, overwriting any existing local copies. The files remain available on the remote site for other team members to get or check out. If you have not yet defined a remote site, this button may be grayed-out to indicate that it is not available for use.

- Put File(s) copies the selected files from the local site to the remote site without changing the file's checked-in or checked-out status. If you have not yet defined a remote site, this button may be grayed-out to indicate that it is not available for use.

- Check Out File(s) transfers a copy of the file from the remote server to your local site, overwriting any existing copies. The file is marked as checked out on the server. The check out feature makes collaborating on a Web site easier. You can check in and check out files on the remote server; then others can see when you're working on a file and know that they will be unable to edit that file at the same time. This option is not available if file check-in and check-out is turned off for this site. If you have not yet defined a remote site, this button may be grayed-out to indicate that it is not available for use.

- Check In transfers a copy of the local file to the remote server and makes the file available for editing by others. The local file becomes read-only. This option is not available if file check-in and check-out is turned off for this site. If Enable File Check In and Check Out is turned off in the Site Definition dialog box, getting a file transfers a copy of the file with both read and write privileges. If you have not yet defined a remote site, this button may be grayed-out to indicate that it is not available for use.

INTEGRATED FILE EXPLORER

The integrated file explorer makes it much easier to access and work with files that may be located outside of your site's root folder.

1) Collapse the Site—Lights of the Coast folder in the Local Files pane of the Site window by clicking the arrow (Macintosh) or the minus sign (Windows) next to the site folder.

Collapse the folder to see the Computer (Macintosh) or Desktop (Windows) icon just below your site folder without having to scroll down in the window. The icon is visible in the Site panel whether or not the site folder is collapsed.

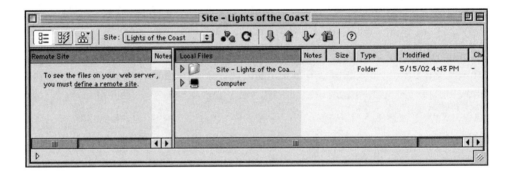

2) Click the arrow next to the Computer icon (Macintosh) or plus sign next to the Desktop icon (Windows) to open the integrated file explorer and browse your computer files.

Dragging and dropping files between your Site folder and your Computer or Desktop will create copies of the files dragged in the new location. If you drag and drop files inside of the Site folder, those files will be moved to the new location.

NOTE *If you need to drag and drop files to or from the Site folder and the Computer (Macintosh) or Desktop (Windows), you must do so within the Dreamweaver Site window. You cannot drag items out of the Site window into folders in the Finder (Macintosh), in My Computer (Windows), or in Windows Explorer File Manager (Windows) or vice-versa.*

You can open files in other programs by double-clicking them. Dreamweaver will use the program that it associates with the file you chose to open it.

NOTE *You can change the associated programs by choosing Edit > Preferences and selecting File Types/Editors from the category list. Select, add, or delete file extensions in the extensions list, and use the editors list to define which programs to use when opening files with the selected extensions.*

You should collapse the Computer icon (Macintosh) or Desktop icon (Windows) and expand the Site—Lights of the Coast folder when you are done and ready to move on to the next exercise.

ADDING NEW FOLDERS AND FILES TO A SITE

You can create new folders and pages in your site directly from the Site window. This allows you to quickly set up your site's file and folder structure. You can immediately create pages that act as placeholders and go back to add their contents at a later time.

1) In the Local Folder pane of the Site window expand the Lesson_06_Sites folder and Control-click (Macintosh) or right-click (Windows) on the right of the title for the Lesson_06_Sites folder.

A context menu opens, displaying a variety of options relative to the selected file or to the entire site if no file is selected.

NOTE *You can access this context menu at anytime using Control-click (Macintosh) or right-click (Windows). The options available to you in this menu will change depending on the item you have selected. The context menu is a quick way to access many of Dreamweaver's functions and can help speed up your production.*

2) Choose New Folder from the context menu.

A new, untitled folder is added within the Lesson_06_Sites folder. Since you just created the folder, the name is highlighted and displayed with a heavy line around the text field to indicate that you are able to name the folder.

3) Type history and press Return (Macintosh) or Enter (Windows) to name the new folder.

The new folder displays the name you have just given it.

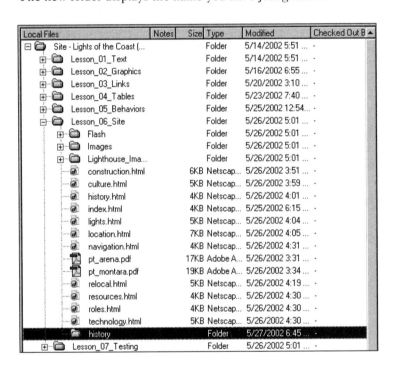

TIP *Clicking elsewhere in the Site window will cause the name to become deselected. If that happens and you need to type the name of the folder, you will need to click the name of the folder, pause, and then click it again. Don't double-click: you don't want to open the folder. You just need to select the title so you can edit it.*

4) In the Local Folder pane of the Site window, Control-click (Macintosh) or right-click (Windows) on the right of the title for the history folder you just created in the Lesson_06_Sites folder.

You are clicking next to the folder in which you want a new folder or file to appear.

The context menu opens.

5) Choose New File from the context menu.

A new, unnamed document is created in the history folder. The name field is highlighted, indicating that you need to type a name for this document.

6) Type background.html and press Return (Macintosh) or Enter (Windows) to name the new file.

Don't forget to include the .html extension for the filename. All HTML documents must have the .html (or .htm) extension.

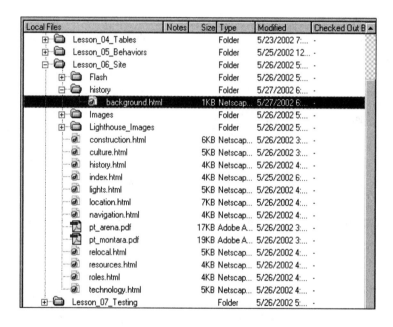

NOTE   *If your filenames are too long for the Local Files column, they will appear to be cut off. This is just in the display of the Site window. You can see the full filename by rolling over it and waiting for the name to pop up.*

CREATING A SITE MAP

A **site map** gives you a visual representation of a selected portion of your site. It does not display all the pages in your site; rather, it starts with a page that has been defined as the home page and shows you all pages that the home page links to. It will continue down the hierarchy of links until it reaches a dead-end page—one with no links. If you have "orphaned" pages that cannot be reached through direct paths from the home page, they will not be displayed in the site map.

1) In the Local Folder pane of the Site window, select index.html in the Lesson_06_Sites folder. Choose Site > Site Map View > Set As Home Page (Macintosh) or Site > Set As Home Page from the Site window (Windows).

You will not see the result of this command until you create the site map. Now that you have defined the home page, you can create the site map. A home page must be created in order to give the site map a starting point.

TIP *Alternatively, you can Control-click (Macintosh) or right-click (Windows) the file and choose Set As Home Page from the context menu in order to select the file to be designated as the home page of the site.*

The files used in this exercise have been created for you using the techniques you have learned so far in this book.

NOTE *Home pages are often called index.html because browsers will display files named index.html (or any known extension variation such as .html or .shtml) as the default page.*

2) Click Site Map button on the Site window toolbar and choose Map Only from the drop-down menu.

SITE MAP DROP-DOWN MENU

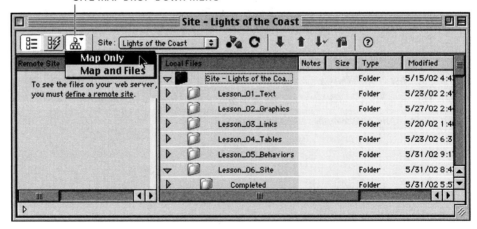

NOTE *Any time you resize the window, the view will revert to Map and Files. You will have to reselect Map Only in that case.*

The site map is a graphical representation of your site; the home page is displayed at the top level of the site map. A link from one page to another is indicated by a line that is drawn from the file containing the link to every page that it links to. Arrowheads at the ends of this line point to each linked page. Pages that contain links are displayed with a plus or minus sign just to the left of the file. Clicking the plus sign displays a list of the linked pages, each with their own plus signs. Broken links (ones that don't work) are displayed in red type. External links, such as email links and URLs, are blue and display a small globe.

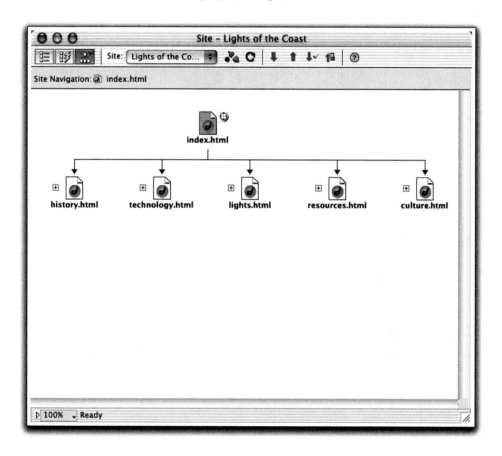

By default, Dreamweaver displays the site map horizontally. If the home page has many links, there might not be enough room on the site map to show all the pages. You can change the number of columns and the column width to make the site map fit a single page for easier viewing. You can also switch the layout to a vertical format.

3) In the Site window, choose Site > Site Map View > Layout (Macintosh) or View > Layout from the Site window (Windows).

The Site Definition dialog box opens, displaying the Site Map Layout options.

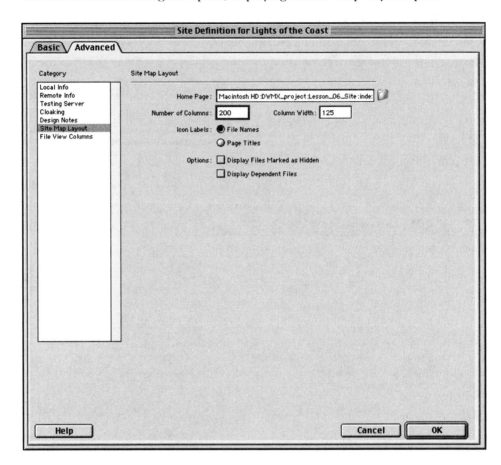

4) In the Number of Columns text field, type 1 and click OK.

The site map is regenerated to show all the linked pages in a single column.

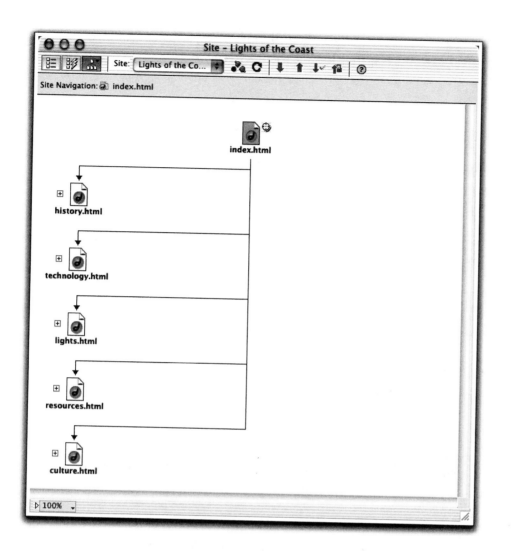

TIP *When you are using Map and Files View, you can completely collapse the Local Files pane by clicking on the bar that separates the two panes and dragging it to the right. You can drag it all the way up to the right edge of the scroll bar, but not past. If you try to drag it past the right edge of the scroll bar it won't work. This may help to create as much space as possible to view large image maps. Simply drag the bar back to its original position to reopen the Local Files pane. This is a quick way to switch your views.*

5) Choose Site > Site Map View > Save Site Map > Save Site Map As JPEG (Macintosh) or File > Save Site Map from the Site window (Windows).

You can save the site map as a graphic to be used in documentation.

The Save Site Map dialog box opens so you can save the site map as a graphic. At times, you may need to share the site map with people outside Dreamweaver. The option to save the site map as a graphic makes it easier to show that site map to others. On Macintosh computers, you can choose whether to save the graphic in PICT or JPEG format. On Windows computers, you can choose to save the site-map graphic in either BMP or PNG format.

TIP *If Save Site Map is grayed out, go back to the Site window and click the empty white space of the site-map pane to make sure it is active. Then go back and choose the Save Site Map command again. If you click in the Local Files pane and cause it to become active, you will not be able to access the site map functions. You will need to reactivate the pane displaying the site map by clicking in that pane.*

6) In the Filename text box, type lighthouse_site.jpg **(Macintosh) or** lighthouse_ site.bmp **(Windows). Save the file into the Lesson_06_Site folder.**

The site map is saved as a graphic that can be printed or viewed in an image editor.

VIEWING A SUBSET OF THE ENTIRE SITE

As your site becomes larger and more complex, the site map might become too big to see in the Site window. You can refine the view to show just a selected page and its links.

1) In the Site window, select the history.html page in the site map.

This is the most extensive section in the Lesson_06_Site folder, so viewing it as a subset will let you focus on any pages that can be accessed with history.html as the starting point.

2) Choose Site > Site Map View > View As Root (Macintosh) or View > View As Root from the Site window (Windows).

The site map changes to show the history.html page as the root (the top level) and its links (the second level). Below the site toolbar is a gray bar displaying the hierarchy of the site, beginning with the file you set as the home page and ending with the file that you chose to view as the root. For this exercise, you should see index.html > history.html.

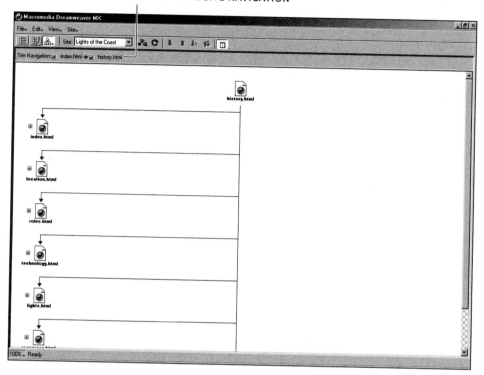

NOTE *This structural site navigation works the same way as breadcrumb navigation, which is used on many sites. **Breadcrumbs** show the visitor the hierarchical path from the main page of the site to the page they are on. They usually appear near the top of the page. Each part of the site listed in the breadcrumb path is normally linked to that section. For example, the breadcrumb navigation for the roles.html page would be <u>Main</u> > <u>History</u> > Roles. In this example, the text "Main" would be linked to the index.html page, and "History" would be linked to the history.html page. "Roles" is not linked—it is at the end of the breadcrumbs which indicates to the visitor that the page being viewed is the Roles page.*

3) Click the Dreamweaver icon to the left of index.html on the Site Navigation bar, the home page for the Lights of the Coast site.

The site root is returned to your home page.

205

LINKS IN SITE MAP VIEW

You can control what files display in the site map by choosing to hide individual linked files. Files are only hidden in the Map View—they are still visible in the Local Files list. You can also make changes to the files by adding or deleting links.

1) Click the plus sign to the left of technology.html in the site map.

The list of files that technology.html links to are displayed.

2) Click the history.html file icon in the list of links in technology.html to select the link to the history.html file.

The file is selected in the Map View.

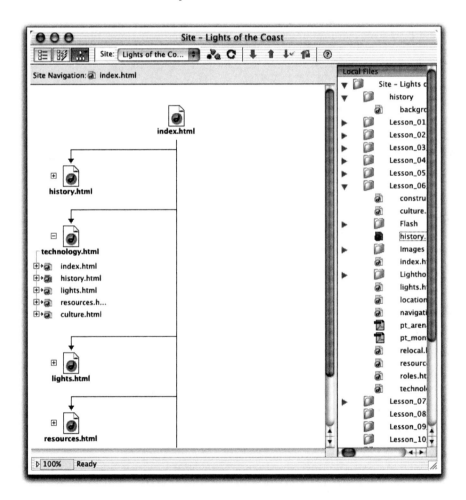

3) Choose Site > Site Map View > Show/Hide Link (Macintosh) or View > Show/Hide Link (Windows).

The history.html file disappears from the list.

4) Choose Site > Site Map View > Show Files Marked As Hidden (Macintosh) or View > Show Files Marked As Hidden (Windows).

This option lets you temporarily view all files marked as hidden. The history.html filename is italicized to indicate that it is a hidden link.

5) With the italicized history.html selected, choose Site > Site Map View > Show/Hide Link (Macintosh) or View > Show/Hide Link (Windows).

The history file is no longer marked as hidden and appears as normal in the site map.

6) Choose the Map and Files view from the Site Map icon on the toolbar. Select the background.html file that you created in the Lesson_06_Sites/history folder from the Local Files pane of the Site window. Choose Site > Site Map View > Set as Home Page (Macintosh) or Site > Set As Home Page from the Site Window (Windows).

You have switched to Map and Files View. The background.html file is now the only file that appears in the Site Map View because it has no links to other pages.

7) Select the background.html file in the Site Map View. Click the Point to File icon and drag it to history.html in the Lesson_06_Sites folder in the Local Files pane. Release the mouse button when the history.html file becomes highlighted.

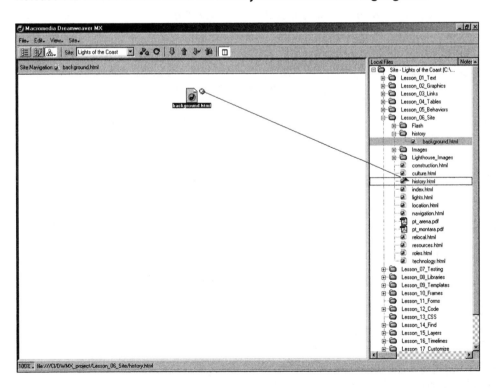

As you drag, the pointer becomes an arrow and a Point to File icon. A line is drawn as you drag from the background.html file to the history.html file. When you release the pointer, history.html shows up in the Site Map View. The link to history.html has been inserted into the background.html document. If you open background.html you will see the link.

TIP *You can also add, remove and change links from the Site > Site Map View submenu.*

8) Select the index.html file in the Lesson_06_Sites folder and choose Site › Site Map View › Set as Home Page (Macintosh) or View › Set as Home Page (Windows).
The index.html file is now defined as the home page again.

MODIFYING PAGES FROM THE SITE WINDOW

As you view pages in the site map and move the pointer over the pages, you'll see information about each page in the status area (bottom left corner) of the Site window.

1) In the site map, place the pointer over the filename technology.html.
The status bar at the bottom of the Site window shows the title and size of the document as well as the date that it was created. Make sure you roll over the filename, not the file icon. The information won't appear in the status bar unless the pointer hovers over the name of the file. You can see by the information that appears on the status bar that the technology.html document is untitled.

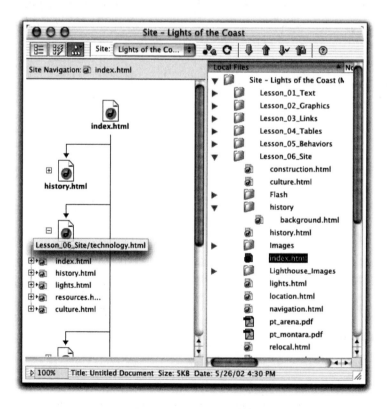

If you forgot to title a page or want to change a title, you can do so in the Site window.

2) Choose Site > Site Map View > Show Page Titles (Macintosh) or View > Show Page Titles from the Site window (Windows) to see page titles instead of filenames in the site map.

The list is regenerated to display the files by title.

3) Click the page title "Untitled Document" once to select it. Pause, and then click the title again.

A rectangle is placed around the title to indicate that it can be edited. Don't double-click; you don't want to open the file. You just need to select the title so you can edit it.

4) Type Lights of the Coast: Technology **as the new title and press Return (Macintosh) or Enter (Windows).**

The site map shows the new title.

NOTE *You can also open a page for editing from Site window by double-clicking the file in either the site-map pane or the Local Folder pane.*

5) Choose Site > Site Map View > Show Page Titles (Macintosh) or View > Show Page Titles from the Site window (Windows) to switch the view from titles back to filenames.

The checkmark next to Show Page Titles will be removed and the files switch back to displaying their filenames.

6) In the Local Files pane of the Site window, select relocal.html. Click the filename relocal.html.

TIP *You may want to shrink the left pane by dragging the bar between the two panes to the left. This will give you more room to work with in the Local Files pane, making it easier to see the files.*

The filename becomes highlighted at the first click, and a rectangle appears around the filename indicating that it can be edited at the second click.

NOTE *When you need to change the name of one of your files, you should change the name in the Site window to preserve the link information maintained by Dreamweaver. If you change the filename outside Dreamweaver in either an HTML file or a graphics file, Dreamweaver has no way to track your changes. If you make the change within the Site window, Dreamweaver updates all pages that link to the file or contain the graphic.*

7) Change the filename to relocation.html and press Return (Macintosh) or Enter (Windows).

The Update Files dialog box opens, listing all the files affected by this name change.

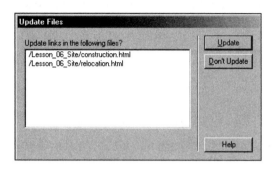

8) Click Update to update the files with the new filename.

The site map and files list now show the new filenames.

NOTE *Dreamweaver makes the filename change within each file in the list. If a file in the list is open, Dreamweaver makes the change but does not save or close the file.*

9) In the Local Files pane of the Site window, open the Lighthouse_Images folder in Lesson_06_Sites.

Only one image, lightshine.jpg, is in the folder. If a file or folder is not in its proper place, you can move the file or folder to its correct location. Making this change in the Site window ensures that all the link information remains correct and intact.

TIP *You can use the scroll bar at the bottom of the Local Files pane to see all the columns.*

10) Drag the lightshine.jpg image's icon to the Images folder, located just above the Lighthouse_Images folder.

Any files that use this image will be affected by the move; you will need to fix the path to the image. The Update Files dialog box opens, asking whether affected files should be updated.

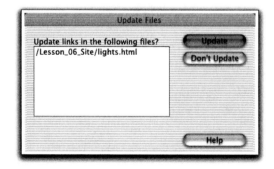

11) Click Update to keep the link to this graphic correct.

The graphic moves to the Images folder. Any references to it in the HTML files are still working.

NOTE *Dreamweaver allows you to customize the Site window by reordering, showing, hiding, or adding columns. To make changes to the columns in the Site window, choose Site > Site Files View > File View Columns (Macintosh) or View > File View Columns from the Site window (Windows). The Site Definition dialog box opens, displaying the File View Columns list. You can use the up or down arrow buttons to change the order of the columns. The Options Show check box controls which columns are displayed in the Site window. You can also add or delete columns, and associate them with Design Notes. You will learn more about Design Notes later in this lesson. The rest of the book assumes that you are using the default arrangement of columns in the Site window and have made no changes.*

CONNECTING TO A REMOTE SITE

In Lesson 1, you created a local site—that is, a folder on your hard drive to store all the folders and files needed for your site. So far you've been developing pages in the local site. For visitors to see your Web pages, however, you need to copy your local files to a remote site. Typically, the remote site is on a server specified by your host, Web administrator, or client, but it could also be on a local network.

1) Choose Site › Edit Sites.

Windows users should use the Site menu located on the Site window.

The Edit Sites dialog box opens.

2) Select your site, Lights of the Coast, and click Edit. Click the Advanced Tab.

The Site Definition dialog box opens.

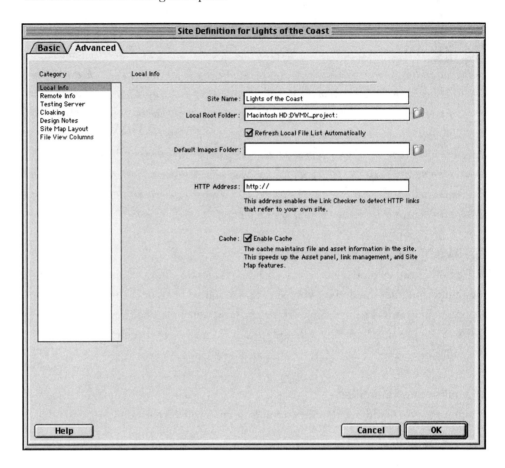

3) In the Category list, choose Remote Info.

The Remote Info section of the Define Sites dialog box is where you will enter information to tell Dreamweaver which remote site to connect to and the attributes of that remote site.

4) From the Access drop-down menu, choose Local/Network.

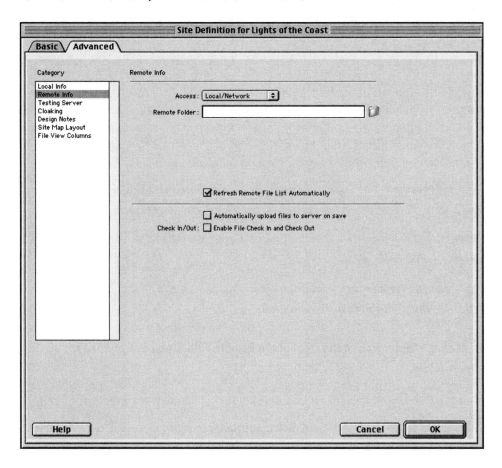

In the following steps, you will create a folder to simulate a remote FTP (File Transfer Protocol) site. This procedure will enable you to experiment with the Get and Put functions, as well as additional site management functions, without the need to have access to a remote server. In many cases the Local/Network option is used when you have access to another computer on a network that will house the remote folder. In this instance, it will be on your own computer.

NOTE *FTP access is a common method of getting files from or putting files on a remote site. Because you may not have access to a remote FTP site while you complete this lesson, the following information is presented as reference material only. Consult your network administrator or host to set these options correctly. The following list of options is available by choosing FTP from the Server Access drop-down menu in the Site Definition dialog box.*

FTP Host: *The host name of your Web server (such as ftp://mysite.com).*

Host Directory: *The directory on the remote site where documents visible to the public are stored (also known as the* **site root**).

Login and Password: *Your login name and password on the server. If you deselect the Save check box, you'll be prompted for a password when you connect to the remote site.*

Use Passive FTP: *Used when you have a firewall between your computer and the server. This option is unchecked by default.*

Use Firewall (in Preferences): *Used if you are connecting to the remote server from behind a firewall. This option is unchecked by default.*

5) Click the folder icon to the right of the Remote Folder text box to specify the remote folder.

The Choose Remote Folder dialog box opens.

6) Choose a location on your hard disk that is outside your root folder, DWMX_project. Click the New Folder button, type LightsRemote for the folder name and select it.

For the Macintosh: Select the LightsRemote folder and click Choose.

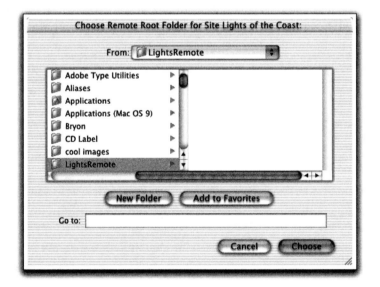

For Windows: Select the LightsRemote folder and click Open. Then click Select to use the LightsRemote folder as your remote folder.

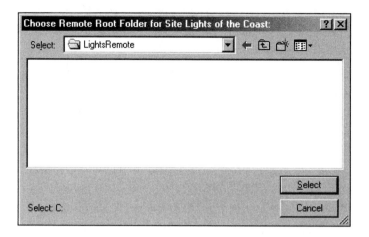

This folder will act as a stand-in for a remote server and, like any remote server, it will be a mirror of the local root folder of your site, DWMX_project, which you defined in Lesson 1. The remote folder must be outside your local root folder.

7) Click OK to save your site information and click Done to close the Edit Sites dialog box. Click the Site Files icon on the Site window.

You can always edit your site information later by choosing Site > Define Sites to open the Edit Sites dialog box, and then selecting the site you want change. For this exercise you left the Refresh File List Automatically box checked, and the Check In/Out options unchecked.

The Site window now displays the empty remote folder in the Remote Site pane of the Site window. The path from your hard disk to the folder is displayed next to the folder icon. You may have to rollover the folder name to see the full path.

At the top of the Site window, you will see a Connect icon, which logs you on to a specified remote server. For this exercise, you've defined a local folder, so the Connect icon button is not active because you are already connected.

NOTE *The Site Export function allows you to select a site from your list of sites and move it to another computer. This is useful for many situations, including sharing sites with other team members or when you need to switch computers. Sites are saved as XML files and all settings from the Site Definition dialog box are retained. To export the current site choose Site > Export. To select a different site to export, choose Site > Edit Sites..., select the desired site from the Edit Sites dialog box, and click Export. The Export Site dialog box will open in which you can name the file and specify the location to save the exported site. The site will be saved with the .ste extension. Do not delete or change this extension. Conversely, you can use the Site Import function to import a site into Dreamweaver. To do so, choose Site > Import. Use the Import Site dialog box to find and select the site. You will be prompted to select a Local Root Folder. You can only import sites that have been exported from Dreamweaver as XML files with the .ste extension. Remember that Export and Import transfer settings from the Site Definition only—you will still need to transfer your root folder with all of your files. If you are using the Local/Network remote access option, you may need to update the path to the remote folder.*

UPLOADING FILES

You can use Dreamweaver to check which are the newest files on your local site. This way, you can update only files that have changed.

1) In the Local Files pane of the Site window, select the top-level folder Site— Lights of the Coast and choose Site > Synchronize.

The Synchronize Files dialog box opens.

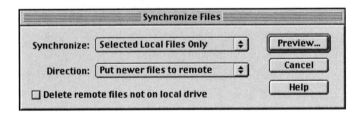

2) From the Synchronize drop-down menu, choose Entire 'Lights of the Coast' Site. From the Direction drop-down menu, choose Put newer files to remote. Click Preview.

Dreamweaver will scan your site and compare the files located in both the local and remote folders. If you have the same files in both, Dreamweaver will compare the modification dates. Files that are newer in your local folder, or that do not exist on the remote, will be transferred to the remote folder. In this case, everything in your local folder will be put to the remote.

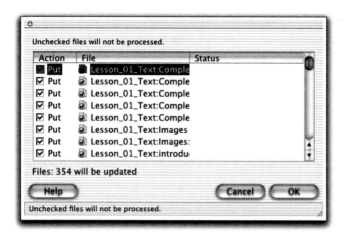

After Dreamweaver is done scanning the local and remote folders, it will open a list of the files that it determines are necessary to upload to the remote. This dialog box lists the action (Put or Get), the filename, and the status. For each file, you have the option to uncheck the action box, which would cause Dreamweaver to skip the file. The number of files to be updated is listed at the bottom of this dialog box.

NOTE *The synchronize function Gets and Puts files, even if you are using Check In/Out. It will not check files in or out, it will merely replace them. You'll learn more about Check In/Out in the next exercise.*

3) Find Lesson_06_Site/history.html in the list and uncheck the Put box for that file.

TIP *You can grab the vertical line separating the File and Status columns on the bar and move it to the right in order to see more of the filenames.*

The history.html file becomes flagged by the word skip in the status column.

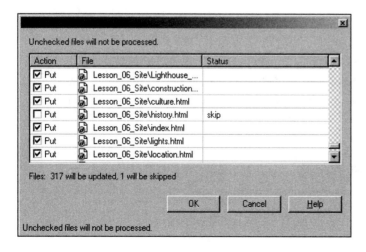

4) Click OK. Click Close when the synchronization is complete.

The Status dialog box appears showing you the progress of the synchronization. All the files in your local folder, except for history.html, are copied to your remote folder, LightsRemote.

This option could take a long time to execute, depending on the size of your site and the number of files that need to be transferred.

TIP *If you have changed only a few files, you might find it quicker to select the updated files and upload them manually so you don't have to wait for files to be transferred that may not need to be copied.*

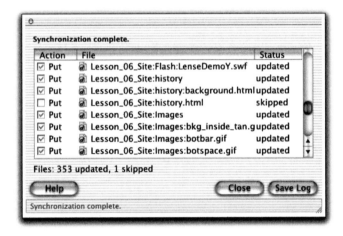

When the transfer is done, the list of site files will inform you how many files were updated.

TIP *You can click Save Log to create a log of the file transfer if you need to keep track of when files were transferred.*

5) Open the lights.html file and click the image of the lighthouse around which the text wraps. Click the Reset Size button on the Property inspector and type Point Montara in the Alt text field. Save and close the file.

This file now has a newer modification date than the lights.html that exists in the remote folder.

Windows Users: When you open the lights.html file the Site window will automatically collapse back into the Site panel in the Files panel group. You will need to click the Expand/Collapse button again after you close lights.html.

6) In the Local Folder pane, select the top-level folder. Choose Site > Site Files View > Select Newer Local (Macintosh) or Edit > Select Newer Local from the Site window (Windows).

Dreamweaver compares the modification dates of all local files with the corresponding file information in the remote site and selects only the newest local files.

The history.html and lights.html files in the Lesson_06_Sites folder should be selected.

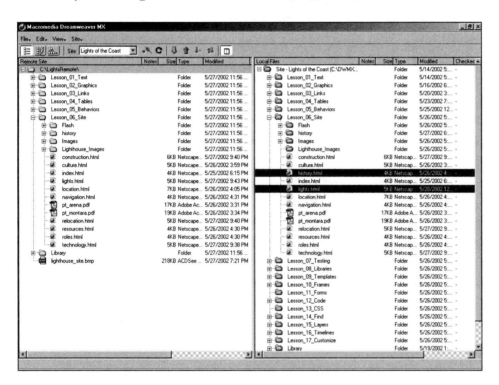

7) Click the Put File(s) button on the Site window toolbar to upload only the two selected files to the server.

The Dependent Files dialog box opens. Your choices are Yes, No, and Cancel. Yes sends any images on the selected pages, along with the HTML pages themselves, to the server. No sends only the HTML pages. If you've changed only the HTML page and the images are already on the server, you have no reason to send the images again, so you should click No. If you have modified an image or added an image to the page, you should click Yes.

N O T E *The Dependent Files dialog box also contains the Don't Ask Me Again check box. If this option has been checked previously, you will not see the Dependent Files dialog box.*

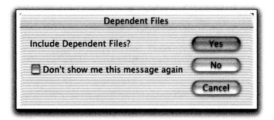

8) Click No if you see the Dependent Files dialog box.

You haven't modified any of the dependent files in this exercise, so it is not necessary to replace them in the remote folder, LightsRemote.

N O T E *Remember that when you modify the size of an image in the Dreamweaver document window, as you did with the lightshine.jpg that had text wrapping around it in the lights.html file, you are only changing the attributes of that object in the HTML. The image source file itself, lightshine.jpg, did not change.*

All the selected files in the local folder are copied to the remote site.

N O T E *If you don't see the Dependent Files dialog box, but want to have the choice, choose Edit > Preferences. Select the Site category and check the two Dependent Files boxes for the options to Prompt on Get/Check Out and Prompt on Put/Check In.*

When the upload has finished, you will see a list of files in the remote-site pane that mirrors the list in the Local Folder pane.

CLOAKING

While you are developing your Web site, you may want to prevent certain files from being uploaded or downloaded. For example, if you have a large number of Flash and QuickTime movies embedded in your pages, you may not want to replace those Flash and QuickTime files in your local folder or on the remote server every time you get or put files.

You can **cloak** folders or file types to exclude them from site transfer functions including Synchronize, Get and Put, and Check In/Out. Cloaked folders and file types are also excluded from site wide operations such as select newer local and newer remote, checking links, search/replace, reports, and library/template updating. Cloaked folder and file types will not appear in the Assets panel lists.

NOTE *Cloaking, like many Dreamweaver Site functions, is not recognized by other FTP programs. As you complete this exercise a Library folder will be created within the Lesson_06_Sites folder and it will not be listed in the Dreamweaver Site window. This Library folder contains the data needed by Dreamweaver to maintain information on the Folders you will cloak in this exercise. This folder takes up very little space and should not be deleted.*

1) In the Local Files pane of the Site window, select the Flash folder that is located in the Lesson_06_sites folder.

This folder contains a Flash file, LenseDemoY.swf.

TIP *A good way to organize your site is to keep all of your media files together in the same folder. For instance if your site has a large number of PDF (Portable Document Format) files, creating a folder solely for PDF files will help keep your site organized and make it easier to maintain.*

2) Choose Site > Cloaking > Cloak.

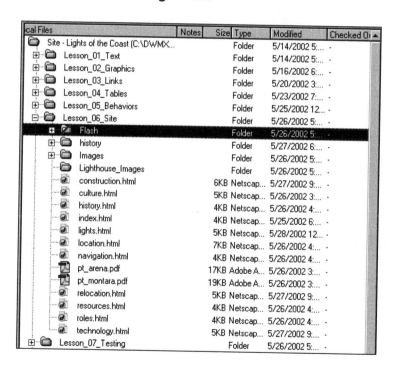

The Flash folder icon is now displayed with a diagonal red line across it in both the Local Files and Remote Site panes of the Site window. The diagonal red line indicates that the file has been cloaked and will be excluded from site operations. If you open the folder you will see that the LenseDemoY.swf file also has a diagonal red line through its file icon.

NOTE *You can uncloak the folder to include it in site operations by selecting the folder and choosing Site > Cloaking > Uncloak.*

3) Choose Site > Cloaking > Settings. Check the Cloak Files Ending With: check box, and then replace the default file extensions listed with .pdf in the text field.

The Advanced tab of Site Definition dialog box will open with the Cloaking category selected.

You cannot cloak individual files; you must cloak either entire folders or all files of a certain file type.

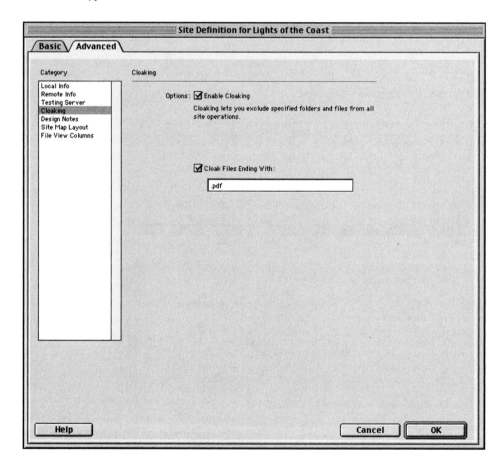

NOTE *You can insert additional file extensions into the text field to cloak more than one kind of file. In order to cloak multiple file types, the extensions must be separated by a space, as demonstrated by the default .png .fla extensions that were originally listed in the text field.*

4) Click OK to close the Site Definition dialog box and click OK when Dreamweaver tells you that the cache will be recreated.

All PDF files contained in the Lights of the Coast project site are now cloaked. There are two PDF files in the Lesson_06_Sites folder that are now displayed with diagonal red lines through their file icons: pt_montara.pdf and pt_arena.pdf. All PDF files are now excluded from site operations.

NOTE *To uncloak file types, choose Site > Cloaking > Settings. On the Site Definition dialog box either remove the specific extension from the text field for the file type that you want to uncloak, or uncheck the Cloak Files Ending With: check box to uncloak all file types.*

5) Choose Site › Cloaking › Enable Cloaking to remove the checkmark from Enable Cloaking.

TIP *You can also choose the Cloaking category from the Site Definition dialog box and uncheck the Enable Cloaking check box to disable cloaking for the site.*

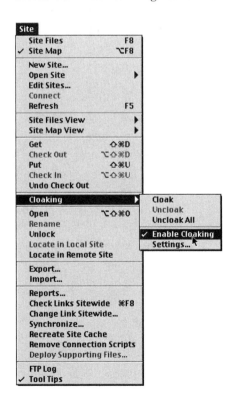

The checkmark is removed from the Enable Cloaking option to indicate that Cloaking is now disabled for the "Lights of the Coast" project site. This is an easy way to temporarily remove cloaking from your site's folders and files. If you choose Site > Cloaking > Enable Cloaking again, cloaking will become enabled again and all previously cloaked folders and files will be recloaked. Cloaking is enabled on all sites by default. You must have cloaking enabled in order to cloak folders and file types.

NOTE *You can also uncloak all folders and file types simultaneously by choosing Site > Cloaking > Uncloak All. This option will leave cloaking enabled and remove cloaking from all folders and files in your site. You will not be able to automatically recloak folders and files if you have used the Uncloak All function. If you only want to suspend cloaking temporarily, you should disable cloaking as demonstrated in step 4.*

CHECKING IN AND CHECKING OUT

If you are working on a team, the Check In/Out options can make collaborating on a Web site much easier. When this feature is activated, if a team member checks out a file for editing, Dreamweaver locks the checked out file on the remote server so that no one else on the team is able to edit the file until it is checked back in. As long as the entire team is using Dreamweaver and all team members enable Check In/Out, use the Site window and are connected to the remote server, the Check In/Out feature lets your group know when someone else is working on a specific file, preventing accidental overwriting of material or duplicate efforts.

1) Choose Site > Edit Sites.
The Define Sites dialog box opens.

2) Choose the Lights of the Coast project site in the list and click Edit.
The Site Definition dialog box opens for the "Lights of the Coast" site.

3) Choose Remote Info in the Category list.
The remote-site information is displayed.

4) Check the Enable File Check In and Check Out check box.

One additional check box and two additional text boxes appear. Files become checked out automatically as you open them if Check Out Files When Opening is checked. You must be connected to the remote site for this feature to function properly. If you are not connected, Dreamweaver connects to the remote site automatically.

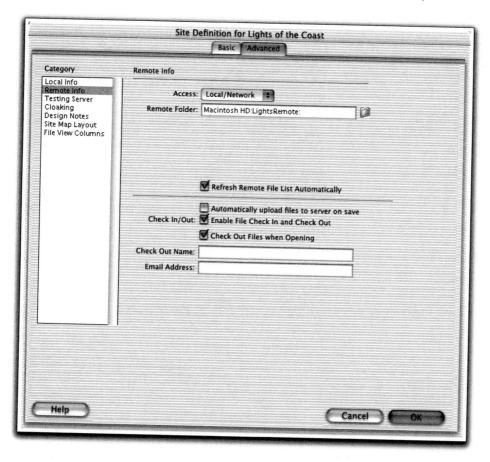

The additional text boxes are Check Out Name and Email Address.

5) Type a Check Out name and your email address in the appropriate text fields. Click OK in the Site Definition dialog box and Done in the Define Sites dialog box.

Your Check Out name is only for group reference; it can be your full name or simply a user name. This name will display in the Checked Out By column of the Site window when you check out a file. Your email address is available to allow team members to contact you with questions.

6) In the Site window, select the index.html page in the Local Folder pane and click the Check In icon at the top of the window. Do the same for the location.html page. Click No if asked whether you want to include dependent files.

Dreamweaver uploads the selected files to the remote site. In the Local Folder pane of the Site window, the files are marked with a small lock icon to let you know the files have been checked in and will need to be checked out for you to edit them locally.

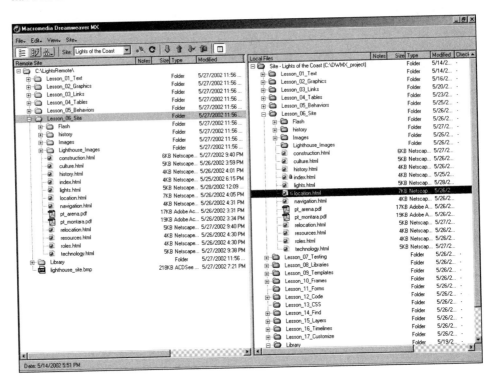

When you are working with a group of people and using the Check In/Check Out feature, it is important for everyone to use the Check In and Check Out File(s) icons instead of the Get File(s) and Put File(s) icons to upload and download files.

If you already have a local copy of your remote site, you must check in each local file for the check-in/check-out feature to work properly. When you enable Check In/Out, keep in mind that your files are not automatically checked into the remote server. The check and lock icons will indicate the status of a file. Check is for files that have been checked out, lock is for files that have been checked in. If a file has neither a check nor a lock, then it has no Check In/Out status. Such an unmarked file will be available to open or edit. If you are working with team members and using Check In/Out, it is a good idea to check in your entire site once you enable Check In/Out so that no unmarked files will be opened and edited accidentally.

7) In the Site window, select the location.html page in the local panel. Click the Check Out File(s) icon at the top of the window. Click No if asked whether you want to include dependent files.

To ensure that you will be working with the most recent version, the file is downloaded to your local site. The file is marked in both the local and remote panes with a small green checkmark next to the file icon, indicating the file has been checked-out by you. The Checked Out By columns in both the local and remote panes show your Check Out name in the form of a clickable link to your email address. Files checked out by other members of your team are displayed with a red checkmark, indicating that you will be unable to check those files out until they have been checked back in.

If you attempt to open a file that someone else has checked out, Dreamweaver will inform you that the file is already checked out and give you several options. You can cancel opening the file, open the file to view it, or override the checkout.

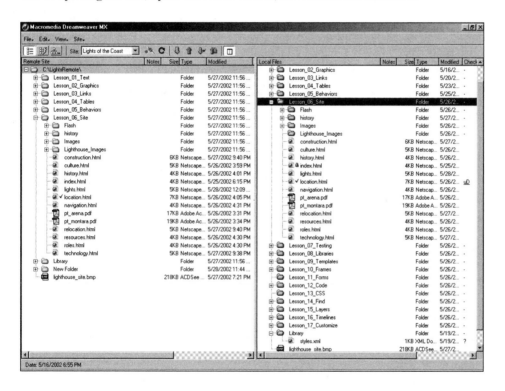

MANAGING YOUR SITE

NOTE *For the Check In/Out feature to work properly, everyone on your team should be using Dreamweaver. This feature is not recognized by other FTP programs. Other programs will be able to overwrite files, negating the purpose of checking files in and out. When you use the Check In/Out feature, FTP programs will be able to see the files that Dreamweaver creates: For each file that is checked out, an LCK file is created on the server, letting Dreamweaver know that file is checked out. For this exercise, you may be able to see the locations.html.lck file in the Finder (Macintosh) or Windows Explorer (Windows). Don't delete these files! They take up very little space and are required for the functionality of Check In/Out.*

8) In the Site window, select the location.html page in the local panel. Click the Check In icon at the top of the window. Click No if asked whether you want to include dependent files.

This file is now checked in and cannot be edited until it is checked out again.

9) Choose Site > Edit Sites, select the Lights of the Coast site and click Edit. Select the remote category and uncheck the Enable File Check In and Check Out box.

Since you are not creating the Lights of the Coast project site with a team, the Check In/Out feature is not necessary. The rest of this book assumes that you have Check In/Out disabled.

The index.html and location.html files still appear with a lock icon.

10) Select both index.html and location.html. Choose Site > Unlock (Macintosh) or File > Turn Off Read Only (Windows).

The lock icons disappear, and the files are now accessible again.

TIP *The Unlock (Macintosh) and Turn Off Read Only (Windows) are also available in the context menu which you can pull up with Control-click (Macintosh) or right-click (Windows).*

USING DESIGN NOTES

Design notes are useful for keeping track of information related to your files. These notes are for your information only; they are hidden text files that cannot be accessed or displayed in browsers by the users of your site. You can share information with your co-workers easily by uploading design notes to the remote server. These notes can be used with all files on your site, including HTML and image files.

1) In the Site window, select the construction.html file and choose File > Design Notes.

> **TIP** *You can also attach a design note from the Site window by double-clicking the Notes column for the selected file or choosing the option from the context menu, which you can access with Control-click (Macintosh) or right-click (Windows).*

The Design Notes dialog box appears. You can use this method to attach a design note to a file when it is selected in the Site window or when the file is open in the document window. The Basic Info tab displays information about the file to which the note will be attached, and the path of that file in the site. You can change the status of the file by making a choice from the Status drop-down menu.

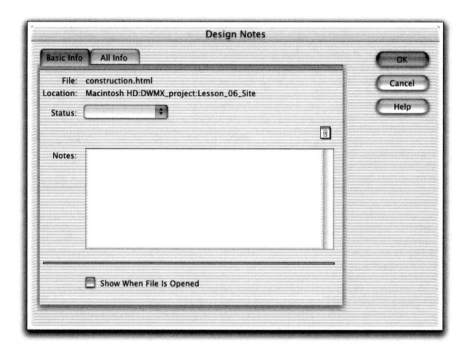

> **NOTE** *The Design Notes option in the Category column of the Site Definition dialog box allows you to turn design notes on or off. By default, both the Maintain Design Notes and the Upload Design Notes for Sharing check boxes are checked. Dreamweaver automatically uploads or downloads the design notes for any file you get, put, check in, or check out from the remote server when the Upload Design Notes for Sharing check box is checked.*

2) Click the Date icon above and to the right of the Notes text box.

The date is inserted into the first line of the Notes text box. Use this area to enter any important information about your files.

A check box at the bottom of this window allows you have this note displayed when the file is opened. You can check the box for this exercise.

3) Click OK.

The Design Notes dialog box closes, and the note is attached to the construction.html file with the information you added. The Design Notes icon is displayed as a yellow text bubble in the Notes column, located to the right of the filename, indicating that a note is attached to the file.

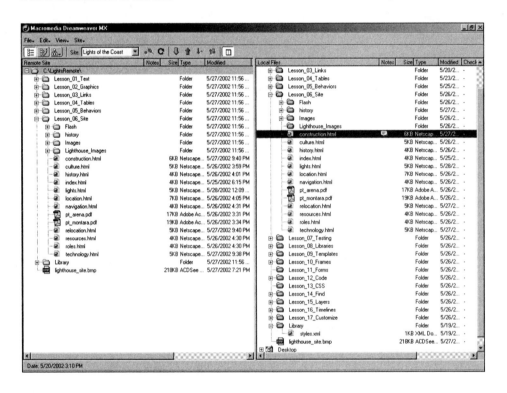

TIP *Double click the Design Notes icon (the yellow bubble) to reopen the Design Notes dialog box in order to edit the note.*

ON YOUR OWN: LIFE ALONG THE FAULTLINE

The Exploratorium's Life Along the Faultline Web site explored the science behind earthquakes in recognition of the 10-year anniversary of the Loma Prieta earthquake of 1989. The site features articles and activities concerning earth science and retrospective looks back at the devastating natural disaster. The 1906 feature focused on the historical 1906 San Francisco earthquake, giving visitors a glimpse of the past through personal accounts, photographs, and earthquake facts.

http://www.exploratorium.edu/faultline/
Credits: © Exploratorium,
www.exploratorium.edu
Earthquake photographs © Karl V.
Steinbrugge Collection, Earthquake
Engineering Research Center,
University California, Berkeley.

Exploratorium Web team members used Dreamweaver extensively during the production of the Faultline Web site and continued to use it after the site was completed for site maintenance. The Site window, which you have used throughout this lesson, played a major role in the day-to-day upkeep of the Web site.

In this bonus activity, you will carry out Web site maintenance on your own. The files you will need for this exercise are located in the Bonus/Lesson_06 folder, which include nearly the entire 1906 feature. You should use the Site window to solve the following issues:

- A number of images are in a separate folder called images. All the images should be in the 1906_images folder.

- Some pages do not have titles. They should all be titled Exploratorium: Faultline: 1906.

- The mission.html document is in the 1906_images folder; it needs to be moved to the Bonus/Lesson_06 folder.

- The 906_7.html has a misspelled filename. It should be 1906_7.html.

For more practice, try recreating some of the pages in the 1906 feature from scratch using the existing ones as guides.

WHAT YOU HAVE LEARNED

In this lesson, you have:

- Performed site-management functions within the Site window, including creating new files, renaming files, and moving files (pages 192–199)

- Created a site map, viewed it horizontally and vertically, used it to manage your files, and learned how to save the site map as an image (pages 200–207)

- Customized the Site window and edited the columns (pages 208–211)

- Used the Update Files dialog box to ensure that your paths and links stay correct when you moved files (pages 210–211)

- Learned the difference between a local site and a remote site, how to use local/network and FTP to connect to servers, as well as how to define and edit both kinds of sites (pages 211–215)

- Set up a connection to a local/network folder as your remote site (pages 211–216)

- Copied files to and from a remote site using the Select Newer Local command to save time (pages 216–219)

- Enabled cloaking to prevent certain file types from being uploaded or downloaded (pages 220–223)

- Used the Check In/Out Options for collaboration (pages 224–228)

- Attached a design note to a file, edited design notes, and learned to use them to share information with team members and keep track of file status and versions (pages 228–230)

accessibility and testing

LESSON 7

Up to this point in the lessons, you have tested Web pages by previewing them in the browser as you completed each exercise. As you built individual pages or sections, you had a chance to see how those pages looked and make modifications as needed. Before making a site available to the public or to your intended audience, however, you should go further and test your entire site. Take the extra time to be sure you've worked out all the potential problems. If you have access to a testing server, it's a good idea to load the site onto that server and access the pages from all computer types and from as many versions of browsers as you can find. Test the pages under real user conditions. If you think a majority of your users will be using a dial-up modem, make sure you use a dial-up modem to test the speed at which the pages load. If you are the primary Web developer, have others test your pages. Watch how other people try to navigate your site. Make sure to test every link and fix any broken ones.

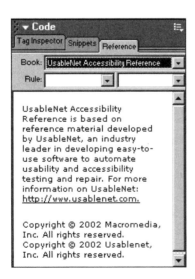

In this project, you will use Dreamweaver to test Web pages for accessibility. You will also test the links in your project site and use reports to determine how your site is functioning and what browsers, if any, may have problems accessing your site.

Remember that users probably don't think like you do—try to prepare for the unexpected as you check the entire site. Analyze what possible paths a visitor might take. Make a list of potential tasks your viewers might perform (searching for and buying an item, looking for contact information, etc.), and go step by step through what those visitors will need to do in order to complete the task.

Ideally you should not begin the testing process when the Web site is finished—by starting the testing process early and incorporating it as a part of the production process, you can catch problems quickly and deal with them. If you wait until the end, after you've put hours of work into your site, it is possible that you might catch an error that will require many hours of time to fix throughout the site. If you can discover such problems early on, you will be able to address them and save yourself and your Web team a great deal of time.

On any site, large or small, the task of thorough testing can be daunting. You've worked hard on the content and the design, but if users get frustrated because of broken links, pages that don't work in their browsers, or pages that are large and very slow to load, you've lost them. In this lesson, you will learn how to use Dreamweaver in your testing process by running reports on your site to find out if the pages are compatible with certain browsers. You'll also learn how to check links throughout the site and test for accessibility.

WHAT YOU WILL LEARN

In this lesson, you will:

- Test your site for browser compatibility
- Test the links in your site
- Create site reports

APPROXIMATE TIME

This lesson should take about one half hour to complete.

LESSON FILES

Media Files:
Lesson_07_Testing/Images/…(all files)

Starting Files:
Lesson_07_Testing/…(all files)

GENERATE SECTION 508–COMPLIANT CODE

Section 508 is an amendment to the Rehabilitation Act of 1973, which requires Federal agencies to account for the needs of people with disabilities when developing, procuring, maintaining, or otherwise using electronic and information technology. The goal is to ensure that all users have an equal opportunity to access the content made available through technology such as the Internet. Section 508 defines the standards that are necessary in order for those who have disabilities to be provided with comparable information and services as that which is available to non-disabled users. While Section 508 is not enforced upon the private sector, it is important for all Web sites to adhere to the practice of creating compliant code wherever possible for many reasons. Disabilities ranging from poor or failing eyesight to color blindness or even total blindness affect a significant portion of the population—and therefore, your audience.

One solution would be to create an alternative, text-only page for every page of content on your site. While this would provide appropriate and functional pages that can be specifically tailored to the needs of the disabled, this solution may not be feasible or even necessary for every site (particularly given issues of the kinds of content and services offered, the amount of space available, time and resources needed to create additional pages, and increased requirements for site maintenance). There are a number of solutions you can work into your pages without creating a duplicate site and with no visual impact on your page designs. Dreamweaver provides you with an easy way to incorporate such solutions to create Section 508–compliant Web pages through the use of elements in the code such as **<alt>** tags, descriptions, and summaries. You've already used two of these objects: You inserted an accessible image in Lesson 2, and you inserted an accessible table in Lesson 4. You can also insert Form objects, Frame objects, and Media objects with accessibility attributes. To turn these accessibility options on or off, choose Edit > Preferences and select Accessibility from the list of categories. You will work with forms in Lesson 11 and frames in Lesson 10.

TESTING FOR ACCESSIBILITY

You can run reports on pages within your sites to determine how well they stack up in terms of compliance with accessibility standards.

1) Open access_check.html from the Lesson_07_Testing folder. Choose Site › Reports, select Current Document from the Report On drop-down menu on the Reports dialog box, and select the Accessibility box in the HTML Reports section. Leave all other options unchecked and click Run.

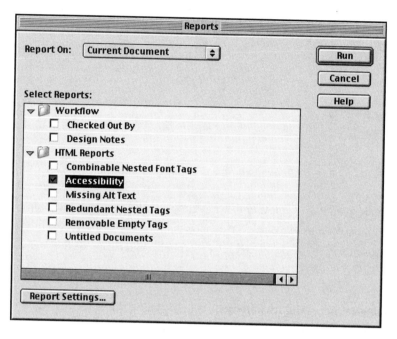

A list of results displays in the Results window. Each item indicates the filename of the document it was found in, the line number where the item can be found in the code, and a brief description of the item.

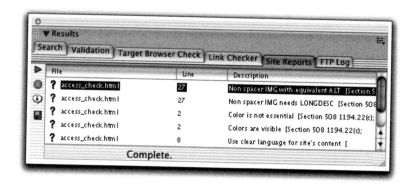

2) Select the third item in the list, which begins with "Color is not essential." Click the More Info icon on the left side of the Results window.

A more detailed description appears in the Reference panel, located in the Code panel group. This description will give you specifics about the particular accessibility rule in question, as well as suggestions for ways to make your pages more accessible.

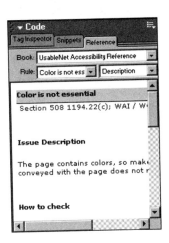

Dreamweaver provides you with a number of Reference panels through which you can learn more about the code used to create Web pages. The UsableNet Accessibility Reference provides you with a quick way to get a thorough explanation of the many standards created by Section 508.

3) Verify that UsableNet Accessibility Reference is selected on the Book drop-down menu at the top of the Reference panel. From the Rule drop-down menu on the Reference panel, choose Spacer IMG with Valid ALT.

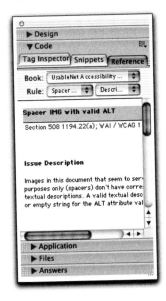

The description of the selected accessibility standard appears in the Reference panel. Displayed in green just above the text description is the specific location of this accessibility standard in Section 508. The description gives you information about the necessity of creating blank `<alt>` tags for all spacer and decorative (non-essential) images used.

This panel will be particularly helpful for developing accessible Web sites once you start working directly in the code, as you will learn in Lesson 12.

You'll be using the Results window throughout this lesson, so you can leave it open. You can close the access_check.html file.

CHECKING BROWSER COMPATIBILITY

Many elements you can add to your Web pages will only work in the later versions of browsers. CSS and layers, for example, are only supported in 4.0 or later browsers. Before making a site available to the public, you should test your pages so you have a chance to fix any errors and be sure your audience will be able to view the pages as they are intended to be seen. To develop an accessible site, you can identify target browsers and design your pages with those browsers in mind. Current browsers support tables and frames, but earlier versions of browsers do not. If you know or suspect that a significant number of your users are still using Netscape Navigator 3.0, for example, you would want to test your pages in that browser. If your pages are geared toward people who may be using hand-held devices, readers, or ways other than standard browsers to access your pages, you should test your site with those devices and software applications.

In this exercise, you will use the Target Browser feature in Dreamweaver to test the HTML in your pages against a browser profile and determine whether or not that browser supports the code in your page. You can run a browser check on a saved file, a folder, or the entire site. Dreamweaver only reports the errors—it does not make any changes to your files.

1) Open the check_browser.html file from the Lesson_07_Testing/Check_Browser folder.

In the following steps, you will run a target browser check on this file.

2) Choose File > Check Page > Check Target Browsers.

The Check Target Browsers dialog box opens.

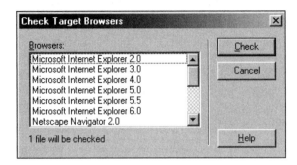

3) Choose Netscape Navigator 3.0 from the list to check against the page, and then click Check.

You can choose more than one browser in this dialog box. Make multiple, non-contiguous selections by using Command-click on the Macintosh or Ctrl-click in Windows. Make contiguous selections by using Shift-click on both Macintosh and Windows.

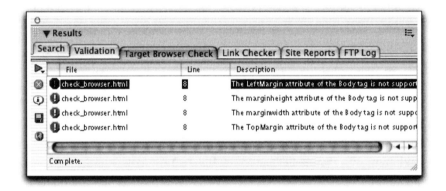

The test runs, and a report is displayed in the Target Browser Check tab of the Results dialog box. This report lets you know that the margin attributes used on this page are not supported in Netscape 3.0, which simply ignores those attributes.

TIP *You can double-click an instance in the Target Browser Check tab of the Results dialog box to view that item on the page or in the code.*

4) Click the Browse Report icon on the left side of the Results dialog box.

The report is now displayed in a browser window. You can close the check_browser.html file and leave the Results window open.

5) Select the Lesson_07_Testing/Check_Browser folder in the Site window.

In the following steps, you will run a target browser check on this folder.

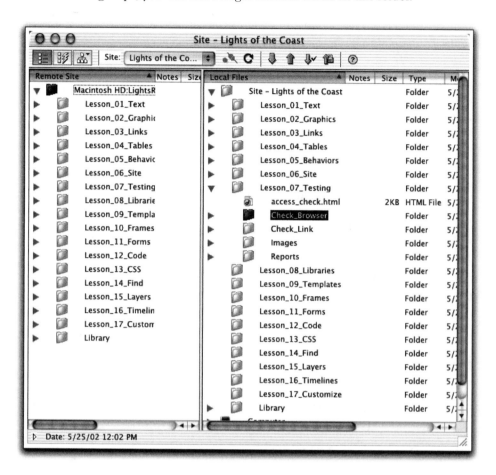

6) Click the Target Browser Check tab in the Results window and click the green arrow in the upper left corner of the Target Browser Check tab. Choose Check Target Browsers for Selected Files/Folders in Site from the drop-down menu (Windows).

NOTE *Macintosh users can alternatively choose File > Check Page > Check Target Browsers to open the same Check Target Browsers dialog box.*

The Check Target Browsers dialog box opens.

TIP *If you need to open the Results window, you can choose Window > Results > Target Browser Check.*

7) Choose the Internet Explorer 5.5 from the list to check against the pages in the selected folder. Then click Check.

The test runs and a report is displayed in the Target Browser Check Tab of the Results dialog box.

NOTE *If you want to save this report, you need to save it from the browser.*

There will be differences in the way your site displays in every browser version. You may have to make trade-offs on how the pages appear. Certain JavaScripts, for example, will produce error messages in browsers that do not support them. Other JavaScripts will simply not work, and the visitor may never know it. To reach the widest audience possible, you will want to create a Web site that is error-free for older browsers. It is far better for visitors to miss certain features than to have error messages appear. If your audience uses a wide variety of browsers, you may want to make sure the navigation of your pages does not rely on features that may not be supported in older browsers, or provide alternative pages for those who are not using the latest versions.

You can leave the Results window open.

CHECKING LINKS IN YOUR SITE

It is not uncommon for a Web designer to add, delete, or change the filenames of pages in the site during the development process. It is easy to overlook a page that links to a deleted or renamed file. Your users will get very frustrated if they get the "404: File Not Found" error message indicating that a page is missing when they click a link.

In this exercise, you will use the Check Link feature to find those missing links. Dreamweaver can only verify links to files within the site. External links are listed, but it is up to you to test those links and make sure the external link is a valid URL.

1) Open links.html from the Lesson_07_Testing/Check_Link folder. Choose File > Check Page > Check Links.

The Link Checker tab of the Results dialog box opens. Broken Links may be selected by default when you run Check Links, and any broken links will be displayed in the Broken Links column. If Broken Links is not selected, choose it from the Show drop-down menu.

In this exercise, only one broken link is displayed in the list.

242

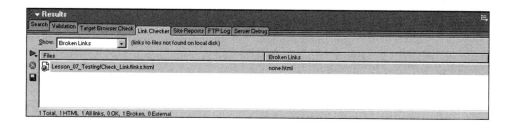

TIP *You can also use the keyboard shortcut Shift+F8 to open the Link Checker report window.*

2) Select the broken link (none.html).

The filename highlights, and a folder icon appears to the right of the broken link.

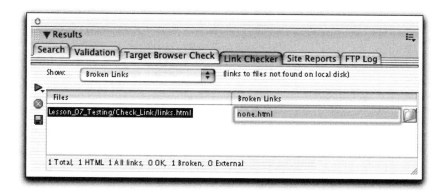

3) Change none.html to culture.html. Then press Return (Macintosh) or Enter (Windows).

TIP *You can also click the folder icon and browse to the correct file to link to.*

If there are other broken references to this file, a dialog box opens asking if you want to fix the other references as well. Click Yes to have Dreamweaver fix all the references to this file. Click No to have Dreamweaver fix only the current reference.

NOTE *You can also check files or folders by selecting them in the Site Window and choosing File > Check Links. If you want to view the document or fix the links by using the Property inspector, double-click the filename in the Link Checker window to open the file.*

You can save and close this file and leave the Results dialog box open.

CHECKING FOR ORPHANED FILES

In the process of creating a Web site, you build new files as well as revise and replace old ones. Throughout the development phase, you may develop multiple versions of certain files or end up disregarding other files entirely. An orphaned file is one that is included with the site files, but which is not used on your site. These may be HTML files that have no links pointing to them, or images that haven't been used on any pages.

1) In the Site window, select the local root folder for your project Web site.

In order to run an Orphaned files report, you must first run a link check on the entire site.

2) In the Link Checker tab of the Results dialog box, choose Broken Links from the Show drop-down menu and click the Check Links icon (the green arrow) for a drop-down menu. Choose Check Links for entire site.

A larger list will appear in the dialog box.

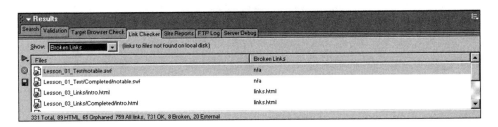

3) From the Show drop-down menu, choose Orphaned Files.

A list of orphaned files appears in the dialog box.

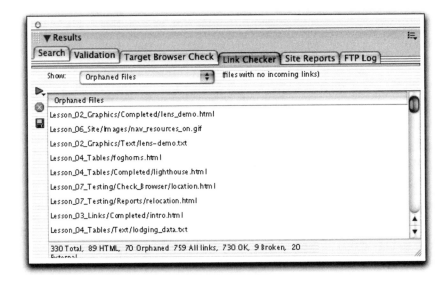

Deleting orphaned files can reduce the amount of disk space used by your site. It is particularly helpful to perform regular maintenance on large sites. Identifying and removing all orphaned files can have a great impact on speed, size, and functionality.

NOTE *It is advisable to thoroughly review the list of orphaned files. You may have files that you want to keep on your site that are not linked to or used in any other file.*

For this exercise, do not delete any of the orphaned files listed. The files in the "Lights of the Coast" project site are needed for completion of this book's lessons and some may appear to be orphaned files.

GENERATING REPORTS FOR A SITE

While testing your site, you can compile and generate reports on several HTML attributes by using the Reports command. This command lets you check several options, including searching for untitled documents and redundant nested tags. You can run reports on a single document, a folder, or the entire site to help you troubleshoot and find potential problems before publishing your site.

1) Select the Reports folder in the Lesson_07_Testing folder in the Site window. Choose Site > Reports.

The Reports dialog box opens.

2) Choose Selected Files In Site from the Report On drop-down menu. Leave all the options in the Workflow area unchecked. Check all the options in the HTML Reports area except for accessibility.

The Workflow options are most useful when you are collaborating with a Web team and need to quickly see who has checked files out and what design notes have been created.

The HTML Reports options check for combinable nested font tags, accessibility, missing alt text, redundant nested tags, removable empty tags and untitled documents.

You can choose to run reports on the Current Document, Entire Local Site, Selected Files In Site, and Folder.

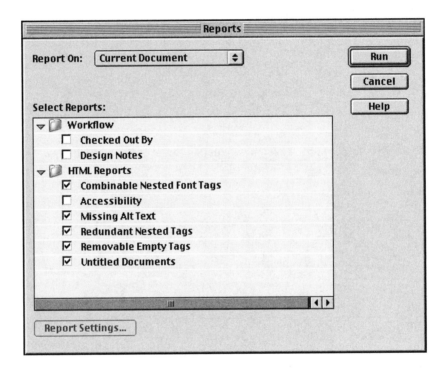

3) Click Run to create the report.

A list of results displays in the Results window. In this case, Dreamweaver alerts you that the relocation.html document has not been given a title.

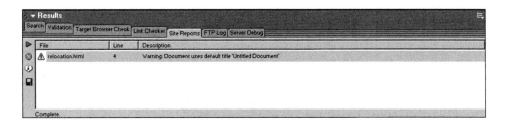

4) Click Save Report on the bottom left corner of the Result window and save the report in the Lesson_07_Testing folder.

All reports are saved as XML files with the .xml file extension.

The Reports command lists problems in your pages but does not fix them.

TIP *After running the reports, you can use Clean Up HTML on any open documents by choosing Commands > Clean Up HTML. This command fixes many, but not all, of the problems found in the site report. A dialog box will appear with a number of items you can choose to have Dreamweaver remove: empty tags, redundant nested tags, non-Dreamweaver HTML comments, Dreamweaver HTML comments, and specific tags. You can also choose to combine nested* **<font>** *tags when possible and to show the log upon completion. The log will give you a detailed list of what changes were made to the document. More information about this feature will be given in Lesson 12 when you work with the code.*

ON YOUR OWN: S.F. BLACK & WHITE GALLERY

The SF Black & White Gallery is located in downtown San Francisco and specializes in black and white photography. The gallery uses Dreamweaver to create and maintain its Web site.

http://www.sfblackandwhite.com
Credits: © SF Black & White Gallery

248

Testing is a big part of site maintenance. It is important to know who can access your site. The reports you used near the end of this lesson can also be extremely useful, particularly when you are working with a team.

In this bonus activity, you will run tests on some of the pages from the SF Black & White Gallery's Web site on your own. The files you will need for this exercise are located in the Bonus/Lesson_07 folder. For this activity you should complete the following:

- Run the Check Target Browser.
- Generate Reports for each page.

WHAT YOU HAVE LEARNED

In this lesson, you have:

- Discovered the requirements for creating accessible Web pages and how Dreamweaver MX can help (pages 236–239)
- Used browser profiles to test individual pages, folders, or an entire site for browser compatibility and find out if there are any errors or unsupported tags (pages 239–242)
- Tested the links in your pages to quickly find any broken links within your site (pages 242–243)
- Checked for and viewed a list of orphaned files (pages 244–245)
- Created site reports to find common problems in your site such as redundant nested tags and untitled documents (pages 245–247)

using libraries

LESSON 8

There are many items and groups of items that you may need to create and repeat on multiple pages throughout your Web site. These items may include, but are not limited to, navigation, copyright information, headers, and footers. Dreamweaver lets you store these often-used content items as **library items**. Creating library items for these elements will allow you to quickly and easily insert the same content into many documents. If you need to change information, such as copyright dates that may appear on a large number of pages throughout your site, library items will make it possible for you to edit the content and, with a single command, update all documents that reference it. Without a library item, you would have to open each page and modify the information

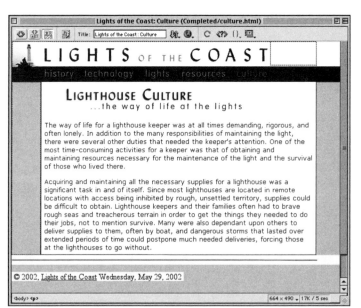

In this project, you will add a library item to a page. After you modify the library item, you will use the update feature in order to quickly and efficiently make the same changes to all pages containing that item on the site.

individually. On a small site, this may not be difficult; however, on a very large site it would be very time-consuming and greatly increase the probability of errors. Library items provide a way for you to maintain consistency and automate the process of updating your site. Library items enable you to repeat certain elements on pages that can still have different layouts. Effective use of library items can be a timesaver not only in the development stage of your Web site, but in the ongoing maintenance tasks, as well.

To see examples of the finished pages for this chapter, open culture.html, lights.html, and technology.html from the Lesson_08_Library/Completed folder.

WHAT YOU WILL LEARN

In this lesson, you will:

- Learn when and why to use library items
- Create and insert a library item
- Recreate a library item
- Edit an existing library item
- Update all references to a library item
- Detach a library item
- Create and modify a library item containing behaviors

APPROXIMATE TIME

This lesson should take about one hour to complete.

LESSON FILES

Media Files:
Lesson_08_Library/Images/…(all files)

Starting Files:
Lesson_08_Library/culture.html
Lesson_08_Library/lights.html
Lesson_08_Library/technology.html

Completed Project:
Lesson_08_Library/Completed/culture.html
Lesson_08_Library/Completed/lights.html
Lesson_08_Library/Completed/technology.html

NOTE *Library items contained within the completed folders have been named with the _completed suffix in order to differentiate them from the library items that you will create in this lesson. The original library items are not included—if you would like to see them, follow the steps in the section "Recreating a Library Item."*

CREATING A LIBRARY ITEM

You can create a library item by selecting one or more elements in a document and adding them to the library. When you do this, Dreamweaver converts the selection into non-editable content that is linked to the corresponding library item. The following exercise demonstrates this process.

1) Open Lesson_08_Library/culture.html.

Library items can only include content that appears between the `<BODY>` and `</BODY>` tags. They can include any document elements such as text, tables, forms, images, Java applets, plug-ins, or ActiveX elements.

NOTE *Cascading Style Sheet (CSS) references (for example, `<SPAN CLASS="green">` `green text </SPAN>`) are preserved in library items, but the style will not appear when the library item is inserted in a document unless the style sheet containing that style is linked to the document. The Library panel offers a visual reminder of this (in addition to a warning message) by displaying the text as it would appear if the style sheet were omitted. The best way to make sure style sheet information is included is to use external style sheets and remember to link them to all documents that need to make use of their styles. CSS is covered in Lesson 13.*

2) Select the copyright text, the email address, the modification date, and the horizontal rule.

TIP *Be sure to select the space that is just before the copyright character. Because this document has margins of 0 defined, this space is necessary to provide a buffer between the edge of the browser window and the copyright text. If you want to use a similar space on your own documents you will need to use what is called a non-breaking space. Typing a space on a new line won't actually put a space in the HTML document, so you need to use the non-breaking space instead. To insert a non-breaking space, you can use the keyboard shortcut Option+Space (Macintosh) or Ctrl+Shift+Space (Windows). You can also choose the Characters tab on the Insert bar and click the Non-Breaking Space icon (second from the left). Non-breaking spaces can also be used to insert more than one space—HTML documents only recognize one standard space, and pressing the space bar multiple times will have no effect after the first space is inserted.*

The text and horizontal rule are highlighted.

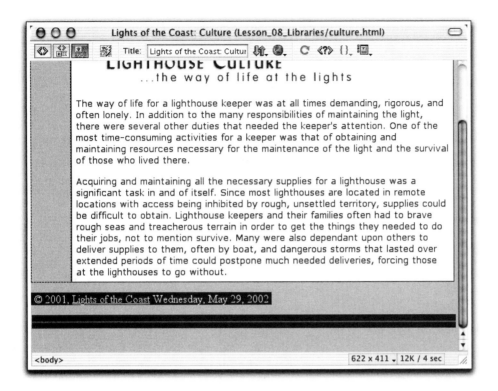

In order to create a library item out of multiple elements, those elements must form a contiguous selection in the document. If you need noncontiguous items to function as a library item does, you will need to create multiple library items.

The copyright text, email address, and modification date are standard information that might be used at the bottom of all pages within a Web site. Libraries can be very useful for this type of information.

A library item containing relative paths (such as links to pages or images) can be placed in any level of your site's directory structure—it does not have to reside on the same level as the original library item. In the sample directory structure shown in the following figure, a library item called Lens created in lightsource.html, containing a link to the image lens.jpg located in the media folder, will work when inserted into beacon.html because the path to the image (media/lens.jpg) is the same for both lightsource.html and beacon.html. The path is the same for both files because they are located in the same level of the site directory structure; both files are on the top level, directly inside the root folder Site-Libraries Example. The path media/lens.jpg tells the browser that the lens.jpg image is located in the media folder inside the current directory. The current directory is the folder in which the file that the browser is reading is located. In this case, the current directory is the folder in which the files that use the path media/lens.jpg (lightsource.html and beacon.html) are located—the Site-Libraries Example folder.

The same Lens library item would also function correctly if it were used in ship.html because Dreamweaver will automatically determine the appropriate path. The correct path for ship.html would be ../media/lens.jpg. The ../ at the beginning of this pathname tells the browser to go up one level in the folder directory structure—so the browser would look inside the site root folder, which is the next level up from the A folder. The browser will then look in the media folder for the lens.jpg image.

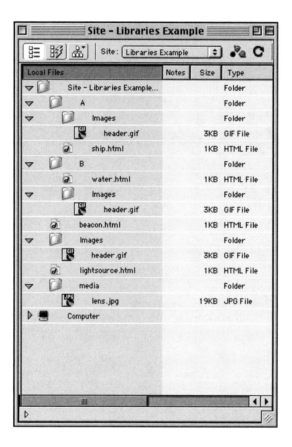

NOTE *If a library item called Ship2 were to be created in ship.html with the path ../media/lens.jpg, then it would have the same path if it were placed in any file within folder A. It will also have the same path if it were placed in any file within folder B, such as water.html, because the path from a file in folder B to the lens.jpg image in the media folder (../media/lens.jpg) would be the same as the path from a file in folder A because the files in folders A and B are on the same level of the directory structure in this sample site.*

Without a library item, a path in beacon.html to the image header.gif located in the top-level images folder inside the lighthouse site in the previous example would work in ship.html only if the image header.gif is duplicated inside the images folder in folder A. In this case, beacon.html and ship.html would be using the same path to access a different copy of the image. A library item, however, would automatically calculate the correct path.

3) Choose Window > Assets to open the Assets panel in the Files panel group. Click the Library button on the bottom left of the Assets panel to open the Library portion of the Assets panel.

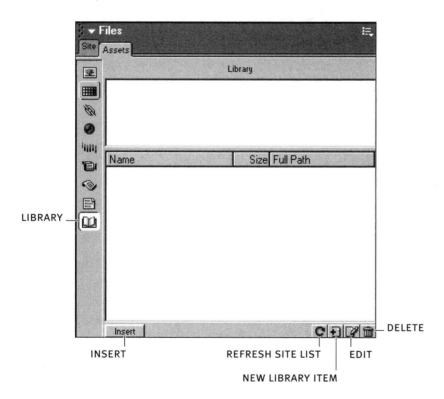

The Library category of the Assets panel opens. This is where you will manage all of your library items.

4) Drag the selected objects from the document window to the lower half of the Library panel.

TIP *You can also click the New Library Item icon at the bottom of the Library category of the Assets panel or choose Modify > Library > Add Object to Library in order to create a new library item.*

A new Untitled icon appears and is highlighted on the Library panel. A preview of the library item, created from the elements you selected in step 2, appears at the top of the panel.

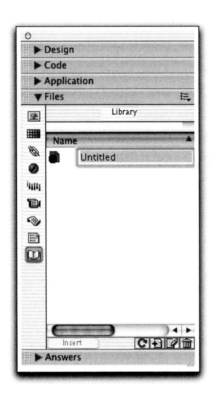

NOTE *When you create a library item, Dreamweaver creates a folder named Library at the top level of your local root folder and stores each library item there. This Library folder and the library files it contains are only stored locally; they do not need to be uploaded to a server unless you wish to share them with other members of your Web team. Dreamweaver saves each library item with the .lbi file extension.*

5) Type copyright for the new library item, and then press Return (Macintosh) or Enter (Windows).

The library item is now known as copyright in the Library panel. You should give your library items descriptive names. The names are for your reference only and will not be displayed to the user in a browser window.

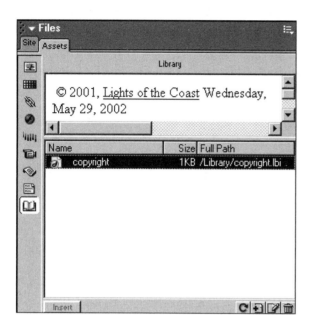

When you deselect the text in the culture.html document window, it has a pale yellow background. The yellow background indicates the text is linked to a library item and is not directly editable. This block of text is now considered one item, so clicking any part of it will select the entire library item. Leave the culture.html document open for the next exercise.

PLACING A LIBRARY ITEM ON A PAGE

Placing a library item in a document inserts the contents of the library item file and creates a reference to that library item. When you insert a library item, the actual HTML is inserted, which means the content appears even if the library item is not available in the Library folder. Dreamweaver inserts comments in the code around the item to show the name of the library file and the reference to the original item. The comments and reference are not visible in the browser window. The reference to the external library item file is what makes it possible to update the content on an entire site all at once simply by changing the library item.

257

1) Open lights.html and place the insertion point on a blank line at the bottom of the document.

In the following steps, you will place into this document the library item you created in the previous exercise.

NOTE *If the Library panel is not visible, choose Window > Assets and click the Library icon in the Assets panel. The Assets panel is located in the Files panel group.*

2) Drag the copyright file icon from the Library panel to the bottom of the document window.

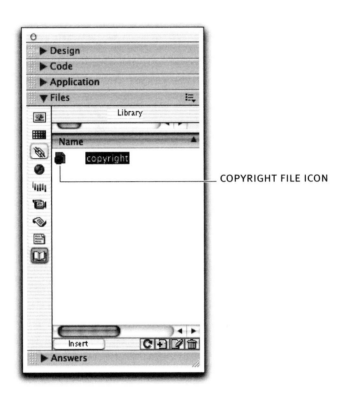

COPYRIGHT FILE ICON

TIP *Alternatively, you can select the copyright library item and then click Insert at the bottom left corner of the panel to insert the item into the Library.*

The text and rule are added to the document. The copyright library item is shown with a yellow background; the color will not be displayed in the browser. While library items are highlighted with yellow by default, the color can be changed or turned off completely in the Preferences dialog box. This item cannot be modified directly on the page. You will modify library items in the next exercise.

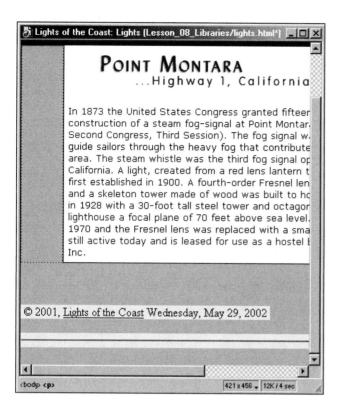

Use library item properties in the Property inspector to see the name of the source file and to perform maintenance functions for the library item that is selected in the document window. The Property inspector has several options:

- **Src**: Displays the filename and location of the source file for the library item. You can open the library item for editing with the Open option. You must save the file to keep the changes you make.

- **Detach from Original**: Breaks the link between the selected library item and its source file. The content of the library item becomes editable, but it can no longer be updated by the library update functions.

- **Recreate**: Overwrites the original library item with the current selection. Use this option to create library items again if the library file isn't present, the item's name has been changed, or the item has been edited.

You can save and close the culture.html document.

3) Open technology.html and place the insertion point on a blank line at the bottom of the document.

You will place a detached copy of the library item with copyright information on this page so it is editable in the document.

4) Hold down Option (Macintosh) or Control (Windows) and drag the copyright file icon from the Library panel to the document.

The library content is copied into the document but is not linked to the library, so there is no yellow highlighting. The elements can be modified directly on the page since they are not connected to a library item. Since these elements are detached, they will not be updated if any changes are made to the original library item.

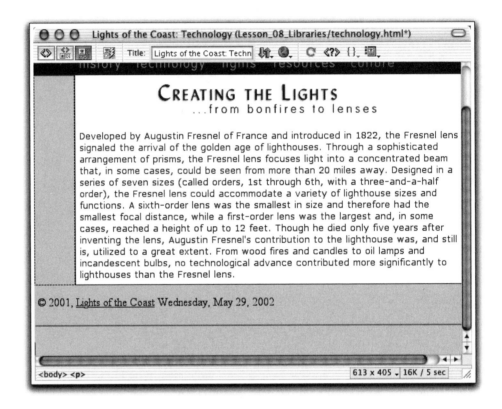

You can save and close the technology.html document. Save the lights.html document, but leave it open for the next exercise.

RECREATING A LIBRARY ITEM

If a library item is accidentally deleted from the Library category of the Assets panel and you still have a page showing the library item, you can recreate it.

1) In the lights.html document, select the library item at the top right of the page by clicking once on the introduction image.

This library item that you will recreate is a simple table with three images, just like one you created in Lesson 4. The entire item is selected and grayed out to show that it cannot be edited within the document. Although this element was marked as a library item in the document window, it does not appear in the Library category of the Assets panel.

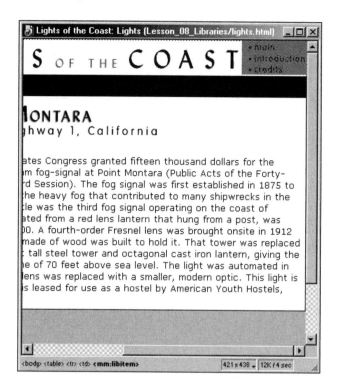

NOTE *You are unable to see any of the yellow highlights on this library item because there is no space between the images in the table. The highlight that indicates a library item shows up around the items contained in a library item—it does not display over the top of an image.*

2) Click Recreate on the Property inspector.

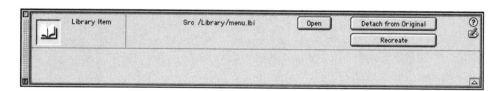

The library item file is recreated with the item name used on this page; it will now show up titled as "menu" in the Library category of the Assets panel.

TIP *You can also Control-click (Macintosh) or right-click (Windows) to open a context menu that contains the Recreate option and other choices related to the selected library item.*

You can close the lights.html document.

MODIFYING A LIBRARY ITEM

When you edit a library item, you need to edit the item's file in the Library folder. Editing a library item changes the library item only. When you finish editing, Dreamweaver prompts you to update all the pages in the site that use the item, letting you choose whether or not to make these changes throughout the entire site. Dreamweaver accomplishes the update by searching for comments that reference the library file you just edited, and then replacing the old HTML with your new HTML. If you remove the library comments, the HTML is no longer associated with the library item and cannot be changed by updating the library item.

NOTE *Any modifications to the library item must be made through the Assets panel. If you want to edit the content directly in a document, you must first break the link to the library item. To do this, use the Detach from Original button on the Property inspector, or hold down Control (Windows) or Option (Macintosh) when inserting the item.*

1) Double-click the copyright file icon on the Library category of the Assets panel.

NOTE *If the Library category of the Assets panel is not open, choose Window > Assets and click the Library icon on the Assets panel.*

Dreamweaver opens the copyright library item for editing. When library items are inserted on a page, they take on the properties of that document; text and link colors change according to the default colors set for the document (unless you have specified the font color in the library item).

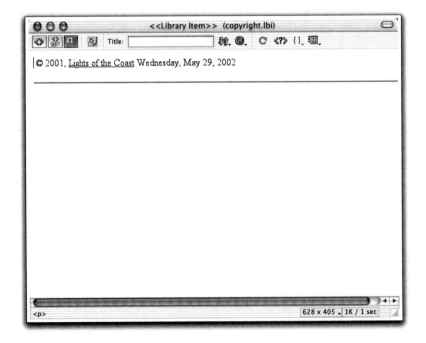

TIP *Alternatively, you can select copyright on the Library panel, and then click Edit on the panel. You can also select the library item on a page and click Open in the Property inspector.*

2) In the document window, select the horizontal rule and move it in front of the space at the beginning of the copyright line in order to move it above the copyright line. Save the document.

The Update Library Items dialog box opens.

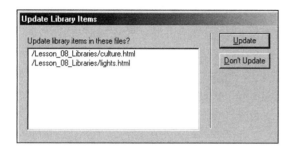

3) Click Update to update all the documents in your site that use the copyright library item.

The Update Pages dialog box shows which pages have been updated with your changes.

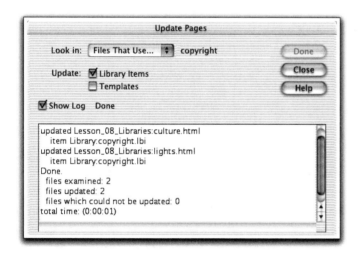

NOTE *If you have a large site, you might prefer to wait to update your site with all your changes at once. In that case, click the Don't Update button when you save the library item.*

4) Click Close to close the Update Pages dialog box.

The horizontal rule should be in its new location in both culture.html and lights.html.

UPDATING LIBRARY REFERENCES

If you choose not to update your pages at the time you edit a library item, but decide do so later, Dreamweaver lets you do all the updating with a single command. For instance, you may want to wait to update pages at a later time if your Web team members have pages checked out that contain library items.

NOTE *If you are using Check In and Check Out and you want to make updates to pages using a library item, Dreamweaver will ask you if you want to check out the pages containing that library item. You must say yes to allow Dreamweaver to check out the file if you want it to be updated.*

1) Open the copyright library item from the Library panel. Change the copyright date to 2002 and save the document. Click Don't Update in the Update Library Items dialog box.

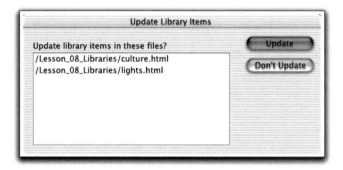

Neither culture.html nor lights.html will show the new copyright date yet.

2) From the menu bar, choose Modify > Library > Update Pages.

The Update Pages dialog box opens.

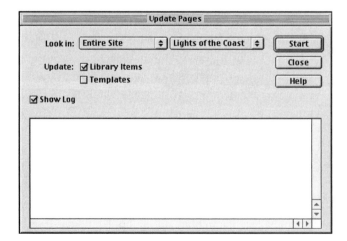

3) In the Look In drop-down menu, verify that Entire Site is chosen.

The menu to the right will display the current site, Lights of the Coast. You are choosing to update all files that use the copyright library item.

4) In the Update check boxes, verify that the Library Items box is checked and the Templates box is unchecked. Check the Show Log box and click Start.

The Update Pages dialog box shows which files were updated.

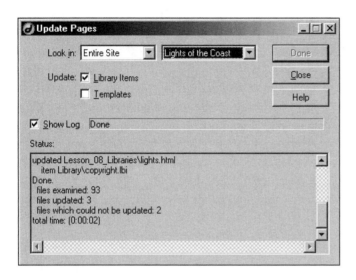

NOTE *For this exercise, the Update Pages dialog box will show that two files were not updated—those two files are the final examples in the Completed folder.*

5) Click Close to close the dialog box.

The new copyright date appears in both culture.html and lights.html.

CREATING A LIBRARY ITEM CONTAINING BEHAVIORS

Since library items must be contained within the **<BODY>** of the document and cannot contain or reference any items outside the **<BODY>**, JavaScript cannot be used in library items if the script requires code between the **<HEAD>** and **</HEAD>** tags of the document because those tags are located before the **<BODY>** tag. There is one exception however. Because behaviors are predefined JavaScripts for which Dreamweaver will insert the corresponding JavaScript functions into the **<HEAD>**, you can use Dreamweaver's behaviors in library items, even though the necessary JavaScript requires code to be placed between the **<HEAD>** and **</HEAD>** tags of the document. Although the code required in the **<HEAD>** is not included in the library item, Dreamweaver will automatically place the code into the **<HEAD>** whenever the library item is placed into a document.

1) Open technology.html and click the history navigation graphic near the top of the page, beneath the main "Lights of the Coast" title. Use the Tag Selector at the bottom of the document window to select the table by clicking the `<table>` tag that is closest to the history image.

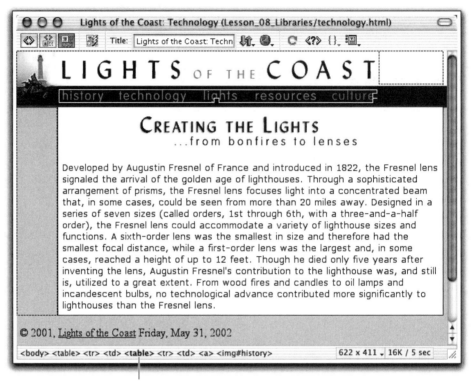

SELECTED ⟨TABLE⟩ TAG

This will be the rightmost **`<table>`** tag beneath the copyright line. This table contains rollovers that were created for each image. Rollovers and other behaviors were covered in Lesson 5.

2) Click the new library item icon at the bottom of the Library category of the Assets panel. Type navigation for the new library item, and then press Return (Macintosh) or Enter (Windows).

The library item contains certain portions of the code necessary for the behavior, including the event, as well as the action to call when the event occurs. It does not contain any of the JavaScript functions that are required to be placed between the **<HEAD>** and **</HEAD>** tags of the document. You worked with events and actions in Lesson 5.

3) Insert this new library item at the top of the page in the culture.html document by clicking in the black bar below the Lights of the Coast title graphic, selecting the navigation library item and clicking Insert on the Library category of the Assets panel.

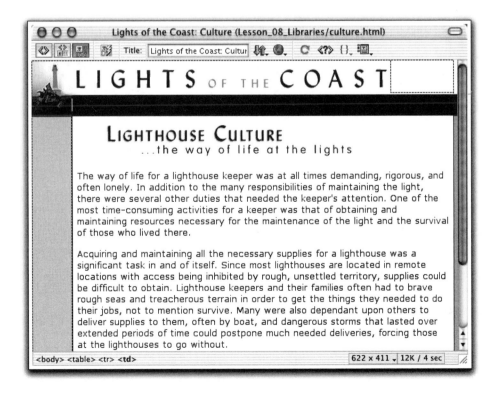

267

The JavaScript functions that are required for the rollover in this library item are automatically inserted between the **<HEAD>** and **</HEAD>** tags of the document. While these functions are not included in the library item, they are inserted because Dreamweaver recognizes certain portions of the code in the library item as behaviors and automatically inserts the required code into the **<HEAD>**. You will learn about working with the code in Lesson 12.

NOTE *If you write your own JavaScript that use functions between the **<HEAD>** and* *</HEAD> tags of the document, you can use the Call JavaScript behavior (available at the top of the Events menu on the Behaviors panel) to execute the code. A behavior must be used in a library item in order for Dreamweaver to insert the corresponding functions.*

You can save and close the culture.html document. Leave the technology.html document open for the next exercise.

MODIFYING A LIBRARY ITEM CONTAINING BEHAVIORS

Library items that contain behaviors require a more complex editing process than items that do not contain behaviors. The options on the Behaviors panel are grayed out while you are editing a library item so you can't modify a behavior from the Library panel. You must first detach the item from a page in order to make your changes. You can then delete the original item and create a new one from the modified elements. The following steps demonstrate how to edit these kinds of library items.

1) In technology.html, click the history image to select the navigation library item at the top of the document.

You created a library item from this table in the previous exercise. The whole library item becomes selected.

2) Make a note of the name of the library item; then click Detach from Original in the Property inspector. Dreamweaver will warn you that this item will no longer be able to be updated if you detach it; click OK to continue.

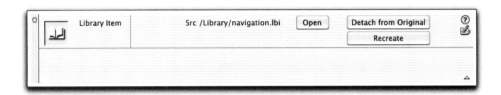

The name of this library item is "navigation." It is important to remember the exact name so that when you make this table a library item again, any links to the library item in the rest of your site will remain correct. Now that you have detached the item, you can edit the rollover.

3) Select the technology image and choose Window > Behaviors to open the Behaviors panel.

This rollover uses the wrong graphic when it swaps. In the following steps, you'll change the graphic from a lens image to a lighthouse image.

4) Double-click the existing Swap Image action in the list of attached behaviors on the Behaviors panel.

TIP *Make sure you double-click the Swap Image action, not the Swap Image Restore action.*

The Swap Image dialog box opens.

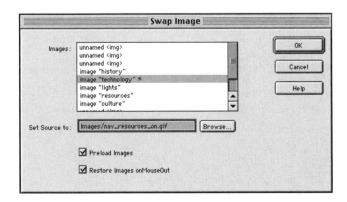

5) In the Swap Image dialog box, click Browse and find nav_technology_on.gif. Choose the image by clicking Open (Macintosh) or Select (Windows). Click OK to close the Swap Image dialog box.

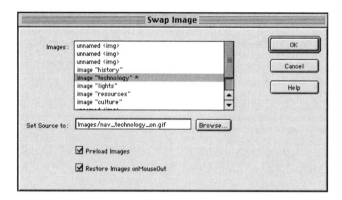

The Swap Image dialog box closes, and the rollover now uses the correct image.

6) Select the original library item, navigation, in the Library panel. Then click the Delete icon at the bottom of the panel. Click Yes when that dialog box asks whether you are sure you want to delete the library item.

The original library item is now deleted. Because it is not possible to edit behaviors directly in a library element, you have to delete the original item and replace it with a corrected version.

7) Click the history navigation graphic near the top of the page, underneath the main "Lights of the Coast" title. Again, use the Tag Selector at the bottom of the document window to select the table by clicking the ‹table› tag that is closest to the history image.

You will use this table to replace the original library item.

8) Click the new Library Item icon at the bottom of the Library panel and name the library item exactly as the original was named: navigation.

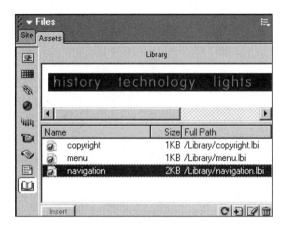

The modified elements are now stored in the Library folder.

9) Choose Modify > Library > Update Pages. In the Look In drop-down menu, verify that Entire Site is chosen. In Update check boxes, verify that the Library Items box is checked and the Templates box is unchecked. Check the Show Log box and click Start.

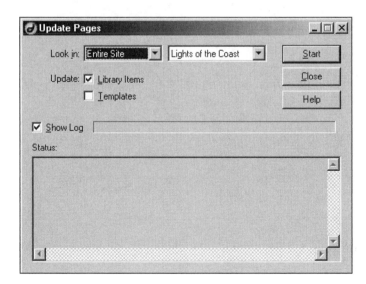

The pages in the rest of the site that once used the original navigation library item are now updated with the new version.

10) Click Close to close the dialog box. Save the technology.html document and test your pages in the browser.

Both technology.html and culture.html will now use the correct rollover image.

ON YOUR OWN: ORIGINS—THE HEART OF THE MATTER

The Heart of the Matter is a feature of the Exploratorium's Origins Web site that explores CERN, home to the world's largest particle accelerator and more commonly known as the place where the Web was born. The slideshow features photographs of CERN.

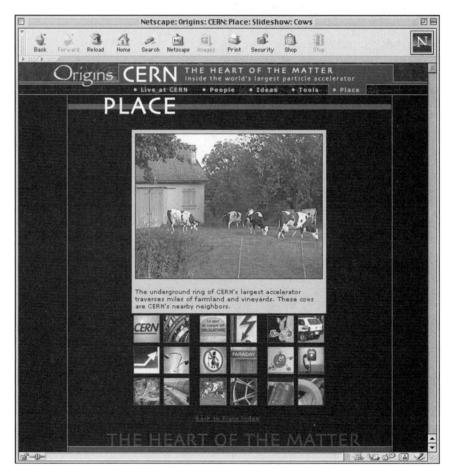

http://www.exploratorium.edu/origins/cern/
Credits: © Exploratorium, www.exploratorium.edu

The Exploratorium Web team used Dreamweaver to create the Origins: CERN Web site. Library items played a big part in the development of the site, allowing designers to create a footer that would be consistent throughout the site.

In this bonus activity, you will recreate the library items used in the Origins: CERN Web site on your own. The files you will need for this exercise are located in the Bonus/Lesson_08 folder. Examine the Completed file before you get started. You should recreate the library item as you did earlier in this lesson with the page that contained a library item that was not shown in the Library portion of the Assets panel. After recreating the library item, change the copyright date to 2002 and update all the pages that contain it.

WHAT YOU HAVE LEARNED

In this lesson, you have:

- Learned how to use library items for elements that need to be repeated on many pages within a site (pages 250–254)

- Created a library item using the Library category of the Assets panel, inserted it on a page with a link to the library item, and inserted it on another page without a link to the library item (pages 252–260)

- Used the Property inspector to recreate a library item that was missing from the Library panel (pages 260–261)

- Edited an existing library item from the Library panel and applied the changes to all pages in the site that used that item (pages 262–263)

- Updated all references to a library item (pages 264–265)

- Created and modified a library item containing rollovers in order to include behaviors in a library item and changed those behaviors when needed (pages 265–272)

- Detached a library item in a document so it no longer linked to the original library item in order to make it editable in the document window (page 269)

using templates

LESSON 9

Whether you have a large site with many sections or multiple pages that share a common design, you can create a template to speed up the production process. By using a template, you can change or update the look of your site, changing multiple pages within a few minutes. Templates are useful when you have a team working together to build an area of the site. The Web designer can create a template, inserting placeholders for the parts of the page that can be edited. The overall design of the page remains locked.

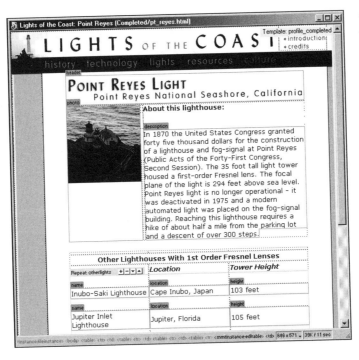

In this lesson, you will create a template from an existing page, build other pages using that template, and modify the pages by editing the template.

The advantages of templates are best seen in two situations: when you have a section or set of pages that need to use an identical design and layout, or when a designer creates the look of the pages but content editors add the content to the pages. If you simply want pages with the same headers and footers but different layouts in between, use libraries (covered in Lesson 8). Libraries allow you to have certain elements or groups of elements repeated throughout your site, giving you more control over the layouts of the individual pages while templates enable you to make use of the same layout and design. But if you want to use the same design on several pages, use templates. For example, say you have an online catalog of your products and you want all the pages to look the same except for the product picture, description, and price. If you create a template, you can have your team build the pages and each page will look the same.

To see examples of the finished pages for this chapter, open pt_arena.html, pt_cabrillo.html, pt_reyes.html, and pt_reyes_photos.html from the Lesson_09_Templates/Completed folder.

WHAT YOU WILL LEARN

In this lesson, you will:

- Create a template
- Add editable regions to the template
- Remove editable regions from the template
- Create optional regions
- Insert repeating regions
- Change the template highlight colors
- Build multiple pages based on the template
- Update a site by changing the template
- Define editable tag attributes
- Create a nested template

APPROXIMATE TIME

This lesson should take about one hour to complete.

LESSON FILES

Media Files:

Lesson_09_Templates/Images/...(all files)

Starting Files:

Lesson_09_Templates/profile.html
Lesson_09_Templates/images_table.html

Completed Project:

Lesson_09_Templates/Completed...(all files)

NOTE *The templates used to create the files in the Completed folder are profile_completed.dwt and profile_photos.dwt. These two files are located in the Completed/Template_Files folder, so that they will not conflict or be confused with the template files you will be creating in this lesson. The correct location for these files would be the Templates folder that will be created by Dreamweaver as you work through this lesson. If you need to use the templates for the completed files, you should move them into the Templates folder.*

CREATING TEMPLATES

A template should define the layout and design of the subsequent pages you will create from it. In this lesson the template you will create provides the navigation, site identity, and look and feel of the profiles section of the "Lights of the Coast" project site.

When creating a template, your first step will usually include the development of the page design—which has already been done for you in this project—and saving that design as a template.

You can build a template page from scratch, or you can take an existing HTML page and save it as a template. In this exercise, you are creating a series of Web pages, each profiling a different lighthouse. You will start with a page that has already been created, then save the file as a template and create other pages from it in the following exercises.

1) Open profile.html in the Lesson_09_Templates folder.

In this document the materials that would be placed in the content areas and which are intended to change from page to page, have been represented with descriptive placeholders.

2) Choose File > Save As Template.

The Save As Template dialog box opens. You can select the site in which you want to save the template. For this project, you should save it within the "Lights of the Coast" site.

Dreamweaver automatically names the template "profile"—the name of your file. For this exercise, use this automatic name. It accurately describes the purpose of the template.

TIP *If you want to change the name of the template, type the new name in the Save As text field. The template name is only for your reference. Try to use names for your templates that are as descriptive as possible.*

This page has now been saved as a template, and you will be able to use it to build other pages later in this lesson.

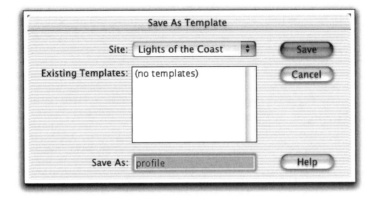

3) Click Save to close the dialog box.

Your template has been added to your site and saved in the Templates folder with an extension of .dwt. Dreamweaver automatically adds the Templates folder if one doesn't already exist. Leave this file open to use in the next exercise.

The Assets panel is now open to the Templates category. The template you just created appears in the list. Any templates you create in this site in the future will appear in this list, as well. The file you are working with is now profile.dwt, and the top of the document window will display <<Template>> (profile.dwt).

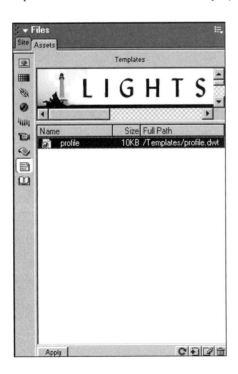

278

NOTE *Instead of saving a page as a template from one that was already created as you just did, you can also create a new, blank template by choosing Window > Assets and selecting the Templates icon on the Assets panel. Click New Template at the bottom of the Templates Assets panel and a new, untitled template will be added to the list of templates in the panel. While that template is still selected, enter a name for the template.*

ADDING EDITABLE AREAS TO A TEMPLATE

The second step in creating a template is to define the areas of the page that should be editable in documents that are based on the template.

As a rule, all areas of a template are locked. If you want to change information on pages that use the template, you need to create "editable" areas or regions. In many Web sites, these regions are often content areas. Everything in the template that is not explicitly defined as editable is locked in pages that are based on the template. You can make changes to both the editable and locked areas while editing the original template, but on a page built from a template, you can change only the editable regions.

1) In profile.dwt, select the placeholder image called "title" (located in the top row of the table for the profiles content). Use the Tag Selector at the bottom of the document window to select the cell that contains the image by clicking the <td> tag closest to the image.

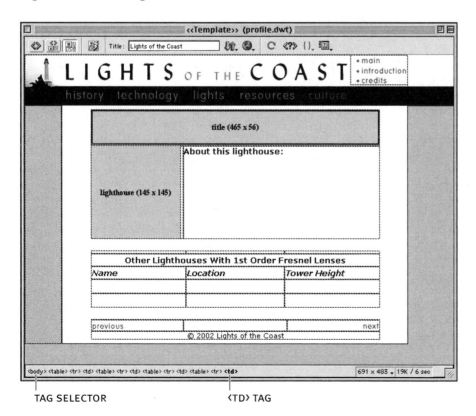

TAG SELECTOR   ⟨TD⟩ TAG

279

This section of the page needs to be editable so you can change the content in subsequent pages.

NOTE *If the file <<Template>> (profile.dwt) is not already open, choose Window > Assets and choose the Templates category. The template you just created in the previous exercise—profile.dwt—appears in the list as "profile." In the Assets panel, double-click the name of the template to open it. Alternatively, you can select the name in the Assets panel list and click Edit at the bottom of the panel.*

2) From the Templates tab on the Insert bar, click the Editable Region icon.

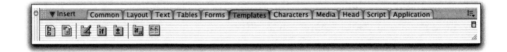

The New Editable Region dialog box opens.

3) Type header for the name and click OK.

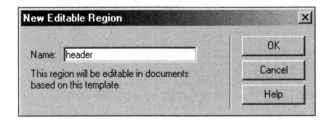

Don't use any special characters (quotation marks, brackets, etc.) for region names. Make each name unique—you can't use the same region name more than once in the same template.

Since you selected the table cell when you defined the editable region, the entire cell appears outlined in blue with a tab at the top displaying the name of the editable region. If you do not see the region names and outlines, choose View > Visual Aids > Invisible Elements.

NOTE *Multiple table cells cannot be designated as a single editable region. If you need multiple cells to be editable, you must either make the entire table editable, or break it up into several editable regions. If you try to select multiple cells within a table and make them editable, the whole table will become an editable region.*

4) Click inside the cell containing "About this lighthouse:" located below the header cell you just defined as editable. Position the insertion point after the colon (:) and press Return to create a new paragraph. Don't select the cell. Click the Editable Region icon on the Templates tab of the Insert bar and name the region description**.**

A new editable region is created inside the cell. You'll see the same blue outline with a tab at the top displaying the name of the editable region, and the word "description" will be placed inside the editable area. Later, when you apply this template to a document, you will select the text inside this area and replace it with text, images, or other content.

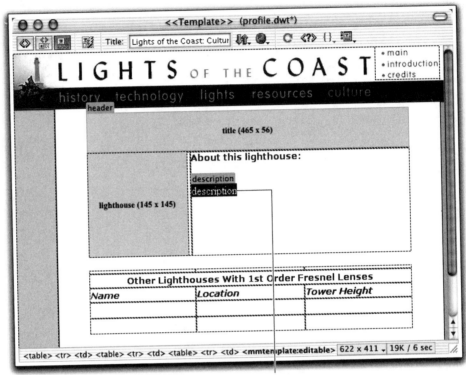

REGION NAME

NOTE *With this method, anything in the cell before or after selection in the blue outline will be uneditable in documents based on the template.*

5) Use the Tag Selector, as you did with the cell for the title placeholder, to select the cell for the lighthouse image placeholder. Click the Editable Region icon on the Templates tab of the Insert bar and name the region photo.

The names of all editable regions that you create are listed at the bottom of the Modify > Templates menu. A checkmark will appear next to an editable region in this list if one is selected, if the insertion point is in the region, or if an item in that region is selected.

6) Select the Next button in the table at the bottom of the page and click the Editable Region icon on the Templates tab of the Insert bar. Name the region next. **Do the same for the Previous button, naming the region** previous; **and for the cell with the copyright information, name the region** copyright.

NOTE *When you define the next and previous buttons as editable regions, the main table of the document may become selected when you click OK. This is due to the fact that these buttons are rollovers (the Swap Image Behavior is applied to each). Simply click outside the main table to deselect it.*

Anything that will need to change, including links, needs to be in an editable region.

When creating links in your original template file, use the folder icon to browse for the link or use the Point-to-File link creator. Both are located on the Property inspector. Don't type the link directly into the link field on the Property inspector, this can cause the links in your template to not work properly. Since templates are saved in the Templates folder, the pathnames may be different than you would expect. Dreamweaver is able to automatically generate the correct path when you direct it to the linked file using either of the two suggested methods.

7) Save your file.
The region names appear on tabs above all the outlined areas to help you identify which areas you've designated as editable.

NOTE *Many of the tools and features available for creating and editing your original templates will only be available in the Design View, which you have been working in. Some template controls are not available if you are in Code View, which you will work with in Lesson 12. If you are working in Code View and find yourself unable to perform certain template operations, switch to Design View.*

Leave this file open to use in the next exercise.

REMOVING EDITABLE REGIONS

You have designated certain areas of the template as "editable." You can also lock them again. In locked areas, elements cannot be changed directly on a page that has been created from the template. Any elements located in locked areas must be edited on the original template file itself.

1) In profile.dwt, click the tab for the region copyright **in the document window in order to select it.**

The Tag Selector at the bottom of the document window displays the template markup `<mmtemplate:editable>`.

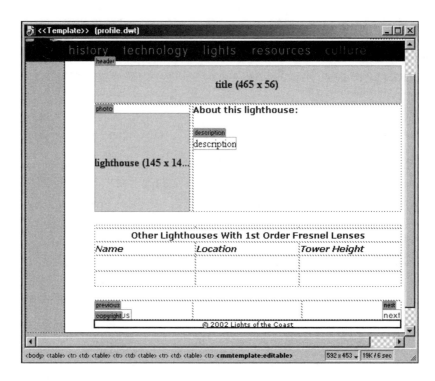

NOTE *If profile.dwt is not open, double-click the profile template in the Templates category of the Assets panel. You can use the Assets panel to move, rename, and delete template files. Use caution when deleting template files, since they cannot be recreated as easily as library items.*

2) Choose Modify > Templates > Remove Template Markup.

The outline designating the copyright cell as editable disappears and that portion of the template is now locked. Now it cannot be changed in files that are based on this template.

NOTE *If you remove an editable region from a template that has already had subsequent pages built from it, any of those pages that you modified previously in the editable region will be changed when you update the pages after saving the template (you will learn how to update pages later in this lesson). Any modifications to the region would be deleted on those pages because the area of the previously editable region changes to reflect the area as it appears in the template.*

284

CREATING OPTIONAL CONTENT

The optional content feature allows you to define whether the content is hidden or displayed in the pages based on the template. It enables you to set conditional or specific values for displaying content. You control these values through template parameters and conditional expressions.

1) In profile.dwt, select the table for "Other Lighthouses With 1st Order Fresnel Lenses" and the line of blank space above it by clicking just to the right of the table and dragging upwards and to the left until the pointer rests in the space created by the blank line above the table.

The table will look grayed-out to indicate that it has been selected along with the line break element before it. This table will be optional on pages that use the profile template.

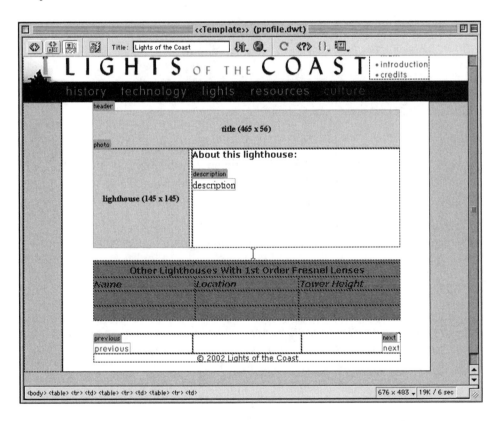

285

2) Click the Optional Region icon on the Templates tab of the Insert bar.

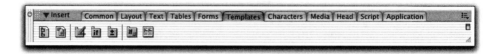

The New Optional Region dialog box opens with the Basic tab active.

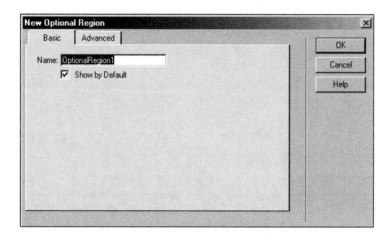

3) In the Basic tab of the Optional Content dialog box, uncheck the Show by Default box. Click OK to close the dialog box.

When creating your own Web site, if the content you define as optional will be used on the majority of your pages, you should leave this box checked. In this lesson, however, only one of the pages will use this content, so it is easier when creating subsequent pages if this content is hidden by default.

In this example, you are using the default name for the optional region.

NOTE *If you have already created an optional content region elsewhere on the page, the Advanced tab of the Optional Content dialog box lets you link that existing optional content region with the new one that you are creating. The Advanced tab also lets you create Template Expressions.*

INSERTING REPEATING REGIONS

A **repeating region** is an area on the page that needs to be duplicated one or more times. Repeating regions can be particularly useful when you need to have multiple entries, possibly a varying number, placed on pages built from your templates. Repeating regions allow you to have specific control over the appearance of tables with multiple entries. In this exercise, the table listing other lighthouses will use repeating regions.

1) In profile.dwt, select the two empty rows at the bottom of the table for "Other Lighthouses With 1st Order Fresnel Lenses."

Outlines appear around the cells to indicate they are selected.

2) Click the Repeating Region icon on the Templates tab of the Insert bar.

The New Repeating Region dialog box opens.

```
┌──────────── New Repeating Region ────────────┐
│                                               │
│  Name : [ RepeatRegion1          ]    [  OK  ]│
│                                               │
│  This region will appear multiple times in    │
│  documents based on this template.   [ Cancel]│
│                                               │
│                                      [  Help ]│
└───────────────────────────────────────────────┘
```

3) Name the region otherlights and click OK.

The rows you selected become outlined in a light blue color and a tab at the top of the outline displays the name "otherlights." The highlight color for repeating regions is the same as the highlight color for optional regions and lighter than the color for editable regions.

TIP *When developing your own Web sites, you may want to change the color of the highlighted regions if they don't show up against the colors used in your page. You can do so by choosing Edit > Preferences and select the Highlighting category. Click the Editable Regions color box and select a highlight color, or enter the hexadecimal value directly into the text field. Do the same as needed for the other highlight colors. The editable region color appears in the template itself and in documents based on the template; the locked region color appears only in documents based on the template. The default colors are blue (#66CCCC) for editable regions and pale yellow (#FFFFCC) for locked regions. You can click Show to enable or disable the display of these colors in the Document window. These highlight colors will only show in the document window if the option to view invisible elements is enabled. If invisible elements such as the highlighting on template regions do not appear in the document window, choose View > Visual Aids > Invisible Elements.*

4) Select the first cell in the bottom row, in the same column as the word "Name," in the empty row that you just made a repeating region. Click the Editable Region icon on the Templates tab of the Insert bar and type name for the region name.

TIP *To select the cell easily, place the pointer in the cell and click the last <td> tag on the Tag Selector.*

In order to make changes within a repeating region in any subsequent documents that are based on your profile template, the repeating region must contain as many editable regions as necessary.

NOTE *If a spacer row like the one used in this example is not placed between the top of the repeating region and the editable regions it contains, then it may be difficult to see the outline around this cell that designates it as an editable region. The outline and tab surrounding the top row, which indicate the row is defined as a repeating region, may obscure the outline of the editable region below. The spacer cell, however, will be included as part of each instance of the repeating region in the documents based on the profile template. If it is difficult to see the outline or tab indicating an editable region, you can confirm that the cell you made editable is indeed an editable region by clicking inside the cell and looking at the Tag Selector. The bold* **<td>** *tag corresponds to the cell you clicked in. Preceding that* **<td>** *tag will be the template markup* **<mmtemplate:editable>**.

5) Repeat step 4 for the next two cells in the bottom row, naming them location and height. Save the file.

Your document should look like the example shown here.

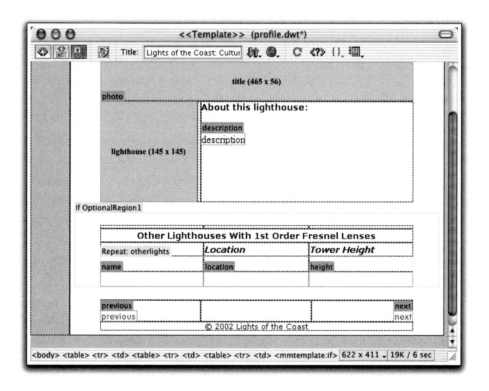

You can save and close the profile.dwt file.

BUILDING PAGES BASED ON A TEMPLATE

The third step in creating a site that makes use of templates is to create the actual pages that are based on your original template.

In this exercise, you will create new pages that use the profile template you created in the previous exercises of this lesson. These pages will inherit the contents of that original template. The only portions of the page you can change in these new pages will be those parts you defined as editable in the template.

The graphics you need for building the pages are located in the Lesson_09_Templates/ Images folder.

1) Choose File > New and select the Templates tab in the New Document Dialog box.

The New Document dialog box opens. In the Templates portion of the box, a list of the sites you have defined and a list of all the templates you've created for the chosen site appears.

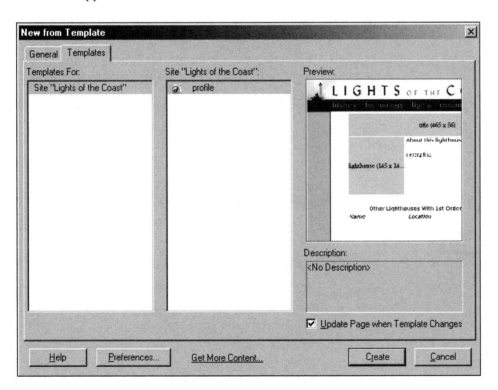

2) Choose profile from the list of templates for the "Lights of the Coast" site, leave the Update Page when Template Changes box checked, and then click Create.

A new page is created from the template. Although this document displays the inherited content, it still needs to be saved.

3) Save the file as pt_arena.html in the Lesson_09_Templates folder. Change the title of the page to Lights of the Coast: Lights: Point Arena.

In the new page, you'll see the highlight color of the locked regions (the default color is pale yellow) on the page. You can also see the template name on a tab of the same color at the top right of the document window.

The pointer will change to a circle with a line through it when you roll over it or try to click any of the locked regions. This indicates that those areas are not editable.

4) Replace the title placeholder in the header region by double-clicking on the placeholder image, then choosing the pt_arena_header.gif image to replace it with. Replace the lighthouse placeholder in the photo region with the pt_arena_img.jpg image and give it a 1-pixel border.

The placeholder images are now replaced with real content in this template-based document.

5) Open the pt_arena.txt file from Lesson_09_Templates/Text. Select and copy all of the text and paste it within the description region of your pt_arena.html file, replacing the text "description."

The text appears within an outlined border. The border color is the color of the editable regions. A tab at the upper left corner of the region displays the name of the region. When the region name is displayed within the cell as it is here, you should delete the title before placing text or images so that the title of the editable region does not remain on the page.

6) Format the description text with Verdana font, size –1.

NOTE *If the text causes the table to expand, you won't be able to get the table to shrink back to the proper size by clicking outside the table as you would do in a regular document. Since this document is based on a template, you will have to close and reopen the file in order for tables to adjust to the proper size in regard to their contents.*

Your page should now look like the following figure.

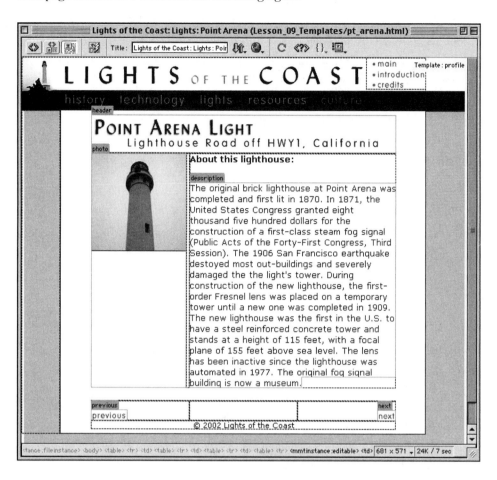

You can save and close the pt_arena.html file.

7) Repeat steps 1 through 6 to create pt_cabrillo.html and pt_reyes.html. Use the text from the pt_cabrillo.txt and pt_reyes.txt files in the Text folder and the images from the Images folder.

The Point Cabrillo images are pt_cabrillo_header.gif and pt_cabrillo_img.jpg.

The Point Reyes images are pt_reyes_header.gif and pt_reyes_img.jpg.

You have now created three pages from the profile template. You can close the pt_cabrillo.html file. Leave the pt_reyes.html file open for the next exercise.

CONTROLLING OPTIONAL CONTENT

In the profile template, you defined the table for a list of other lighthouses with 1st Order Fresnel lens as an optional region that would be hidden by default on pages based on that template. When you create and edit new pages using a template, you can show or hide any optional content areas that were created in the original template. In this exercise, you will prepare to develop the optional content for the Point Reyes Lighthouse profile by displaying the region.

1) In the pt_reyes.html document, choose Modify > Template Properties.

The Template Properties dialog box opens.

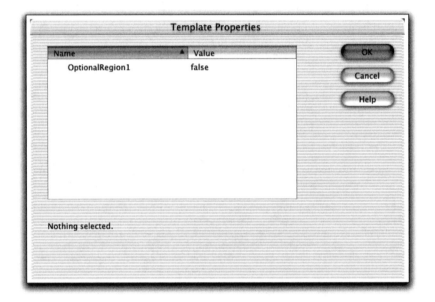

2) Select OptionalRegion1 from the list of names.

Once you've selected the region, options become available beneath the list boxes.

3) Check the Show OptionalRegion1 check box.

The value listed for OptionalRegion1 in the list of values changes from false (hidden) to true (shown).

4) Click OK to close the Template Properties dialog box.

You return to your document, and the table you created in the optional region on the profile template is now displayed in the pt_reyes.html document. Keep this file open for the next exercise.

ADDING REPEATING ENTRIES

The table for "Other Lighthouses With 1st Order Fresnel Lenses" that is now displayed in the pt_reyes.html document contains the repeating region you created in the profile template. In this exercise, you will use the repeating region to insert entries for five lighthouses.

1) In the "name" editable region in the pt_reyes.html document, located on the now visible optional region, type Robben Island Lighthouse; **type** Table Bay, South Africa **in the "location" editable region; and type** 59 feet **in the "height" editable region. Format each entry as Verdana, –1.**

The editable regions you placed in each cell allow you to enter content into the repeating regions.

2) On the Repeat:otherlights tab, click the plus sign (+) button.

TIP *You may have to roll over the text Repeat:otherlights on the tab in order to get the pointer to change to an arrow, which will allow you to click the button.*

A duplicate of the repeating region is added below the row in which you typed the information for the Robben Island Lighthouse. Since both the spacer row and the row for the information were selected when you defined the repeating region, the spacer row is included (making it easier to see the buttons on the repeating region tab). If you had selected only the last row for the information, there would be no spacer row.

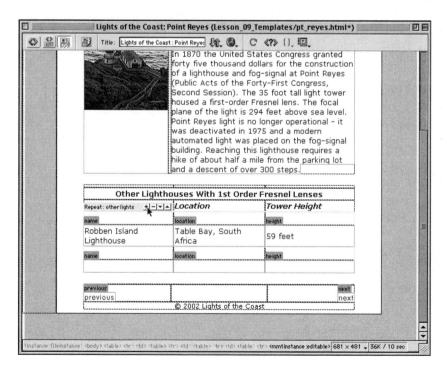

293

The four buttons on the repeating region tab allow you to add, delete, and change the order of the entries in this region.

3) Use the lighthouse information that follows to add four more entries to the table.

NAME	LOCATION	TOWER HEIGHT
Inubo-Saki Lighthouse	Cape Inubo, Japan	103 feet
South Stack Lighthouse	Holyhead Island, UK	197 feet
Jupiter Inlet Lighthouse	Jupiter, Florida	105 feet
St. Bees Lighthouse	St. Bees Head, UK	56 feet

You now have five entries of lighthouse information in this table.

4) Place the insertion point in the cell for the Inubo-Saki Lighthouse. Use the up arrow button on the Repeating Region tab to move this entry up to the top of the list.
The arrow buttons allow you to move the entries up or down in the region.

5) Use the up and down arrow buttons on the repeating region table to adjust the remaining entries in the table so the names appear in alphabetical order. Save the file.

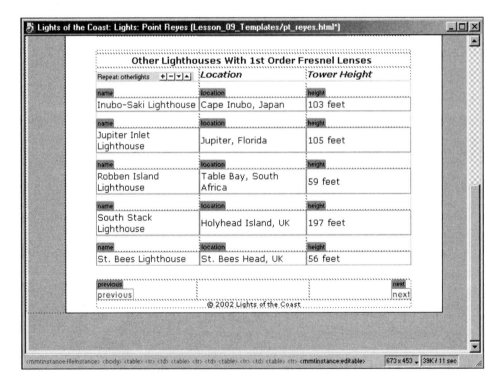

You can close the pt_reyes.html file.

MODIFYING A TEMPLATE

The use of a template makes it very easy to build multiple pages using the design of your original template. The person creating the page can just add the content that changes from page to page, but will not be able to make changes to any of the locked areas.

The real time savings comes when you need to make changes to all the pages that were built using the template. Without a template, you'd have to edit each page. With the use of a template, you simply edit the original template file to update all the pages built with the template.

1) In the Templates category of the Assets panel, double-click the profile template you've been using.

The original template you created earlier in this lesson opens.

2) Select the Lights navigation button, located on the black bar near the top of the page. Click the folder icon next to the Link text box in the Property inspector and browse to find the lights.html file in the Lesson_09_Templates folder.

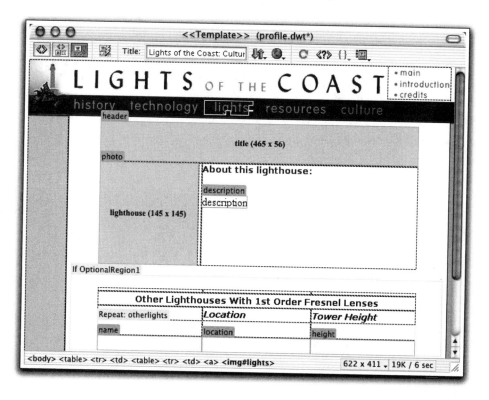

The Lights navigation button is now linked to the correct file.

295

3) Save the template.

Since you have made changes to the template, the Update Template Files dialog box opens, displaying a list of all the files that have been built from this template.

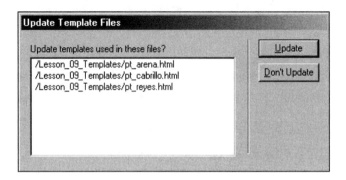

4) Click Update to modify all the pages with the change you just made. Close the log of updates that appears.

TIP *When creating your own Web sites, if you wish you can choose Don't Update. You can then update the pages later by choosing Modify > Templates > Update Pages.*

The pt_arena.html, pt_cabrillo.html, and pt_reyes.html documents that you created earlier from the template will all be updated with the new link. The ability to update all pages associated with a template can be very useful. If you have a navigation section of the template with graphics for links (like the Lights of the Coast pages you've been working with), you can set those graphics and their links in the template. If the links change, you simply change the template, and all pages designed with the template are updated.

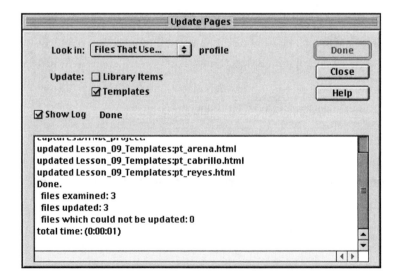

NOTE *You can detach a page from a template by choosing Modify > Templates > Detach From Template. A detached page is completely editable, but it will no longer be updated if the template is changed. You can also uncheck the Update Page When Template Changes check box on the New Document dialog box to create a copy of the page, completely independent from the template. This creates a page that functions much like stationery and does not have any template markup. Pages created in this manner will not be updated if the template changes.*

5) Open the pt_arena.html file and preview it in the browser.

The link to the Lights page should work on this page, as well as on the other two pages, pt_cabrillo.html and pt_reyes.html, that you built from the template.

NOTE *If you want to create content that is controlled by CSS (covered in Lesson 13) you should use an external style sheet in order to make it possible to update the style sheet without having to update the template.*

CREATING EDITABLE TAG ATTRIBUTES

Editable tag attributes allow you to define tags that can be changed in the subsequent documents based on the original template.

1) In the profile template, profile.dwt, click to place the insertion point in the white space to the right of the first table containing the header, photo, and description editable regions. Select the last <td> tag in the Tag Selector.

The document window now outlines the cell that provides the white background for all the tables you have created by clicking the **<td>** tag in the Tag Selector.

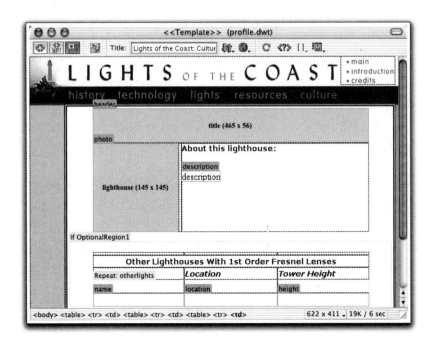

2) Choose Modify > Templates > Make Attribute Editable.

The Editable Tag Attributes dialog box opens.

3) In the Editable Tag Attributes dialog box, select BGCOLOR from the Attribute drop-down menu.

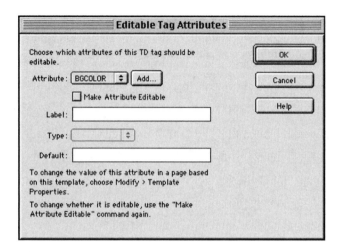

The BGCOLOR attribute only appears in this menu because a background color was defined for the cell (also known as table data or **<td>**). In order for an attribute to appear, you must set that attribute initially.

NOTE *If you want to define an attribute as editable, and it is not listed in the Attribute drop-down menu, you can click Add and enter the name of the attribute you would like to add. Attribute names must be typed in uppercase. If you define the attribute first as you did in this exercise, then the Label, Type, and Default settings will be set automatically. Adding an attribute yourself requires you to be familiar with HTML tags and their attributes. You can use the Reference panel, located in the Code panel group, to learn more about tags and their attributes. For example, if you select TD in the Tag drop-down menu on the Reference panel, you can learn about that tag's attributes by clicking the Description drop-down menu and selecting one of the tag attributes, such as bgcolor.*

4) Click the Make Attribute Editable check box. Leave the Label, Type, and Default settings as they are and click OK. Save the profile template, click Update, close the Update Pages dialog box and close the file.

The Editable Tag Attributes dialog box closes. The background color of the main cell is now an editable tag. The color of the background in the profile.dwt document will change because of the code used to make that attribute editable in the files that

298

use the profile template. The profile.dwt template may not display as expected if you preview it in the browser after making bgcolor attribute editable. In order for Dreamweaver to create the necessary template markup that allows it to control all documents based on the template, the code displayed in the Bg text field is `@@bgcolor@@`. This kind of markup is necessary for the template to function and will not cause viewing irregularities in the final documents that are based on the template.

NOTE *To relock a tag that has previously been defined as editable, you must select the tag and choose Modify > Templates > Make Attribute Editable. Select the attribute you want to lock from the Attribute drop-down menu and uncheck the Make Attribute Editable check box.*

MODIFYING AN EDITABLE TAG ATTRIBUTE

The ability to create editable tag attributes makes the possibilities for creating templates much greater. You can potentially make a wide variety of tag attributes editable which will give you a great deal of control over the individual documents created from your original template. Attributes such as background color, alignment, and size can increase the usefulness and flexibility of your template-based documents.

1) Open the pt_cabrillo.html document and choose Modify › Template Properties.
The Template Properties dialog box opens, and the bgcolor tag attribute that you made editable in the previous exercise now appears in the Name list. You can see in the Value column that the default setting for this attribute is #FFFFFF.

2) Select the bgcolor attribute.

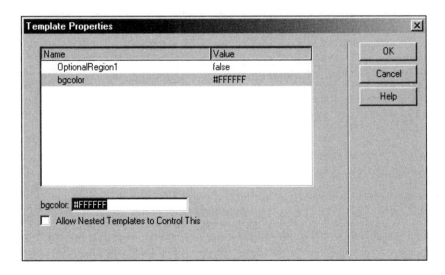

Options for editing the tag appear below the list. In this case, you are provided with a text field in which you can change the color.

3) Replace #FFFFFF in the bgcolor text field with #99CC99 and click OK to close the dialog box.

The color of the cell is now changed to light green.

You can save and close the pt_cabrillo.html file.

TIP *Knowing HTML will help you to make the most of editable tag attributes. If you don't know HTML, using the Reference panel will help you to understand the different tags and the functions of their attributes. Defining the attribute before you choose to make it editable will also help. If you do know HTML, you will be able to make use of a very powerful template feature.*

300

CREATING NESTED TEMPLATES

A **nested template** is one that inherits a master layout from a base template. You can create a base template with the main content that should appear on all pages, and then use a nested template to create specific content or a layout style for a certain section in your site. If you have an additional section in which you want to use a different layout while keeping the main site components such as main navigation, footer, and header, you can create another nested template that is also based on your main template. Nested templates are most useful for creating a series of page styles with variations in their layout and design that derive their common content from a main template. You will need to make some modifications to the profile template in the following steps before you can create the nested template.

1) Open the profiles template, profile.dwt, from the Assets panel. Select the first table that contains the header, photo, and description regions. Click the Optional Region on the Templates tab of the Insert bar. Title the region mainTable **and click OK.**

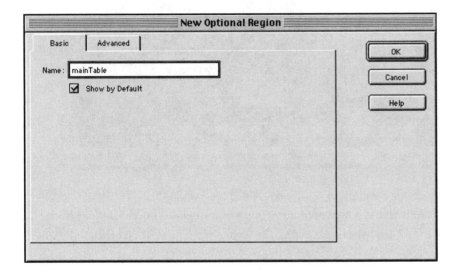

You've left the Show by Default option checked because most documents that you would want to create based on the profile template will need that table.

You have made this table an optional region so you will be able to discard it when you create a nested template.

2) Place the insertion point to the right of the main table you just made an optional region. Select the `<mmtemplate:if>` tag in the Tag Selector and press the right arrow key once. Press Return (Macintosh) or Enter (Windows) to create a second paragraph below the optional main table. Click the Optional Region on the Templates tab of the Insert bar. Title the region nestedArea, **uncheck the Show by Default check box, and click OK. Double-click inside the nestedArea region and click the Editable Region on the Templates tab of the Insert bar. Title the region** photoTable **and click OK.**

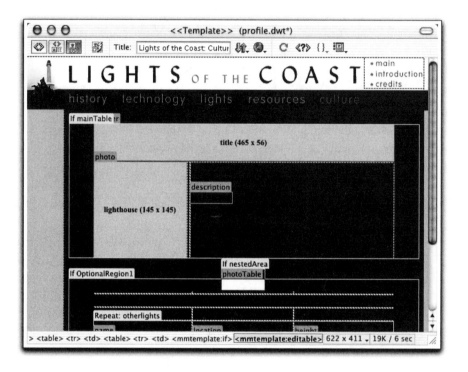

This empty, editable optional region will allow you to place content in this space in your nested template without affecting the layout of the pages that are based on the original profile template.

3) Save the profile.dwt document and click Update to update all pages which use the profile template. Close the Update Pages dialog box and the profile.dwt document.
Now that you have modified the original profile template, you are ready to create the nested template in the remaining steps.

4) Choose File > New. From the Templates tab, locate the profile template and click Create.
A new page using the profile template is created. You are going to use the profile template as your base template in this exercise.

5) Choose File > Save As Template and name the nested template you are creating profile_photos.

By saving the document you created from the original template as a template itself, you are creating a nested template. Now that you have created the nested template, you will edit it. Dreamweaver will automatically add the extension.

6) Choose Modify > Template Properties. Select nestedArea from the list and check the Show nestedArea check box below the list. Select mainTable from the list and uncheck the Show mainTable check box below the list. Click OK to close the dialog box.

The mainTable region is hidden and the nestedArea now appears on the page. Most of the page is locked, as it was defined in the original template. You now need to create editable regions in the nested template.

7) Open images_table.html. Select and copy the table on the page. Replace the text nestedArea in the photoTable region on the profile_photos.dwt document by selecting it and pasting the copied table. Close the images_table.html document.

In this example, you are creating a page with photographs of the Point Reyes Lighthouse. This page needs to have many of the same elements as the other documents in the Lighthouse Profiles section, yet it also needs to have a substantially different layout due to the type of materials that will be contained on the page.

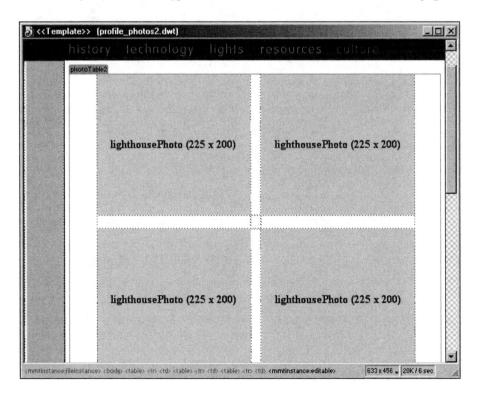

303

8) Select each of the placeholder images and make them individual editable regions.

The table on this page uses a layout specifically designed to display additional photographs of the lighthouses. You can use region names of photo1, photo2, and so on.

9) Save and close the profile_photos.dwt template document. Choose File > New and select the Templates tab. Choose profile_photos.dwt and click OK. Save the new document as pt_reyes_photos.html.

You have now created a document based on a nested template that is controlled by the base profile template you created at the beginning of this lesson.

10) Place the following photos in the pt_reyes_photos.html document: pt_reyes1.jpg, pt_reyes2.jpg, pt_reyes3.jpg, pt_reyes4.jpg, pt_reyes5.jpg, and pt_reyes6.jpg. Give each image a 1-pixel border.

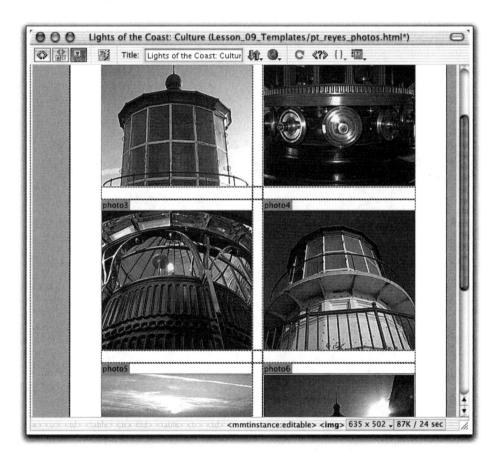

You can save and close the pt_reyes_photos.html document.

WHAT YOU HAVE LEARNED

In this lesson, you have:

- Created a template from an existing page by saving the page as a template (pages 277–278)

- Added editable areas to the template in order to allow changes to be made on pages built from that template (pages 279–283)

- Removed editable areas from the template in order to prevent changes from being made on pages built from that template (pages 283–284)

- Created optional content areas that could be shown or hidden in subsequent pages (pages 285–286, 292)

- Inserted repeating regions that allow pages based on the template to have as many or as few entries as needed (pages 286–288, 293–294)

- Changed the template highlight colors for both editable and locked regions (page 287)

- Built multiple pages based on the template in order to create pages with the same layout (pages 289–291)

- Made changes to the template and updated multiple pages within the site to reflect those changes (pages 295–297)

- Created and used editable tag attributes for more control over specific elements (pages 297–300)

- Nested a template to create a variation on the main layout that is still controlled by the original template (pages 301–304)

creating
frames

Frames are created by splitting the browser window into rectangular areas that contain independent HTML content. Frames are commonly used to define navigation and content areas for a page. Typically, the navigation area remains constant and the content area changes each time a navigation link is clicked. This use of frames can be extremely helpful to a user for navigation through a site. This can also make a site easier to modify since there is only one navigation page to update. On the other hand, frames can degrade a Web site if they are poorly implemented: They may be confusing and disorienting to users if they do not provide a clear site structure, they may make it difficult for users to bookmark or find their way back to a previous page, or they may make the content difficult to view if they are not properly sized and formatted.

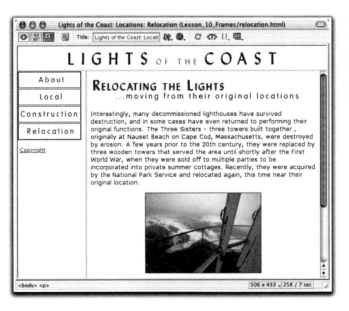

In this lesson, you will create and change the properties of framesets and frames, resize frames, and use links to control their contents.

When a user views a Web page that has been created with two frames, the browser is actually using three separate files to display the page: the frameset file and the two files containing the content that appears inside each of the two frames. A **frameset** is an HTML file that is invisible to the user and defines the structure of a Web page with frames. A frameset stores information about the size and location of each frame, along with the names of the files that supply the content for each of the frames. Each frame is a separate HTML file. Frames have borders that can be turned off so the frames are not readily apparent to the user, or they can be turned on to clearly split the window into different panes. Other options include scroll bars and the possibility of allowing the user to resize the frames by dragging the borders.

In this lesson, you will work with frames to create a Web page with a navigation area and a content area. You will develop a set of pages that will all appear in the content frame when the user selects a link from the navigation frame, and you'll learn how to target links to different frames. You will also learn how to include content for browsers that do not support frames.

To see an example of the finished page for this chapter, open locations.html from the Lesson_10_Frames/Completed folder.

WHAT YOU WILL LEARN

In this lesson, you will:

- Create a frameset
- Save a frameset
- Create frames and nested frames
- Resize frames
- Change frameset and frame properties
- Create documents within frames
- Create a navigation bar
- Target frame content
- Create NoFrames content

APPROXIMATE TIME

This lesson should take about one hour to complete.

LESSON FILES

Media Files:

Lesson_10_Frames/Images/…(all files)

Starting Files:

Lesson_10_Frames/Text/…(all files)

Lesson_10_Frames/copyright.html

Completed Project:

Lesson_10_Frames/Completed/about.html

Lesson_10_Frames/Completed/construction.html

Lesson_10_Frames/Completed/copyright.html

Lesson_10_Frames/Completed/local_history.html

Lesson_10_Frames/Completed/locations.html

Lesson_10_Frames/Completed/nav_bar.html

Lesson_10_Frames/Completed/relocation.html

Lesson_10_Frames/Completed/title_bar.html

CREATING A FRAMESET

A frameset defines the overall look of the framed page—the number of frame areas on the page, the size of each frame, and the border attributes. In this lesson, you will create a Web page consisting of two frames. The left frame will hold navigation elements that remain constant. The right frame will display pages with content that is relative to the links clicked in the navigation frame.

There are two ways to create a frameset in Dreamweaver: You can manually insert the frames, or you can choose from several predefined framesets. If you choose a predefined frameset, the frameset and frames are automatically set up for you. This is a quick way to create a layout using frames because most of the work is done for you. You just need to name the individual pages.

In this exercise, you will use a predefined frameset to make a Web page that uses frames.

1) Create a new basic HTML file, but do not save it.

You must insert frames into the document in order for this page to become a frameset.

2) Choose View > Visual Aids > Frame Borders.

A thick border will appear around the page edges in the document window.

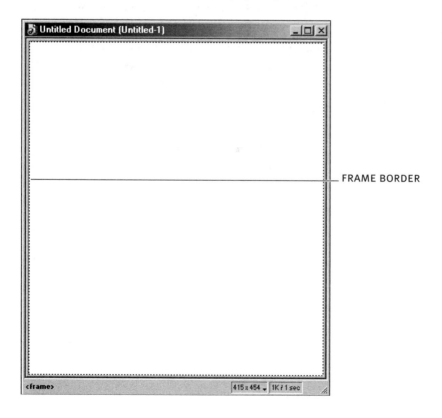

FRAME BORDER

3) Click the Top Frame icon on the Frames tab of the Insert bar.

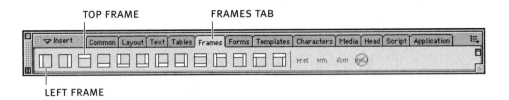

TOP FRAME   FRAMES TAB

LEFT FRAME

The page is divided into two frames: a short frame on the top and a taller frame on the bottom. A thin gray line marks the division.

NOTE *To insert frames manually, drag the border surrounding the page into the document window. The document will become split horizontally (if you drag from the top or bottom of the border) or vertically (if you drag from the left or right sides of the border). If you drag the border from the corner, the document will become divided into four frames. You can also choose Modify > Frameset > Split Frame Left, Right, Up, or Down.*

4) Click to place the insertion point in the bottom frame. Click the Left Frame icon on the Frames tab of the Insert bar.

This creates another frameset inside the bottom frame. This second frameset is called a **nested frameset** because it is inside another frame. The single bottom frame has now been divided into two frames: a narrow frame on the left and a wider frame on the right. Several of Dreamweaver's predefined framesets use nested framesets. You can use combinations of these predefined framesets as you have done in this exercise to come up with any frame layout you want.

NOTE *If you selected the wrong frames configuration or need to reduce the number of frames in your frameset, you can remove the extra frames by dragging the border of the unwanted frame to the edge of the page or atop another frame. The extra frame will disappear.*

Your page should now look similar to the example shown here.

Leave this file open to use in the next exercise.

SAVING A FRAMESET

When you have the page set with the number of frames you want, you need to save the frameset. The frameset and the files for each frame need to be saved before you can preview the page in a browser. If you attempt to preview the page in the browser prior to saving, Dreamweaver displays a message stating that all documents need to to be saved in order to preview. The frameset file is the one you reference when linking to this Web page. You can save each file individually, or you can save all open files at once. In this exercise, you will save only the frameset.

1) In the document window, click the border around the edges of the document window to select the frameset.

TIP *You can also select the frameset by choosing Window > Others > Frames and then clicking the outermost border enclosing the frames in the Frames panel. The Frames panel shows you a simplified version of the structure of frames in the document.*

In the document window, all frame borders within the frameset are outlined by a dotted line, and the Tag Selector at the bottom of the window displays <frameset>. The document's title bar shows "Untitled Document (UntitledFrameset-1)," and the Property inspector shows the frameset properties. The number (-1, -2, etc.) of your untitled document may vary depending on how many new documents you have created.

NOTE *If only one frame is selected, only that frame border will appear in the document window with a dotted line. In documents that have nested framesets, only the frames in the selected frameset display with a dotted line.*

In the Frames panel, framesets are displayed with a thick border, and frames are displayed with a thin border.

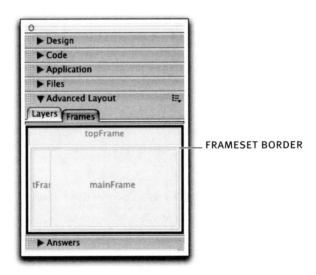

FRAMESET BORDER

2) Choose File > Save Frameset As and save the file as locations.html in the Lesson_10_Frames folder.

The document's title bar shows the file name and location is Lesson_10_Frames/locations.html.

NOTE *The default, temporary name given to the frameset was UntitledFrameset-1.html.*

3) With the frameset still selected, type Lights of the Coast: Locations **for the page title.**

If you don't have the frameset selected when you title the page, you are titling one of the pages in the frameset—not the frameset file. The document title bar displays the selected page title and the filename. If you have the frameset selected, the document title bar displays the frameset title and filename. Refer to the Frames panel to check what is selected; this will help ensure you are working within the frame or frameset that you intend to edit.

Leave the locations.html file open to use in the next exercise.

RESIZING FRAMES IN A FRAMESET

You can use the Property inspector to specify the size of your frames, or you can simply drag the borders in the document window to perform the same task. In addition to specifying a size in the Property inspector, you can also determine how browsers will allocate space to frames when there is not enough room to display all frames at full size.

1) In the document window, position the pointer over the horizontal border between the top and bottom frames. When the pointer changes to a double arrow, click the border once to select the first frameset.

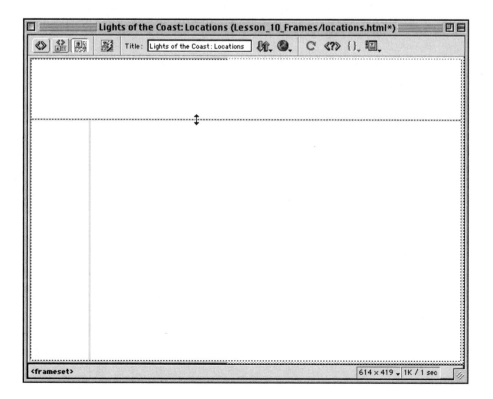

The frame borders in the document window will become dotted. The Tag Selector will display **<frameset>**, and the Frames panel will show the outermost frameset border selected.

The Property inspector shows the Frameset properties. The Property inspector will change depending on whether you have selected a frameset or a frame. In order to change the size of the frames, you will need to make sure you have selected the frameset.

NOTE *Click the expander arrow on the Property inspector to view all Frameset properties if they are not already visible.*

2) Drag the border between the top and bottom frames until the top frame is 50 pixels high.

Use the Row Value in the Property inspector to check the height, or type **50** in the Row Value text field to get the exact height. Make sure Pixels is selected from the Unit drop-down menu.

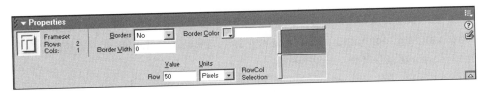

3) With the outer frameset still selected, click the bottom row in the RowCol Selection area on the Property inspector to select the bottom frame of the frameset. Next to the Row Value text field, verify that Relative is selected from the Unit drop-down menu.

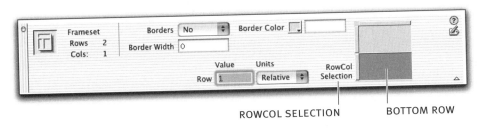

ROWCOL SELECTION   BOTTOM ROW

This will allow the bottom row to expand or contract depending on how large the user's browser is and how much space is left after the top row has been allocated the 50 pixels that were assigned to it. By default, Dreamweaver will automatically place a 1 in the Row Value text field. If you view the HTML code for the frameset size you will see `frameset rows="50,*"`. The 1 in the Row Value text field, in conjunction with the Relative unit chosen from the menu, is the same as the asterisk (*) in the code; it represents a size that is relative or proportional to the other rows in the frameset.

4) In the Frames panel, click the nested frameset, represented by the thick inner border around the two columns in the bottom row, to select it. In the visual representation of the frame on the Property inspector, click the left column in the RowCol Selection area to select the left frame.

The left column in the Property inspector darkens to indicate it has been selected. Use these tabs to select the columns or rows in a frameset.

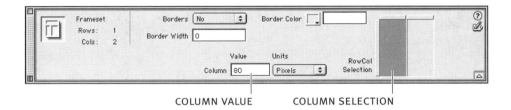

COLUMN VALUE   COLUMN SELECTION

5) In the Column Value text field of the Property inspector, type 150 and press Return (Macintosh) or Enter (Windows). Verify that Pixels is selected from the Unit drop-down menu.

The left frame's width is adjusted to 150 pixels.

NOTE *When you are deciding how to resize the frame, keep these unit options in mind:*

Pixels: *This option sets the absolute size of the selected column or row to the number of pixels that you enter. It is the best option for any frame that needs to have a set size. If other columns or rows are defined by a different Unit option, those other columns or rows are allocated space only after rows or columns specified in pixels are their full size.*

Percent: *This option specifies a percentage that the current column or row should take up in its frameset. Columns or rows specified with units set to Percent are allocated space after columns or rows with units set to Pixels and before columns or rows with units set to Relative.*

Relative: *This option specifies that the current column or row will be allocated space using the current proportions relative to the other columns and rows. Columns or rows with units set to Relative are allocated space after columns or rows with units set to Pixels and Percent, but they take up all remaining space. If you set the bottom or the right frame to relative, the frame size changes to fill the remaining width or height of the browser window.*

315

6) In the Property inspector, click the tab above the right column to select the right frame of the nested frameset. Next to the Column Value text field, verify that Relative is selected from the Unit drop-down menu.

This will allow the right column to expand or contract depending on how large the user's browser is and how much space remains after the left column has been allocated the 150 pixels assigned to it.

7) Save the frameset by choosing File > Save Frameset.

If this command is not available, first select the outer frameset by clicking the border between the top and bottom frames.

NOTE *If you have the frameset selected, Command+S (Macintosh) or Control+S (Windows) saves the frameset only.*

Leave the locations.html file open to use in the next exercise.

SPECIFYING FRAME PROPERTIES

When you create a frameset, get in the habit of naming each frame. The name you assign to a frame does not name the file that appears in the frame—it just identifies the framed area of the document for your reference. Naming your frames is important when you create links to display pages within a framed area. In the previous exercise, you used the predefined top and left framesets. Each frame in the frameset has already been given a default name. In this exercise, you will change the name to reflect the future content of the frame.

1) Select the top frame by clicking inside the top frame in the Frames panel.

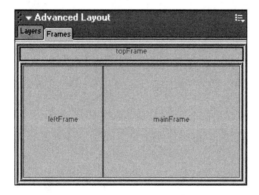

TIP *If the Frames panel is not open, choose Window > Others > Frames.*

The Frames panel shows a dark border around the top frame with the name "topFrame" shown in the center. The Property inspector displays frame properties for topFrame.

Remember that selecting the top frame is different from placing the insertion point in it. If the pointer is in the top frame, it will be the active frame; however, you won't be able to make changes to the frame properties. In order to affect the properties of the frame itself, it needs to be selected.

TIP *You can also Shift+Option-click (Macintosh) or Alt-click (Windows) in the top frame in the document window to select the frame.*

2) In the Frame Name text field on the Property inspector, type title to replace the default name topFrame. Press Return (Macintosh) or Enter (Windows), or click in the document window to apply the name.

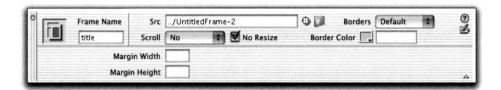

The Frames panel displays the word "title" in the top frame. You can always refer to the Frames panel for the name of a particular frame.

NOTE *Don't use spaces, hyphens, periods, or special characters in the frame name, and don't begin the name with an underscore.*

3) Verify that No is selected in the Scroll drop-down menu and that the No Resize box is checked on the Property inspector.

The scroll option defines when scroll bars appear and applies to both vertical and horizontal scroll bars. The Auto setting will display scroll bars whenever there is not enough room in the frame to display the content of the page. The Default option is the browser default setting, which is usually Auto. Be careful how you set this option—if it is set to No and the frame is not large enough to display all the contents, the user will be unable to scroll to see the rest of the content; if it is set to Yes and the contents fit within the frame, scroll bars that are grayed out will still take up space on the page even though it isn't possible to scroll.

No Resize locks the size of the frame when viewed in the browser. If this option is unchecked, users will be able to drag the frame borders in their browser window.

Regardless of whether this option is checked or unchecked, it will not affect your ability to resize frames within Dreamweaver.

4) Select the bottom left frame and name it nav. Scroll should be set to No and the No Resize box should be checked.

On the Property inspector, notice that the Borders drop-down menu has Default selected. The predefined framesets that you used to create the page layout are automatically set to have no frame borders. When the Default setting is selected for the Borders option of an individual frame, that frame uses the setting of the parent frameset. If another setting (Yes or No) is selected, then the frame will override the setting of the parent frameset.

The Frames panel displays the name "nav" in the bottom left frame.

5) Select the bottom right frame and name it content. Scroll should be set to No and the No Resize box should be checked.

On the Property inspector, notice that the text fields for Margin Width and Margin Height are blank. This is the default for the predefined framesets you used to layout your page. Margin Width sets the left and right margins of the frame in pixels. Margin Height sets the top and bottom margins of the frame in pixels. Leaving them blank will use the browser default, which may vary in size depending on the browser version and type.

The Frames panel displays the name "content" in the bottom right frame.

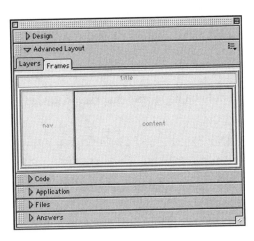

6) Choose File > Save Frameset.

When you change Frame properties, you are actually modifying the frameset, locations.html. Frame and frameset properties are both defined within the frameset.

Leave the locations.html file open to use in the next exercise.

CREATING AND EDITING FRAMES CONTENT

Remember that the content of a frame is a separate HTML page. You can create the page on its own or within the constraints of the frame. Using the frameset to help you design the pages that will be contained in each frame is always a good idea. That way, you don't create a page that's too wide or too narrow for the frame. Your users will find the pages difficult to view if they have to scroll in multiple directions to see all the content.

In this exercise, you will add content to each page in the frameset.

1) Place the insertion point in the title frame (the top frame).

The document title bar changes to show that this is an untitled, unsaved document.

2) Choose File › Save Frame. Save the file as title_bar.html in the Lesson_10_Frames folder and title it Lights of the Coast: Locations: Title. In the Page Properties, set the background to white, and type 0 into all four margin-text fields.

The document title bar changes to reflect the title and filename for the document in this frame. The title is actually unneccessary because the browser will use the title of the frameset in the browser window. Still, it is good practice to always title your documents. That way, if this page is opened in a window by itself for any reason, it will contain a title.

3) Insert the lights_title.gif from the Lesson_10_Frames/Images folder into the title frame and center it.

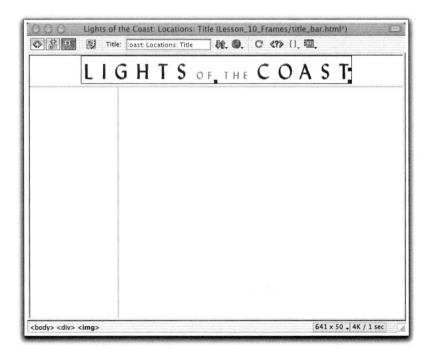

Save this document again. As you edit your pages, remember to save often. When you use the Save command, you are only saving the currently selected file. This does not save the frameset; you must do this separately. If you want to save a file located in another frame, just click inside its frame in the document window and then save. Refer to the Frames panel to check which frame you are saving.

4) Place the insertion point in the content frame (the right frame). Save the file as about.html in the Lesson_10_Frames folder and title it Lights of the Coast: Locations: About. Choose Modify > Page Properties to set the background of the document to white and the text to black. Set the links to #330000, the visited links to #333333 and the active links to #660000.

The document title bar changes to reflect the title and filename for the document in this frame.

5) In the about.html document, place the about_header.gif at the top of the document. Copy the text from Lesson_10_Frames/Text/about.txt and paste it on a new paragraph line below the graphic header. Format this text as Verdana, –1.

This is the content page that will correspond with the About link that you will create on a navigation bar later in this lesson.

6) Place the about_lights.jpg image from the Lesson_10_Frames/Images folder on a new paragraph line below the text, center the image and give it a 1-pixel border. Save the file.

Your content frame should now look like the example shown here.

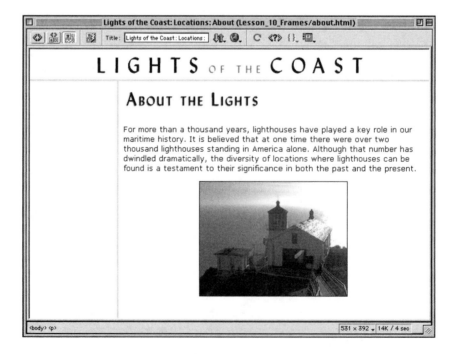

CREATING OTHER CONTENT DOCUMENTS

You now need to create additional documents to open in the content frame.

1) Choose File > New to create a new HTML document. Save the file as local_history.html in the Lesson_10_Frames folder and title it Lights of the Coast: Locations: Local History. **Choose Modify > Page Properties to set the background to white and the text to black. Set the links to #330000, the visited links to #333333, and the active links to #660000.**

The document title bar changes to reflect the title and filename for the document.

2) In the local_history.html document, place the location_header.gif at the top of the document. Copy the text from Lesson_10_Frames/Text/local_history.txt and paste it on a new paragraph line below the graphic header. Format this text as Verdana, –1.

This is the content page that will correspond with a Local History link, you will create on a navigation bar later in this lesson.

3) Repeat steps 1 and 2 to create construction.html in the Lesson_10_Frames folder. Title it Lights of the Coast: Locations: Construction. **Use construct_header.gif for the graphic header and construction.txt for the text.**

This is the content page that will correspond with a Construction link you will create on a navigation bar later in this lesson.

4) Repeat steps 1 and 2 to create relocation.html in the Lesson_10_Frames folder. Title it Lights of the Coast: Locations: Relocation. **Use relocate_header.gif for the graphic header and relocation.txt for the text.**

This is the content page that will correspond with a Relocation link you will create on a navigation bar later in this lesson.

You can close local_history.html, construction.html, and relocation.html. Leave the locations.html file open to use in the next exercise.

ADDING A NAVIGATION BAR

A **navigation bar** is a set of images used to link to pages in your site. Navigation bars are similar to simple rollovers (covered in Lesson 5) in their ease of use. Navigation bars, however, allow you to add up to four states for each image to display, based on user interaction. The first state of an image in a navigation bar is known as Up Image and appears when the page first loads. The second state of an image is called Over Image and is displayed when the user rolls over the image. (These states are the same two that occur in a simple rollover.) In a navigation bar, you have two additional states that you can use. When the user clicks the image, the third state, Down Image, is displayed. The fourth state of an image, Over While Down Image, is displayed when the user rolls over an image after the image has been clicked.

The navigation bar is effective for adding user feedback. You can make the third image look like a "clicked" button, indicating that it has been selected. Users will then understand what pages they are looking at based on the selected button. When the user is on a home page, for example, the Home Page button could look like the clicked button, while all of the other buttons would be in their normal states. When the user clicks another button, the user goes to that page; that page's button is in the clicked state, and the Home Page button returns to normal. On each visited page, the appropriate button appears to be clicked, and the others are back to their normal states.

NOTE *To use navigation bars without frames, you can create them on one page and then copy them to the other pages in your site. Then you will need to modify the behaviors for each button on all the other pages.*

1) Place the insertion point in the nav frame (the bottom left frame). Save the file as nav_bar.html in the Lesson_10_Frames folder and title it Lights of the Coast: Locations. Choose Modify > Page Properties to set the background to white and the text to black, and type 0 into all four margin-text fields. Set the links to #330000, the visited links to #333333, and the active links to #660000.

The document title bar changes to reflect the title and file name for the document in this frame.

2) Place the insertion point in the nav frame. Choose Insert > Interactive Images > Navigation Bar.

Clicking in the nav frame will enable you to edit the nav_bar.html document. This will be your navigation frame. It will contain links to various pages that will appear in the content frame to the right. These will be the links you target to open files in the content frame.

The Insert Navigation Bar dialog box opens.

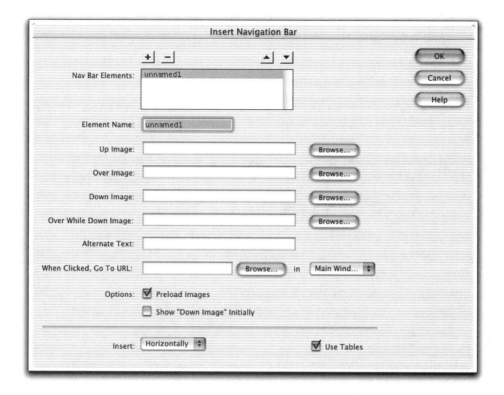

3) In the Element Name text field, type about as the name of the first image in the navigation bar to replace the unnamed1 element name.

The graphics you need are located in the Lesson_10_Frames/Images folder.

4) Click the Browse button next to the Up Image text field and locate the about.gif file. Click the Browse button next to the Over Image text field and locate the about_2.gif file. Click the Browse button next to the Down Image text field and locate the about_3.gif file. Click the Browse button next to the Over While Down Image text field and locate the about_4.gif file.

These different image states will display according to the user actions. The image you chose for the Over Image option will display in the browser when the viewer rolls over the image you chose for the Up Image option. The Up Image is the first state and the original image the user will see.

5) Click the Browse button next to the When Clicked, Go To URL text field, and choose the about.html file in the Lesson_10_Frames folder. In the drop-down menu initially displaying Main Window, choose content.

The file named in When Clicked, Go To URL is the link to which the user will be directed.

6) Choose Vertically from the Insert drop-down menu. Leave Preload Images checked, leave Show "Down Image" Initially unchecked, and leave Use Tables checked.

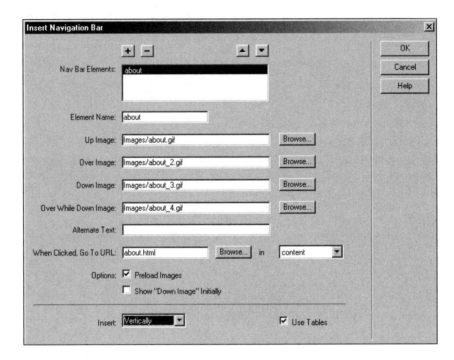

The Insert Vertically option inserts a vertical table that contains your buttons when you exit the dialog box.

As you make changes in the dialog box, the name of the element being changed appears in the Nav Bar Elements list at the top of the dialog box.

7) Click the plus sign (+) button at the top of the dialog box to add more buttons. Repeat steps 3 through 5, entering the images for local, construction, and relocation.

For the local image, link to local_history.html; for the construction image, link to construction.html; and for the relocation image, link to relocation.html.

TIP *You can click the up and down arrow buttons, located above the Nav Bar Elements list, to adjust the order of the buttons if necessary.*

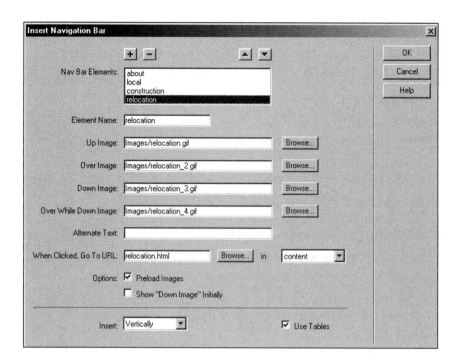

8) Click OK when you finish.

The table with all your buttons ready to go is placed in the document.

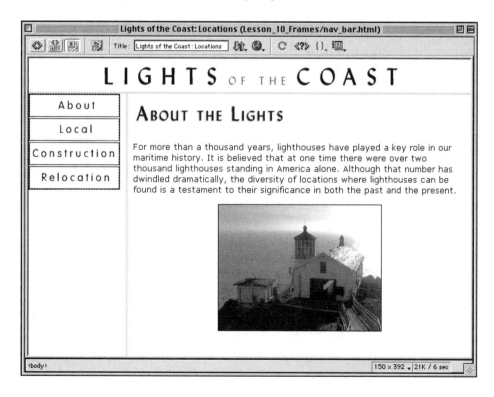

NOTE *If you need to make any changes to the navigation bar, you can choose Modify > Navigation Bar to open the Modify Navigation Bar dialog box. The Modify Navigation Bar dialog box is the almost exactly the same as the Insert Navigation Bar dialog box in which you created the navigation bar several steps earlier. The only differences are that the Modify Navigation Bar dialog box does not provide the option to choose whether the navigation bar is inserted horizontally or vertically, or the option to use tables when inserting the navigation bar.*

You will be able to navigate to all four pages from the nav frame. The button for each page will appear in the Down Image state when you are on that page.

OPENING AN EXISTING PAGE IN A FRAME

You've already started several content pages, so you need to make sure they fit in the content frame. You can open those files directly in the frame to check or edit them.

1) In the locations.html document window, click inside the content frame.

This is the frame in which you want the about, local_history, and relocation pages to appear.

2) Choose File > Open in Frame. Choose local_history.html from the dialog box.

The page is loaded into the content frame and is available for editing.

3) Place the local_history.jpg image from the Lesson_10_Frames/Images folder on a new paragraph line between the first two paragraphs and center the image. Give the image a 1-pixel border and save the file.

Depending on the size of the text and of the window in which your frameset is displayed, the content on this page may require scrolling. With the frame properties set to auto scroll, the browser will use scroll bars only if they are needed.

4) Open construction.html in the content frame. Place and center the construction.jpg image on a new paragraph line between the first two paragraphs. Give the image a 1-pixel border and save the file.

You might have noticed the Save All Frames command in the File menu. Exercise caution when using this command. It saves all open pages contained in your frames and the frameset. Remember that the frameset is the file you use when linking. The number of frames and the files that initially appear within each frame are defined in the frameset. If you choose File > Save All Frames while you are editing other pages within the frames (by using File > Open in Frame), you will redefine the frameset.

5) Open relocation.html in the content frame. Place and center the relocation.jpg image on a new paragraph line between the first two paragraphs. Give the image a 1-pixel border and save the file.

Your page should now look like the example.

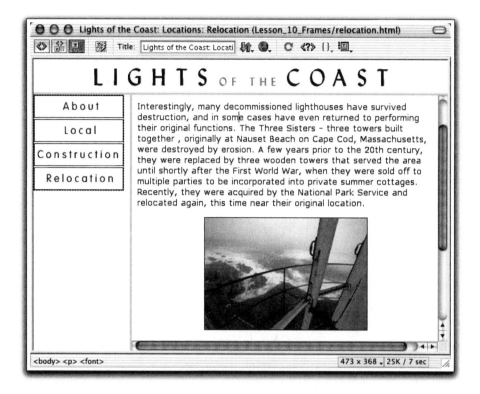

CHECKING FRAME CONTENT

As you create and edit pages within a frame, it's easy to accidentally place the wrong content in a frame. You can use the Property inspector to ensure that the correct pages will be loaded into each of the frames for the initial view of your Web page.

1) Select the title frame by clicking the top frame in the Frames panel. In the Src text field on the Property inspector, make sure title_bar.html is selected. If it isn't, click the folder icon to find and select it.

The Property inspector shows Frame properties for the title frame.

2) Select the nav frame by clicking the bottom left frame in the Frames panel. In the Src text field on the Property inspector, make sure nav_bar.html is selected. If it isn't, click the folder icon to find and select it.

The Property inspector shows Frame properties for the nav frame.

3) Select the content frame by clicking the bottom right frame in the Frames panel. Next to the Src text field on the Property inspector, click the folder icon to find and select about.html.

The relocation.html was selected because it was the last document that you worked with in this frame. The about.html file is the document you want to appear in the content frame of the final frameset. The Property inspector shows frame properties for the content frame.

CONTROLLING FRAME CONTENT WITH LINKS

After you have created the content document pages, you need to link the navigation elements to the pages that should display in the content area of your Web page. To get the content to appear in its proper location, you need to target the link.

1) In nav_bar.html on a new paragraph line below the navigation table, type Copyright and format it as Verdana, –2. Place a non-breaking space before the word "Copyright" by pressing Option+Space (Macintosh) or Ctrl+Shift+Space (Windows). Select "Copyright" and create a link to copyright.html by typing copyright.html in the link text field on the Property inspector.

By default, links are targeted to the frame or window in which they are located. However, you want this link to open in the content frame, not the nav frame.

2) In the Property inspector, select content from the Target drop-down menu.

This option forces the Copyright document to be placed in the content frame (the bottom right frame) when the Copyright link is clicked in the browser. Whenever you create a new frame, the name of that frame is automatically added to the Target drop-down menu.

> **NOTE** *If you are working on a document that will be loaded in a frame, and you are not working on it inside the frameset as you are in this exercise, you won't have the option in the Target menu to select the names of any frames. Dreamweaver only displays the names of frames that are available in the current document in the target menu. In this case, you will need to type into the target text field the exact name of the frame you want to target.*

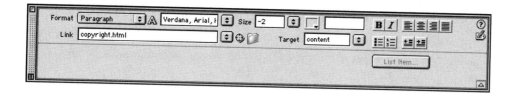

There are other options available in the Target drop-down menu. _blank loads the linked document in a new, unnamed browser window. _parent loads the linked document in the parent frameset of the frame that contains the link. If the frame containing the link is not nested, the linked document loads into the full browser window. _self loads the linked document in the same frame or window as the link. This target is implied, so you usually don't have to specify it. _top loads the linked document in the full browser window, thereby removing all frames.

3) Save the file and preview it in the browser.

When previewing your frames pages in the browser, you may get a dialog box informing you that all the frames need to be saved. You can click OK to save all frames. All frames and the frameset must be saved in order to preview the pages in the browser.

When you click the Copyright link, the copyright.html document displays in the content frame.

TIP *If your pages don't appear in the frames you expect them to, check to see that you have selected the correct frame from the Target drop-down menu in the Property inspector for each link.*

When you created the navigation bar, you defined where the linked pages would appear in the drop-down menu that was located just to the right of the When Clicked, Go To URL drop-down menu in the Navigation Bar dialog box. The links should open all of the pages in the content frame—if not, you will need to correct the target using the drop-down menu on the Navigation Bar dialog box.

CREATING NOFRAMES CONTENT

In Dreamweaver you can create content that will be ignored by frames-capable browsers, and displayed in older and text-based browsers or in other browsers that do not support frames. The NoFrames content you create is placed in the frameset file. When a browser that doesn't support frames loads the frameset file, the browser displays only the NoFrames content.

1) Open the about.txt document, select and copy all of the text. In the locations.html document, select the frameset.

The locations.html document is the page the browser will load initially, so the NoFrames content will be specified here.

2) Choose Modify › Frameset › Edit NoFrames Content.

The document window changes to display the NoFrames page, and the words "NoFrames Content" appear at the top. This is still the locations.html document, you are just seeing a different view of the page's content.

3) Create the NoFrames content in the document window by pasting in the text you copied from the about.txt text file.

Alternative content can contain elements from a standard html page. It will be enclosed between the **\<noframes\>** and **\</noframes\>** tags. Only browsers that do not support frames will see this content. The content should be relatively simple— browsers that do not support frames are likely to not support JavaScript, image maps, and other types of complex elements. Some Web sites use NoFrames content to provide simple alternative pages or to direct users to a text-based version of the Web site, while other sites use NoFrames content to display a message to users that the site is only available to frames-capable browsers.

N O T E *You cannot open other documents while you are editing NoFrames content, so you must copy the necessary text before hand.*

4) Choose Modify > Frameset > Edit NoFrames. Choose File > Save All and close all of your documents.

The document window changes to hide the NoFrames content and returns to the normal view of the frameset document.

N O T E *When you finish editing the NoFrames content, you might be inclined to close the window because you can't see the original document. If you do, you will close the frameset and all the frame pages. You will then have to open them up again if you wish to continue editing them.*

ON YOUR OWN: SOUTH OF MARKET CHILD CARE, INC.

The South of Market Child Care Web site was created by a team of students from the Multimedia Studies Intensive Program at San Francisco State University. The team included Kathleen Donahue, Destiny Goings, David Lazarus, and Enrica Lovaglio.

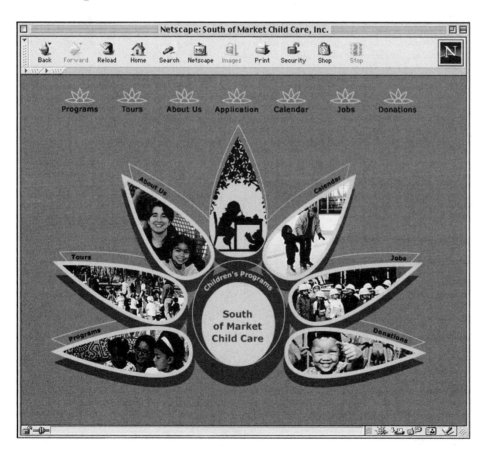

331

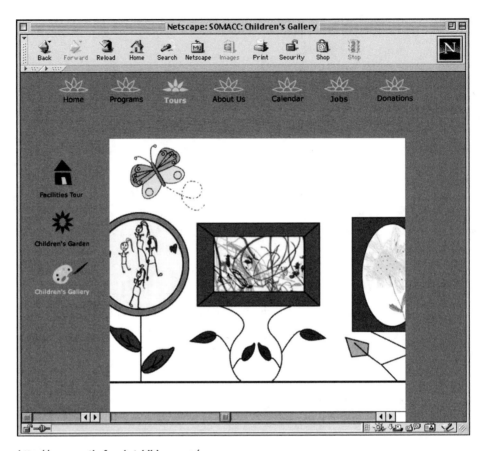

http://www.southofmarketchildcare.org/

Credits: Used With Permission of South of Market Child Care, Inc., San Francisco, CA.

The design team utilized Dreamweaver's tools for developing frames to create the Children's Gallery page.

In this bonus activity, you will recreate the frameset and the pages it contains for the Children's Gallery of the South of Market Child Care Web site on your own. The files you will need for this exercise are located in the Bonus/Lesson_10 folder. Examine the Completed file before you begin and see how it was constructed. Start by creating the frameset page and then move on to creating the individual frame pages. You can view the final file in the Bonus/Lesson_10/Completed folder.

WHAT YOU HAVE LEARNED

In this lesson, you have:

- Created a frameset to define the layout of frames within your document (pages 309–311)

- Saved a frameset and learned how to save other frames individually, as well as how to save them all at once (pages 311–313)

- Created frames and nested frames to modify the layout of your page using predefined framesets (pages 313–315)

- Resized frames by dragging borders in the document window and changing the dimensions in the Property inspector (pages 313–316)

- Changed frameset and frame properties using the Frames panel and the Property inspector (pages 316–318)

- Created documents within frames by inserting elements directly into the frames and by opening existing documents in the frames (pages 319–321)

- Created a navigation bar within a frame that linked to each of the featured pages and caused them to be displayed in the content frame (pages 322–327)

- Targeted frame content into other frames to control where the pages appear (pages 328–329)

- Created NoFrames content for browsers that are unable to display frames (pages 329–331)

creating
forms

Web sites often need to collect information from their visitors, for purposes that may include feedback, registration, polls, and e-commerce. From gathering different types of information to creating an opportunity for those visitors to interact with your site, forms provide the necessary user interface that enables you to obtain data. Forms allow you to ask visitors for specific information or give them an opportunity to send feedback, questions, or requests to you. A form contains fields in which users enter information. These fields can be text fields, radio buttons, check boxes, menus, or lists.

Form data is usually sent to a database on a server, to an email address, or to an application that will process it. Data sent by a form is a continuous string of text

In this project, you will build a form with various text fields, check boxes, radio buttons, submit and reset buttons, and a menu.

from the information typed by the user. CGI (Common Gateway Interface) scripts are commonly used to process form data. CGI is a standard protocol that acts as the communication link between the data from the form and the server. Talk to your Web administrator to get information about what CGI scripts your server uses.

To see an example of the finished page for this lesson, open lights_quiz.html from the Lesson_11_Forms/Completed folder.

WHAT YOU WILL LEARN

In this lesson, you will:

- Create a form on a Web page
- Add single-line text fields
- Add a multi-line text field
- Add check boxes
- Add radio buttons
- Add list/menu items
- Add buttons
- Validate a form
- Create a jump menu
- Test a form

APPROXIMATE TIME

This lesson should take about one hour to complete.

LESSON FILES

Media Files:
Lesson_11_Forms/Images/lights_title.gif
Lesson_11_Forms/Images/spacer.gif

Starting Files:
Lesson_11_Forms/buoys.html
Lesson_11_Forms/gps.html
Lesson_11_Forms/lights_quiz.html
Lesson_11_Forms/radar.html
Lesson_11_Forms/related_navigation.html
Lesson_11_Forms/sonar.html

Completed Project:
Lesson_11_Forms/Completed/lights_quiz.html
Lesson_11_Forms/Completed/related_ navigation.html

BUILDING YOUR FORM

Before adding individual fields, you must place a form on the page. The form will contain fields for users to enter information into, and it will specify what should be done with the data. In this exercise, you will create the form area.

1) Open the lights_quiz.html document from the Lesson_11_Forms folder. Position the insertion point on the blank line below the text "Test your knowledge about lighthouses..." and click the Form icon from the Forms tab on the Insert bar.

TIP *You can also insert a form by choosing Insert > Form.*

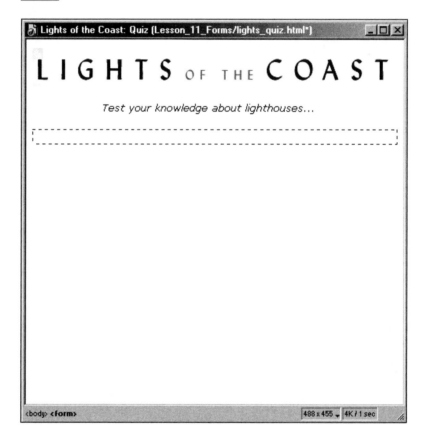

Red dotted lines visually identify the form area in the document window; that area is defined by the **<form>** and **</form>** tags in the code. These red lines are invisible elements that are displayed only in Dreamweaver; when you view the page within a browser, there will be nothing to mark the form area. These red lines are not draggable. The size of the form area depends on what you place inside the form, and it will expand as much as necessary to accommodate the contents.

FORM

NOTE *If invisible elements are not turned on, a message box appears letting you know that you won't be able to see the form. Click OK to close the message box, and then choose View > Visual Aids > Invisible Elements so you can see the red dotted boundary of the form. If invisible elements are turned on, you will not see the warning message.*

2) Select the form by clicking the red dotted line.

The Property inspector changes to display form properties. There are several options on the Property inspector.

NOTE *If the Property inspector is not visible, choose Window > Properties.*

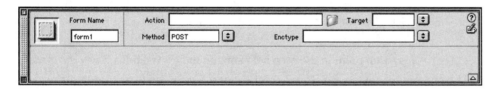

Form Name lets you give the form a name if you want to control it with a scripting application such as JavaScript. Dreamweaver assigns generic names automatically in a numeric order: form1, form2, etc.

NOTE *Because you may not have access to a CGI script while you complete this lesson, the following information is presented as reference material only. You should leave the Action text field empty and you should not change the Method.*

Action tells the browser what to do with the form data. It specifies the path or URL to the location and name of an application (usually a CGI script or a dynamic page) that will process the information when the user clicks the Submit button. CGI scripts are located on the Web server that processes the data sent by a form.

Method defines how the form data is handled: GET, POST, or Default. Data sent by a form is a continuous string of text from the information typed by the user. GET appends form contents to the URL specified in the Action text field; that information is therefore visible in the browser's address bar. GET is not a secure method of transferring data, so it should not be used for sensitive information such as credit card or social security numbers. The GET method can send only a limited amount of information because restrictions are often imposed on the lengths of URLs by browsers and servers. This limitation can vary, so the GET method is also not a good choice for forms in which the visitor may have entered a lot of information—long forms will lose any information exceeding the size or length restriction. The POST method, on the other hand, is capable of sending far more information and is more reliable and secure. It is the most common method used in scripts to send form data. POST uses an HTTP request to send the form value in the body of a message. Default uses the browser's default method, which is usually GET.

Talk to your ISP (Internet Service Provider) or Web administrator to get the information you need to set the Action and Method options to work with the scripts used on your server. You won't need this information in order to complete this lesson.

3) Place the insertion point in the area between the red dotted lines. Click the Insert Table icon from the Common category of the Insert bar. In the Insert Table dialog box, make the table 12 rows, 3 columns, and 600 pixels wide. Set the border to 0, the cell padding to 5, leave the cell spacing at 0, and click OK.

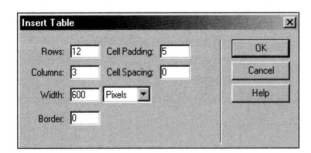

The table will improve the layout of the form and make it easy to align text or images with the form fields to label them. You can place a table inside a form or you can place a form in a table, but the table must completely contain or be contained by the form.

NOTE *Typing or verifying that a "0" is placed in the cell padding and cell spacing text fields is different from not having any value in those text fields. If there is no value, then the default of 1 pixel is used—even though the number 1 does not display in the fields.*

4) Click in the first cell of the top row and use the W text field on the Property inspector to set the width to 284 pixels. Place the insertion point in the center cell of the top row and set the width to 2. Set the width of the third cell of the top row to 284 pixels.

Defining the widths of columns before putting text or objects into them can help hold the size of the cells while you insert the necessary objects.

5) Place the insertion point in the left cell of the first row. Insert spacer.gif from the Lesson_11_Forms/Images folder and set the width of the image to 284 pixels and the height to 1 pixel. Insert spacer.gif into the center row, setting the width of the image to 2 pixels and the height to 1 pixel. Insert spacer.gif into the right cell, setting the width of the image to 284 pixels and the height to 1 pixel.

These spacer gifs will hold the size of the table cells to the desired dimensions. Spacer gifs are often needed to force table cells to hold to their proper dimensions. Without the spacer gifs, cells may collapse or expand depending upon the text they contain—even though you have set their widths. The size of the spacer gifs accounts for the cell padding that you applied to the cells. There will be 5 pixels of cell padding applied to each side of every cell. The total size of the left and right columns then will be 294 pixels each (284 for the spacer gif, plus 5 pixels of cell padding on the left, plus 5 pixels of cell padding on the right).

6) Select the cells in the left column of rows 2, 3, 4, and 5. From the Horz pop-up menu of the Property inspector, choose Right to right-justify all four cells. Select corresponding cells in the right column and choose Left from the Horz pop-up menu.

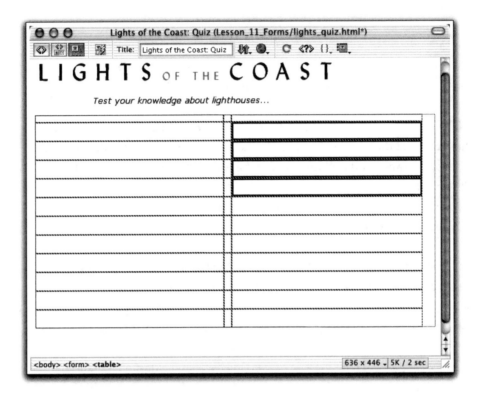

These four cells on the left will contain the text that labels the form fields. You will add the labels to the table as you add the form fields, beginning with the first cell in the next exercise. The four cells on the right will contain the form fields themselves.

7) Merge all three cells in row 6. Repeat this step for rows 7, 8, and 9.

TIP *You can merge the cells as you did in Lesson 4 by selecting the cells and pressing the Merges selected cells using spans button on the lower left of the Property inspector, or by choosing Modify > Table > Merge cells.*

The first five rows have three cells each. Rows 6 through 9 now have a single cell each.

8) Select cell rows 10 through 12 in the left column. From the Horz pop-up menu of the Property inspector, choose Right to right-justify all three cells. Select the cells in the right column of rows 10 through 12 and choose Left from the Horz drop-down menu.

These cells will also contain text labels on the left and form fields on the right.

9) Save the document.

You have now completed the layout of the table that will present your form. The center column will act as a spacer column to prevent the text labels and the form fields from being too close together. Your document should now look like the example shown here.

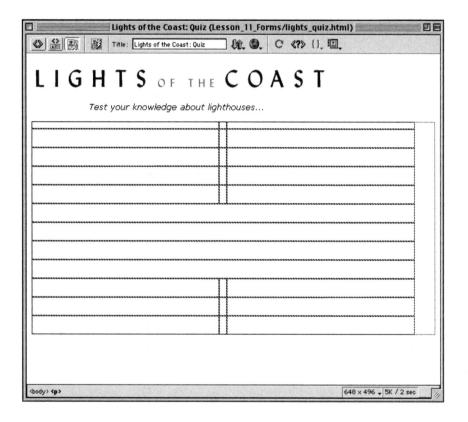

NOTE *You can have multiple forms on one page. However, it is not possible to nest a form inside of another form in HTML. Because of this restriction, Dreamweaver prevents forms from becoming accidentally nested by disabling the insertion of one form into another form. The option to insert a form will not be grayed-out, but no form will be inserted if you attempt to place one form inside of another. If form tags have been inserted manually within a form, Dreamweaver will highlight the tags that are incorrect to bring the error to your attention.*

ADDING SINGLE-LINE TEXT FIELDS

Text fields are for gathering information that the user can type in. Typical single-line text fields collect names, portions of addresses, and email information from users.

You must place all form fields and buttons within the red dotted lines; otherwise, they will not be a part of the form. If you try to insert form fields outside of the red lines, Dreamweaver will display an alert box with Yes or No options asking if you want to add a form tag. If you choose No, the field or buttons will not function as a part of any form.

1) In the lights_quiz.html document, type Name: in the left cell of row 2 and press Tab twice.

It is very important to provide labels for all of your form objects (text fields, check boxes, etc.) so your visitors will know what information they are supposed to enter into those fields. Without labels, forms can be very confusing.

The Tab key moves the insertion point to the next table cell. The next cell is the center cell, so you need to press the Tab key twice to move into the right cell where you will place the form field.

2) Click the Text Field icon on the Forms tab of the Insert bar.

> **TIP** *You can also choose Insert > Form Objects > Text Field.*

TEXT FIELD

A single-line text field is placed in the form. The Property inspector displays Text Field properties whenever a text field is inserted or when you click on a text field in the document window. The default Type option is Single line.

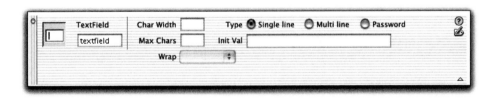

Leave the Init Val text field blank for this exercise. The initial value option enables you to set text that will appear in the text field when the page loads. Although the user will be able to change this text, use this option with caution. Users who want to get through the form quickly may accidentally skip a field that already has text in it, perhaps thinking they have already filled it out. Init Val can, however, help give the user an example of the kind of information that is being requested of them.

3) Select the text field that you just inserted and replace textfield with name in the Name text field on the Property inspector.

When the form is submitted, the name of the text field identifies the information that was entered into the field. In this case, "name" signifies that the information entered into this field is the visitor's name. Names are required for all fields. Do not use any spaces or special characters in the name, and remember that names are case-sensitive. Dreamweaver assigns generic names automatically in a numeric order: textfield, textfield2, etc.

It is important to remember to name all of your fields with short, descriptive names. Suppose you have two text fields on a page with labels next to them prompting the user to enter a home phone number into one field and a work phone number into the other. If those fields are named textfield and textfield2, their names will not give you any indication as to which number is the home number and which is the work number. On the other hand, by giving the fields more descriptive names, such as worknumber and homenumber, you can avoid confusion over the identity of the information.

4) In the Char Width text field on the Property inspector, type 40.

The width of the text field increases to show approximately 40 characters. The initial width of the text field is approximately 24, even though the text field is blank. The actual size of the text field in the browser will vary because it is dependent upon the size to which the user has set their browser's default text. The height of the text field is also determined by the browser's default text size.

5) In the Max Chars text field on the Property inspector, type 50.

Max Chars limits the total number of characters a user can enter. Initially this text field is blank, and the number of characters a user can enter is unlimited. You may need to limit the number of characters if you are sending information to a database in which the number of characters for a field is limited in the database definition.

NOTE *If the Max Chars value is larger than Char Width, users can continue to type and the text will scroll within the area. The scrollable area ends at the Max Char value.*

6) Type Email in the left cell of row 3 and press Tab twice. Add a single-line text field in the right cell and name the field email. Set the Char Width to 40 and the Max Char to 70.

This field will accept the user's email address.

> **TIP** *Be careful when setting the Max Char for fields that accept information such as email addresses and URLs. Users won't be able to enter a complete URL or any other information if that information is longer than the Max Char value, because they won't be able to type past the limit you set.*

7) With the email field still selected, type Enter your email in the Init Val text field on the Property inspector.

The initial value defines any text that appears in the text field when the visitor loads the page. Visitors can replace the initial value text with text of their own. Initial values are useful for prompting users to enter information or displaying example text. However, initial values may be a disadvantage if a visitor skips over the field because it looks like it has already been filled out.

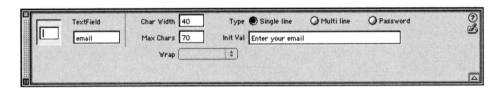

8) Save the file and preview it in the browser.

Leave this file open for the next exercise.

> **NOTE** *A regular text field displays the information in the browser as you type it in. A password text field looks the same as any other text field, but the text displayed on the screen is hidden by bullets or asterisks as you type. The password option only hides the text in the field from someone looking over your shoulder as you type—it does not encrypt or secure your data. To encrypt data, you must have secure server software running on the Web server. You should talk to your Web administrator for detailed information on securing data. To create a password field, insert a standard single-line text field and select Password for the Type option on the Property inspector. This option causes asterisks or bullets to appear when a user enters data in this field. Password text fields can be only single-line text fields. The Max Chars value for passwords should be set at the limit for passwords on your server.*

ADDING MULTI-LINE TEXT FIELDS

Multi-line text fields make it easier to collect larger amounts of information from a user by providing a text area with multiple lines in which the visitor can type. Typical multi-line text fields collect comments and feedback from visitors. In this exercise, you will place a multi-line text field in the table inside the form.

1) In the lights_quiz.html document, type Describe how a Fresnel lens works: in the left cell of row 4 and press Tab twice.

The multi-line text field will be inserted in same column as the single-line text fields from the previous exercise.

2) Click the Text area icon on the Forms tab of the Insert bar.

> **TIP** *You can also insert a multi-line text field by choosing Insert > Form Objects > Textarea.*

A multi-line text field is placed in the form and the Property inspector shows Text Field properties.

> **TIP** *You can convert a single-line text field to a multi-line text area by selecting the text field and choosing Multi line in the Type option on the Property inspector.*

3) In the Name text field on the Property inspector, replace textfield with fresnel. In the Char Width text field, type 40.

When you use multi-line text fields, you will see an additional option on the Property inspector. The Wrap drop-down menu is only available for multi-line text fields. It is grayed-out for both single-line and password text fields. Wrap specifies how text that is typed into a multi-line field is displayed if there is more text than will fit in the visible area.

The options are Default, Off, Virtual, and Physical. You can leave it set to Default for this exercise.

- Default will use the browser default. This option is selected automatically when you select Multi line for the Type option.
- Off will stop text from wrapping to the next line. Text will continue on one line until the Return key is pressed.
- Virtual will wrap text to the next line, but wrap will not be applied to the data when it is submitted.
- Physical will wrap text to the next line, and wrap will be applied to the data when it is submitted.

4) Type 4 in the Num Lines text field on the Property inspector.

This option dictates how many lines will appear in the scrollable area. It does not limit the number of lines users can enter.

5) In row 5, type What is your favorite lighthouse and why? in the left cell and insert a multi-line text field into the right cell. Name the field favorite and apply the same attributes that you set for the previous multi-line text area in steps 3 and 4.

Your document should now look similar to the example shown here.

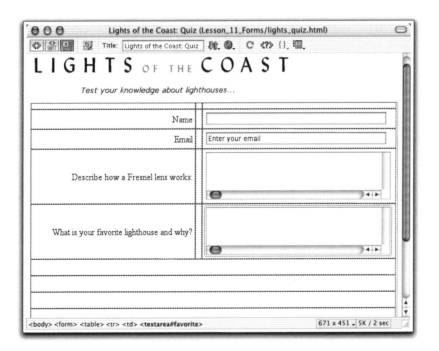

6) Save the file and preview it in the browser.

Leave this file open for the next exercise.

ADDING CHECK BOXES

Check boxes allow users to choose one or more options in a group of related items. Check boxes are typically used when you want the user to choose as many of the listed options as desired. If you want your user to choose only one selection, then you should use a radio button as demonstrated in the exercise that follows this one. In this exercise, you will insert a group of check boxes.

1) In the lights_quiz.html document, type Which of these fuel sources have been used in lighthouses? (Check all that apply) in row 6 of the table. Add a line break after the text by pressing Shift+Return.

Recall from Lesson 1 that a line break will move the insertion point to the next line without inserting a blank line as a regular paragraph return would do.

2) Click the check box icon on the Forms tab of the Insert bar.

TIP *You can also choose Insert > Form Objects > Check Box.*

A check box is inserted into the form, and the Property inspector displays CheckBox properties.

3) In the document window, type Sperm whale oil after the check box. Select the check box again by clicking it.

The Property inspector displays the CheckBox properties again.

4) In the Name text field on the Property inspector, replace "checkbox" with whale. In the Checked Value text field, type yes.

When the visitor to the page checks the Sperm whale oil check box, the name and value will be passed to the CGI and the *yes* value will indicate that the *whale* check box has been selected.

347

5) Position the insertion point on a line below "Sperm Whale Oil" and insert a line break. Repeat steps 2 through 5, adding check boxes and text for Hydrogen, Kerosene, and Solar Power, each on a separate line. In the Name text field on the Property inspector, replace "checkbox" each time with hydrogen, kerosene, and solar, respectively. Type yes in each Checked Value text field.

Your document should now look similar to the example shown here.

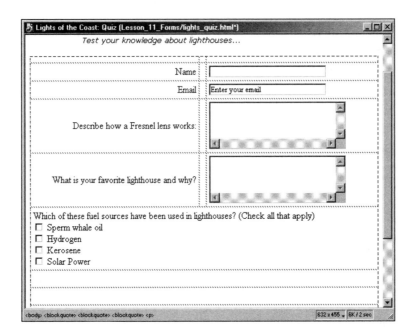

6) In row 7, type Which of the following have contributed to making lighthouses obsolete? and insert a line break. Type the following four choices, each on a separate line with its own check box: radar, global positioning systems, navigational buoys, and all of the above. In the Name text field on the Property inspector, replace "checkbox" each time with radar, global, buoys, and all, respectively. Type yes in each Checked Value text field.

As you continue to insert form objects, the table will expand downward to accommodate its content. As this happens, the red dotted line of the form may appear to overlap the table and not be pushed down along with the bottom of the table. If this happens, just click outside the table in the document window in order to cause Dreamweaver to refresh the table.

Leave this file open for the next exercise. You can save and preview the file in a browser.

NOTE *When inserting text labels in the document for your form objects, make sure the text is close enough to the corresponding button or field and not too close to other form objects. This will help to avoid confusing your Web site visitors.*

348

ADDING RADIO BUTTONS

Radio buttons are a group of options. Selecting one option automatically deselects all other options. Typical uses for radio buttons are credit card selections and yes/no answers. In this exercise, you will insert a group of radio buttons into the table.

1) In the lights_quiz.html document, type Who invented the Fresnel lens? in row 8 of the table.

In the next step, you will place the radio buttons on the same line as this text.

2) Insert a line break and click the radio group icon on the Forms tab of the Insert bar.

TIP *You can also choose Insert > Form Objects > Radio Group.*

The radio group dialog box appears.

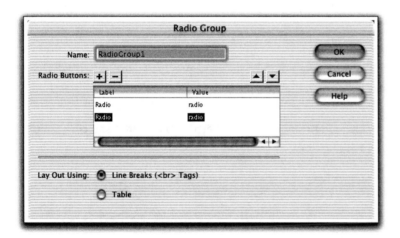

3) In the radio group dialog box, type whoInvented in the Name text field.

When using radio buttons, you must use the same name for each group of items. Radio buttons are meant to allow only one selection.

NOTE *If you insert radio buttons one by one (either by using the insert Radio Button icon on the Insert bar or by using the Insert > Form Objects > Radio Button menu option), you can make those buttons all part of the same group by giving them the same name. Using the same name for multiple radio buttons indicates that those buttons are part of the same group. If the names are not the same, the radio buttons will be treated as different groups and negate the purpose of using radio buttons. You can also insert a single radio button, but keep in mind that once your visitor clicks the button, the only way for that visitor to deselect the button will be to reset the form.*

349

Also keep in mind that names are case-sensitive, so "whoInvented" is not the same as "whoinvented."

4) Click the first instance of "Radio" in the Radio Buttons list area and replace that text with Thomas Jefferson. Click the second instance of "Radio" and replace it with Argand Fresnel.

By default, every Radio Group has at least two radio buttons. You can add more as needed. Clicking an instance in the Label or Value lists will highlight the text and allow you to change it.

5) Click the plus (+) button and replace the new instance of "Radio" with Augustin Fresnel. Add one more entry to the list: Benjamin Franklin. In the Value column, replace each instance of "radio" with the same text as contained in the corresponding Label.

You can add or delete entries by using the plus (+) and minus (–) buttons. You can also adjust the order of entries by selecting them and using the arrow buttons to move them up or down in the list.

When the form is submitted, these values will be sent to the script that processes the form on the server. It is also important to be sure you give each radio button a different value so you know which option the user chose.

6) Leave the line breaks option selected in the Lay Out Using area and click OK to close the Radio Group dialog box.

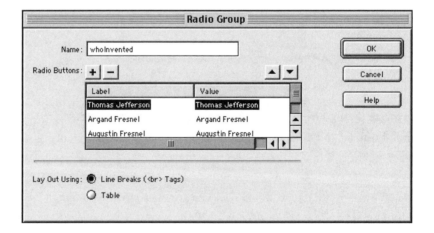

The line breaks option places the radio buttons in your document with each entry on a separate line. The table option inserts a table with each entry in a separate row.

To test the radio buttons, click each one in the browser. When you click one to select it, the other one should deselect. You must preview the file in the browser to see the effect; form objects will not appear selected or checked in the Dreamweaver document window.

Save lights_quiz.html and leave the file open for the next exercise.

ADDING LIST/MENU ITEMS

A list/menu enables users to pick options from a scrolling list or a menu. A scrolling list gives you the option to allow users to make multiple contiguous or noncontiguous selections. A menu restricts users to one selection. In both types, items chosen by the user will be highlighted.

1) In the lights_quiz.html document, type Unique markings are painted on lighthouses to: in row 9 of the table. Insert a line break and type (select the most appropriate options—make multiple selections with Command-click on the Macintosh and Ctrl-click on Windows).

In the following steps, you will place a scrolling list with six menu options just below the text you typed in this step.

2) Click at the end of the first line you typed in step 1, insert a line break, and click the List/Menu icon on the Forms tab of the Insert bar. On the Property inspector, select List for the Type option and change Height to 4. Check the Allow multiple check box for the Selections option.

TIP *You can also choose Insert > Form Objects > List/Menu.*

A small menu is inserted into the form, and the Property inspector displays Menu properties. Dreamweaver inserts a drop-down menu by default. You've changed the format to a scrolling list. You must change the height to a value that is greater than 1 for the form object to change from a menu to a list.

The list format has an additional option that is not available in the menu variation. You can choose to allow or not allow multiple selections by checking or unchecking the Allow multiple check box for the Selections option. This option is unchecked by default. If you check the selections box, users can make multiple noncontiguous selections by using Command-click on the Macintosh and Ctrl-click on Windows. Users may make contiguous selections by using Shift-click on both Macintosh and Windows. If you decide to allow multiple selections, it is a good idea to inform your visitors that they are able to make multiple selections, as well as tell them how to do so. Many users may not know these commands. It is always best to provide your visitors with all the information and tools they will need in order to interact with your site.

You can also set a height for the scrolling list by typing in the Height text field the number of lines you want to be visible. If you leave the Selections check box unchecked, be sure to enter a line height value of more than 1; otherwise, the scrolling list will display as a menu. You should always define the height for a scrolling list; if you don't, the number of lines displayed will be the browser default, which varies.

3) In the Name text field, replace select with markings and click the List Values button on the Property inspector.
The List Values dialog box opens. This dialog box is the same for both List and Menu entries.

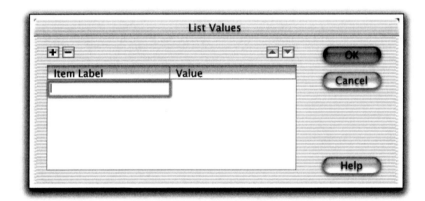

4) Click the plus sign (+) button to add an entry. In the Item Label field, type scare away birds and then press Tab.
The longest item in the list values box determines the width of the list/menu.

5) In the Value field, type scarebirds.
This text is sent to the CGI or server to indicate that the option has been selected.

6) Press Tab or click the plus sign (+) at the upper left of the dialog box to add another option to the menu.

Use the minus sign (–) to delete items from the List Values box.

7) Repeat steps 4 through 6, adding hide them in the fog, make them look different, make them beautiful, make them visible, **and** camouflage them **to the list. Change the Value field to match the name of each region using** fog, different, beautiful, visible, **and** camouflage, **respectively.**

Use the arrows above the Value field if you want to reorder the list.

TIP *When you have multiple entries to add, you can press Tab after entering a value to automatically add a new entry.*

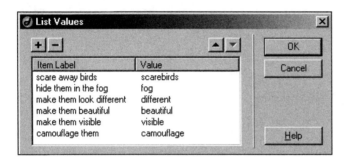

8) Click OK to close the dialog box.

The list shows the regions you just added.

An additional option on the Property inspector for list/menu items is the Initially Selected box. You can choose to have any one of the items in the list be selected when the page loads. This might not be desirable for scrolling lists, but for menu items it is helpful to have a sample choice or instruction such as "Choose one…" appear on the first line.

NOTE *If you choose an item to select initially, there is no way to deselect it. In order to deselect it, you would need to open the List Values dialog box, delete the item that was selected, and add it to the list again.*

9) Save the file and preview it in the browser.

Leave this file open for the next exercise.

ADDING BUTTONS

Forms usually have two buttons: one to send the form data (Submit) and one to clear the form (Reset). The Submit button tells the browser to send the data according to the Action and Method specified. The Reset button clears all the information from the fields on the page.

1) In the lights_quiz.html document, position the insertion point in the right cell of the last row of the table and click the Button icon from the Forms category in the Insert bar.

TIP *You can also choose Insert > Form Objects > Button.*

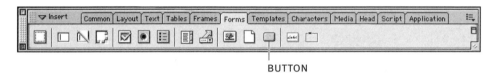

BUTTON

A Submit button is placed in the form, and the Property inspector displays Button properties. Since a submit button is the default, you do not need to change any of the options for this button.

2) Position the insertion point in the left cell of the last row of the table and add another button to the page.

A second submit button is placed in the form. The only difference is the name—this button is called submit2 because no two buttons can have the same name. The only form objects that can have the same name are radio buttons that are supposed to be in the same group. The button you are working with in this exercise is different because it cannot be grouped with other buttons and it will have its own action assigned to it in the next step.

3) Choose Reset form as the Action on the Property inspector.

The text in the Label text field will automatically change to Reset. The Button Name however, stays the same.

This action will cause all text fields, check boxes and radio buttons to clear and revert to their original state when the page was first loaded in the browser.

The third Action option is None. Unlike Submit and Reset, the None button option has no action attached to it. It can be used in conjunction with a script in order to perform another task. A JavaScript, for example, can be used to perform calculations such as totals or interest and return the end value to the user.

4) In the Label text field, type Clear Form and in the Button Name text field, type Reset.
It is a good idea to name your buttons clearly, with consideration for your users' expectations. Submit and Reset are standard form-button labels that people understand because of their widespread use.

5) Save the file and preview it in the browser.
Your document should now look similar to the example shown here.

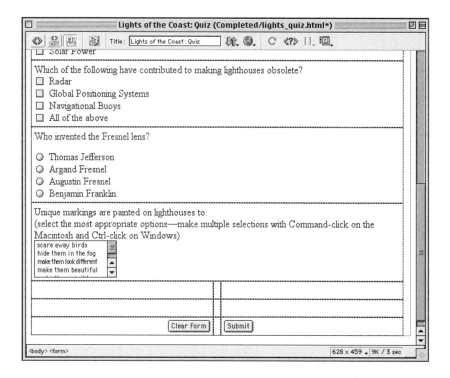

Leave this file open for the next exercise.

VALIDATING FORMS

The Validate Form behavior checks the contents of text fields in a form to ensure the user has entered the proper information. Whether accidentally or intentionally, users sometimes enter the wrong information or skip a field entirely. Instead of waiting until the form has been sent, you can check data as the user enters it or just before the form has been sent to the server.

In this exercise, you will add a behavior that will check the information typed into a form to be sure all required text fields have been filled out and that the information is the right type of data.

1) In the lights_quiz.html document, click the email field that you placed in the third row of the table to select it. Open the Behaviors panel in the Design panel group.

TIP *You can also choose Window > Behaviors to open the Behaviors panel.*

The Behaviors panel opens.

2) Click the plus (+) button and choose Validate Form from the drop-down menu on the Behaviors panel.

The Validate Form dialog box opens with a list of the form fields in the document; the first field in the list is selected by default.

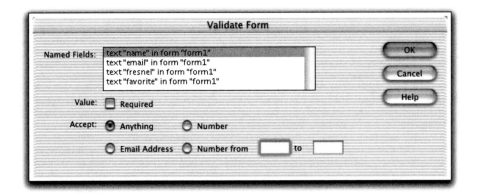

3) Select the email text field from the Named Fields list on the dialog box. Check the Required box for the Value option.

This specifies that it is necessary for the email field to contain data. The Validate Form action is added to the Behaviors panel with the onBlur event. Now an error message will be displayed if the user tabs to the next field without filling in this one. The onBlur event is activated when the user leaves the text field. In this example, if the user tabs to the next field in the form, leaving the email text field blank, an error message will be displayed. If the user clicks into specific fields (not tabbing through the form), this initial validation check is ignored.

NOTE *While it may seem like a good idea to validate each field as the user moves along through the form, use care—it may annoy your visitors. Many people skip certain questions and come back to them later, after filling out the rest of the form.*

4) Choose Email Address from the Accept options and click OK.

This option will check whether or not the text field contains an @ symbol. This only checks whether @ was included—it can't check that an email address actually exists.

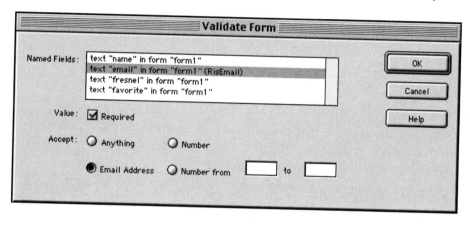

NOTE *The Number option specifies that the field should contain only numbers. The Number from option specifies that the field should contain a number that is within the given range of numbers. This is particularly useful for years.*

5) Select the Submit button in the document window. Click the plus sign (+) button on the Behaviors panel and choose Validate Form from the drop-down menu.

The Validate Form action is added to the Behaviors panel with the onSubmit event.

6) Select the Name text field from the Named Fields list and select Required from the Value option. Select Anything from the Accept option.

Anything specifies that the field is required, but that it does not need to have a certain type of data. Now when the user clicks the Submit button, the checks will be made.

NOTE *If you set an initial value for a text field, validating that field will not be useful (particularly if you select the Anything option) because there is already text in the field.*

7) Click OK. Save the file and test it in your browser.

Click in the email field, and then press Tab without entering any data. You will see an error message generated by the Validate Form behavior. You may not want to rely on the individual field check to validate a form, because if you click to place the insertion point in another field, you will not see an error message—it only works if the user moves into the required field. If the visitor does not use the Tab key and never places the insertion point into the required field, then the error message will not display.

NOTE *To add the email field to the checks that occur when the Submit button is clicked, open the Validate Form dialog box again by double-clicking the Validate Form action in the Behaviors panel. Select the email field and the desired option. Click OK when you are done.*

TESTING YOUR FORMS

You can send a form to an email address even if you don't have a CGI script running on your server. This method should be used only to test your forms.

1) In the lights_quiz.html document, select the form by choosing <form> from the Tag Selector. In the Action field of the form on the Property inspector, type mailto: followed by your email address.

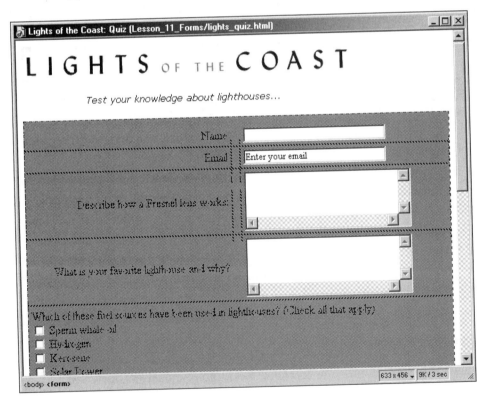

You should remember to include the colon and no spaces. It should appear as *mailto:info@mysite.com* with your email address replacing "info@mysite.com". This is the same way you inserted manual email links in Lesson 3.

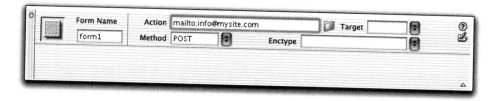

2) Choose POST from the Method drop-down menu and type text/plain into the Enctype text field.

You have set the encode type to plain text; otherwise, the text sent will be encoded into an almost unreadable form.

The enctype defines how the data in the form is encoded. The text/plain value formats the information with each form element on a separate line. Using this value will make it easier to read the results in an email. If you don't define an enctype value, browsers will use a default value that formats the data. Because the default is the one that should be used in most circumstances, you will usually not need to specify an enctype. This example is an exception, because you are sending the data in an email to test the form.

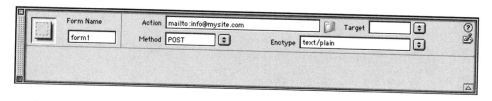

NOTE *To add a subject line to your form, change the Action to this:* mailto:info@mysite.com?Subject=Title for Subject goes here. *The **?Subject=** defines the text that follows as the subject. You can uses spaces in the subject, but do not use any other special characters such as quote marks, apostrophes, periods, or slashes (other than the **?Subject=** that separates the email and the subject) because they will interfere with the HTML code.*

This form action might not work in all browsers. Use it only for testing. You should always use a CGI script to send your forms. If your browser is not configured to send email, you will not be able to test this form in this manner.

3) Save the file and test it in the browser.
You can close this file.

CREATING JUMP MENUS

A jump menu is a drop-down menu that contains links to other pages in your site or to other Web sites. Like regular links, the jump menu can link to any type of file, including graphics or PDF files. The jump menu provides an easy-to-use interface for linking to pages in your site, if you don't make the list too long. A jump menu is embedded in a form and looks like a menu list in the browser.

1) Open the related_navigation.html file from the Lesson_11_Forms folder. Place the insertion point at the end of the line of text "Learn more about navigation:". Click the Jump Menu icon from the Forms category in the Insert bar.

TIP *Alternatively, you can also choose Insert > Form Object > Jump Menu.*

The Jump Menu dialog box opens. By default, there is one item listed in the menu, unnamed1. Dreamweaver assigns generic names automatically in a numeric order: unnamed1, unnamed2, etc.

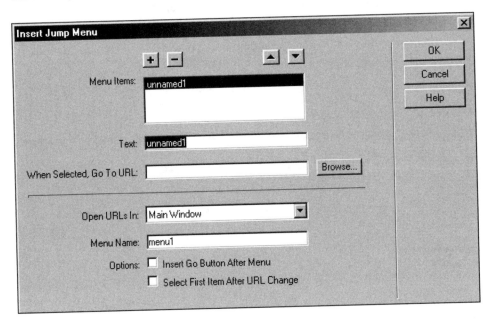

2) In the Text text field of the Jump Menu dialog box, type Pick One. Type # in the When Selected, Go To URL text field.

The first item in the menu list will appear in the first line of the menu. Since the user will see this initially in the menu list, the first line should be a short description of the list or a short instruction to let the user know that this is a jump menu.

3) In the Options area, choose Select First Item After URL Change.

This forces the menu list to display the first menu item in the list when the user returns to this page; otherwise, the list displays the most recent option chosen.

> **NOTE** *The Open URLs In drop-down menu can be used to target links to specific frames, as you did in Lesson 10. For this exercise, you should leave the default Main Window selected.*

4) Click the plus sign (+) button to add a new menu item. Type Radar in the Text field, press Tab, and type radar.html in the When Selected, Go To URL text field. Repeat this step, entering Sonar, sonar.html; GPS, gps.html; and Buoys, buoys.html. Click OK when you are done.

When these items are selected in the browser window, they will link to their appropriate pages. A link will be activated when the user selects the corresponding item.

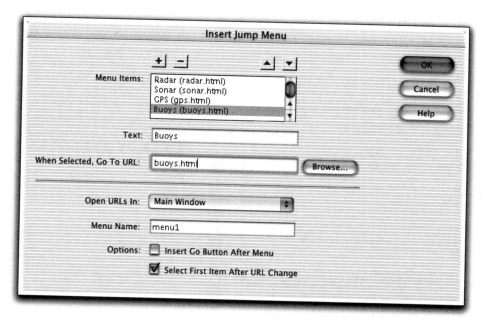

> **NOTE** *If you want to add a Go button to your list, select the Insert Go Button After Menu check box.*

Dreamweaver will automatically insert the required form when you insert the jump menu, as you can see by the dotted red lines. Since the insertion point was at the end of the line of text, the jump menu is created just below the text. If you want the prompt text "Learn more about navigation" to appear on the same line as the jump menu, you need to move that text into the form. Using tables as you did with the lights_quiz.html file will give you more control over the layout of your forms.

TIP *Use the up and down arrow icons to adjust the order of the items in the menu.*

When you click OK the inserted menu may appear to be very short. You'll preview the page in the browser to see how it will really look to a visitor.

5) Save the file and preview it in the browser.

After you create the jump menu, you can make changes by using the Property inspector or the Behaviors panel. The Property inspector gives you limited editing capability, allowing you to change the text the user sees and change the order in which the text appears in the list. For more extensive editing control, select the jump menu in the document window and double-click the Jump Menu action listed on the Behaviors panel.

ON YOUR OWN: THE WOMEN'S BUILDING

The Women's Building Web site was created by a team of students from the Multimedia Studies Intensive Program at San Francisco State University. The team included Debra Belale, Ali Nufire, Wendy Turner, and Jim Zazzera.

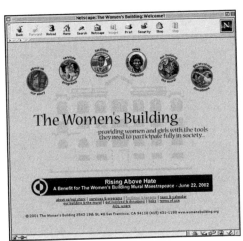 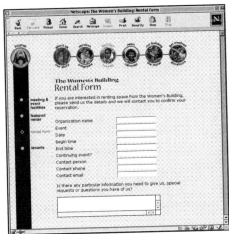

http://www.womensbuilding.org/
Credits: © The Women's Building

The design team utilized Dreamweaver's tools for developing forms to create the rental page.

In this bonus activity, you will recreate the form for the rentals page of the Women's Building Web site on your own. The files you will need for this exercise are located in the Bonus/Lesson_11 folder. Examine the Completed file before you begin and see how it was constructed. Start by creating a new basic HTML page and using the completed form document as your guide. You can view the final file in the Bonus/Lesson_11/Completed folder.

WHAT YOU HAVE LEARNED

In this lesson, you have:

* Created a form on a Web page to place form fields within, enabling visitors to send information to you (pages 336–341)

* Added single-line text fields using options including width and maximum number of characters (pages 342–344)

* Added a multi-line text field and set options for the number of lines, maximum characters, and wrap method (pages 345–346)

* Added check boxes to allow users to select multiple choices (pages 347–348)

* Added radio buttons to limit users to a single choice (pages 349–351)

* Added list boxes and drop-down menus with multiple items and specified an item to be selected initially (pages 351–353)

* Added buttons for Submit and Reset in order for users to send or clear the form (pages 354–355)

* Used a behavior to validate individual fields and multiple fields to make sure that all required fields are filled out with the correct kind of data (pages 356–358)

* Tested a form with a mailto action to be sure it is functioning correctly (pages 358–359)

* Created a jump menu that allows users to navigate through the site (pages 360–362)

editing the code

LESSON 12

You can gain more control over many of the elements on your Web pages once you become familiar with HTML code and how to edit that code or even write it from scratch yourself (otherwise known as **hand coding**). Dreamweaver does a great deal of work for you, saving you time by creating the code in the background while you visually design your pages. However, Dreamweaver is a great deal more than just a visual editor. It provides an extensive array of tools and resources for hand coding and code editing. These features enable advanced programmers to make precise modifications, troubleshoot their documents, and make use of the most recent progress in code development—even if those advances go beyond what is available in Dreamweaver. The ability to introduce items that Dreamweaver may not recognize and the level of

In this lesson, you'll work with a page like this one while you make modifications to the HTML code that is used to create the page.

control that you have over the code makes for a very flexible program that you can use while staying up-to-date in the rapidly changing world of Web development. Even as a beginner, you can make use of these code features and use Dreamweaver's code tools and resources to learn hand coding.

In this lesson, you will learn to edit the code and make use of many of the tools that will enable you to create code by hand. This lesson is intended to give you a basic introduction to the extensive code editing features available in Dreamweaver—a thorough and advanced exploration of these tools is outside the scope of this book.

To see examples of the finished pages for this chapter, open lighthouse_history.html and markings.html from the Lesson_12_Code/Completed folder.

WHAT YOU WILL LEARN

In this lesson, you will:

- Learn to switch document views
- Use the Code View to edit HTML
- Create meta tags and HTML comments
- Use the Tag Selector
- Use the Quick Tag Editor
- Use Snippets
- Clean up HTML
- Clean up Word HTML

APPROXIMATE TIME

This lesson should take approximately one hour to complete.

LESSON FILES

Media Files:

Lesson_12_Code/Images/…(all files)

Starting Files:

Lesson_12_Code/lighthouse_history.html
Lesson_12_Code/Text/markings.html
Lesson_12_Code/Text/point_reyes.html

Completed Project:

Lesson_12_Code/Completed/lighthouse_history.html
Lesson_12_Code/Completed/markings.html
Lesson_12_Code/Completed/point_reyes.html

365

SWITCHING DOCUMENT VIEWS

As you develop your pages, you may need to view the HTML source code generated by Dreamweaver. Perhaps a stray line break or other unseen character is ruining the effect you are trying to achieve, but you can't locate it in the document window. By looking at the HTML source code, you can find and remove the line break easily.

Dreamweaver gives you three views of your document: Design View, which shows all the objects (text, images, tables, and so on) that you have added to your page; Code View, which shows only the HTML source code; and a combination of both Code and Design Views. In the following exercise, you'll look at each of these views.

1) Open the lighthouse_history.html document from the Lesson_12_Code folder. If the document toolbar is not visible, choose View > Toolbars > Document.

The toolbar is displayed at the top of the document window on the Macintosh, and above the document window as its own panel in Windows.

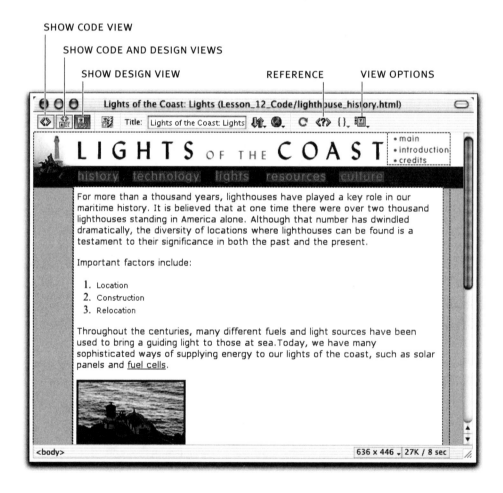

2) Click the Show Code View button in the toolbar.

TIP *You can also choose View > Code.*

In Code View, you don't see the visual elements of the page as they would actually appear in a browser window. Instead, you see the HTML code in a text editor. A number of the document toolbar's controls are particularly useful for extensive code editing. (If you can't see these options, make sure the window is open wide enough.)

- **Refresh Design View**: This feature updates the design view (the visual representation of your page) to reflect any changes you make in Code View.

- **Reference**: This feature allows you to select a tag and use the Reference panel to obtain more information on what the tag does—a good way to learn more about HTML.

- **Code Navigation**: This feature lets you work with JavaScript or VBScript functions. You can choose functions from this drop-down menu or use it to set break points for testing your scripts.

- **View Options**: This menu provides options that adjust the display of Code View. You can add line numbers for each line of code, enable wrapping to eliminate horizontal scrolling and make the code easier to view, and so on. You can customize any of these options by choosing Edit > Preferences > Code Format.

```
Lights of the Coast: Lights (Lesson_12_Code/lighthouse_history.html)          _|□|×|
 1 <!DOCTYPE HTML PUBLIC "-//W3C//DTD HTML 4.01 Transitional//EN">
 2 <html>
 3 <head>
 4 <title>Lights of the Coast: Lights</title>
 5 <meta http-equiv="Content-Type" content="text/html; charset=iso-8859-1">
 6 <script language="JavaScript" type="text/JavaScript">
 7 <!--
 8 function MM_openBrWindow(theURL,winName,features) { //v2.0
 9   window.open(theURL,winName,features);
10 }
11 //-->
12 </script>
13 </head>
14
15 <body bgcolor="#CCCC99" background="Images/bkg_inside_tan.gif" text="#000000" link="
16 <table width="617" border="0" cellspacing="0" cellpadding="0">
17   <tr>
18     <td rowspan="5" valign="top"><img src="Images/nav_lighthouse.jpg" alt="lighthous
19     <td><img src="Images/nav_titlebar.gif" alt="Lights of the Coast" width="465" hei
20     <td><table width="93" border="0" cellspacing="0" cellpadding="0">
21       <tr>
22         <td><a href="index.html"><img src="Images/nav_main.gif" alt="main" width="
23       </tr>
24       <tr>
<body>                                                            1K / 1 sec
```

NOTE *You can also open the Code Inspector, which gives you the same options and controls as Code View. The difference is that the inspector opens in a separate window. To open the Code Inspector, choose Window > Others > Code Inspector or press the F10 key.*

3) Click the Code and Design Views button in the toolbar or choose View > Code and Design.

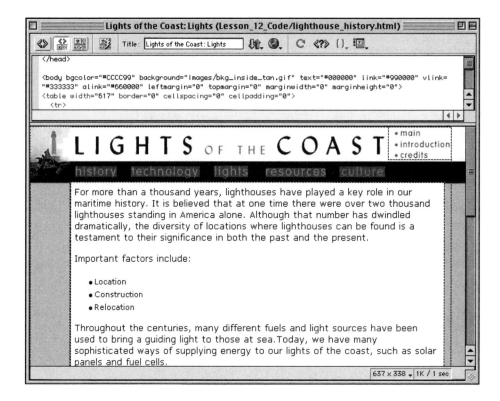

In this view, you can see both the design and the code that creates the page. You can resize the HTML pane by dragging the border between the design and HTML panes. To change the location of the HTML pane, click the View Options button in the toolbar (located at the right end) and choose Design View on Top from the drop-down menu. This menu also contains other options for adjusting the view, including rulers, visual aids, and the grid.

4) Click the Design View button in the toolbar or choose View > Design.

Your document window changes to Design View, which shows you all of the visual elements of your page approximately as they will appear in the browser. As in the other document views, you can access several view options through the toolbar.

In the following exercise, you'll format some text and then change the HTML inserted by Dreamweaver.

EDITING HTML IN CODE VIEW

You can edit the HTML by hand, and Dreamweaver will not overwrite those changes. If a change is made that appears to be wrong, however, Dreamweaver will highlight it to call the code to your attention. There may be many times when you need to adjust the code by hand, as demonstrated in the following steps.

1) In the lighthouse_history.html document, look at the numbered list from "Location" to "Relocation." View the page in Microsoft Internet Explorer and Netscape Navigator. Look carefully at the font and size of the numbers in comparison to the text in the list. Compare between the Dreamweaver document window and each browser.

Notice how the font used for the numbers is different from the text in Explorer. The font for the numbers is the default browser font, not Verdana as is specified in the HTML. The size is also different; Explorer is using the default font size and not the −2 that is specified in the HTML. In Netscape, the font is displayed as expected, in the same font and size as the text contained in the list.

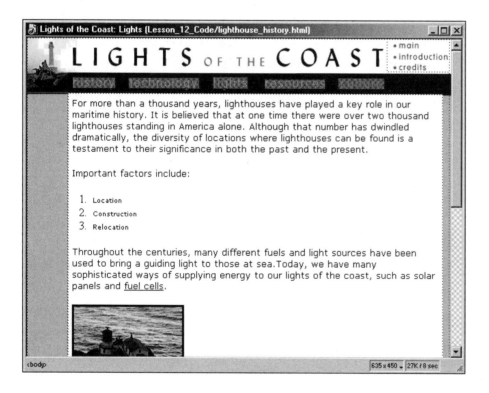

You can also see this difference in the Dreamweaver document window: The list numbers are displayed in the default font and size just like in Explorer.

In this exercise, you will change the placement of the font tags so that you get the same result in Internet Explorer and Netscape.

2) Switch to Code and Design View. Select the list and look at the HTML code. The list will be selected in Code View. You should see the following:

```
<ol>
<li><font size="-2" face="Verdana, Arial, Helvetica,
sans-serif">Location</font></li>
<li><font size="-2" face="Verdana, Arial, Helvetica,
sans-serif">Construction</font></li>
<li><font size="-2" face="Verdana, Arial, Helvetica,
sans-serif">Relocation</font></li>
</ol>
```

The **<li>** tag, which defines the list numbers or letters, is outside the **<font>** tag and, therefore, is not included in the font styling.

3) Select a single <li> tag in the Code View pane. In the document toolbar, click the Reference icon.

The Reference panel is located in the Code panel group and displays information about the tag that you have selected and its function. This feature is a good way to learn more about HTML while creating or working with documents in Dreamweaver. The material used for code reference is the O'REILLY HTML Reference.

NOTE *You can read introductory information about the O'REILLY HTML Reference by using the Book drop-down menu at the top of the Reference panel to select a different book. Then use the Book drop-down menu to select the O'REILLY HTML Reference again. This will cause the HTML reference material to open up to the introductory information, without any tags selected.*

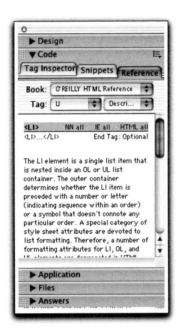

To learn more about any of the HTML tags that you see in Code View, select the tag and click the Reference icon on the document toolbar. You can also choose a tag from the Tag drop-down menu at the top of the Reference panel. For example, selecting DIV from the Tag drop-down menu will present you with information about the **<div>** tag, which you may notice in the Tag Selector at the bottom of the document window when you choose an alignment for text or objects that are located in the cell of a table. An additional drop-down menu, located to the right of the Tag drop-down menu, indicates that the information presented about the **<div>** tag is a description of that HTML tag. You can use this menu to learn more about the attributes that are related to the **<div>** tag. For instance, you could choose align from this menu to learn more about how the **<div>** tag affects alignment.

NOTE *Many of the tabs on the Insert bar contain code elements that can be inserted into the Code View pane of the document window. These code elements appear grayed-out when in Design View, or if the Design View pane is active.*

4) In the Code View pane, move the first <li> tag from the left of the <font size="-2" face="Verdana, Arial, Helvetica, sans-serif"> tab to the right of that tag so that <li> is placed just in front of the text "Location." Click in the Design View pane to refresh the document.

TIP *You can also click the Refresh button that appears on the Property inspector after you've made a change to the code.*

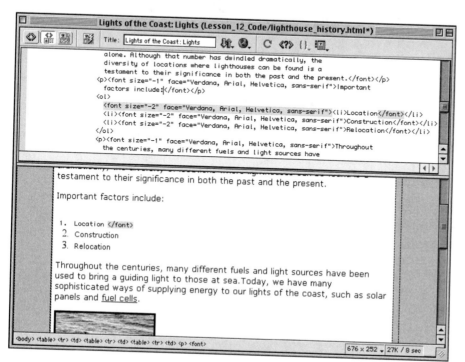

Yellow highlighting now appears on the portion of the code that defines the font. If you make a mistake while editing HTML code, Dreamweaver does not correct the mistake, but it does highlight in bright yellow the code that appears to be invalid. You have to make the corrections yourself. This feature is one of Dreamweaver's advantages, known as **RoundTrip HTML**. The fact that Dreamweaver does not change the code is important, because there may be times when Dreamweaver comes across code that appears to be invalid that you used for a reason. For instance, you can add special tags that your Web server recognizes but that are not standard HTML. Dreamweaver will leave them alone. The Invalid Markup highlight will only appear in Dreamweaver and will not affect what is seen in the browser.

TIP *You can prevent the Invalid Markup highlight from displaying in the Code View by choosing View > Code View Options > Highlight Invalid HTML to remove the checkmark and turn the option off. You cannot turn the Design View highlight of invalid markup off.*

5) In the Design View pane of the document window, click the highlighted </font> tag that appears to the right of "Location."

The Property inspector informs you that the selection is Invalid Markup and lists the problematic tag, along with additional information concerning why the code is invalid and a suggestion for how to remedy the problem.

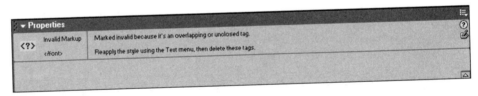

In this case, you will complete the following steps in this exercise to continue editing the code—not follow Dreamweaver's suggestion.

6) In the Code View pane, select and move the </li> tag at the end of the line that contains "Locations" so that it is located in front of the </font> tag. Click the Refresh button on the Property inspector.

The yellow highlighting disappears, and the Design View displays the first number in the list in the same font and size as the term "Location."

TIP *The Code View pane will display with a heavy line around the edges of the pane (Macintosh) or a highlighted margin (Windows) to indicate that it is active.*

7) Move the `<li>` and `</li>` tags for the terms "Construction" and "Relocation" inside the respective `<font>` and `</font>` tags.

The result should look like this:

```
<ol>
<font size="-2" face="Verdana, Arial, Helvetica,
sans-serif"><li>Location</li></font>
<font size="-2" face="Verdana, Arial, Helvetica,
sans-serif"><li>Construction</li></font>
<font size="-2" face="Verdana, Arial, Helvetica,
sans-serif"><li>Relocation</li></font>
</ol>
```

8) Preview your page in the Internet Explorer browser to see the results.

The Dreamweaver document window will now also display the numbers in the Verdana font at the –2 size.

ADJUSTING NEW WINDOW PLACEMENT

You learned how to control the attributes of new windows in Lesson 5 with the Open Browser Window behavior. By editing the HTML in Code View, you can also control the placement of those windows.

1) Preview the lighthouse_history.html document in your primary browser. Click the fuel cells link.

A new browser window opens with the definition of fuel cells. You created new windows like this one using the Open Browser window to select the fuel.html file, but you had no control over the exact placement of the window. You can control the placement by adding certain parameters to the JavaScript code to place the window in an exact location on the visitor's screen.

2) In the lighthouse_history.html document, look in the Code View pane for the code that opens the new browser when the visitor clicks the fuel cells link.

You'll see some code like this:

```
<a href="#" onClick="MM_openBrWindow('fuel.html','definition',
'scrollbars=yes,width=300,height=100')">fuel cells</a>
```

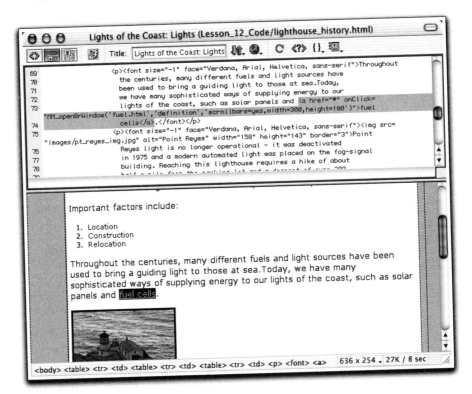

3) After the value of the height parameter, type , (a comma) and the following code:

`screenX=0,screenY=0,top=0,left=0.`

Be sure to type the comma and code after the numeric value of 100 and before the single apostrophe. Do not include any spaces.

The **screenX** and **screenY** parameters are for Netscape 4.0 and later; they position the window at the top and left side of the screen. The **top** and **left** parameters are for Internet Explorer 4.0 and later; they do the same thing as **screenX** and **screenY**. Using a parameter of 0 will place the new window at those coordinates—in the top left corner of the screen.

The resulting code should look like this:

```
<a href="#" onClick="MM_openBrWindow('fuel.html','definition',
'scrollbars=yes,width=300,height=100,
screenX=0,screenY=0,top=0,left=0')">fuel cells</a>
```

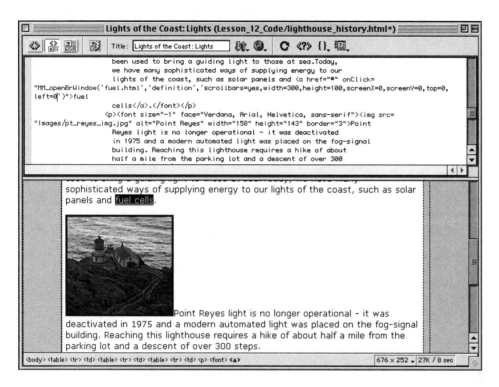

4) Save your page and test it in the browser.

The new window displays at the top and left side of your screen.

TIP *You should close the fuel cells definition window that you viewed earlier before previewing your page.*

5) Change all four parameters to 300, and see the difference when you view the page in the browser.

The new window displays in a different position.

When defining the placement of a new browser window, be careful not to position the window too far down or too far to the right; users who have smaller monitors might not be able to see your window if the coordinates place the window outside the dimension of their screen.

META TAGS AND COMMENTS

You can insert certain elements into your code that will not be displayed in a browser, but are nonetheless important to the document. Meta tags and HTML comments are two examples of these kinds of elements. **Meta tags** are used for many purposes: they identify and describe documents, provide copyright information, identify the authors or creators, redirect visitors to different pages, control the appearance of the document summary in some search engines, as well as affect ranking within search engines. **HTML Comments** are used to make notes in the code, to indicate or explain the use of a particular section of code, or to disable a portion of the document without actually deleting the code.

1) Choose View > Head Content.

The Head Content area appears right above the Design View pane. This is where icons will appear for items that are located in the head of your document, between the **<head>** and **</head>** tags. At this point the items contained in this area include icons for the title of the document, the meta http-equiv tag, and the portions of JavaScript that are required to appear in the head of the document.

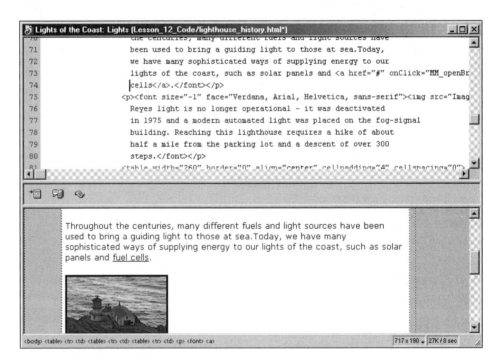

TIP *As you click the icons in the head pane, the corresponding code for those items will highlight in the Code View pane.*

You must be in either Design View or split Code and Design Views in order to view this head content area. If you are in Code View, the View > Head Content option will be unavailable. For this exercise, you should use split Code and Design View.

2) Click the View Options icon on the document toolbar and choose Design View on Top. From the same View Options menu, verify that the line numbers option is turned on. Place the pointer over the bar that separates the Design and Code Views. When the pointer turns into a line with double arrows, click and drag the bar upward to enlarge the Code View and shrink the Design View.

You can now see the head content near the top of your document window, just above the Design View pane. You also now have only a minimal amount of the Design View pane showing, and you can easily see the corresponding code in the Code View when selecting the head area icons.

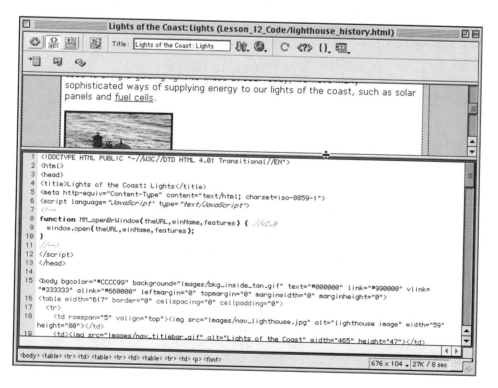

3) In the Code View pane, place the insertion point at the end of line 4, which contains the title of the document, just after the </title> tag, and then press Return (Macintosh) or Enter (Windows). On the Insert bar, click the Description icon located in the Head tab.

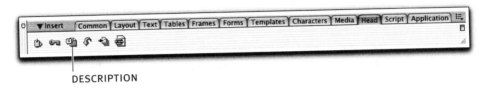

DESCRIPTION

The Description dialog box opens with a text field in which you can type a description of your page. The description meta tag, used to give a brief synopsis to identify your page, is included in search results displayed by some search engines. Adding the description meta tag to your pages is an important part of site promotion.

4) Type Learn how lighthouses have played a key role in maritime history. Click OK.

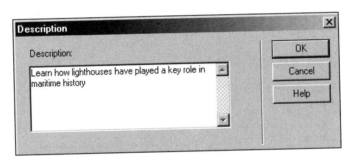

Descriptions should be short—200 characters or less. Most search engines have a cut-off, anything more than their limit will not be used. A good description is a very short, concise indication of the contents of the document.

5) The insertion point should now be at the beginning of line 6. Click the Keywords icon on the Head tab of the Insert bar. Type lighthouses, maritime history, lens, keepers, fuel cells into the Keywords text field.

When developing a list of keywords, you can separate individual words or phrases by commas. Do not repeat the same keyword or phrase over again—using "lighthouse lighthouse lighthouse lighthouse" as a keyword list is considered spamming because of the repetition of the word "lighthouse." Keywords should be representative of what is on your page and also be words that are actually used on your page.

6) Enlarge the Design View pane of your document window by moving the bar between the Design View and the Code View. Place the cursor at the beginning of the paragraph containing the fuel cells link. On the Insert bar, click the Comment icon located on the Common tab.

COMMENT

The Comment dialog box opens.

An HTML comment is text that is placed in the code that the browsers do not read. Comments are not visible to the visitors of your site—unless they look at the source code of your document.

7) Type Lightsource Information and click OK.

The Comment icon appears in the document window and `<!--Lightsource Information -->` is inserted into the code.

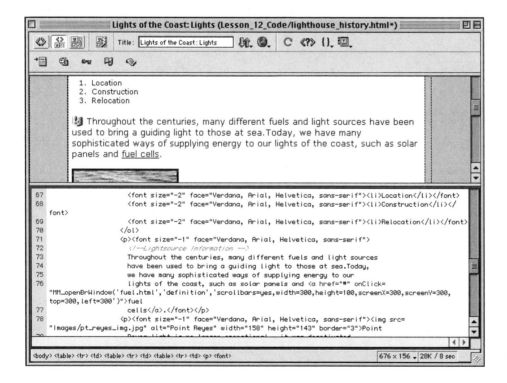

TIP *Selecting the Comment icon will allow you to edit the comment in the Property inspector.*

Comments are often used to mark sections of code in order to indicate the function of that code or to make note of copyright information on certain scripts or other content.

8) Choose View > Head Content to remove the checkmark next to the Head Content view option.

The Head area disappears. The rest of this book assumes that you have the Head Content view option turned off.

USING THE TAG SELECTOR

The Tag Selector enables you to jump quickly through a hierarchy of HTML tags, depending upon what is active, or selected, in the document window. This tool begins with the **<body>** tag and outlines the structure of the tags to the selection. This can be very useful for quickly selecting an item, particularly if it is one that may be difficult to select in the document window.

1) In the lighthouse_history.html file, click anywhere inside the white cell of the nested table that contains the text and images for this page.

Nested tables are particularly hard to select in the document window. You can't easily grab the border of a nested table, especially if the borders are defined as 0. The first step is to place the cursor at a point in the hierarchy of the HTML code that is after the desired table tags.

2) Using the Tag Selector at the bottom of the document window, Control-click (Macintosh) or right-click (Windows) the <table> tag that is second from the right.

This **<table>** tag corresponds to the table that creates the outline effect. This table is the wrong size. The width is 548 pixels, but it should be 558 pixels. The cell padding value is also wrong, which is causing the black outline that should be around the white area to not appear.

380

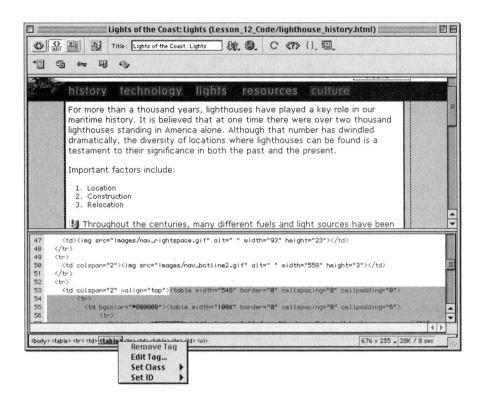

You've worked a little bit in the previous lessons with the Tag Selector. The more you get familiar with the hierarchy of HTML code, the easier it will be to move immediately to the point in the code that you need. The Tag Selector menu gives you additional control and quick access to the tags in the HTML.

3) In the menu that appears, choose Edit Tag.

A small Edit Tag box appears near the Tag Selector with a text field containing the **<table>** tag and the attributes contained within that tag. In the text field, you should see the following:

```
<table width="548" border="0" cellspacing="0" cellpadding="0">
```

4) In the Edit Tag box change the width to 558 pixels and the cell padding to 1.

The resulting code should appear as follows:

```
<table width="558" border="0" cellspacing="0" cellpadding="1">
```

381

5) Press Return (Macintosh) or Enter (Windows).

The changes that you defined are now made to the document, and the Edit Tag box disappears.

NOTE *The Tag Selector menu also allows you to remove tags.*

EDITING CODE WITH QUICK TAGS

Quick Tags give you the ability to rapidly insert HTML tags. This is especially important when you are writing code by hand, as it will help to speed up the process. There are three ways to edit HTML with the Quick Tag Editor. You can insert new HTML code, edit an existing tag, or wrap a new tag around the current selection.

1) In the lighthouse_history.html document, place the insertion point between the image of the lighthouse and the text beginning with "Point Reyes" in the Design View. Click the Quick Tag Editor icon on the upper right corner of the Property inspector.

The Quick Tag Editor opens in the Insert HTML mode because the insertion point was in the document window and there was nothing selected. In order for the Quick Tag Editor to appear in the Insert HTML mode, the cursor must be in the Design View of the document window as if you were going to insert an object.

The Insert HTML Quick Tag Editor opens as a box with a text field and a hints menu that you can scroll through to choose a tag. You will need to pause and wait for the hints menu to appear.

2) Scroll through the list of tags in the hints menu, find and double-click br. Press Return (Macintosh) or Enter (Windows).

The tag **br** is the break tag, and it will appear between the **<** and **>** characters in the Quick Tag text field when you double-click it. After pressing Return (Macintosh) or Enter (Windows), the break will be inserted into the document window at the place the insertion point was located.

The text is now on a line directly below the image.

NOTE *You can also perform more extensive code edits by typing directly into the text field; as you do so, Dreamweaver will automatically make corrections to the code for you.*

3) In the Design View of the document window, select the image of the lighthouse and click the Quick Tag Editor icon on the Property inspector.

The Quick Tag Editor opens in the Edit Tag mode because you had an object in the document selected. The path to the image is initially selected in the Quick Tag text field.

4) Press the Tab key to move from the path of the image to the next attribute. Keep pressing the Tab key until you reach the numeric width attribute. Change the width to 143. Keep pressing Tab until the number 3, which defines the border, is highlighted. Change the border of the image from 3 to 1. Press Return (Macintosh) or Enter (Windows).

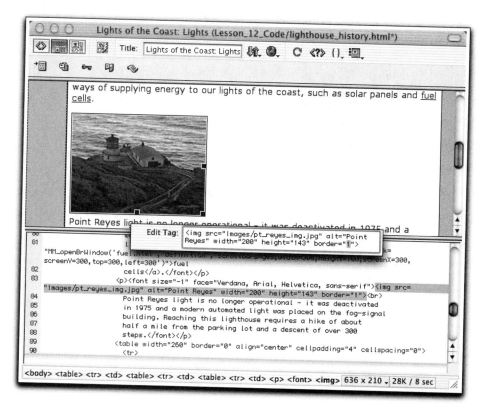

383

The border of the image has now changed from 3 pixels to 1 pixel. Each time you press Tab, the Quick Tag Editor applies the change you just made (if any) and jumps you to the next attribute.

5) Select the image of the lighthouse again and click the Quick Tag Editor icon on the Property inspector. Press Command+T (Macintosh) or Ctrl+T (Windows) to cycle through the three different Quick Tag options until you get the Wrap Tag mode.

Each time you Press Command+T (Macintosh) or Ctrl+T (Windows) the Quick Tag Editor switches to a different mode.

TIP *Depending on what you have selected in the document, the Quick Tag Editor may open in either Edit Tag mode or in Wrap Tag mode. For example, if you select text, the Quick Tag Editor will open in Wrap Tag mode. If you want a different mode, use Command+T (Macintosh) or Ctrl+T (Windows) to select a different option.*

6) Choose center from the Quick Tag Editor menu. Press Return (Macintosh) or Enter (Windows).

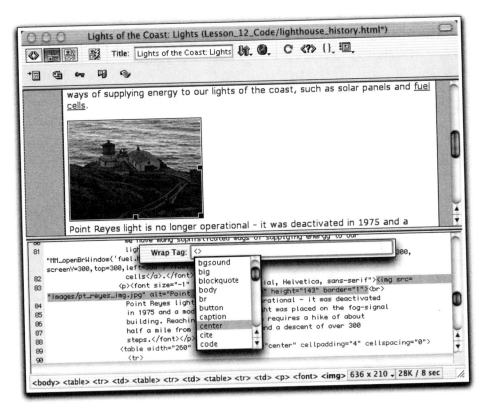

The lighthouse image is now centered. The tags **<center>** and **</center>** have been placed around the image.

> **NOTE** *As you work, the top pane of the Tag Inspector, located on the Code panel, will show the hierarchy of tags in your document. You can select any tag in this tag structure, and the attributes of the selected tag will be displayed in the bottom pane.*

MAKING USE OF CODE HINTS

While you are working in Code View, you can make use of Code Hints to speed up the process of writing code. As you begin to type tags, the Code Hints list appears. This list is a scrolling menu with a large number of tags that you can use to complete the tag or tag attribute. This exercise is an example of how to use the Code Hints for inserting an email link. You have inserted email links in the Design View in previous lessons.

1) In the Design View pane of the lighthouse_history.html document, place the insertion point in front of the word "Contact" at the bottom of the document, located just after the copyright information.

The Code View pane will display that portion of the code. You will see a static cursor located right in front of the word "Contact" in the code.

2) Click in the Code View pane in front of the word "Contact."

The Code View pane is now active, as indicated by the heavy line around the border of the pane.

3) Type ‹ in front of "Contact."

The < character indicates a tag. The Code Hints menu will appear with a list of tags that you can choose from.

> **NOTE** *You can access the Code Hints preferences by choosing Edit > Preferences and selecting the Code Hints category. The options allow you to turn off Auto Tag Completion (enabled by default) and turn off Code Hints (also enabled by default). The Delay slide allows you to set how long Code Hints waits before displaying a list of options. The Menus list box lets you specify the tags to include in the list of tags that appear in the Code Hints list.*

4) Double-click a, the first tag in the list, to insert the tag, and then press the space bar.

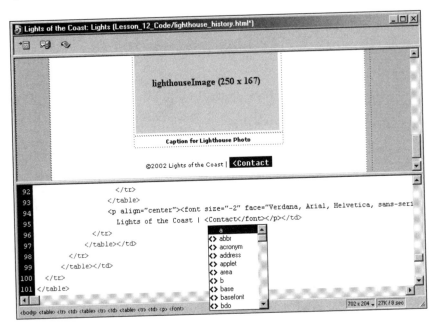

The **a** tag is inserted into the Code View and the Code Hints list pops up again.

5) Scroll down in the list until you find href, the fourth item in the list, and double-click to insert it in the document.

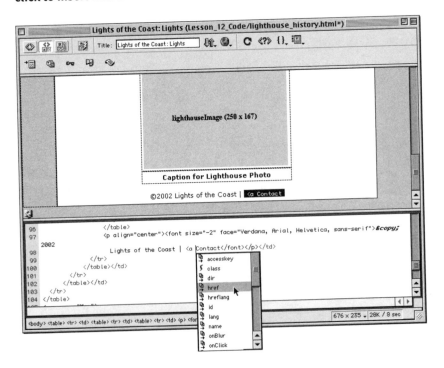

Dreamweaver has inserted **href=""** into the code, which indicates a link. The cursor is automatically placed between the quotes, and the Code Hints list pops up again.

6) Find and double-click mailto: **, the seventh item in the list.**

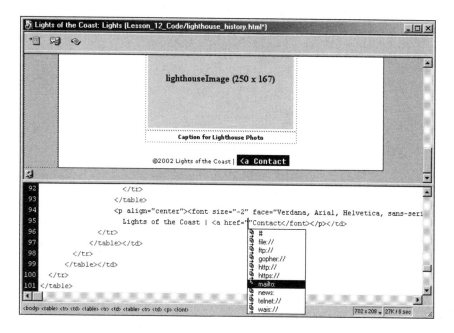

The cursor now appears just outside the ending quote after **mailto:** in the code.

7) Use the left arrow key to move to the left once, so the insertion point is between the colon and the quote. Type your email address. Use the right arrow key to move to the right once so the insertion point is back to the outside of the quote. Then type the > character.

Your email address now appears in the code defining the email link, and Dreamweaver has inserted a closing **</a>** tag.

8) Double click the word "Contact" in the Code View; click and drag it between the open and end tags.

Your code should look like this:

```
<a href="mailto:info@mysite.com">Contact</a>
```

NOTE *Dreamweaver MX includes many new tools for code editing that give users precise control over the development of code. You can store information on standard and custom tags using the Tag Library Editor. This new tool gives you the ability to modify current tags and import new tags into the already extensive database of tags that is integrated in Dreamweaver. Tags are set up in a system of libraries; each library is specific to a different type of code (HTML, CFML, ASP, etc.). You can add or delete libraries. The individual libraries each contain a number of tags for which you can edit the Tag Format: Line Breaks, Contents, and Case. The Preview text field displays the tag according to the options you set. Each tag contains a number of attributes that can be customized as well. Choose Edit > Tag Libraries to open the Tag Library Editor. Use caution when adding, modifying, or deleting tag libraries, tags, and tag attributes. This dialog box is best for advanced Dreamweaver users who have a thorough understanding of the code they wish to alter.*

USING SNIPPETS

In Dreamweaver you can store portions of code, called **snippets**, to be reused. There are a certain number of predefined snippets you can use, or you can create your own from HTML comments, JavaScript, portions of the HTML code, and more. Snippets are particularly useful for code that needs to be used repetitively throughout a site, like an email address or a link. You can either place a snippet directly into the code or have it wrap around a selection.

1) In the lighthouse_history.html document, place the insertion point at the end of the last sentence about Point Reyes, "and a descent of over 300 steps" in the Design View pane.

This is where you will insert a predefined Dreamweaver snippet.

2) Open the Code panel group and select the Snippets tab. Open the Text folder on the Snippets tab and select the Different Link Color snippet. Click Insert at the bottom of the Snippets panel.

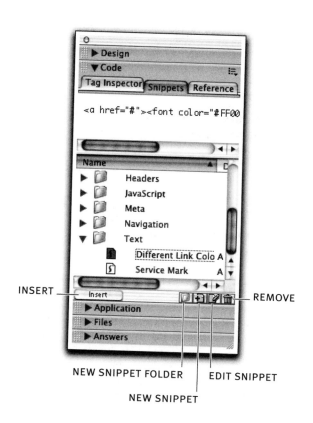

INSERT

REMOVE

NEW SNIPPET FOLDER

EDIT SNIPPET

NEW SNIPPET

This snippet creates placeholder text with a null link in the document.

TIP *You can also drag the snippet to the point in the document where you want it to be placed.*

3) Select the placeholder text "xxx." Locate the code in the Code View pane and change the color in the font tag `<font color="#FF0000">` to #333366, a dark blue.
You can override a page's default link color for individual links by placing the font color tags inside the link tags. For example, `<a href="#"><font color="#333366">Lighthouse</font></a>` will override the default link color, whereas `<font color="#333366"><a href="#">Lighthouse</a></font>` will not. You may have to move the tags manually in Code View to get this effect—or you can just insert the Different Link Color snippet and replace "xxx" with your own text.

4) Select the table at the bottom of the page that contains the placeholder image and corresponding caption.

This is an example of a table that might be used throughout a Web site like the "Lights of the Coast" project site for images and corresponding captions. By creating a snippet that contains this table, you no longer have to recreate the same code every time you wish to include an image and caption combination. You can just insert the snippet quickly and easily. Another advantage is the consistency that will come about from using a snippet—you can use a standard look and layout for the image and caption combinations.

5) Click the New Snippet icon at the bottom of the Snippets panel.

The Snippet dialog box opens.

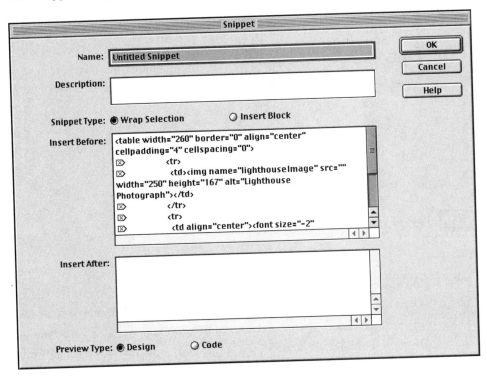

TIP *You can also delete and modify snippets by selecting them and clicking the Edit Snippet or Remove icons at the bottom of the Snippets panel. You can create folders to organize your snippets by clicking the New Snippet Folder icon.*

390

6) Type Image Caption Table **in the Name text field. Type** Table layout for lighthouse images needing captions **in the Description text field. Select Insert Block for Snippet Type and select Design for Preview Type. Click OK.**

The snippet is created and now appears in the Snippets panel. You are now able to insert this snippet into a document whenever you need it by selecting it in the Snippets panel and either dragging it to your document or clicking the Insert button on the Snippets panel.

7) Test your new snippet by deleting the original table at the bottom of lighthouse_history.html and replacing it with the new snippet by selecting the Image Caption Table snippet icon in the Snippets panel and clicking the Insert button. Replace the placeholder image with pt_arena.jpg from the Lesson_12_Code/ Images folder and replace the caption with View from the Point Arena Lighthouse.

Keep the names and descriptions of your snippets as short as possible. The first column in the Snippets panel displays the icons and names, while the second column displays the descriptions. You can roll over a description to see the full description pop-up.

USING CLEAN UP HTML

Throughout the process of creating an HTML document, you may wind up with empty or redundant tags, unnecessary or improperly nested tags, and more problems with the HTML code in your document. Using the Clean Up HTML command gets rid of nearly all of these problematic instances. It is recommended that you run the Clean Up HTML command whenever you finish a page or site.

1) In the lighthouse_history.html document, choose Commands > Clean Up HTML...

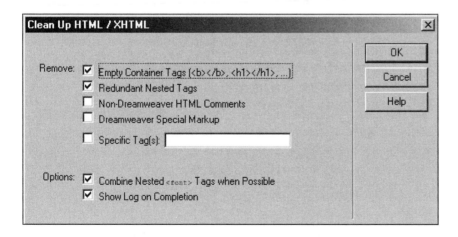

The Clean Up HTML/XHTML dialog box opens. By default, the first two options under the Remove section are checked, and both options under the Options section are checked. The choices in the dialog box are as follows:

- **Empty Container Tags (`<b></b>`, `<h1></h1>`, ...)**: Empty tags such as the example `<b></b>` (where there is nothing between the open bold and end bold tags) given in this dialog box can occur as you format text, particularly when you format, edit, reformat, etc. The more you work on a document, the more likely it is to have these kinds of nested tags. These tags may not cause problems in the browser, but they do take up space and make it harder to read through the code if you are editing in Code View. This option is checked by default.

- **Redundant Nested Tags**: When you have a duplicate set of tags inside of a set of tags that do the same thing, the inner set of tags is redundant because the outside set has already made the definition. If this box is checked, Dreamweaver will remove all instances of a set of duplicate tags since they are unnecessary. This option is checked by default.

- **Non-Dreamweaver HTML Comments**: Any comments that have not been inserted by Dreamweaver will be removed if this box is checked. This includes comments that have been inserted by you using Dreamweaver. Dreamweaver HTML Comments are those that are created by Dreamweaver in order to mark certain objects such as the `<!--#BeginEditable "lighthouse" -->` comment that signifies the editable region "lighthouse" in a template. Templates were covered in Lesson 9. This option is unchecked by default.

- **Dreamweaver Special Markup**: Dreamweaver creates a number of tags that are not standard HTML. These tags include items (like `<mm:libitem>`, which signifies a library item) that indicate to Dreamweaver how specific objects should be handled. Only Dreamweaver recognizes this markup; browsers will ignore it. Use caution when checking this box, as it will cause all tags related to library items, templates, and tracing images to be removed. If this is done, you will no longer be able to update the page using those features. This option is unchecked by default.

- **Specific Tag(s)**: This text field allows you to instruct Dreamweaver to remove particular tags. If you want to remove multiple tags at the same time, separate the tags with commas. This option is unchecked by default.

- **Combine Nested `<font>` Tags when Possible**: As you format text in your documents, `<font>` tags may become nested. For example, you might wind up with something that looks like this:

```
<font size="-1"><font face="Verdana, Arial, Helvetica, sans-serif">
<font color="#336633">Lights of the Coast</font></font></font>
```

The three sets of font tags in this example can be combined into one **`<font>`** and **`</font>`** set, making the code much cleaner and leaner:

```
<font size="-1" face="Verdana, Arial, Helvetica, sans-serif" color="#336633">
Lights of the Coast</font>
```

This option is checked by default.

- **Show Log on Completion**: The log will let you know what items Dreamweaver was able to clean up. This option is checked by default.

NOTE *You can run this command on both HTML and XHTML documents. When cleaning up XHTML, you will have different options available to you.*

2) Leave the default options selected and click OK.

Dreamweaver runs Clean Up HTML and displays a dialog box with the log of what was cleaned up. In this case, the message tells you that there was nothing to clean up.

3) Click OK to close the log. Save and close the lighthouse_history.html document.

Running Clean Up HTML helps to make your code as clean and free of errors as possible. It can potentially help decrease the file size and browser loading time for your document.

NOTE *To further optimize the code in your documents, you can run Validate Markup to examine the code for tag and syntax errors by choosing File > Check Page > Validate Markup or selecting the Validation tab in the Results window and clicking the Validate icon (the green triangle on the left). Any errors found will be displayed in the Results dialog box.*

WORKING WITH MICROSOFT WORD HTML

You may get content for your pages from a variety of sources. Clients or colleagues might send the content in a Microsoft Word file. If the format of the Word document is fairly simple, you can use the copy-and-paste method to import your text into Dreamweaver. If the Word document has formatting such as bullets or tables, you may want to save the document as a Web page (choose File > Save As Web Page in Word 97 or later) and open the resulting HTML file in Dreamweaver. Word inserts a great number of unnecessary tags, however. You can clean up this code in Dreamweaver in one step. The tags that Dreamweaver removes are required to display the page in Word but are not needed in HTML or a browser.

1) Create a new basic HTML document. Choose File › Import › Import Word HTML.
The Select Word HTML File to Import dialog box opens.

> **NOTE** *You must have a Dreamweaver document open in order to access the Import options.*

2) Select the markings.html file from Lesson_12_Code/Text and click Open.
This HTML file was saved from a Word 2001 document. Dreamweaver opens the file in a new document window and automatically opens the Clean Up Word HTML dialog box.

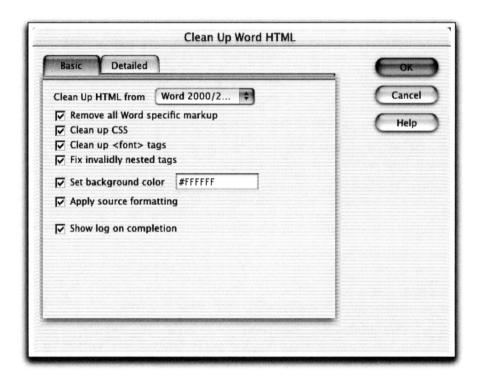

Dreamweaver attempts to determine what version of Word was used to create the HTML. If Dreamweaver is unable to determine the version, you need to choose the correct version from the drop-down menu. For this exercise, choose Word 2000/2002.

The dialog box has two tabs, Basic and Detailed, with several options to check for each. For this exercise, you should use the default setting (all options checked).

The options on the Basic tab are as follows:

- Remove all Word specific markup

- Clean up CSS

- Clean up <font> tags

- Fix Invalidly nested tags

- Set background color

- Apply source formatting

- Show log on completion

The Detailed tab contains additional options to remove all word specific markup and clean up CSS.

3) Click OK. Click OK again to close the dialog box after reviewing the changes made. Save the file as markings.html in the Lesson_12_Code folder.

Dreamweaver displays a dialog box listing all the changes that it made.

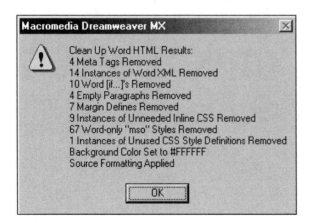

TIP *You can also open the Clean Up Word HTML dialog box by choosing Commands > Clean Up Word HTML.*

PRINTING FROM CODE VIEW

There are many times when it can be difficult to view code online. Dreamweaver allows you to print out the code, a useful feature that can allow you to simply work on a hard copy or share with team members. You will need to have a printer connected to your computer in order to complete this exercise.

1) In the markings.html file, choose File > Print Code.

As long as you have a printer connected to your system you will be able to print by clicking the Print button after specifying the printing options such as number of copies and page numbers.

2) You can close the markings.html file.

ON YOUR OWN: ROBOTICS: SENSING, THINKING, ACTING

The Robotics Web site was the online counterpart to a physical exhibition on Robotics at The Tech Museum of Innovation, located in San Jose, CA.

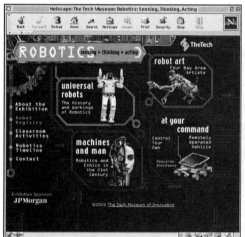 

http://www.thetech.org/exhibits/online/robotics/
Credits: Reprinted by permission of The Tech Museum of Innovation (http://www.thetech.org)

"The ability to easily view the code is very helpful. While the 'wysiwyg' features in Dreamweaver are excellent—there are still occasions when you need to view the code. The split design and code mode in the document window gives us quick access and ability to compare."

—Jim Spadaccini, Ideum

The files you will need for this exercise are located in the Bonus/Lesson_12 folder. For this activity, you should complete the following:

- Run the Clean Up HTML command on all HTML files in the Bonus/Lesson_12 folder

- In clayton.html, adjust the placement of the new window for the "View photographs" link located in the middle of the page, so that the new window appears in the middle of your screen.

- Add the following meta tag keywords to the robot_index.html page: robot, robots, robotics, sensor, sensors, technology, technological, ROV, laws of robotics, sensing, sense, senses, thinks, thinking, think, act, acting, acts, machine, machines, rovers, mechanical, artificial intelligence

- Add the following meta tag description to the robot_index.html page: "Robotics: Sensing, Thinking, Acting, an online exhibition exploring the complex and evolving world of robotics. This site complements and enhances The Tech Museum of Innovation's Robotics floor exhibition by providing interactive media, threaded discussions, activities and more."

WHAT YOU HAVE LEARNED

In this lesson, you have:

- Switched document views and edited the HTML in Code View (pages 366–368)

- Edited HTML code by hand using split Code and Design View (pages 369–373)

- Changed the location of a new browser window by adding x and y coordinates to the code (pages 373–375)

- Inserted keyword and description meta tags (pages 376–380)

- Used the Tag Selector to quickly edit tags (pages 380–382)

- Inserted and edited code using Quick Tags and Code Hints (pages 382–388)

- Created and inserted code using Snippets (pages 388–391)

- Ran the Clean Up HTML command to streamline code (pages 391–393)

- Imported a Word HTML file and used Clean Up Word HTML to remove unnecessary tags (pages 393–395)

- Learned how to print the HTML code (page 396)

using
style sheets

Cascading Style Sheets (CSS) enable you to define how text is displayed on your Web pages. The term "cascading" refers to the ordered sequence of styles. A **style** is a group of formatting attributes, identified by a single name. Styles in HTML documents give you a great deal of control over text formatting. The advantage of using styles is that when you make a change to an attribute of the style, all of the text controlled by that style will be reformatted automatically. You can make adjustments on a wide variety of settings from standard HTML attributes such as font, size, color, and alignment to unique attributes such as the space between characters (tracking), the space between lines (leading), and additional size and font options.

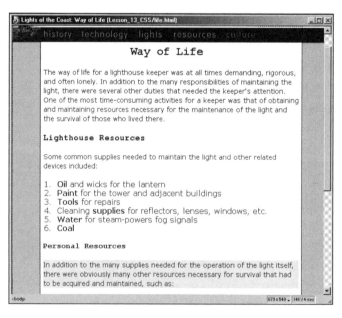

In this project, you will use CSS to apply a variety of format options to text using the three types of styles provided in Dreamweaver: HTML tag styles, custom styles, and CSS selector styles.

Using style sheets, you can, for example, create a paragraph with a half-inch margin, 20 points between the lines, and the text displayed in a 12-point blue Verdana font. This would not be possible without the use of CSS, which is mainly supported by 4.0 or later browsers. Most earlier browsers ignore CSS, although Internet Explorer 3.0 recognizes some style attributes.

You can use an internal style—one that is stored inside the document—when you need to format a single page, or you can use an external style sheet—one that is stored outside of the document and linked to the current page—when you need to control several documents at once in order to keep the same style of text formatting on multiple pages. It is ideal to keep the treatment of text consistent throughout your site because drastic changes in appearance may give viewers the impression they have landed on another site.

To see examples of the finished pages for this lesson, open keepers.html and life.html from the Lesson_13_CSS/Completed folder.

WHAT YOU WILL LEARN

In this lesson, you will:

- Create an external style sheet
- Add styles to an existing style sheet
- Edit a style
- Create a custom style
- Link to an external style sheet
- Create an internal style
- Convert internal styles to external styles
- Convert CSS to HTML

APPROXIMATE TIME

This lesson should take about two hours to complete.

LESSON FILES

Starting Files:

Lesson_13_CSS/keepers.html
Lesson_13_CSS/life.html

Completed Project:

Lesson_13_CSS/Completed/keepers.html
Lesson_13_CSS/Completed/life.html
Lesson_13_CSS/Completed/life_oldbrowsers.html

CREATING EXTERNAL STYLE SHEETS

Style sheets can be stored externally and linked to one or more documents. When you create an external style sheet for a document, the style sheet is automatically linked to the document for which it was created. An **external style sheet** is a text file that contains only style specifications. One advantage of creating an external style sheet for a document is that you can link that style sheet to other documents in the site in order to ensure consistency from page to page.

Another advantage of using an external style sheet is the ability to edit your styles, because any modifications will be made automatically to all documents which link to that style sheet. Use an external style sheet to standardize the appearance of text on multiple pages and to make changes that will be applied to all linked documents. In this exercise, you will create a new style in an external style sheet by redefining an HTML tag. By redefining the Heading 3 (**<h3>**) HTML tag in this exercise, you are telling the browser that any text using the **<h3>** tag should be displayed with the formatting you specify. This is useful because it allows you to alter the basic Heading 3 format so all text that uses the Heading 3 format will be formatted with the style attributes you specified.

1) Open the keepers.html file from the Lesson_13_CSS folder.

This document contains paragraphs, headings, and an unordered list.

NOTE *You should be using the Design View.*

2) Place the insertion point within the "Keeper's Responsibilities" heading. Select the <h3> tag in the Tag Selector at the bottom of the document window.

Look at the Tag Selector at the bottom left of the document window. You'll see the HTML tag **<h3>** that has been applied to the heading. The redefinition of the **<h3>** tag will be the first style you create.

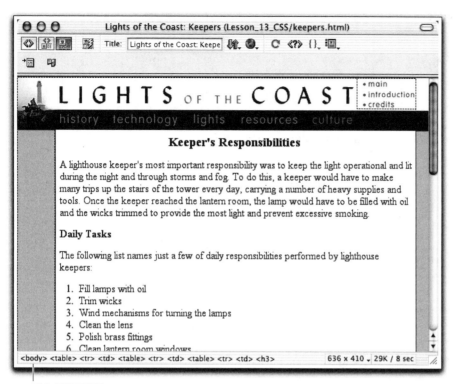

TAG SELECTOR

3) Choose Window > CSS Styles to open the CSS Styles panel.

The CSS Styles panel opens.

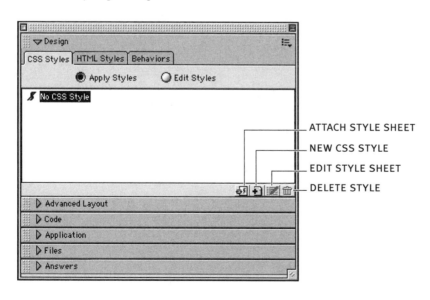

ATTACH STYLE SHEET

NEW CSS STYLE

EDIT STYLE SHEET

DELETE STYLE

TIP *You can also open the CSS Styles panel from the Design panel group.*

4) Click the New CSS Style icon at the bottom of the CSS Styles panel.

TIP *You can also open this dialog box by choosing Text > CSS Styles > New CSS Style...*

The New CSS Style dialog box opens.

5) In the Type area, select Redefine HTML Tag.

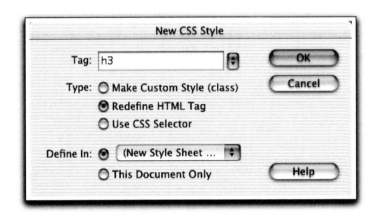

You are going to redefine the **<h3>** tag. Since the **<h3>** tag was selected when you clicked the New CSS Style icon, the **<h3>** tag is automatically selected and shown as h3 in the Tag text field. If h3 is not displayed, choose h3 from the drop-down menu.

TIP *When you are creating a style that redefines an existing HTML tag, you should place the insertion point within the text on the page with that formatting before you create the style. Dreamweaver will then automatically associate the HTML tag with the style you create. In this exercise, you want to make a style for all Heading 3 tags. In HTML, the tag is **<h3>**. Since your insertion point was within the text for the Heading 3 tag, **<h3>** is selected automatically when you create the new style. This is helpful if you are not familiar with HTML.*

6) In the Define In area, select New Style Sheet from the drop-down menu and click OK.
The Save Style Sheet File As dialog box opens.

NOTE *If this is the first style sheet you've created, New Style Sheet is the only option in the drop-down menu. If you have another style sheet defined, you'll also see that style sheet name in the drop-down menu.*

402

7) Navigate to the Lesson_13_CSS folder. Type lighthouse in the Name field and click Save.

N O T E *You won't need to add the extension .css because it will be added for you automatically.*

This creates the external style sheet file and opens the CSS Style Definition for h3 in lighthouse.css dialog box for the selected **<h3>** tag. In this Style Definition dialog box, you define the way you want your Heading 3 tags to appear. The options you want to select for the next step are located in the Type category. Make sure the Type category is selected in the Category list on the left side of the dialog box.

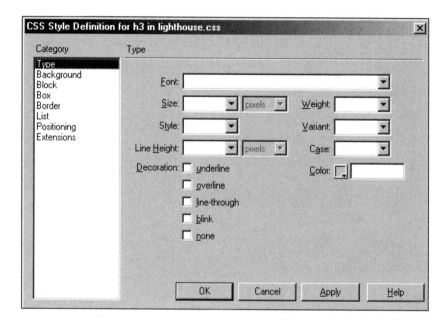

8) For this exercise, select Courier New, Courier, mono from the Font drop-down menu. Select 18 from the first Size drop-down menu and change the measurement to points in the second Size drop-down menu. Select bold from the Weight drop-down menu and select the dark blue color #000033 in the Color area. Click OK.

T I P *To select the color, you can either type the hex color code into the color text field, or you can click the color box—color swatches appear and the pointer becomes an eyedropper that you can use to select a color.*

The changes you have made are now reflected in the first heading on your page. Redefined HTML tag styles are applied throughout the document, so they do not display in the Apply Styles portion of the CSS Styles panel. You can see the redefined HTML tag styles that are applied to a document by looking at the Edit Styles portion of the CSS Styles panel. All redefined HTML tag styles are shown grouped inside of the style sheet that contains them.

NOTE *Dreamweaver has some attributes that are in the CSS specification but are not supported by all current browsers. Make sure you check your styles in both Netscape Navigator and Internet Explorer to see if the attribute you chose is supported.*

Leave the keepers.html file open for the next exercise.

ADDING A STYLE TO AN EXISTING EXTERNAL STYLE SHEET

When you create an external style sheet for a page, it is attached (linked) to that page. You can add new styles to make changes to not only this page but to all pages that use the style sheet.

In this exercise, you will add new styles to the style sheet.

1) In the keepers.html document, place the insertion point within the first paragraph below the "Keeper's Responsibilities" heading.

You will create a style for all paragraphs on the page. The Tag Selector at the bottom left of the document window will display the HTML tag **<p>**, indicating that the insertion point is within the paragraph. The **<p>** tag defines a paragraph.

2) Click New CSS Style on the CSS Styles panel and select Redefine HTML Tag from the Type area. Choose p from the drop-down menu.

The New CSS Style dialog box opens when you click the New CSS Style icon.

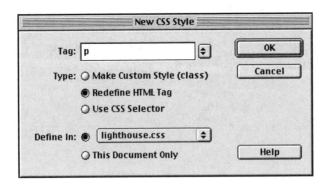

3) In the Define In area, verify that lighthouse.css is selected in the drop-down menu and click OK.

The CSS Style Definition dialog box opens. You are redefining the way text formatted with paragraph tags should appear by using the CSS Style Definition dialog box.

4) Select Verdana, Arial, Helvetica, Sans-serif from the Font drop-down menu. Select 10 from the Size drop-down menu and change the measurement to points in the second Size drop-down menu. Type 17 in the Line Height text field and change the measurement to points. Choose #333300 from the Color area and click OK.

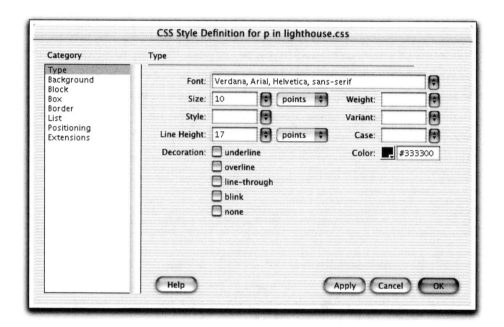

Any text that is contained within paragraph tags in the document appears with the formatting you defined in the external style sheet. Any text that has a different format applied to it, such as the subheading "Daily Tasks," is not affected by the style sheet.

Click Apply to see your selections appear on the page while the dialog box is still open. If you want to make changes, you can do so before closing the dialog box. Click OK when you finish.

5) Click in the subheading "Daily Tasks" and select the <h4> tag in the Tag Selector. Click New CSS Style on the CSS Styles panel, select Redefine HTML Tag from the Type area and click OK. In the Style Definition dialog box, set the font to Courier New, Courier, mono; set the size to 14 points; and set the color to #333366. Click OK.

This subheading is set to the Heading 4 format. You can see the **<h4>** tag displayed in the Tag Selector at the bottom left of the document window, and you can also see Heading 4 displayed in the Format drop-down menu on the Property inspector.

Most of the text on the page has now been formatted with styles. The next section of text is a definition list that still needs formatting.

6) Place the insertion point in the first line of the list "Fill lamps with oil." In the Tag Selector, click <ol>.

This selects the list tag that controls the HTML formatting of the text. By selecting the **<ol>** tag, you will apply the formatting to both the list number and the list item at the same time.

7) Click New CSS Style on the CSS Styles panel, select Redefine HTML Tag from the Type area, and click OK. Make sure ol is displayed in the Tag text field—if it isn't, type ol in the field, deleting anything else that may be there. In the CSS Style Definition dialog box, set the font to Verdana, Arial, Helvetica, Sans-serif; set the size to 12 points; set the style to italic; and set the color to #000000. Click OK.

At this point, your document should look similar to the example shown here, although you may have chosen different formatting attributes for some of the styles.

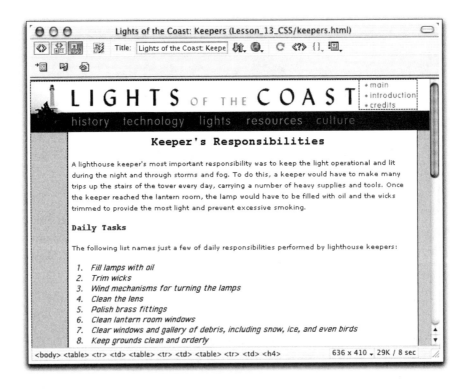

Leave the keepers.html file open for the next exercise.

EDITING AN EXISTING STYLE

You may need to modify the styles that are in an existing style sheet. Editing an external style sheet will affect all documents that use the style sheet. This is useful because the appearance of text can be changed in several pages or an entire site by editing only the external style sheet.

In this exercise, you will edit a style in the external style sheet that you created in the first exercise.

1) Click the Edit Styles radio button at the top of the CSS Styles panel. Select p from the list of styles defined in the lighthouse.css style sheet. Click the Edit Style Sheet icon at the bottom of the CSS Styles panel.

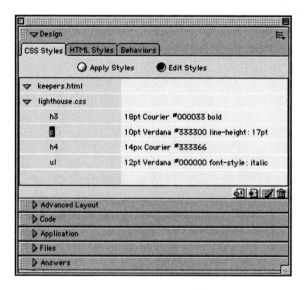

TIP *You can also double-click the p style in the list to open the same dialog box.*

The attributes of all listed styles are displayed in the CSS Styles panel for easy reference.

The CSS Style Definition dialog box opens. This is the same as the CSS Style Definition dialog box you used in the previous exercise to choose formatting attributes.

2) In the CSS Style Definition dialog box, change the size from 10 points to 11 points by typing 11 in the Size text field. Type 19 for the Line Height and click OK.
Your changes are applied to the document. The font size is now slightly larger, and the space between each line of text is greater. This style sheet is not yet used by any other documents; if other documents did use this style sheet, any text in those documents using the **<p>** tag would be formatted according to the modifications you just made.

TIP *You can use the Reference panel to learn more about the CSS elements. Open the Reference panel by choosing Window > Reference. In the Book drop-down menu, choose O'REILLY CSS Reference. Use the Style drop-down menu to choose CSS terms and read their descriptions, or click on a CSS element in your document and use the reference icon on the document toolbar to pull up information about that element in the Reference panel. All references to CSS styles are placed between the **<HEAD>** and **</HEAD>** tags of the document.*

Leave the keepers.html file open for the next exercise.

CREATING CUSTOM STYLES

Custom styles give you more specific control over the formatting of your document. You apply custom styles the same way you apply styles in a word processor: by selecting the text and then applying the style. You can apply the style to blocks of text or to individual words within the text. Custom styles can be created in either external or internal style sheets.

In this exercise, you are going to make a custom style in the external style sheet that will apply a bold style to any text to which you choose to apply it.

1) Click the Apply Styles radio button at the top of the CSS Styles panel. Click New CSS Style icon on the CSS Styles panel.
You can see by looking at the CSS Styles panel that there are no CSS Styles currently defined.

The New CSS Style dialog box opens.

2) Select Make Custom Style from the Type area.

The text field that displayed tags in the previous exercises now becomes a Name text field for creating a custom style. Dreamweaver assigns generic names automatically in a numeric order: .unnamed1, .unnamed2, etc. These names are not very descriptive, and they can be especially unhelpful when you create multiple custom styles. It is best to get in the habit of giving your styles short, descriptive names.

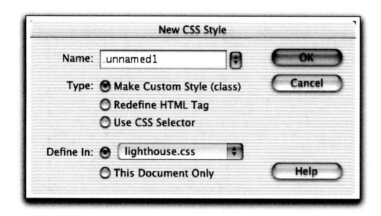

NOTE *If you have switched the style type in the dialog box, the .unnamed1 default name may not display in the text field. If you were to cancel the new style, and click the New CSS Style icon again, you would see the .unnamed1 generic name listed in the text field.*

3) Type .boldstyle in the Name text field for the name of your custom style.

A period before the name is required. If you delete the period, Dreamweaver will automatically include it at the beginning of the name, even if it isn't shown.

4) The Define In area should still show lighthouse.css. If not, choose lighthouse.css from the drop-down menu. Click OK.

The CSS Style Definition for .boldstyle in lighthouse.css dialog box opens.

5) Change Weight to bold, select normal from the Style drop-down menu, and set #663300 for the color. Leave all other options undefined and click OK.

You'll see the custom style you just created displayed on the CSS Styles panel. Only custom styles are displayed in this panel because they are the only styles for which you can select text in the document window and apply a style as if you were using a word processor. HTML tag styles and CSS selector styles are applied automatically when they are defined or changed in the style sheet.

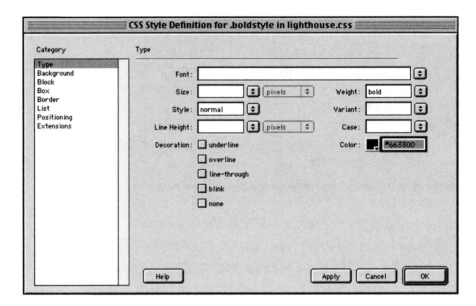

In the next steps, you'll apply the boldstyle custom style you just created to certain items in the numbered list.

6) Select "lamps" in the first line of the numbered list and click the boldstyle custom style on the CSS panel.

The selected text changes to reflect the boldstyle custom style. There are now two styles affecting this text: the external style—the first style applied—redefines the **<ol>** (ordered list) tag; the custom style—the second style applied—specifies bold and color formatting. When you apply more than one style to the same text, those styles might conflict and produce unexpected results. Browsers apply style attributes according to the order in which styles are applied and the following rules:

CSS is applied in an ordered sequence. When two or more styles are applied to the same text, the browser will display the attributes of each style in combination with each other.

410

If there is more than one style applied to the same text with conflicting attributes, the browser uses the specifications from the innermost style (the style closest to the text itself). The most recent styles are nested inside earlier styles. Since the last formatting attributes you apply are physically the closest tags to the text, they take precedence over earlier styles and control the final look of the text. The order of styles is as follows:

- External styles (the style that is farthest away from the text; lowest priority)
- Internal styles
- Custom styles applied to text on the page
- Local formatting, such as bold or italics, applied to text on the page from the Property inspector (the style that is closest to the text; highest priority—overrides any options set in the styles above)

If your document uses an external style sheet, the styles in that sheet are applied across your document. Suppose, for example, the external style sheet has definitions for Heading 3 and Heading 4, and that you've also created an internal style within your document that redefines the Heading 3 tag. The internal style takes precedence if the attributes conflict with those in the external style.

Text formatting applied manually to ranges of text can also take precedence over styles. In the example just presented, suppose that you've used the Property inspector to apply a different color on one of the Heading 3 lines. This is local formatting, and it overrides other styles if they specify color as well. However, the attributes from custom styles overrule attributes from HTML tag styles. To make sure your styles control the formatting for a paragraph, you may need to remove all other formatting settings if they conflict.

7) Repeat step 6 for the following terms in the remaining lines of the numbered list: "wicks", "mechanisms", "lens", "brass", "lantern", "windows", "grounds", "buildings", and "tower".

The custom style changed only the color and weight of the text. The text inherits additional font formatting from the style you defined previously for the paragraph.

NOTE *After you apply a custom style, you might want to remove the style. If you apply the custom style to the entire paragraph, make sure the insertion point is in the paragraph, and then click No CSS Style on the CSS Styles panel. The style and its formatting are removed. If you're removing the custom style that has only been applied to selected text within a paragraph, make sure the insertion point is within a word that uses the custom style, and then click No CSS Style on the CSS Styles panel.*

Your document should now look similar to the example shown here.

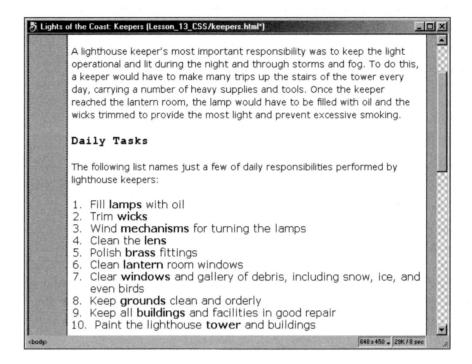

8) Save the keepers.html document.

Leave this file open for the next exercise.

CREATING CSS SELECTOR STYLES FOR LINKS

You can use styles to change the appearance of links on your page. CSS selector styles can be used for controlling the dynamic link tag (**<a>**) with specific attributes for the different states that can be applied to it. The different states of the **<a>** tag are activated when a user performs an action such as clicking the link. In the CSS Selector drop-down menu in the New Style dialog box, Dreamweaver provides four standard states for the **<a>** tag that make it easy to change the formatting of links on your pages. This type of CSS selector is known as a **pseudoclass**.

In this exercise, you will create a CSS selector style in the external style sheet in order to change the look of a link on the page.

1) In the keepers.html document, click New CSS Style on the CSS Styles panel.

The New Style dialog box opens.

2) In the New CSS Style dialog box, select Use CSS Selector in the Type area, choose lighthouse.css from the drop-down menu in the Define In area, and choose a:link from the Selector drop-down menu.

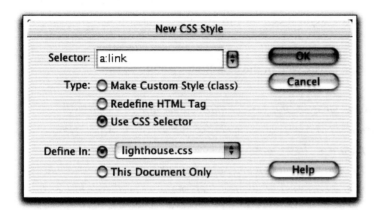

The four states applicable to links appear in the Selector drop-down menu because they change based on user activity. The choices in the drop-down menu are a:link, a:visited, a:hover, and a:active.

- The Active selector controls the link when the link is selected or as it is clicked by the user; the default color is red. It is displayed in the Selector menu as a:active.

- The Link selector controls the normal state of a link; the default color is blue. It is displayed in the Selector menu as a:link.

- The Visited selector controls the link after it has been clicked by the user; the default color is purple. It is displayed in the Selector menu as a:visited.

- The Hover selector controls the link when the user moves the pointer over the link; the default color is red. It is displayed in the Selector menu as a:hover. (This option is not supported by all browsers.)

3) Click OK in the New Style dialog box. In the Style definition dialog box that appears, change the font to Courier New, Courier, mono. Type in 13 points for the size. Use the color box to change the color to #003300 and click OK.

You are using a color other than the default so you can see your style changes.

4) Select the text "Lights of the Coast" at the bottom of the page. Use the Email icon on the Common tab of the Insert bar to apply an email link with your email address.

The email link is displayed with the formatting attributes that you chose in the Style definition dialog box. If there were any other links on this page, or in documents that linked to the same external style sheet, they too would display these formatting attributes.

CSS selector styles are not displayed in the CSS Styles panel.

NOTE *Using CSS selector styles, it is possible to remove the default underline that appears on all links, but this practice is not recommended. When creating Web sites, you need to consider user expectations. Users have become accustomed to underlined links. If you remove the underlines, your users might overlook the links and miss the information. Conversely, if you underline other words in your text, users might try to click them, expecting links. If it is necessary, you can remove the underline in your style definition for the link you just created in this exercise by following these steps: In the lighthouse.css dialog box that you used in this exercise, select a:link and click Edit. In the Style definition dialog box that opens, select None in the Decoration area to remove the underline from the link.*

5) Save the keepers.html document.

Leave this file open for the next exercise.

CREATING CSS SELECTOR STYLES FOR TAG COMBINATIONS

CSS selector styles also enable you to format combinations of tags—tags that appear within other tags. In this lesson, for example, you want to give text paragraphs within a table a different format than the other paragraphs on the page. Since you already created a style for the **<p>** tag, the paragraphs within the table currently reflect that formatting. Place the cursor in the paragraph within the nested table that contains the light source image, and you will see by looking at the HTML code that there are **<td>** tags for the table cell and **<p>** tags for the paragraphs within the cell. The Tag Selector at the bottom left of the document window shows the hierarchy of the code. The last five tags listed are **<table><tr><td><center><p>**: table, table row, table cell, center, and paragraph, respectively.

In this exercise, you will create a style that changes only the formatting of the paragraphs within the table cells so that they look different from the rest of the paragraphs on the page.

1) In the keepers.html document, click New CSS Style on the CSS Styles panel.

The New CSS Style dialog box opens.

2) Select Use CSS Selector in the Type area and type center p in the Selector text field.

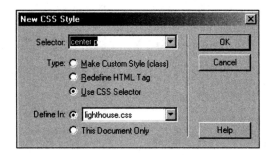

The center p you typed in the Selector text field represents the center tag and the paragraph tags inside it. Wherever this specific combination of tags appears in the document, the formatting you are going to choose in the following steps will be applied. By using center p, you are specifying that only paragraphs that are centered with the **<center>** tag will be affected.

3) Select lighthouse.css in the Define In area and click OK.

The Style definition dialog box opens.

4) Set the font to Geneva, Arial, Helvetica, san-serif. Select 10 points for the size and 14 points for the line height. In the color box, select #000000 and click OK.

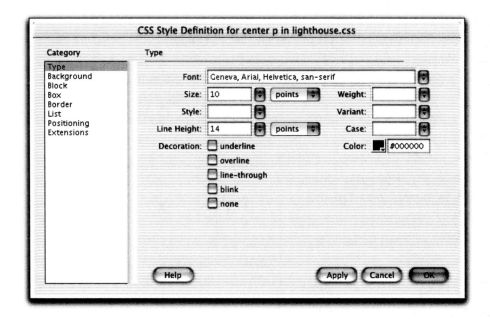

Your changes are reflected in the text that is located in the table.

5) Save your changes and close the file.

Because CSS selector styles allow you to format tags that appear after another tag, the changes you made for the paragraph in the table do not affect the other paragraphs on the page. The text in the table uses a **<p>** tag that appears between the **<center>** and **</center>** tags in the HTML code, so the center p CSS selector style is applied to that text. The paragraphs outside the table, however, do not have center applied to them, so that text remains unaffected by the selector style.

LINKING TO AN EXISTING EXTERNAL STYLE SHEET

You now have an external style sheet with several style definitions. Because it is external, you can use this file for other documents by linking the style sheet to the file you want the style definitions to be applied to. The style definitions, except for custom styles, will be applied automatically to all documents that are linked to this style sheet. You will need to manually apply any custom styles to paragraphs or selected text.

NOTE *Dreamweaver includes a number of predesigned CSS style sheets you can use in your own Web sites. To use one of these style sheets, choose File > New and select CSS Style Sheets from the Category list on the General tab. Select the style sheet you wish to use from the CSS Style Sheets list and click Create. Use these style sheets as-is, or use them as a starting point to develop your own. The new CSS document will open in Code View. You should save the new CSS document with the .css extension. You can link your documents to it using the steps in this exercise.*

1) Open the life.html file from the Lesson_13_CSS folder.

In the following steps, you will link this document to the external style sheet you've been working with so the text formatting will be consistent between both pages.

2) Click the Attach Style Sheet icon at the bottom of the CSS Styles panel.

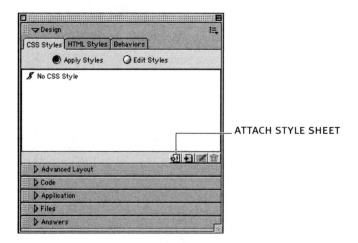

ATTACH STYLE SHEET

The Link External Style Sheet dialog box opens.

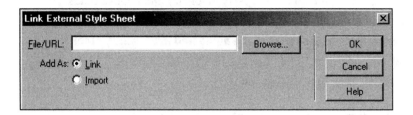

3) Click Browse and locate the lighthouse.css file you created at the beginning of this lesson in the Lesson_13_CSS folder using the Select Style Sheet File dialog box. Click Open to select the file. Verify that Link is selected from the Add As options in the Link External Style Sheet dialog box and click OK.

The external style sheet has now been linked to this document. Any tags in the current document are changed to the styles in the external style sheet.

N O T E *The Import Add As option does not work with Netscape Navigator.*

Notice that not all the text in life.html has changed from its default formatting. The document had some HTML tags that were not included in your style sheet. In the following steps, you will edit the external style sheet to add the HTML tags that appear in this new page.

4) Using steps 5 through 7 from the *Adding a Style to an Existing Style Sheet* exercise earlier in this lesson, create styles with format attributes of your choice for the heading "Personal Resources" and the bulleted list that appear on the life.html page. When you create the style for the Personal Resources heading, make sure <h5> is selected in the Tag Selector. When creating the style for the bulleted list, make sure <ul> is selected in the Tag Selector.

The **<ol>** tag that you redefined earlier in the lesson indicated an ordered list (or numbered list); the **<ul>** tag that you are redefining in this exercise corresponds to the unordered list (or bulleted list).

The text on the page changes as you specify styles for the heading and bullet list.

417

5) Select the word "Oil" in the numbered list near the top of the page. Click the Toggle CSS/HTML Mode button on the Property inspector and choose boldstyle from the drop-down menu, which initially shows No CSS Style. Continue to apply the boldstyle custom style to the terms in the numbered list "Paint", "Tools", "supplies", "Water", and "Coal". Click the Toggle CSS/HTML Mode button when you are done to switch back to the HTML Mode.

If the number 6 in the last line of the list displays the boldstyle when you are setting the term "Coal" to use that style, you may need to edit it in Code View, as you did in Lesson 12. You can switch to Code View and copy the **<span class="boldstyle">** tag from in front of the term "Water" and paste it in front of "Coal". Then copy the **</span>** tag from after the term "Water" and paste it just after "Coal". Your code will look like this:

```
<li><span class="boldstyle">Coal</span></li>
```

Save this file and leave it open for the next exercise.

CREATING INTERNAL STYLES

Internal styles are used only in the current document. If you want to create style definitions for only one page in your site, you should create an internal style. If you want your site to have a consistent look, you should use an external style sheet and link that style sheet to each document.

In this exercise, you will add an internal style that will be available only for the current document.

1) In the life.html document, click New CSS Style on the CSS Styles panel.
The New Style dialog box opens.

2) Select This Document Only in the Define In area and change the Type to Make Custom Style (class).
"This Document Only" specifies that you are adding a new internal style.

3) Type highlight in the Name text field and click OK.

The Style definition dialog box opens.

4) In the CSS Style Definition dialog box, click Background in the Category list on the left.

The CSS Style Definition dialog box changes to display background options.

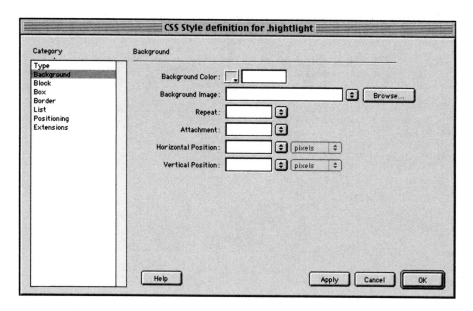

5) Change the color in the Background Color field to pale green (#CCFFFF) and click OK.

NOTE *There are a total of eight categories available for style definition. You've used two: Type (basic text format options such as font, size, and style) and Background (options for background appearance such as color and image). Information on the other six categories follows:*

- *Block provides additional text spacing and positioning options.*

- *Box provides additional options to control placement.*

- *Border provides options to control borders.*

- *List provides options to control the formatting of ordered and unordered lists.*

- *Positioning provides options for CSS layers.*

- *Extensions provides additional options that are not widely supported.*

The highlight custom style you just created appears in the CSS Styles panel. There are now two custom styles: boldstyle and highlight. Notice the icon to the left of each name. The custom style in the external style sheet (boldstyle) has a small link image on the icon to represent the link to the external style sheet.

NOTE *You will see these styles listed in the Apply Styles portion of the CSS Styles panel. You can switch to this view by clicking the Apply Styles radio button at the top of the CSS Styles panel.*

EXTERNAL STYLE SHEET ICON ——
INTERNAL STYLE SHEET ICON ——

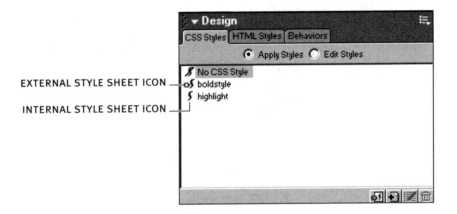

6) Select the paragraph of text below the "Personal Resources" heading and click the highlight style on the CSS Styles panel to apply the style.
The text appears to be highlighted with the pale color.

7) Save the life.html file, and then open the keepers.html file.
Look in the CSS Styles panel. You will not see the highlight custom style you just created because it is an internal style and appears only in the document where it was created.

NOTE *To remove internal or external styles, click the Edit Style Sheet icon on the CSS Styles panel to open the Edit Style Sheet dialog box. Select the style you want to remove and click Remove. If the style is an internal style, it is deleted from the document. If you remove an external style sheet, the link to the style is removed from the document. The actual external style sheet file is not deleted from your site.*

You can close the keepers.html file and leave the life.html file open for the next exercise.

420

CONVERTING INTERNAL STYLES TO EXTERNAL STYLES

If you have a document with internal styles and you decide you want to use those styles in other pages, you can easily export those styles to an external style sheet.

1) In the life.html document, choose File > Export > CSS Styles...

The Export Styles As CSS File dialog box opens.

2) Name your style sheet lifestyle.css and click Save.

An external style sheet with just the highlight style is created from the internal styles in the current document.

If you want to use this external style sheet in your current document, first remove all internal styles, and then click the Attach Style Sheet icon at the bottom of the CSS Styles panel to link to the external file you just created.

NOTE *While working in Dreamweaver, you can hide the effects of a style sheet. To hide the effects of a particular style sheet choose Design Time Style Sheets from the context menu in the upper right corner of the CSS Styles panel. Click the plus sign (+) button to add a style sheet to the Show Only at Design Time text field. Any Style Sheets added to this text field will be displayed in Dreamweaver. Click the plus sign (+) button to add a style sheet to the Hide at Design Time text field. Any style sheets added to this text field will not be displayed while you work in Dreamweaver. This will not affect the display in any browser—documents will still use all style sheets they are linked to when viewed in the browser.*

CONVERTING CSS TO HTML

CSS is a great way to control the text throughout your Web site, but not all browsers are capable of CSS. Earlier browsers will ignore CSS formatting. If you decide to use CSS, you may want to convert your page to 3.0 browser–compatible files in order to display the page with formatting as close to the CSS styles as possible. You can then use the Check Browser behavior to redirect users based on their browser version (as you did in Lesson 5). This exercise shows you how to convert from CSS to HTML tags.

1) In the life.html document, choose File › Convert › 3.0 Browser Compatible.

The Convert to 3.0 Browser Compatible dialog box opens.

2) Select CSS Styles to HTML Markup and click OK.

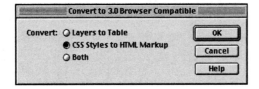

The converted file is opened in a new, untitled document, and your original file remains unaltered. The styles that were applied in the keepers.html document are reproduced as closely as possible using standard HTML tags. However, it is not possible to convert some types of CSS formatting to HTML tags. For example, line height (also known as **leading**) has no equivalent in HTML. There is no way to adjust the spacing between lines of text with the standard HTML formatting attributes. Any attributes that cannot be converted will be discarded.

NOTE *After the file is converted and placed into a new document, any changes made to the original won't be reflected in the converted document. Changes made by editing the CSS styles will not appear in converted 3.0 browser–compatible documents. You will have to reconvert the original document to match the edits as closely as possible.*

3) Save the document as life_oldbrowsers.html.

You can close all open files.

NOTE *If you are proficient in writing HTML and know how to write CSS, you can create a CSS page from scratch by choosing File > New and selecting the CSS document type from the Basic Page category on the General tab. A new document will open in which Code View will be the only available viewing mode. For more information about CSS, choose O'REILLY CSS Reference from the Book drop-down menu on the Reference panel located in the Code panel group.*

ON YOUR OWN: PROJECT DISCOVER

The Project Discover Web site was created by a team of students from the Multimedia Studies Intensive Program at San Francisco State University. The team included Brian Garcia, Nicole Holdorph, Dorcia Lu, and Chris Wiedenmayer.

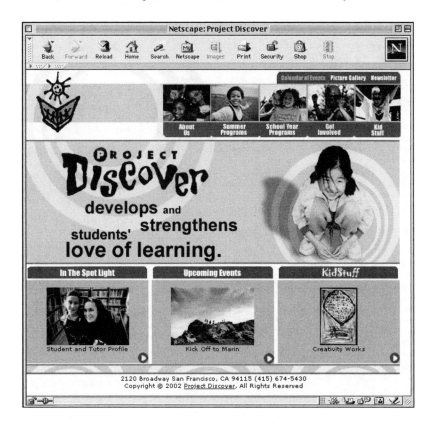

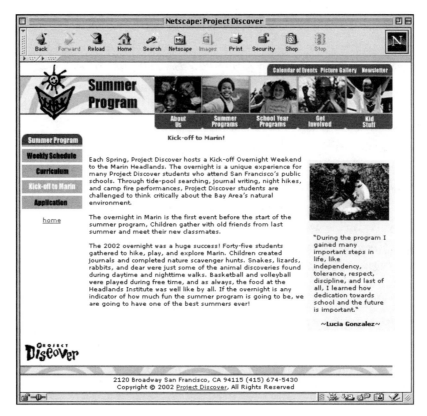

http://www.projectdiscover.org

Credits: © Project Discover

The files you will need for this exercise are located in the Bonus/Lesson_13 folder. For this activity, you should create an external style sheet and attach it to summer.html and marin_summer.html. This style sheet should define the Heading 4 as #3366CC and bold style and the paragraph text as Verdana, #000000 and 10 points.

WHAT YOU HAVE LEARNED

In this lesson, you have:

- Created an external style sheet specifying text formatting that can be used to maintain consistency in the look of text throughout a Web site (pages 400–403)

- Added multiple styles to an existing style sheet by redefining HTML tags (pages 404–406)

- Edited a style in the external style sheet to affect all documents linked to it (pages 407–408)

- Created a custom style that can be applied to different kinds of text formats (pages 408–412, 414–416)

- Created CSS selector styles to change the appearance of links on the page (pages 412–414)

- Linked to an external style sheet from another document to use the same text formatting (pages 416–418)

- Created an internal style to use the same text formatting quickly and easily (pages 418–420)

- Converted internal styles to external styles so they can be used by other documents (page 421)

- Converted CSS to HTML to make the pages compatible with 3.0 browsers (pages 422–423)

using find and replace

LESSON 14

The Find and Replace feature in Dreamweaver provides you with a powerful searching tool. You can search the current document, a specified folder, or an entire site. The extensive options enable you to search for text, HTML tags, or even limit your search to certain attributes within HTML tags. After you've found what you are looking for, you can modify or replace it. The Find and Replace feature can save a lot of time when you need to make massive changes to a document or an entire site.

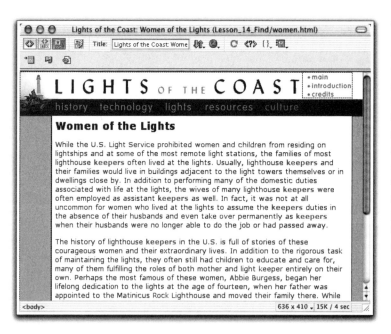

In this project, you will use find and replace to change words in this document. You will also adjust the formatting attributes of text in this document by using find and replace to automate the process of linking to an external style sheet and applying a custom style to text.

In this lesson, you will use find and replace to make a wide variety of changes to several documents. You will use find and replace to apply CSS styles and attach external style sheets to a number of documents all at once. You'll find and replace text, change text formatting, learn to save your searches to use at a later time, find dates, and replace names.

To see examples of the finished pages for this lesson, open women.html and ca_lights.html from the Lesson_14_Find/Completed folder.

WHAT YOU WILL LEARN

In this lesson, you will:

- Find and replace text
- Find text within HTML tags
- Use find and replace to apply a custom style
- Use find and replace to attach external style sheets
- Save and reuse your search settings
- Search for patterns in text
- Find variations of a name

APPROXIMATE TIME

This lesson should take about one hour to complete.

LESSON FILES

Starting Files:

Lesson_14_Find/women.html
Lesson_14_Find/ca_lights.html
Lesson_14_Find/light_style.html

Completed Project:

Lesson_14_Find/Completed/…(all files)

SEARCHING YOUR DOCUMENT

In this exercise, you will perform a simple search in order to find and replace words in the text of a document.

1) Open the women.html file from the Lesson_14_Find folder. Place the insertion point at the end of the header "Women of the Lights."

This document refers to "lite house keepers" throughout the text, when it should actually be "lighthouse keepers." You'll replace that text in this exercise.

2) Choose Edit › Find and Replace.

The Find and Replace dialog box opens.

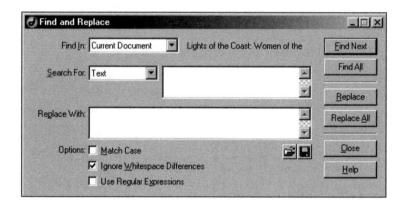

3) In the Find In drop-down menu, choose Current Document. In the Search For drop-down menu, choose Text. In the Search For text field, type lite house keepers. In the Replace With text field, type lighthouse keepers. Uncheck the boxes for all three options.

TIP *Selecting a portion of text before opening the Find and Replace dialog box will automatically cause the selected text to appear in the Search For text field.*

Find in Current Document will search the entire document. This can only be used from a single document while it is open. The Find In drop-down menu also has additional options:

- Entire Local Site will search the whole current site.

- Selected Files in Site will search files you specify and should be used while viewing the site window so you can select the files.

- Folder will allow you to browse in order to select a folder and search all the contents of that folder.

There are three other options at the bottom of the Find and Replace dialog box:

- Match Case limits the search to the exact case of the words. If the Match Case box is checked, a search will look for only the exact phrase you entered.

- Ignore Whitespace Differences ignores all spaces. If this is checked and you are searching for two words, Dreamweaver will also find all instances where those two words have additional spaces between them.

- Use Regular Expressions provides patterns to describe character combinations in the text. Use this option to select sentences that begin with "The" or attribute values that contain a number.

4) Click Find Next.

The first occurrence of the phrase after the insertion point is highlighted.

5) Click Replace.

The phrase is changed to "lighthouse keepers," and the next occurrence of the phrase is highlighted.

TIP *When replacing text in your document, it is recommended that you click Replace first and check the new text to make sure you typed the correct information in the Replace field. After you verify the search criteria, then use Replace All.*

The Results window opens. It may be blank initially; you should leave it open.

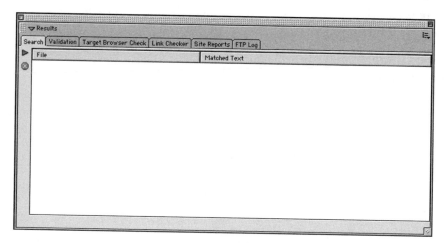

6) Click Find All.

Three more instances of the text you are searching for are found and displayed in the Results window. Double-clicking an item in this list will highlight the instance in the document window.

7) Click the green arrow on the left of the Results window.

The Find and Replace dialog box opens again.

NOTE *Dreamweaver remembers the settings from your most recent search. If you close and reopen the dialog box, the text and options you set the last time the dialog box was open will still be there.*

8) Now click Replace All on the Find and Replace dialog box.

The remaining text is all changed and a message box appears, reporting the number of items found and replaced in your document.

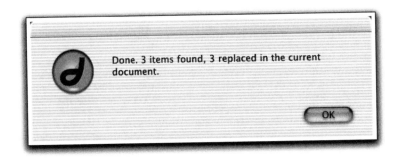

The Find and Replace dialog box will automatically close once it has finished searching for and replacing text.

9) Click OK to close the message box. Click the context menu in the upper right corner of the Results window and choose Clear Results; then close the Results window. Save the women.html document.

Leave this file open for the next exercise.

REMOVING HTML TAGS

In this same file, the text "Lighthouse Keepers" is italicized. The italic attribute has been applied using local formatting. Local formatting is applied using the Property inspector to define the text attributes as opposed to using CSS. In this exercise, you will use find and replace to remove the HTML font tag that defines the italic attribute.

In a later exercise, you will use find and replace to apply a custom CSS style to the text, but first you need to remove the local formatting. Remember that in CSS styles, local formatting overrides any internal or external styles, so if you want to apply CSS styles, you will need to remove the local formatting first.

1) In the women.html document, select the first occurrence of the text "lighthouse keepers" in the text "the families of most lighthouse keepers often lived at the lights."

The text you have selected is italic.

2) Click Show Code and Design Views on the toolbar to view the HTML for the text.

NOTE *Selected text in the document is also selected in the code window. This makes it easier to spot the text and the corresponding HTML code.*

On line 53, the HTML tag that controls the italic of the text is the **<em>** tag which appears just before the selected text and the **</em>** tag which appears just after the selected text. You will use find and replace in this exercise to strip these tags, removing both tags at once from each instance of italicized text in this document.

3) To make sure the first find selects the first tag, click anywhere before the opening <em> tag in the Code View.

If your insertion point is inside of or after the opening italic tag (**<em>**) that defines the attribute, Dreamweaver will bypass that tag. You need to place the insertion point before the tag in the HTML code in order to include the first instance of the italic text in your search.

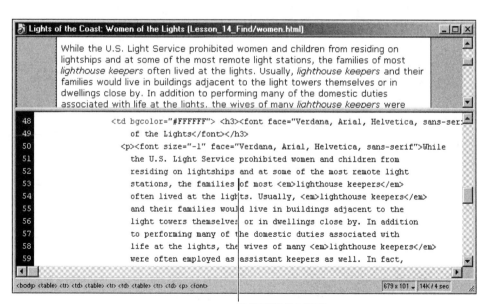

INSERTION POINT

4) Choose Edit > Find and Replace to open the Find and Replace dialog box. Change the Search For drop-down menu to Specific Tag.

NOTE *You can also use the shortcut Ctrl+F (Windows) or Command+F (Macintosh) to open the Find and Replace dialog box.*

Choosing Specific Tag allows you to search Dreamweaver for a certain tag. The dialog box will change to reflect this search method. A set of options to choose from will be displayed in order to narrow the search and look for tags with specific attributes.

5) Select em from the list of HTML tags in the drop-down menu to the right of the Specific Tag selection.

TIP *You could also type "em" in the Search For text field instead of using the drop-down menu.*

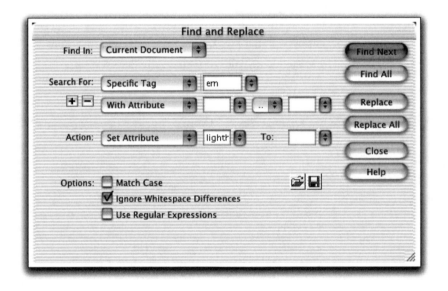

Dreamweaver will search for all italic tags in the women.html file.

6) Click the minus sign (–) button to remove the tag modifier option. Choose Strip Tag from the Action drop-down menu and uncheck all three additional Options.

Since you are looking for a simple tag with no attributes, the modifiers are unneeded.

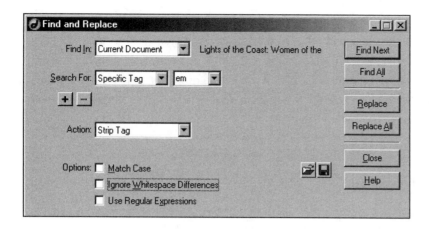

7) Click Find Next to select the first occurrence, and then click Replace. Verify that the italic tag (<em>) was removed, and then click Replace All. Click the context menu in the upper right corner of the Results window and choose Clear Results.

All italic tags within the document are removed. The Find and Replace dialog box closes automatically.

8) Locate and select the first instance of green text in the second paragraph of the women.html document. In the Code View pane, click anywhere before the opening `<font color="#006633">` tag just before the selected text.

The name "Abbie Burgess" is set to a green color. The HTML tag that controls the color of the text is the `<font color="#006633">` tag that appears before the selected text in the Code View pane.

9) Choose Edit > Find and Replace to open the Find and Replace dialog box. Make sure the Search For drop-down menu is set to Specific Tag and select font from the tag drop-down menu.

You will remove the color attribute of the `<font>` tag from the document in the following steps.

10) Click the plus sign (+) button below the Search For area.

Several drop-down menus and text fields appear that will allow you to make very specific selections. Use these menus and text fields to limit your searches and find unique occurrences of a tag. The additional options here include a number of qualifiers for an attribute; the ability to choose a specific attribute that can be used with the selected tag; less than (<), greater than (>), and not equal to (!=); and a place to set a value for the desired tag. The options in the drop-down menus will vary depending upon the tag that you have selected. In this exercise, you have chosen to look for font tags.

11) Make sure that With Attribute is selected in the drop-down menu directly below the Search For field and select color from the drop-down menu to the right of it. In the drop-down menu to the right of color, make sure = is selected. In the next drop-down menu to the right, type #006633. In the Action drop-down menu, select Strip Tag. Deselect the check boxes for Match Case, Ignore Whitespace Differences, and Use Regular Expressions.

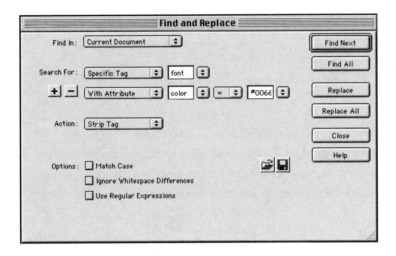

Since you want to remove only the tags that have color applied, you are looking specifically for the **<font>** tag with the attribute of color. You have limited the search further by typing the hex value for the color in the last field. Make sure you include the # sign in front of the hexadecimal code in this field.

NOTE *You can continue to add additional modifiers by clicking the plus sign (+) button. For this exercise, you should use only the single modifier.*

12) Click Find Next to select the first occurrence, and then click Replace. Verify that the <font color="#006633"> tag was removed, and then click Replace All.
The green color attribute is discarded from any text with that color throughout the entire document.

13) Click OK to exit the message box that reports the number of items replaced. Save the file. If a list of results appears in the Results Window, click the context menu in the upper right corner of the Results window and choose Clear Results; then close the Results window.
The Find and Replace dialog box closes automatically after the items have been replaced.

Leave the women.html file open for the next exercise.

USING FIND AND REPLACE TO APPLY A CUSTOM STYLE

Now that you have removed the local italic and color formatting from the text, you can apply a custom CSS style to the document. In this exercise, you will use find and replace to locate the text in the HTML Source window and apply the HTML tags for the custom style.

1) In the women.html document, link to the external style sheet light_style.css located in the Lesson_14_Find folder by clicking the Attach Style Sheet icon on the CSS Styles panel.

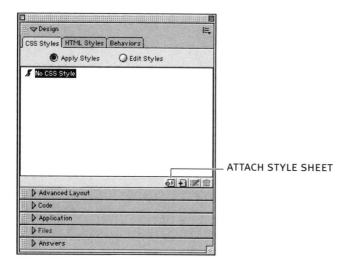

ATTACH STYLE SHEET

If the CSS Styles panel is not visible, choose Window > CSS Styles.

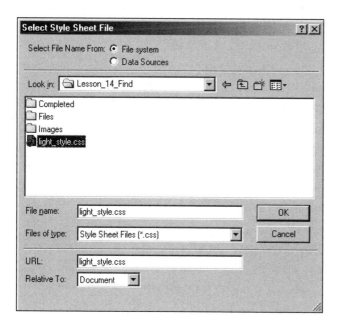

435

This style sheet has two custom styles already created. You need to attach the style sheet first before you can apply the custom styles.

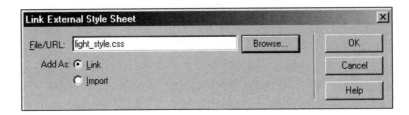

2) Select the first occurrence of the word "keepers" in the body text. Click the boldcolor custom style from the CSS Styles panel to apply it to the selected text.

The text changes to reflect the bold and brown attributes that are defined by the custom style.

3) Choose Edit > Find and Replace, change the Search For drop-down menu to Source Code, and type keepers in the text field.

The dialog box that appears will change to reflect the Source Code search method.

4) Leaving the Find and Replace dialog box open, look at the HTML for the custom style you just applied in step 2.

You should see `<span class="boldcolor">keepers</span>`.

5) Copy all the HTML in the Code View beginning with `<span class="boldcolor">` and ending with `</span>`.

436

You must have the Code View pane visible or be in Code View to copy the HTML along with the text; otherwise, you get just the text and no HTML. You should now have **`<span class="boldcolor">keepers</span>`** selected.

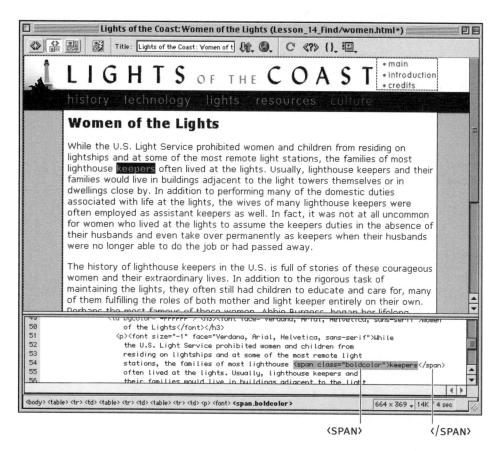

<SPAN>   </SPAN>

6) Return to the Find and Replace dialog box. Paste the HTML code you copied in step 5 into the Replace With text field. Uncheck the three additional options.

Dreamweaver will replace all occurrences in the text with this code.

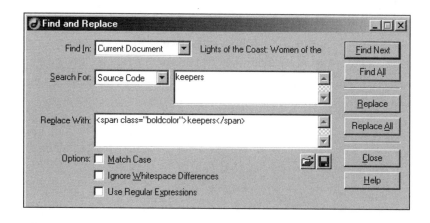

7) Click Find Next to select the next occurrence of the word "keepers." Click Replace to change the text and add the HTML. Verify that the change is correct. Click Replace All to change all occurrences in your document. Click OK to close the message box that reports the numbers of changes made.

The Property inspector will let you know that changes have been made to the code. Once you click OK the document refreshes and the changes are visible.

All instances of the "keepers" are now formatted with the boldcolor CSS style. Using find and replace to apply styles in this way can save you a lot of time.

The Find and Replace dialog box closes automatically.

NOTE *When using this method, you will need to be certain that there no occurrences of the word that you are replacing (in this case it is "keepers") in the code anywhere but in the text. If any images were named "keepers," or if "keepers" was part of a pathname, you would have problems with your code. When in doubt, use the Replace button rather than the Replace All button so you can double-check the item to be replaced.*

8) Save this document. If a list of results appears in the Results Window, click the context menu in the upper right corner of the Results window and choose Clear Results; then close the Results window.

Look back to the first occurrence of "keepers" where you manually applied the custom style. You should see that now you have two **<span>** tags applied to this text because find and replace added the extra tag. Although the word appears to display properly in Dreamweaver, you need to remove the extra tag. You can manually remove the custom style by selecting the text in Design View, choosing None from the CSS Styles panel and then reapplying the style, or you can choose Commands > Cleanup HTML. Make sure Redundant Nested Tags is selected in the Cleanup HTML dialog box and click OK. Dreamweaver will remove the extra **<span>** tags.

You can close the women.html file.

USING FIND AND REPLACE TO ADD EXTERNAL STYLE SHEETS

In Lesson 13, you created an external style sheet and attached that style sheet to another document. The steps to add a style sheet to a document are not difficult, but they could be time-consuming if you need attach one to multiple pages or an entire site. By using find and replace, you can accomplish that task in a matter of minutes.

In this exercise, you will attach the external style sheet light_style.css to multiple pages.

Macintosh users: For this exercise, you do not need to open a document.

Windows users: For this exercise, you will need to create a new, basic HTML page. You must have a document window open in order to run the Find and Replace function.

1) Choose Edit > Find and Replace.

The Find and Replace dialog box opens showing everything you set in the previous exercise. If you do not have a document window open, then you must have the Site window open in order to choose Find and Replace.

NOTE *You should verify that the Lights of the Coast site is the selected site if you have other sites defined.*

2) Change the Find In drop-down menu to Folder and click the folder icon to the right of the text field.

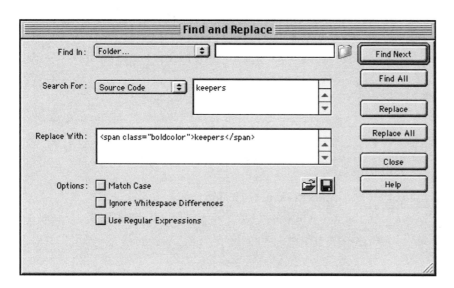

The Choose Search Folder dialog box opens.

3) Locate the Files folder in the Lesson_14_Find folder. On Macintosh, select the Files folder (but do not open it) and click Choose. In Windows, open the Files folder and click Select.

There are two HTML documents in the Files folder that need to have the external style sheet attached.

4) Make sure that the Search For drop-down menu is set to Source Code. In the Search For text field, type </head>. In the Replace With text field, type the following code: <link href="light_style.css" rel="stylesheet" type="text/css"></head>.

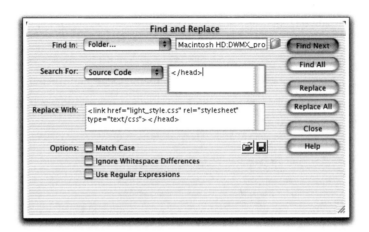

When you use the Attach Style Sheet icon, Dreamweaver adds the **<link>** tag within the **<head>** tag. You are using find and replace to search for the end head (**</head>**) tag and then add the **<link>** tag before it by replacing it with the **<link>** tag followed by a **</head>** tag.

> **NOTE** *To get a new line when you are within the Replace With text field, press Shift+ Enter (Windows) or Shift+Return (Macintosh). Using the Enter or Return key alone activates the Find Next button in the dialog box.*

5) All the Options should be unchecked. Click Find Next.

The first document in the folder in which Dreamweaver finds the **</head>** tag opens in Code View. Dreamweaver will select the **</head>** tag.

6) Click Replace.

Dreamweaver makes the replacement, then automatically finds the next document in the folder and opens it in Code View with the **</head>** tag selected.

7) Click Replace. Close the Find and Replace dialog box. Save and close both open documents, keepers.html and life.html. If a list of results appears in the Results Window, click the context menu in the upper right corner of the Results window and choose Clear Results. Then close the Results window.

The style sheet is attached to both documents.

Windows users should leave open the blank document created at the beginning of this exercise.

SAVING AND REUSING YOUR SEARCH CRITERIA

You might want to save your search criteria for other documents in your site, especially with complex search criteria. Saved search criteria, known as **queries**, are saved in the Configuration/Queries folder inside the Dreamweaver folder by default. They can, however, be saved in different places.

In this exercise, you'll save your search query in the Lesson_14_Find folder. For this exercise, Macintosh users do not need to open a document. Windows users must have a document open—you should still have the blank document open from the previous exercise.

1) Choose Edit > Find and Replace. Click the Save Query icon in the Find and Replace dialog box.

The Find and Replace dialog box will have the same settings that were used in the last exercise to attach the light_style.css style sheet to documents.

The Save Query icon looks like a floppy disk icon. This option makes it possible for you to save and reuse complex searches.

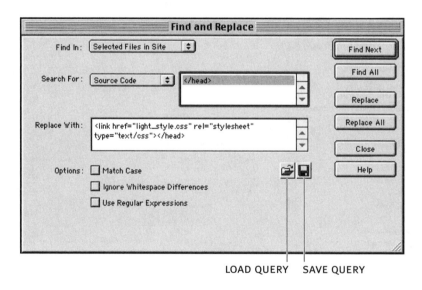

LOAD QUERY   SAVE QUERY

2) In the Save Query to File (Macintosh) or Save Query (Windows) dialog box, locate and open the Lesson_14_Find folder. Then type addStyle in the File Name text field and click Save.

Find queries have a .dwq extension; Replace queries have a .dwr extension. The extension is automatically added for you. The default location for the file to be saved is in the Queries folder inside the Configuration folder. The Configuration folder is located in the Dreamweaver program folder.

Now that you have saved the addStyle query, it will be available to you anytime you need to run the same Find and Replace function in other documents. To save your own searches, set up your search and test it. Then follow steps 1 and 2 in this exercise.

3) Click the Load Query icon in the Find and Replace dialog box.

The Load Query icon looks like an open folder icon next to the disk icon.

You will now load a new Query that has already been saved for you.

4) In the Load Query (Windows) or Load Query from File (Macintosh) dialog box, locate and Open (Macintosh) or Select (Windows) the highlight_query.dwr query in the Lesson_14_Find folder.

This query will look for "keeper" and add the highlight custom style from the external style sheet you just added to the files in the folder.

5) From the Find in: drop-down menu, choose Selected Files in Site. Leaving the Find and Replace dialog box open, use your Site window to select keepers.html and life.html in the Files folder.

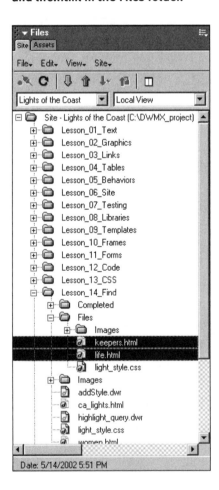

Dreamweaver will use the search criteria you loaded from the highlight_query on both documents selected in the Site window.

NOTE *You can Shift-Click to select contiguous files, or Command-click (Macintosh) or Ctrl-click (Windows) each file name to select noncontiguous files in the Site window.*

6) Click Replace All to make the changes in the selected files. Click the context menu in the upper right corner of the Results window and choose Clear Results; then close the Results window.

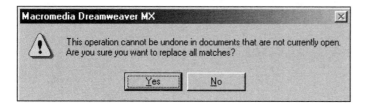

You can click OK on the dialog box informing you that this operation cannot be undone in documents that are not currently open. The Find and Replace dialog box will close automatically when done.

Both keepers.html and life.html are updated to include the highlight custom style on any "keeper" text.

SEARCHING AND REPLACING WITH REGULAR EXPRESSIONS

Regular expressions are control characters that describe character combinations or patterns in text. For example, if you want to find all occurrences of years from 1700–1799, the pattern is "17" followed by any combination of two numbers from 0–9. You can use a number of special characters to define the search pattern. For example, the backslash (\), dollar sign ($), and question mark (?) are special characters. It is important to know these characters; if you are looking for such special characters in your text, you need to precede the character with a backslash to indicate it is part of the character search and not used as a special character.

NOTE *Appendix A contains a table with all the special characters, regular expressions, and their meanings.*

In this exercise, you will use patterned searches in a document.

1) Open the ca_lights.html file in the Lesson_14_Find folder and choose Edit › Find and Replace.

TIP *You can also use Command+F (Macintosh) or Ctrl+F (Windows) to open the Find and Replace dialog box.*

The Find and Replace dialog box opens.

2) Select Current Document in the Find In drop-down menu. Set the Search For drop-down menu to Text. Check the Use Regular Expressions option box.

Notice that Ignore Whitespace Differences is completely disabled when you select Use Regular Expressions.

NOTE *The Ignore Whitespace Differences option, when selected, treats all whitespace as a single space for the purposes of matching. For example, with this option selected, "this text" would match "this text" but not "thistext". This option is not available when the Use Regular Expressions option is selected; you must explicitly write your regular expression to ignore whitespace. Note that P and BR tags do not count as whitespace.*

3) In the Search For text field, type 17\d\d.

Be sure to type backslashes (\), not forward slashes (/), when you enter 17\d\d into the text field.

NOTE *The Replace With text field may still contain the code* `<span class="highlight">` `keeper</span>` *that was used in the previous exercise. You'll change this in the following steps; it will not affect the initial search.*

The first search will look for all years from 1700–1799. The ca_lights.html file contains a list of years that are mostly after the 1800s. In this exercise, you will draw attention to the few years in the 1700s by applying the bold attribute to any year from 1700–1799. You want to skip the other years such as 1821 or 1901. To search for any number between 0–9, you use \d (known as a wildcard) as the search pattern. Because you want to limit the search to only the 1700 years, you are preceding the pattern character with the explicit text "17." See Appendix A for more regular expressions to use for search patterns.

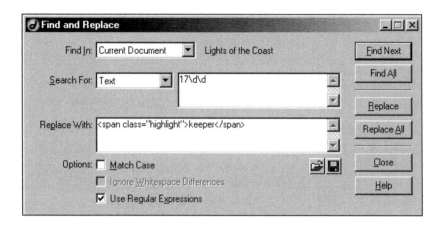

TIP *To distinguish decimal numbers from years—19.09 for example—when searching in the document, include a period in your search. A period is also a special character, so you need to precede it with a backslash in your search.*

4) Click Find Next.

Dreamweaver will select the first year (1783) in the document window.

5) Continue to click Find Next several times to see what gets selected.

Any years in the 1800s or 1900s are not selected because they don't match the exact pattern.

6) In the Find and Replace dialog box change the Search For drop-down menu to Source Code.

The search now takes place in the Code Inspector, which will open up in a separate window.

In the Replace With text field, you will add the bold tags (<b> and </b>) around the text in the search. However, if you were to type <b>17\d\d<\b>, the text in the document window would be changed to 17\d\d. It would literally change the numbers in the year to \d. Instead, you need to isolate the search as a pattern by surrounding the pattern in parentheses.

7) In the Search For text field, insert a left parenthesis before the text and a right parenthesis after the text, like this: (17\d\d).

The parentheses create the first pattern.

8) In the Replace With text field, type ‹b›$1‹/b›.

To reference the pattern you created in the previous step, you use $1 in the Replace With text field. This adds the bold tags around the results of the first pattern search. If you were to create several patterns, the next pattern, as indicated by the parenthesis, would be referenced in this text field with $2 and so on in a sequential manner.

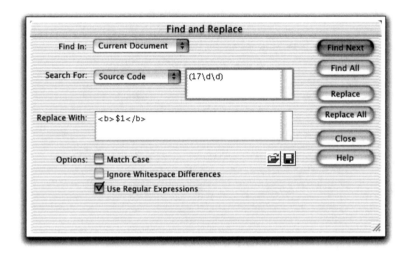

9) Click Find Next, and then click Replace.

The bold tags are placed around the year in the Code Inspector. Click in the Document window to see the results.

10) Click Replace All to find and replace all occurrences in the document. Save the ca_lights.html document. Click the context menu in the upper right corner of the Results window and choose Clear Results; then close the Results window.

Leave this file open for the next exercise.

FINDING VARIATIONS IN A NAME

You can also look for variations in a name. For example, some of these lighthouses are located in California, but the name of the state is written in various formats throughout the page: ca, Ca, california, and California. You want to make the format consistent and change it to California.

1) In the ca_lights.html document, choose Edit > Find and Replace. Change Search For to Text and type C\w* built in the Search For text field.

The \w searches for any alphanumeric character after the C, and the asterisk means you want to find any number of alphanumeric characters. Adding "built" limits the search even further by causing Dreamweaver to search for instances that match

C\w* and which are followed by the word "built." For instance, "C\w* built" will find "Ca built," "California built," and other variations of the character 'C' followed by any number of alphanumeric characters and the word "built." If you were to leave off "built", the search would also find items such as "Cape" and "Cabrillo" in the document.

2) In the Options, make sure Match Case is unchecked and check the Use Regular Expressions box.

If Match Case were selected, then the search would be limited to finding only words that begin with an uppercase C. In this exercise, you want to find both the uppercase and lowercase instances of California, so you are leaving Match Case unchecked.

3) In the Replace With text field, type California built. Place the insertion point at the beginning of the text in the document window, click Find Next to find the first occurrence, and then click Replace to change it.

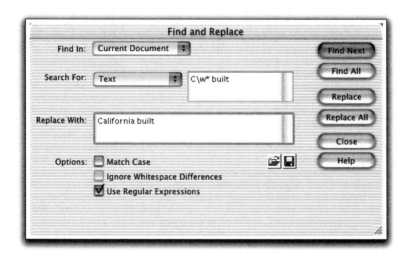

The first version of the state name is found in this document and replaced with California.

Dreamweaver selects the second instance of a "c" followed by "built": "chusetts built." You don't want to change this one because it is not a version of the CA state name.

4) Click Find Next. Continue to replace all the remaining versions of the CA state name. Save the ca_lights.html document.

You can close this document and the Results window.

ON YOUR OWN: REVEALING BODIES

The Revealing Bodies Web site was the online counterpart to the award winning Revealing Bodies Exhibit at the Exploratorium in 2000. The Web site featured in-depth explorations into certain aspects of the floor exhibit, as well as a number of Web casts.

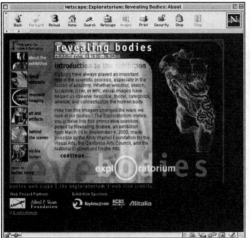 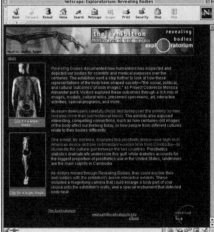

http://www.exploratorium.edu/bodies/
Credits: © Exploratorium, www.exploratorium.edu

The files you will need for this exercise are located in the Bonus/Lesson_14 folder. For this activity, you should complete the following:

• In many of the pages the word "body" has been misspelled as "bode." Use find and replace to replace all instances of "bode" with "body."

• Some of the images are broken. The source of the broken images is revealingbodies_images, whereas the images are actually located in the images folder. Use find and replace to search the code and replace all instances of "revealingbodies_images" with "images" to fix the problem.

WHAT YOU HAVE LEARNED

In this lesson, you have:

- Found and replaced text using detailed options to quickly modify a document (pages 428–430)

- Found text within HTML tags and learned how to change it using find and replace (pages 430–434)

- Used find and replace to quickly apply a custom style to a document (pages 435–438)

- Used find and replace to attach external style sheets to multiple pages within a site (pages 438–440)

- Saved your search settings for later use and loaded saved queries (pages 441–443)

- Searched for patterns in text using regular expressions to find specific text like dates and names (pages 443–446)

- Found multiple variations of a name and replaced them with one version (pages 446–447)

creating layers

LESSON 15

A **layer** is a rectangular container for HTML content that you can position at an exact location in the browser window. Layers can contain a wide variety of elements: text, images, tables, and even other layers. Anything you can place in an HTML document you can also place in a layer. Layers are especially useful for placing elements atop each other or making them overlap. Layers are supported by 4.0 or later browsers only. They can control layout and appearance when used in combination with CSS, and they provide interactivity when used in combination with behaviors and timelines.

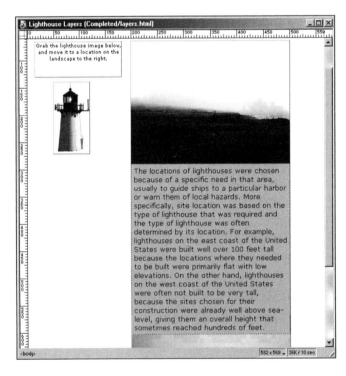

In this project, you will create layers, place text and images in them, move them to exact locations on the page, and change their properties.

In this lesson, you will learn several ways to create layers in Dreamweaver. You will draw a layer on the page to the size you want and place a layer on the page using a predetermined width and height. You will learn to modify layer attributes including size, placement, and visibility. You will also convert your layers to tables in order to make it possible for users with older browsers to view your pages.

To see an example of the finished page, open layers.html from the Lesson_15_Layers/ Completed folder.

WHAT YOU WILL LEARN

In this lesson, you will:

- Create layers

- Name layers

- Modify layer sizes and locations

- Use layers to control content on your page

- Change the stacking order of layers

- Nest and unnest layers

- Change layer visibility

- Set rulers and grids

- Use a JavaScript fix for a Netscape bug

- Make pages designed with layers compatible with earlier browsers

APPROXIMATE TIME

This lesson should take about one hour to complete.

LESSON FILES

Media Files:
Lesson_15_Layers/Images/…(all files)

Starting Files:
Lesson_15_Layers/Text/…(all files)

Completed Project:
Lesson_15_Layers/Completed/layers.html
Lesson_15_Layers/Completed/layers_table.html

CREATING LAYERS

There are several different ways to create layers. Which method you choose may depend on how you plan to use the layer and where you plan to place it.

1) Create a new document. Save the file as layers.html in the Lesson_15_Layers folder. Title the document Lighthouse Layers. Set the background to white and the text to black in the Page Properties dialog box.

In this exercise, you will create several layers on this page and insert content into them.

NOTE *You should be using Design View for this lesson.*

2) Verify that the Standard View icon is selected on the Layout tab of the Insert bar.

STANDARD VIEW

You must be in the Standard View in order to create a layer.

3) Select Draw Layer on the Common tab of the Insert bar. Move the pointer into the document window; then click and drag to create a new layer on the right side of the page.

DRAW LAYER

The pointer changes to a crosshair (+) when you move the pointer into the document window. After you drag and release the pointer, the new layer displays as a rectangle.

You should now see a layer marker at the top of the document window. It will appear blue when it is selected and yellow when it is not selected. If the layer marker isn't visible, choose View > Visual Aids > Invisible Elements.

NOTE *You can use the layer marker for selecting the layer, but if your layer is positioned at the top left of the document window, the marker could get in the way and may appear to shift the position of the layer. This shift only happens in the document window; when the page is viewed in the browser, all elements will be in their correct positions. Turn the markers off by using View > Visual Aids > Invisible Elements. A check next to the command in the menu indicates the option is on.*

By default, the layer code is inserted at the top of the page, just after the **<BODY>** tag. There are two tags you can set for your layers using the Tag drop-down menu in the Property inspector: **<DIV>** and **<SPAN>**. The **<DIV>** tag is the most common, allowing the largest possible audience to be able to view your layers. Dreamweaver uses the **<DIV>** tag by default to create layers that use absolute positioning to determine the placement of the layer in relation to the top and left sides of the browser window. The **<DIV>** tag is a block-level element. **<SPAN>** uses relative positioning to determine the placement of the layer depending upon the position of other elements around it. The **<SPAN>** tag is an inline element.

NOTE *Dreamweaver recognizes two additional tags, **<LAYER>** and **<ILAYER>**, but it does not provide the option to use these tags to create layers. These tags were only supported in Netscape Navigator 4. Netscape no longer supports these tags, and Internet Explorer has never supported them. The Design View will not render or display the layer, although it will insert a layer marker for the layer.*

4) Position the pointer over the border of the layer. When the pointer turns into a hand (Macintosh) or four outward-facing arrows (Windows), click to select the layer.
The layer is now shown with a square tab at the top left. This tab is the layer selection handle. The black squares on the borders of the layer are sizing handles.

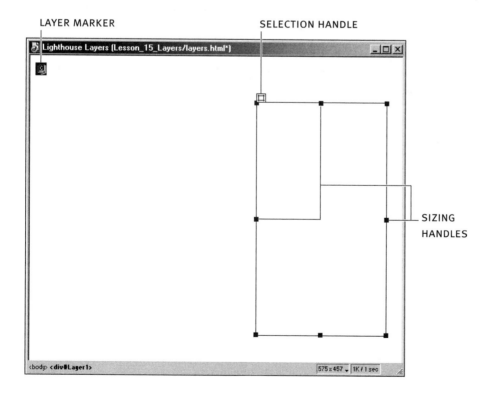

LAYER MARKER   SELECTION HANDLE

SIZING HANDLES

5) Place the insertion point inside the layer. Insert a table into the layer with the following attributes: 1 column, 1 row, 300 pixels wide, 5 cell padding, and 0 cell spacing. Open locations.txt from the Lesson_15_Layers/Text folder, copy all the text, and paste it into the table you created inside the layer.

The text will paste into the layer at the insertion point. The layer will expand if necessary to accommodate all the text. Layers expand to show you all of their content unless you change the overflow setting in the Property inspector. The length of this layer listed on the Property inspector is still the same as when you first inserted the table, when it had no text. The actual length of the layer will vary since the size of the text will vary depending on the system, browser, and font settings that the visitors to your page are using.

6) Place the insertion point in the document outside the layer. Click the Draw Layer icon on the Common tab on the Insert bar to draw a small second layer on the left side of the page. Insert the PMlight70.gif image, from the Lesson_15_Layers/Images folder, into the layer.

The layer will expand if necessary to the dimensions of the image. The layer will not change size if it is larger than the image.

TIP *To draw multiple layers continuously without clicking Draw Layer more than once, hold down Command (Macintosh) or Ctrl (Windows) as you draw the first layer. You can continue to draw new cells until you release the modifier key.*

If the insertion point is within a layer when you insert the layer, the new layer will be nested inside the other layer. Nested layers can cause problems in browsers, so it is best to avoid using them.

At this point, your document should look similar to the example shown here.

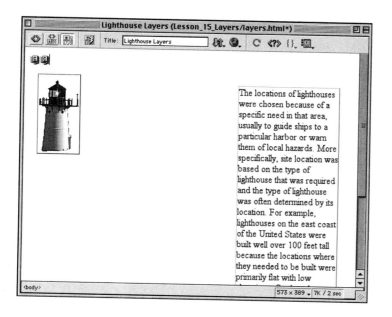

NOTE *Layers that are not selected and not activated will be displayed with a faint, thin gray line marking their borders. You can turn this on or off by choosing View > Visual Aids > Layer Borders. A check next to the command in the menu indicates the option is on.*

7) Place the insertion point in the document outside the first and second layers and choose Insert > Layer. Insert the rocks-ocean.jpg image, from the Lesson_15_Layers/ Images folder, into the layer.

The layer appears in the top left corner of the document window with the default width and height specified by the layer preferences.

NOTE *Dreamweaver's default is 200 pixels for the width and 115 pixels for the height, but you can change this in the Layers category of the Preferences dialog box. To open the Preferences dialog box choose Edit > Preferences and choose the Layers category.*

A third layer marker appears after the first two markers to show where the layer code has been inserted.

8) Drag the Draw Layer icon from the Insert bar into the document window and drop it outside the existing layers. Insert the landscape.jpg image, from the Lesson_15_Layers/Images folder, into the layer.

TIP *Don't drop the Draw Layer icon into another layer; that would cause the layers to be nested.*

A fourth layer with the default width and height will be created in the top left corner of the document window, over top and offset slightly to the right of the last layer you created.

9) Save the layers.html document.
Leave this file open for the next exercise.

NAMING LAYERS

Dreamweaver assigns generic names automatically in a numeric order: Layer1, Layer2, etc. These names are not very descriptive, especially when you create complex pages with multiple layers. It is best to get in the habit of giving your layers short, descriptive names.

1) In the layers.html document, choose Window > Others > Layers.
The Layers panel, located in the Advanced Layout panel group, gives you a list of the layers on the page. You can use it to select a layer, name a layer, change the layer's visibility, change the stacking order, or select multiple layers on the page. When you create a layer, it is placed at the top of the list on the Layer panel, before other layers, if there are any. If the layer is hidden or placed off the page, the Layers panel is the only method for selecting the layer.

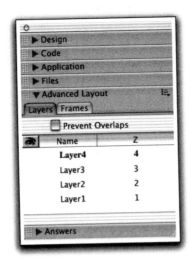

TIP *If the insertion point is inside a layer, that layer's name will appear in bold on the Layers panel and the selection handle will appear in the document window to indicate that the layer is active but not selected.*

The four layers you just created are named Layer1, Layer2, Layer3, and Layer4.

2) Double-click the Layer1 layer in the Layers panel, type textlayer for the layer name, and press Return (Macintosh) or Enter (Windows). Double-click the Layer2 layer in the panel, type lighthouse, and press Return (Macintosh) or Enter (Windows). Don't change the name for the Layer3 layer. Double-click the Layer4 layer in the panel, type landscape, and press Return (Macintosh) or Enter (Windows).

Do not use spaces or special characters (including the underscore character) for layer names. A layer name must be unique—don't assign the same name to more than one layer or to a layer and another element, such as a graphic. It is a good idea to use a consistent naming scheme for all layer names.

NOTE *You can also type the name in the Layer ID text field on the Property inspector if the layer is selected.*

As you assign the layers names, they become selected in the document window. A selected layer will appear to be in front of the other layers. You can click in the document window, outside of all layers, to deselect a selected layer.

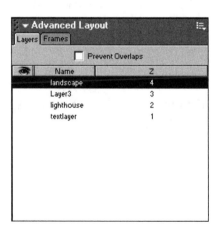

3) Save the layers.html document.

Leave this file open for the next exercise.

MODIFYING LAYERS

After you create a layer, you might want to add a background to it, move it around, or resize it. One of the advantages of using layers is that you can place them in precise locations on the page. You can use the Property inspector and type in numbers for placement, and you can align layers to other layers. You need to select a layer first before you can make any modifications to it. There are several methods for selecting a layer. Which method you use may depend on the complexity of your layout.

1) In the layers.html document window, position the pointer over the textlayer layer's border and click the border line when the pointer turns into a hand (Macintosh) or four outward-facing arrows (Windows).

NOTE *If no layers are selected, Shift-clicking inside a layer will select it, whereas simply clicking inside a layer places the insertion point in the layer and activates it, but does not actually select the layer itself. Other ways to select a single layer are to click the yellow layer marker that represents the layer's location in the HTML code (invisible elements must be showing) or to click the name of the layer in the Layers panel.*

The layer becomes selected, and square, black sizing handles appear around the layer. The textlayer layer appears above the other layers while it is selected. A dotted line (Macintosh) or a solid line (Windows) appears around the name of the selected layer in the Layers panel. The Property inspector changes to reflect the selected layer. To see all properties, click the expander arrow in the lower right corner of the Property inspector.

NOTE *To delete a layer, select it and press Delete (Macintosh) or Backspace (Windows).*

2) Resize the textlayer layer by typing 300px for the width in the W text field of the Property inspector and pressing Return (Macintosh) or Enter (Windows).
In the Property inspector, the W and H text fields display the specified width and height of the layer. Resizing a layer will change these values. The default unit of measurement is px (pixels).

NOTE *You can also specify the following units: pc (picas), pt (points), in (inches), mm (millimeters), cm (centimeters), or % (percentage of the parent's value). The abbreviations must immediately follow the value, with no space between (for example, 3mm). Pixels or percentage are the recommended units.*

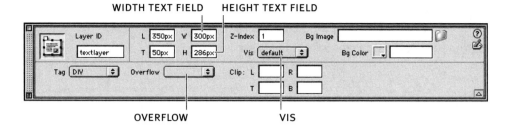

WIDTH TEXT FIELD   HEIGHT TEXT FIELD

OVERFLOW   VIS

You can also resize the layer by dragging any of the sizing handles.

TIP *To resize the layer one pixel at a time using the keyboard, select the layer and press Option+right-arrow key (or any arrow) for Macintosh or Ctrl+right-arrow key (or any arrow) for Windows. To resize the layer by the current grid increment, press Shift+Option+ right-arrow key (or any arrow) for Macintosh or Shift+Ctrl+right-arrow key (or any arrow) for Windows. See the Grid and Ruler Settings exercise later in this lesson to learn how to set the grid increment.*

As you have seen while inserting the text and images, layers will expand to fit their content. When the content of the layer exceeds the specified size, the original values for width and height will be overridden. The Overflow setting on the Property inspector controls how layers behave when this occurs. There are four Overflow options: visible, hidden, scroll, and auto. Visible, the default option, will increase the size of the layer, expanding it down and to the right as much as is needed for all of its contents to be visible. Hidden maintains the size of the layer and clips any content that doesn't fit without providing scroll bars. Scroll will add scroll bars to the layer whether or not the contents exceed the layer's size. Auto will make scroll bars appear only when the contents of the layer exceed its boundaries. You may need to click the expander arrow on the Property inspector to make these options visible.

NOTE *You can also set the clipping area to specify the part of the layer that is visible. The clipping area can be smaller, larger, or the same size as the layer. Use the Property inspector to define the visible area by typing values in all four Clip text fields: L (left), T (top), R (right), and B (bottom). Any content outside of the clipping area will be hidden. This setting is available with all four Overflow options.*

3) With the textlayer layer still selected, type 350px **in the L text field and** 50px
in the T text field on the Property inspector. Select the landscape layer and type
25px **in the L text field and** 100px **in the T text field.**

TIP *The layer position can be off the page if the values in L and T are set to negative
numbers. You might do this if you want to animate the layer and want it initially placed
off the page. You will animate layers in Lesson 16.*

LEFT TEXT FIELD   TOP TEXT FIELD

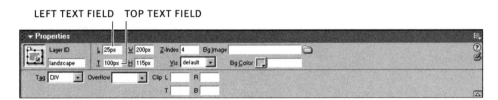

Be sure to use the L and T text fields on the top half of the Property inspector.
Do not use the Clip text fields for this step. The L text field on the top half of the
Property inspector defines the space between the layer and the left side of the
browser window. The T text field on the top half of the Property inspector defines
the space between the layer and the top side of the browser window.

TIP *You can also drag the selection handle or border of the selected layer to move it to a
different location on the page. To move a layer from the keyboard one pixel at a time, select the
layer and use the arrow keys. Hold the Shift key and press an arrow key to move the layer by
the current grid increment.*

**4) Select the lighthouse layer in the layers panel and drag the selection handle in
the document window down on the page so the layer appears underneath the landscape layer. Select the Layer3 layer and drag in underneath the lighthouse layer.**
You can use any of these methods to move layers atop each other. When layers are
hidden by other layers that appear atop them, you will need to use the layers panel
or the layer markers to select the layer you want to modify. You can also adjust the
order in which layers are overlaid (their stacking order), as demonstrated in the
next exercise.

NOTE *If your document contains* **<LAYER>** *or* **<ILAYER>** *tags (Netscape 4.x layers only), those layers are indicated by a layer marker with an 'N' on the marker. If you select a* **<LAYER>** *or* **<ILAYER>** *layer in the document window, the Property inspector will display radio buttons for you to choose from: Top, Left or PageX, PageY. These two options allow you to position a layer in relation to its parent. Top, Left places the layer in relation to the top left corner of its parent (the outer layer if it is a nested layer, or the document window if it is not nested). PageX, PageY places the layer in the absolute location relative to the top left corner of the page, whether or not it is a nested layer. As mentioned previously, these tags are now discontinued; they are not support by either Netscape or Explorer.*

Your document will now look similar to the example shown here.

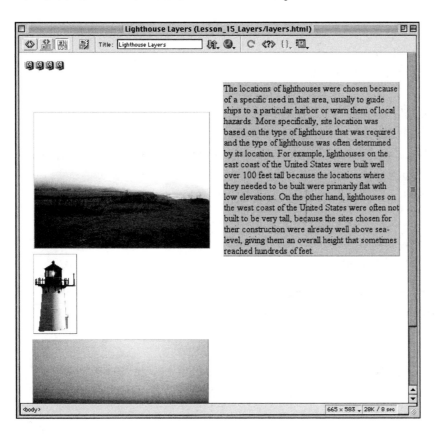

5) Select the textlayer layer. In the Property inspector, click the Bg Color box and select pale tan, or type #CCCC99 into the text field.

BG IMAGE

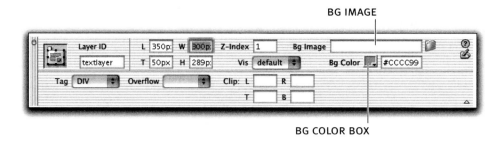

BG COLOR BOX

The background of the layer changes to pale tan.

There are two options for the backgrounds of layers. When using either option, test your pages in all browsers—the results may not be what you expect, depending on the content of the layer. In this case, you have text in the layer. When viewed in the browser, the size of the text can vary greatly depending upon the visitor's browser and system. The text may exceed the defined length of the layer, in which case the background may be either too big or too small. To avoid this, you can assign the same pale tan color to the background of the table. Another way to solve the problem is to use CSS to define an absolute size for the text. For this exercise, you may want to set the background of the table to #CCCC99 in order to avoid this problem.

Bg Image specifies a background image for the layer. Type the path for the image in the text field or click the folder icon to select a source image. The background of a layer might not display in all browsers.

Bg Color specifies a background color for the layer. Leave the text field blank or choose no color (the empty color swatch with a red line through it) at the top of the color menu to specify transparency.

6) Select the landscape layer, and then press and hold down the Shift key while selecting the textlayer layer by clicking on the border of that layer.

TIP *You can also hold down the Shift key and click the layer name in the Layers panel to select multiple layers. If the Layers panel is not visible, you can choose Window > Layers to display the Layers panel.*

Since multiple layers are selected, the most recently selected layer appears with black handles—the other layer has outlined handles.

462

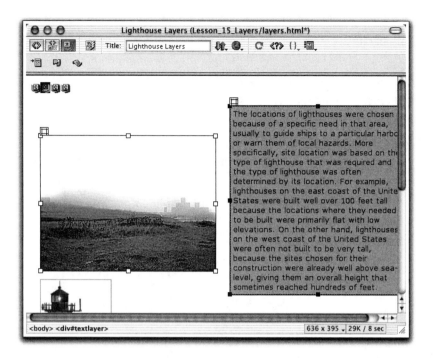

NOTE *To resize multiple layers at once, select two or more layers in the document and choose Modify > Align > Make Same Width or Make Same Height. The first selected layers change to the width or height of the last selected layer. You can also enter width and height values in the Property inspector to apply the values to all selected layers.*

7) Choose Modify › Align › Top.

When you choose an alignment option, all the selected layers are aligned to the last layer selected. The alignment options in this menu also include Left, Right, and Bottom.

The tops of the textlayer and landscape layers are now aligned to each other.

8) Save the document.

Leave this file open for the next exercise.

CHANGING THE STACKING ORDER OF LAYERS

You can use either the Property inspector or the Layers panel to change the stacking order of layers by adjusting the z-index of each layer. The **z-index** determines the order in which layers are drawn in a browser. A layer with a higher z-index number appears to be laid atop layers with lower z-index numbers. Values can be positive or negative. This is particularly useful when you have overlapping layers and you need to specify which layer(s) will be atop others. It is also possible for more than one layer to have the same z-index number, in which case the layer that appears in the code first will appear on top.

1) In the layers.html document, select the lighthouse layer and drag it upward until it partially overlaps the landscape layer. Preview your page in the browser.

The PMlight70.gif image that you inserted into this layer was created with a transparent background and saved in the GIF image format, which supports transparency. In this exercise, you will adjust the stacking order of the layers to make this layer appear above the landscape layer.

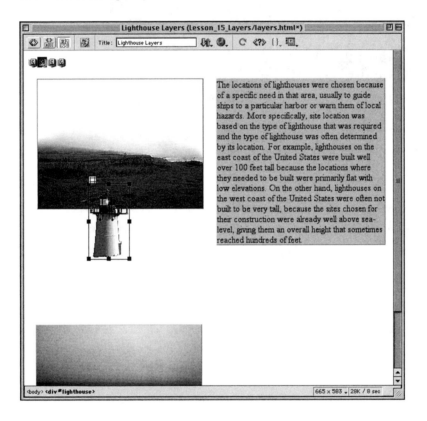

2) In the layers.html document, select the landscape layer in the Layers panel and drag it downward in the list. Stop dragging and release the layer when a thin black line appears between the lighthouse and textlayer layers in the Layers panel.

You will see the changes applied in the Layers panel—the landscape layer now appears between the lighthouse and textlayer layers. The z-index numbers on the layers panel will also change automatically. It can be easier to change the stacking order when you move layers in the Layers panel, since Dreamweaver automatically changes the z-index values, than it would be to change the z-index values yourself via the Property inspector.

464

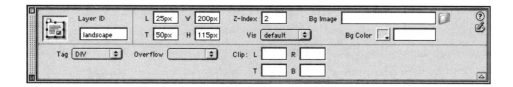

The landscape layer's z-index text field located on the Property inspector has changed from 4 to 2.

3) Select the lighthouse layer and move it up in the document window, positioning it so that the lighthouse image appears to be on the ground near the cliff.

Your document will now look similar to the example shown here.

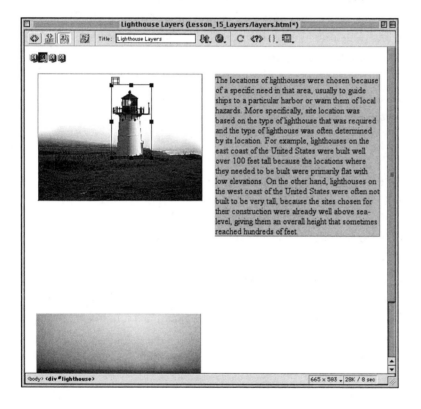

Save this file and leave it open for the next exercise.

NESTING AND UNNESTING LAYERS

There may be times when you want to nest or unnest a layer. This exercise demonstrates the process of nesting and unnesting layers. **Nesting** is a way to group layers together. A nested layer moves with its parent layer and inherits the parent's visibility. Although the concept of nested layers sounds like a good idea, especially when creating animations (covered in Lesson 16), it is not recommended because the results may be unreliable. Be cautious, because nested layers may not display correctly in all browsers. The more layers that you have nested, the longer it will take the browser to display them and the more likely they will be to display incorrectly. If you do choose to nest layers, test your pages with all browsers to be sure the result is what you expect.

NOTE *The top (T) and left (L) values in the Property inspector for a nested layer are relative to the parent layer, not the top left corner of the page. T and L specify the location of the layer from the top left corner of the page or parent layer.*

1) In the layers.html document, use the Layers panel to select the Layer3 layer and drag it over the textlayer layer while pressing Command (Macintosh) or Ctrl (Windows). When the dotted line (Macintosh) or solid line (Windows) appears around the Layer3 layer name, release the textlayer.

TIP *Don't release when the area between the layers is highlighted—doing so changes the stacking order of the layers instead of nesting the layers.*

In the Layers panel, the Layer3 layer appears indented below its parent layer, textlayer. Next to the textlayer layer is a downward-pointing blue triangle (Macintosh) or a minus sign (–) button (Windows) that allows you to see the nested layer. You can collapse this view by clicking the triangle (Macintosh) or minus sign (Windows) to display only the parent layer with a triangle pointing to the right (Macintosh) or a plus sign (+) button (Windows). You can click the plus sign or blue triangle again to show the list of nested layers. The position of the Layer3 layer in the document window will shift to be directly beneath the textlayer layer because the left value of the Layer3 layer is now relative to its parent layer, textlayer.

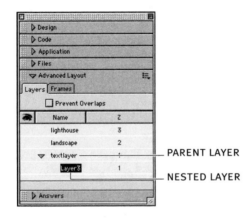

PARENT LAYER

NESTED LAYER

466

In the document window, the layer icon representing the nested Layer3 layer will appear at the top of the textlayer layer, just above the table. The space created by this icon is seen in Dreamweaver only, if you have visual aids enabled. The icon will not be seen in, nor will it take up space in, the browser window.

If you preview the layers.html file in the browser window, you will notice the differences that occur in the display of layers between browsers. In Netscape Communicator 4.75, the background color of the textlayer layer extends to encompass the Layer3 layer and the lighthouse layer is displayed in the upper left corner of the browser window. In Internet Explorer 5, the lighthouse layer displays in the correct position, but the background color of the textlayer does not extend to encompass Layer3. The display will vary depending on the system (Macintosh OS 9, Macintosh OS X, or Windows) and browser in which you are viewing the page.

NOTE *You can also create a layer within an existing layer by selecting Draw Layer on the Insert bar and drawing the layer within an existing layer. For this to work, Nest When Created Within A Layer must be selected in the Preferences. To change the Preferences, choose Edit > Preferences and select the Layers category.*

2) On the Layers panel, select the nested Layer3 layer and drag it above the textlayer layer so a thin black line shows just above the textlayer layer.

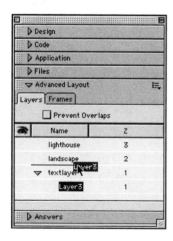

The nesting of a layer is removed, and the layer no longer appears indented in the Layers panel. The Layer3 layer is now moved back to its original location in the document window.

3) Save the layers.html document.

Leave this file open for the next exercise.

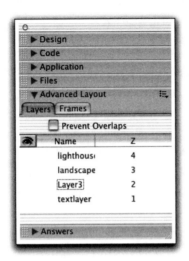

CHANGING LAYER VISIBILITY

You can change layer visibility in order to show or hide a layer. This can be useful when using layers to add user interactivity. You may need to change the visibility of a layer if you are creating dynamic content that displays in response to user interaction. For example, you can use timelines (covered in Lesson 16) to hide a layer until the user clicks a button or rolls over an image.

1) Select the Layer3 layer in the layers.html document. Click in the column to the left of the Layer3 name in the Layers panel to change the visibility of that layer. Click until you see a closed eye icon.

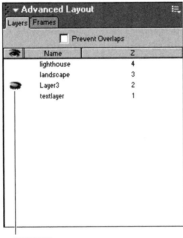

HIDDEN

468

TIP *To change the visibility of all layers at once, click the eye icon at the top of the column.*

There are three visibility options on the Layers panel: inherit, visible, and hidden.

- Inherit uses the visibility property of the layer's parent. For this option, there is no icon displayed in the visibility column.

- Visible displays the layer contents, regardless of the parent's value. For this option, there is an open eye icon displayed in the visibility column.

- Hidden displays the layer content as transparent, regardless of the parent's value. If you set a layer to hidden, the layer markers and the Layers panel may be the only ways for you to select that layer. For this option, there is a closed eye icon displayed in the visibility column. Even though you have set the Layer3 layer to hidden, you will still see scroll bars because hidden layers take up the same space as if they were visible.

On the Property inspector, there is a fourth visibility option: Default does not specify a visibility property, but most browsers interpret this as inheriting the parent's value.

VIS

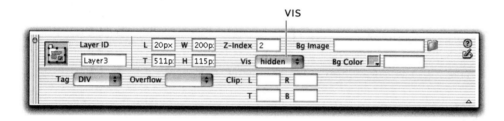

NOTE *Choose Edit > Preferences and select the Layers category to set the default visibility for new layers.*

2) Save the layers.html document.

When the Layer3 layer is selected, you will be able to see it in the document window. When it is not selected, the layer will disappear, making the document window look just like it will in the browser.

Leave this file open for the next exercise.

SETTING GRID AND RULER OPTIONS

When you work with layers, you might want to use grids and rulers as visual guides for placement of layers on your page.

1) In the layers.html document, choose View > Grid > Show Grid.

The grids will display in the document window. A check next to the command indicates the option is on.

2) Choose View › Grid › Snap To Grid.

This option will turn snapping on or off. A check next to the command indicates the option is on. When this option is on, the layers will snap to the grid lines when you move them close.

3) Select the lighthouse layer, then press the Shift key and select the landscape layer. Move them to the right so that four of the grid boxes are showing between the edge of the document window and the left edge of the landscape layer.

The landscape layer will appear to be on top of the lighthouse layer while you move them because you selected the landscape layer last. Once you click off of the layers in a blank area of the document window, the lighthouse layer will appear above the landscape layer again.

The landscape layer will have snapped to the grid line. The L value of the landscape layer should now be 200px. You may be able to see the faint gray border of the landscape layer just to the left of the grid line in the document window. The layer is actually aligned exactly with the grid line even though the border appears to be 1 pixel to the left of the grid line; the 1-pixel gray layer border that you see is a Dreamweaver visual aid which does not display in the browser.

TIP *You can change the grid setting by choosing View > Grid > Grid Settings.... The Edit Grid dialog box will appear in which you can change the color, set the spacing value and units (pixels, inches, or centimeters), and switch the grid display to lines or dots. The grid can be useful when you need to align layers.*

4) Choose View › Rulers › Show.

The rulers will display in the document window. A check next to the command indicates the option is on. The units for rulers can be changed by choosing View > Rulers > Pixels, Inches, or Centimeters. A check next to a unit of measure indicates which one is set.

5) Select the textlayer layer and move it just below the landscape layer. Format the text in the textlayer as Verdana, −1.

The background color or the textlayer layer should touch the landscape layer. This may be difficult to see in the document window since the layer borders visual aid is turned on.

470

6) Preview the page in the browser. If necessary, adjust the T value of the textlayer layer so there is no white space between the landscape layer and the background color of the textlayer layer.

You can also temporarily turn off the layer borders visual aid by choosing View > Visual Aids > Layer Borders. The rest of this lesson assumes you have the layer borders visual aid turned on.

NOTE *The zero point is the point where the horizontal and vertical rulers intersect. The default location for the zero point is the upper left corner of the page, where the top and left sides of the page meet. You can set the zero point to a different location by clicking in the square between the vertical and horizontal rulers, dragging the zero point downward and to the right, and then releasing. When the zero point is moved to a point inside the document, you will see negative values appear upwards and to the left of the zero point. Choose View > Rulers > Reset Origin to reset the zero point.*

Notice when you preview the file that the browser window continues to scroll past the end of the text. This is due to the hidden Layer3 layer.

7) In the Layers panel, select the Layer3 layer, click the layer selection handle in the document window, and press Delete (Macintosh) or Backspace (Windows).

Your document should now look similar to the example shown here.

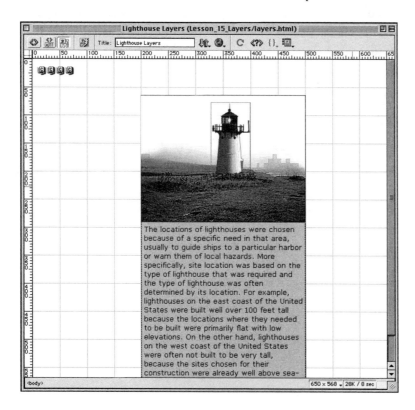

8) Choose View › Grid › Show Grid to remove the check mark and hide the grid.

The rest of the book assumes you have the grid turned off. You can either turn off the rulers or leave them on. Save this file and leave it open for the next exercise.

USING THE DRAG LAYER BEHAVIOR

Layers can be combined with behaviors to enable your visitors to interact with your page. The Drag Layer behavior makes it possible for the visitor to grab a layer in the browser window and move it to a different spot on the page. This is a great way to create interactive games or teaching tools with elements that can be moved by the user.

1) Place the insertion point at the end of the text in the textlayer layer. Click the `<table>` tag in the Tag Selector at the bottom of the document window. Press the right arrow key once to move the insertion point after the table. Click the Image icon on the Common tab of the Insert bar and insert the rocks-ocean.jpg image.

The rocks-ocean.jpg image that you used previously in Layer3 is now in the textlayer, just below the table containing the text.

2) Select the lighthouse layer. Type the following values: set the width of the lighthouse layer to 70px, the height to 131px, the left value to 50px, and the top value to 140px. Create a layer just above the lighthouse layer. Name it grab and type Grab the lighthouse image below and move it to a location on the landscape to the right. Format the text as Verdana, –2. Click the center alignment button on the Property inspector.

You adjusted the dimensions of the lighthouse layer to make it exactly the same size as the image it contains. The new grab layer should not overlap any other layers.

Your document should now look similar to the example shown here.

472

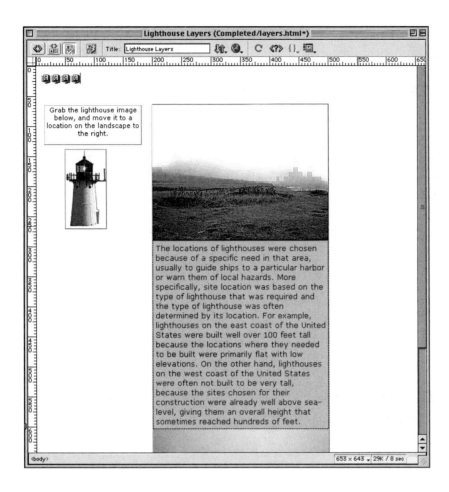

It is a good practice to be sure to let your visitors know whether an item can be moved. Now that you've included text to let the visitor know the lighthouse image is draggable, you can apply the behavior.

3) Click the <body> tag in the Tag Selector at the bottom of the document window to select it.

The Drag Layer behavior cannot be applied directly to a layer, so you will apply it to the document's **<body>** tag.

N O T E   *You can also apply the Drag Layer Behavior to other tags, like link* **<a href>** *that can be either inside or outside of a layer.*

4) In the Behaviors panel, click the plus sign (+) button and select the Drag Layer action from the Actions drop-down menu.

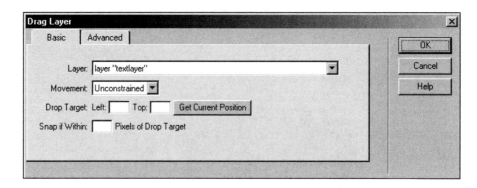

The Drag Layer dialog box appears with the Basic tab active.

NOTE *The Drag Layer action will not be available if you have a layer selected. If it is grayed out, you should make sure the **<body>** tag is selected.*

5) Select layer lighthouse from the Layer drop-down menu. Choose Constrained from the Movement drop-down menu.

Four text fields will appear to the right of the Movement drop-down menu: Up, Down, Left, and Right.

6) Type 70 in the Up text field, 22 in the Down text field, 0 in the Left text field, and 390 in the Right Text field. Leave the text fields for Drop Target and Snap if Within blank.

The coordinates will allow the visitor to place the lighthouse only within the area of the landscape image. The amount of allowable movement will be relative to the original position of the lighthouse layer. You are restricting the visitor to moving the lighthouse only 70 pixels upward of where it is now, only 22 pixels downward, and so forth.

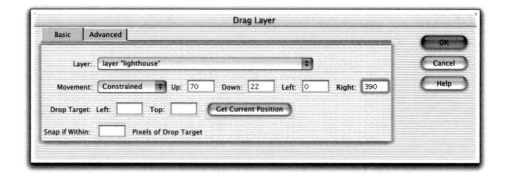

NOTE *If you had chosen Unconstrained from the Movement menu, the visitor would be able to move the lighthouse image anywhere on the page.*

You can use the Constrain option to control the direction and amount of pixels in which the visitor is able to drag a layer. You could restrict the visitor to moving the layer only in a horizontal direction by setting the Up and Down text fields to 0 so that the image could not be moved up or down. Likewise, you could restrict movement to a vertical direction by the Left and Right text fields to 0.

NOTE *If you have a target area where you want the visitor to place the layer, you can specify that location by typing into the Drop Target text fields the left and top values that the layer should have in its target position. You can make it easier for a visitor to place the layer in the target location by causing the layer to snap to the target location if the layer is moved within the range of pixels that you specify; use the Snap if Within text field to set the snap-to range.*

7) Click OK. Save the file and preview it in the browser.

Test out the movement of your lighthouse image by trying to move it. Notice that you can move it only within the region specified by the numeric values you entered in step 6.

NOTE *The Advanced tab on the Drag Layer dialog box allows you to specify an area of the image as a handle that the visitor can use to grab and move the layer. It also gives you control over what happens to the z-index of the layers when the layer is moved. You also have the option to call additional JavaScripts while the layer is moving, when the layer is dropped, or when the layer snaps to the target. This gives you the ability to create a more interactive experience for the visitor.*

CONVERTING LAYERS TO TABLES

Layers can be an easy way to design your page; however, because not all browsers support them, your audience may be limited. Earlier browsers display layer contents without any positioning and without any control as to the placement. If you decide to design your page using layers, you may want to convert the layers to a table to provide an alternate page for those viewers with browsers that do not support layers. After you have converted the layers to a table, you can switch to Layout View to complete any design changes. You can then use the Check Browser behavior to redirect users based on their browser version (as you did in Lesson 5).

The following exercise shows you how to convert layers, but the recommended method of creating tables is using Layout View to draw tables and table cells or Standard View to create tables (as you did in Lesson 4).

475

A few restrictions apply when you're converting layers to tables: You can't have nested layers, and the layers can't overlap. If these conditions exist, Dreamweaver displays an alert and will not create the table. You also cannot convert a single layer—the entire page will be converted.

NOTE *Another way to convert your layers to pages that are compatible with older browsers is to choose File > Convert > 3.0 Browser Compatible. This method will open the converted file in a new window.*

1) In the layers.html document, choose File > Save As and type layers_table.html **in the Name text field. Save the file in the Lesson_15_Layers folder.**

The layers in this document will be converted and replaced with a single table.

NOTE *The conversion to a table will remove the layer names.*

2) Click in the document window. On the Layers panel, select Prevent Overlaps. Move the lighthouse layer to the left of the landscape layer.

Overlapping layers cannot be converted to a table. If you select this option before you begin drawing layers, Dreamweaver will prevent them from overlapping. By using the Prevent Overlaps option, you can move layers as close as possible to other layers.

If you already have layers that overlap, checking the Prevent Overlaps check box will not move those layers. You will have to move them in order to stop them from overlapping.

Once you start moving the lighthouse layer, Dreamweaver will prevent any overlap.

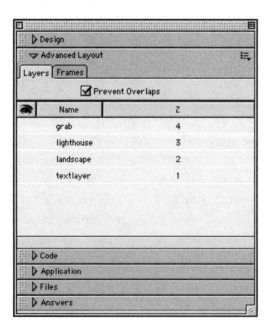

3) Choose Modify > Convert > Layers to Table.

The Convert Layers to Table dialog box opens with several options.

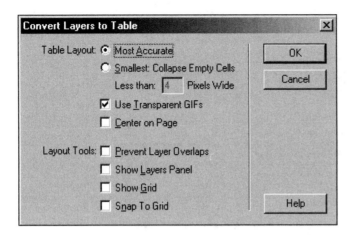

- Most Accurate will create a table cell for every layer plus any additional cells that are necessary to preserve the space between layers.

- Smallest: Collapse Empty Cells specifies that the layers' edges should be aligned if they are positioned within the specified number of pixels. If this option is selected, the resulting table may have fewer empty rows and columns.

- Use Transparent GIFs will fill the last row of the table with transparent GIFs. This ensures that the table will display the same way in all browsers. When this option is selected, you cannot edit the resulting table by dragging its columns. When this option is deselected, the resulting table will not contain transparent GIFs, and its appearance might vary slightly in different browsers.

- Center on Page will center the resulting table on the page. If this option is deselected, the table is left aligned.

- Layout Tools will allow you to set any desired layout or grid options.

4) Keep the default settings of Most Accurate and Use Transparent GIFs. Click Center on Page and click OK.

If you have any layers that overlap you will get a warning dialog box, informing you that Dreamweaver cannot convert the layers to a table. If this happens, go back to your document and make sure none of the layers overlap.

Any hidden layers will be deleted. After you convert your layers to a table, you can make any necessary adjustments to the table.

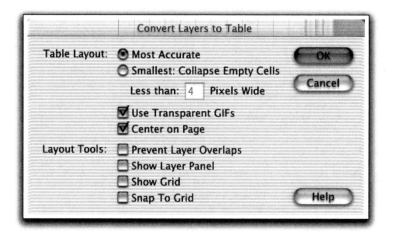

NOTE *You can also convert a table to layers by choosing Modify > Convert > Tables to Layers while in Standard View. The Convert Tables to Layers dialog box opens, and you can select the desired options and then click OK. Empty cells in the table will be ignored and not converted to layers. Any content on the page outside the table will be converted to a layer.*

USING THE NETSCAPE RESIZE LAYER FIX

Netscape 4.*x* versions have a problem with layers when you resize the browser window: The layer changes its shape when the browser window is resized. This can cause problems with your page when the user resizes the browser window. You can fix the problem by inserting the Resize Layer Fix JavaScript code into your document when you add layers. The code fixes the Netscape problem and will not affect Internet Explorer.

1) In the layers_table.html document, choose Commands > Add/Remove Netscape Resize Fix.

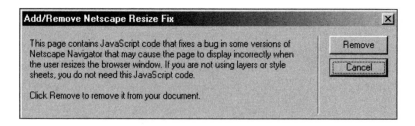

In the Add/Remove Netscape Resize Fix dialog box that opens, depending on whether or not the script is in the document, you can either add or remove the JavaScript code. The code will cause the page to reload if the user resizes the browser window. Dreamweaver will add this code to your page automatically. If it is not in a page that uses layers, you can add it easily with this dialog box.

2) Click Remove.

When you convert layers to a table, you should use the Add/Remove Netscape Resize Fix option to remove the JavaScript code you added in the previous exercise, because it is no longer needed.

3) Save the layers_tables.html document.

You can close this file.

WHAT YOU HAVE LEARNED

In this lesson, you have:

- Created layers by drawing them in the document window and by inserting default, pre-sized layers (pages 452–456)

- Named layers to keep track of them in the Layers panel (pages 456–457)

- Selected single and multiple layers, modified their sizes and locations, and aligned them relative to each other (pages 458–463)

- Used layers to control the placement and display of content on your page (pages 462–463)

- Changed the stacking order of layers in order to specify the order in which they display from top to bottom (pages 463–465)

- Nested and unnested layers to understand how layers can work in groups or become nested accidentally (pages 465–468)

- Changed layer visibility to hide and show entire layers (pages 468–469)

- Set rulers and grids to help when moving layers on the page (pages 469–472)

- Combined layers with behaviors to let users interact with your pages (pages 472–475)

- Made pages designed with layers compatible with earlier browsers by converting the layers to a table (pages 475–478)

- Learned to insert or remove a JavaScript to remedy a Netscape bug that causes viewing problems with layers (pages 478–479)

animating
with timelines

LESSON 16

HTML pages are generally motionless unless you add an animated GIF or a Macromedia Flash movie. You can roll over a button that might appear to move slightly as it swaps out with another image, but it remains static on the page. With Dynamic HTML (DHTML), you can add more extensive animations to your Web page. These animations are controlled with JavaScript within the HTML page, without the need of a plug-in. The limitation on DHTML animations is that users must use a 4.0 or later browser to view the pages.

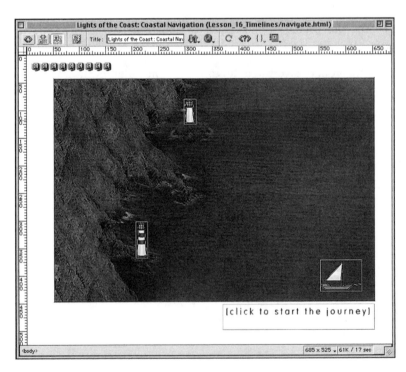

In this project, you will create an animation by placing multiple layers in a timeline, and you will use keyframes to control visibility and create movement.

All objects that you want to include in an animation must be contained in layers. The layers are placed in a timeline, which allows you to create a path of movement and control timing. The **timeline** consists of a series of frames, much like frames in a movie. Each frame displays on the Web page at a specific point in time, depending on how many frames per second you specify and how long the animation is. You can control the placement and properties of each layer in a frame. A frame can also trigger a behavior during the animation.

To see an example of the finished pages for this lesson, open ship.html and navigate.html from the Lesson_16_Timelines/Completed folder.

WHAT YOU WILL LEARN

In this lesson, you will:

- Add layers to the timeline

- Make layers move around the page

- Alter the timeline with keyframes

- Change the speed and duration of the animation

- Record the path of a layer as you move it

- Control when the animation starts

- Change the visibility of layers during the animation

- Add behaviors to the timeline

- Make it possible for the viewer to start the animation

APPROXIMATE TIME

This lesson should take about two hours to complete.

LESSON FILES

Media Files:
Lesson_16_Timelines/Images/…(all files)

Completed Project:
Lesson_16_Timelines/ship.html
Lesson_16_Timelines/navigate.html

ANIMATING OBJECTS

To create animations on your Web pages, you need to use layers and the Timelines panel. This exercise demonstrates how to add objects in layers to a timeline and how to work with those elements once they are a part of the timeline.

1) Create a new page and save it as ship.html in the Lesson_16_Timelines folder. Title the document *Lights of the Coast: Racing Ships*. Choose Modify > Page Properties, select waterBKG.jpg as the background image, set the text to black, and click OK.

In the following steps, you will animate an image on this page.

2) Click the Draw Layer icon on the Insert bar and draw a small layer on the bottom left side of the page. Use the Layers panel to name the layer yellow.

> **TIP** *If the Layers panel is not visible, you can open it by choosing Window > Others > Layers or using the keyboard shortcut F12.*

DRAW LAYER

Layers must be used to create an animation using timelines. Keep in mind that using layers will limit your audience to those using 4.0 or later browsers.

3) Select the yellow layer. On the Property inspector, type 78px in the W text field and 58px in the H text field. Insert the ship_Y.gif image from the Lesson_16_Timelines/ Images folder into the layer.

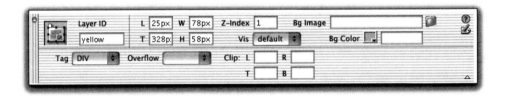

You have set the width and the height of the layer. To move an object (such as text or a graphic), the object must be contained in a layer.

> **NOTE** *Objects such as images can be added to the timeline without placing them in a layer, but you will not be able to animate their positions.*

4) Choose Window > Others > Timelines to open the Timelines panel.

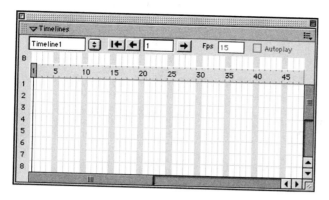

The Timelines panel represents the properties of layers and images over time.

Each row on the Timelines panel is called an **animation channel** and represents elements on the page. Because you can only animate layers, each row on the timeline can only contain layers. You can use the Timelines panel to control a layer's position, dimension, visibility, or stacking order.

Each column on the Timelines panel is called a **frame** and represents a unit of time. Frame numbers indicate the number of frames each animation occupies.

5) Select the yellow layer. Choose Modify > Timeline > Add Object To Timeline to put the layer on the timeline.

TIP *You can also use the layer selection handle to grab the layer and drag it from the document window into the Timelines panel.*

When you use Modify > Timeline > Add Object To Timeline, the layer is added to the Timelines panel in the first Animation channel (the first row). When you drag a layer into the Timelines panel, the layer will appear in whichever animation channel (row) that you drop it into.

A message box appears to tell you what layer attributes the Timelines panel can animate. You can close the message box.

A horizontal blue animation bar appears in the new channel on the timeline and displays the name of the layer in the bar. You should see the word "yellow" displayed in the bar. If you see the name "Image1" in the animation bar, you added the image, not the layer, to the timeline. Delete the bar from the timeline and try again.

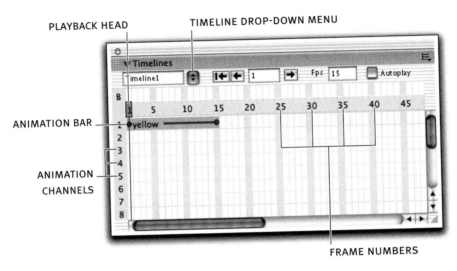

If you were to continue to add layers to the timeline using the Modify menu, the next layer would be placed in the next Animation channel, in the row below the first bar.

NOTE *You can also add more timelines to a page by choosing Modify > Timeline > Add Timeline. The timeline drop-down menu allows you to select a timeline if you have created more than one.*

6) You can move animation bars on the Timelines panel by dragging the solid area of the bars. For this exercise, make sure the animation bar is positioned in the first row, starting in frame 1 with the red playback head in the first frame.

Since you used the Modify menu to add the layer to the timeline, the animation bar will be in the first row and begin at frame 1. If you drag a layer into the Timelines panel, you can drop it anywhere; you may need to adjust the placement of the animation bar.

Animation bars show the duration of each object. A single row can include multiple bars representing different objects. Different bars cannot control the same object in the same frame. The animation bar can be relocated to any frame and any channel. The initial placement of the animation bar in the channel is based on the position of the playback head. The playback head shows which frame of the timeline is currently displayed on the page. If the playback head is in frame 1, the animation bar begins in frame 1; if the playback head is in frame 8, the animation bar begins in frame 8. As you move the animation bar, the playback head will also move.

7) Save the file.

Leave this file open for the next exercise.

USING KEYFRAMES

All animations are controlled by keyframes. **Keyframes** are the pivotal instances that define what happens in the animation. After you place a layer on the timeline, you use keyframes to control the movement of that layer on the page. A keyframe marks a point in the animation when a change is made to specified properties (such as position or size) for the layer. Dreamweaver interpolates values—that is, it creates the values needed for all frames between keyframes in order to come up with the path of the layer. The path line that is automatically generated between the keyframes is based on the values and locations of the layers at the keyframes.

By default, there will always be a beginning keyframe and an ending keyframe, which are indicated by open circles at the beginning and end of the animation bar. An animation with only these two keyframes will move in a straight line. To create an animation that doesn't move in a straight line, you need to add keyframes at other frames in the timeline.

In this exercise, you will select the last keyframe and move the layer on the page to the ending position of the animation. That movement will control the animation of the layer from the first keyframe to the last keyframe.

1) In the ship.html document, click the keyframe marker at the end of the *yellow* animation bar in the Timelines panel to select the last keyframe.

The playback head jumps to that frame. The keyframe turns dark to indicate it is selected; the rest of the animation bar remains lighter.

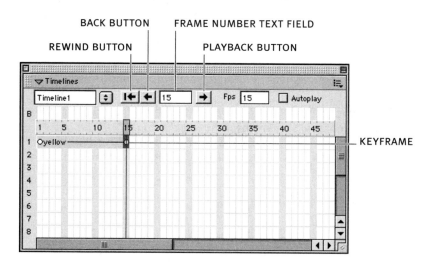

485

2) In the document window, use the layer selection handle to drag the yellow layer slightly upward and to the right side of the page.

When you release the mouse button, you should see an animation line extending from the first location to the last. If you don't see the animation line, you didn't select the last keyframe before moving the layer. Since you are only using two keyframes in this exercise, the animation will move in a straight line.

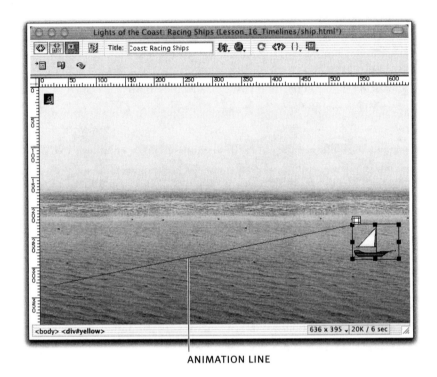

ANIMATION LINE

3) Click Rewind on the Timelines panel, and then hold down Play to preview the animation on the page.

When you click the Rewind button, the yellow layer will jump back to its original position in the document window, and the playback head will move to the first frame in the Timelines panel.

If you click the Play button once, you will see the layer move one frame per click, and the playback head will advance one frame to the right. When you click and hold the play button, you will see the animation play continuously. The animation will repeat for as long as you continue to hold down the Play button.

As the animation plays, the playback head shows which frame of the timeline is currently displayed on the page.

486

TIP *You can also use the Back button to move one frame to the left or back. Hold down the back button to play the timeline backward.*

4) To make the animation play when the page loads in the browser, select Autoplay in the Timelines panel.

AUTOPLAY   BEHAVIORS CHANNEL

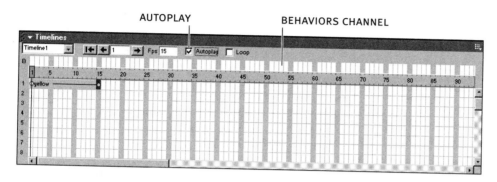

Autoplay uses JavaScript to make a timeline play when the page loads. A behavior is attached to the page's **<body>** tag; the behavior automatically executes the Play Timeline action when the page loads in a browser. A message box appears when you click Autoplay, alerting you that the Play Timeline action is being inserted in the **<body>** tag of your document using an onLoad event. The onLoad event will cause the animation to begin once the document has finished loading in the browser. Click OK to close the message box. You might not see the message box if the option to not display the message box again was selected previously.

NOTE *If you select Loop on the Timelines panel, a behavior is added in the last frame that returns the playback head to frame 1 and plays the timeline again. The behavior is added to the Behaviors channel and appears as a dash above the last frame. You can edit the parameters for this behavior to define the number of loops by selecting the dash in the Behaviors channel and double-clicking the corresponding action in the Behaviors panel. A dialog box will allow you to set how many times the animation will loop and in what frame it will begin to loop.*

Events don't have to start at the beginning of the timeline. You can use the timeline to delay action on the page until a certain time after the page loads by moving the animation bar to the right to create the desired number of empty frames.

5) Save your file and test it in the browser.

The ship should move from the beginning point to the ending point and then stop. You can click Refresh or Reload in the browser to see the animation again. The ship image is an animated gif, which gives the animation more movement.

NOTE *Users with a Macintosh and Internet Explorer 5.0 might notice a trail of pieces of the ship image as the ship moves across the screen. Internet Explorer 5.0 on a Macintosh is unable to calculate the layer dimensions as it moves across the page if the layer is the same size as the image. To fix this, you will need to change the size of the yellow layer (or the layer you are animating) to make it larger than the image. When the layer is on the timeline, you have to change the size of the layer at each keyframe. Use the Property inspector to exactly match the sizes of the layer at each keyframe. If you have a timeline with more than two keyframes, it might be easier to remove the layer from the timeline and start again.*

Leave this file open for the next exercise.

POSITIONING AN OBJECT

In this exercise, you will change the ship animation so it comes into the browser window from the left and moves out of the browser window to the right.

1) In the ship.html document, select the first keyframe on the animation bar for the yellow layer in the Timelines panel. Click the selection handle of the yellow layer in the document window and use the arrow keys to move the layer to the left and off the screen.

The arrow keys will move the layer one pixel at a time. Holding down the Shift key and pressing an arrow key will move the layer by the current grid increment.

TIP *You can also type a negative number in the L (Left) text field at the top of the Property inspector to move the ship layer off the screen.*

L TEXT FIELD

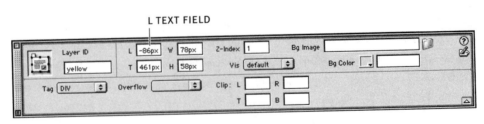

You have selected the first keyframe and moved the ship layer to the left where it is not visible. This will cause the animation to come into the browser window from the left. The top left corner of the browser is the zero point (covered in Lesson 15), where Dreamweaver's horizontal and vertical rulers intersect when they are visible. Anything to the right or down from that point is a positive value; anything to the left or up from that point is a negative value. In order to make the yellow layer begin outside of the visible window of the browser you have set the starting point of the layer to a negative horizontal value. You've placed this value in the L (Left) text field because the horizontal location of a layer on a Web page is defined by its distance from the left side of the browser window.

NOTE *You can select any frame or keyframe by clicking it in the animation bar, or by typing the desired frame number into the frame number text field. The frame text field is a good indication of the exact frame that is selected.*

2) Select the last keyframe on the animation bar for the yellow layer in the Timelines panel. Type 700px in the L text field of the Property inspector and press Return (Macintosh) or Enter (Windows) to move the layer to the right, off the screen.
Selecting the last keyframe and moving the yellow layer to the right where it is not visible will cause the animation to move out of the browser window to the right. Selecting a keyframe in the Timelines panel will automatically select the corresponding layer in the document window. Keep in mind that whether the yellow layer moves out of the browser window or simply stops on the far right side of the page will depend on how large the visitor's browser window is open. If it is important for an animation to completely leave the right side of the screen, make sure that the value is large enough to make this happen for those with large monitors.

3) Save your file and test it in the browser.
The ship should come in from the left and move off the screen to the right.

NOTE *You may have to adjust the size of your browser window to less than 700 pixels wide in order to see the ship move off the page, or you can increase the left value of the ship layer to make it move farther to the right.*

4) Drag the last keyframe of the *yellow* animation bar on the Timelines panel toward the right to frame 45. Hold down the Play button to preview the animation.
The animation now lasts longer and has slowed down. By default, animation bars are initially 15 frames long when you add layers to the Timelines panel. The frame numbers show the duration of the animation. You can control the speed and length

of the animation by setting the total number of frames and the number of frames per second (fps). Set the total number of frames by dragging the last keyframe to the right as you did in this exercise. Set the number of frames per second in the Fps text field. The default setting of 15 frames per second is a good average rate to use—faster rates might not improve performance. Browsers always play every frame of the animation, even if they cannot attain the specified frame rate on the user's system.

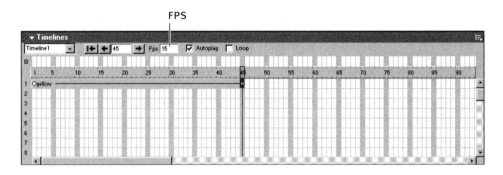
FPS

TIP *If you want to shorten and speed up the animation, drag the last keyframe to the left to shorten the animation bar.*

5) Save the file.
Leave this file open for the next exercise.

CHANGING AN ANIMATION WITH KEYFRAMES
Animating a timeline can do more than just move an object from point A to point B. The important thing to remember is that all movement is controlled by keyframes. For the ship animation, you set the position of the layer for the first and last keyframes, and Dreamweaver calculated the placement for all the frames in between. To make the movement more fluid and follow a more complex path, you need to add more keyframes.

1) In the ship.html document, draw a small layer and place it on the left side of the page, near the horizon line between the water and sky in the background image. Name the layer red. Insert the ship_R.gif image from the Lesson_16_Timelines/ Images folder.
In this exercise, you will animate this layer on a curved path.

2) Select the first keyframe in the *yellow* animation bar on the Timelines panel. Select the red layer in the document window by clicking the layer selection handle. Choose Modify > Timeline > Add Object To Timeline to add it to the timeline.

The red layer now appears in the second animation channel on the Timelines panel, below the yellow animation bar. The red animation bar is 15 frames long.

Since the first keyframe of the yellow animation bar was selected, the red animation bar appears in the second animation channel, directly below the yellow animation bar and begins on the same frame that was selected. If frame 46 had been selected, the red animation bar would be placed on the same animation channel, beginning in frame 46 because the yellow animation bar ends in frame 45.

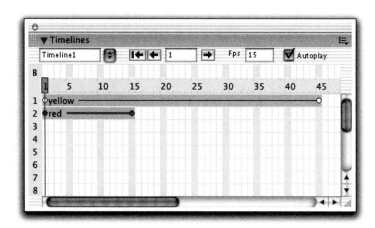

NOTE *The z-index (covered in Lesson 15) determines the order in which layers will overlap each other, designating their level not horizontally or vertically, but in the third dimension. To change it, you can drag one layer below another on the Layers panel. It is easier to adjust the stacking order of the layers before you place them in the timeline. If you wait until you place a layer in the timeline, adjusting the z-index will change the stacking order only for the keyframe that is selected in the timelines panel. This is useful if you want the stacking order of your layers to change over the course of the animation.*

3) In the Timelines panel, select the last keyframe in the red layer and drag it until the red animation bar is the same length as the yellow animation bar. In the document window, move the red layer to the right side of the document window, just in front of the place at which the yellow layer moves off the page.

As you move last keyframe of the red animation bar to frame 45, you may notice the yellow layer in the document window move to the position it will occupy in frame 45, which you defined in the previous exercise.

TIP *You can also choose Modify > Timeline > Add Frame or Remove Frame to add or remove frames on the timeline and make the animation longer or shorter.*

A path line is displayed in the document window for the red layer, and should look similar to the example shown here.

4) Click Rewind, and click and hold the mouse button on Play on the Timelines panel to see the animation.

The red layer should move from left to right, following the yellow ship in a straight, diagonal line. To make the layer move in a curve, you will add more keyframes and move the layer at each new keyframe in the following steps.

5) In the Timelines panel, hold down Command (Macintosh) or Ctrl (Windows) until the pointer changes to a circle. Then click on the red animation bar at frame 10.

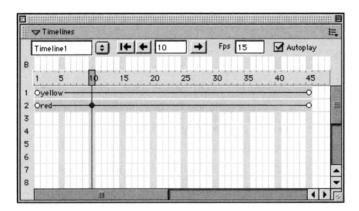

A new keyframe is added at frame 10, as indicated by the small circle shown on the red animation bar at frame 10. You can move keyframes on the timeline by dragging

492

them left or right to new frames. The frame text field will tell you which frame number the selected keyframe is on.

TIP *You can also add a new keyframe by clicking a frame on the animation bar or typing the number of the frame into the frame text field to select it and choosing Modify > Timeline > Add Keyframe. To remove a keyframe, select the keyframe and choose Modify > Timeline > Remove Keyframe.*

6) With the new keyframe selected, move the red layer downward on the page in the document window.

The animation line starts to change shape.

7) Repeat step 6 to add more keyframes at frames 20 and 35, moving the red layer at each new keyframe.

TIP *Right-click (Windows) or Control-click (Macintosh) on the Timelines panel (or use the Timeline drop-down menu) to open a shortcut menu that includes all the relevant commands.*

Your document window will now have a more freeform animation line, similiar to the example shown here.

If you were to extend or shorten the animation bar to change the duration of the red animation, all the keyframes you added would automatically move in order to stay in the same position relative to the other keyframes.

Your Timelines panel will now have more keyframes on the red animation bar.

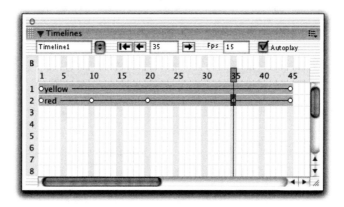

8) Save your file and preview it in the browser.
Leave this file open for the next exercise.

NOTE *To change the start time of an animation, select the animation bar (click in the middle of the bar and not on a keyframe) and drag left or right. Press Shift to select more than one bar at a time.*

RECORDING THE PATH OF A LAYER

The method you just used in the last exercise for animating a layer works great when you want to control the movement of the layer in a few frames. You can also use another method that follows your pointer as you drag the layer on the page. Dreamweaver tracks your movement and creates the keyframes on the timeline for you. Dreamweaver also matches the time you take when dragging the layer. The slower you drag, the more keyframes are added, and the longer the animation bar becomes. You can then alter the time or the keyframes on the timeline.

In this exercise, you will add a third ship to the animation and drag the layer to create the path.

1) In the ship.html document, draw another layer on the page and name it blue. Insert the ship_B.gif image into the blue layer. Select the first frame in the Timelines panel by clicking the 1 in the row of frame numbers.
In the Timelines panel, the playback head moves to frame 1 when you select the first frame.

In the document window, the current position of the blue layer will be the starting point of the animation.

2) Select the blue layer in the document window and choose Modify › Timeline › Record Path Of Layer.

TIP *Complete steps 2 and 3 quickly. Once you choose Record Path Of Layer, you are recording the movement of the blue layer in the document window.*

This option will allow you to create an animation by dragging a layer. Recording the path of a layer will automatically add that layer to the timeline—you do not need to add the layer to the Timeline as you have done in the previous exercises.

3) Click the selection handle and briefly drag the blue layer around the page to form the path of the animation. Then stop dragging and release.

As you drag the layer, a gray dotted line will show the resulting path. You can drag the layer in any direction, cross back over the path you are creating, and vary the speed with which you drag the layer to affect the way the path is recorded.

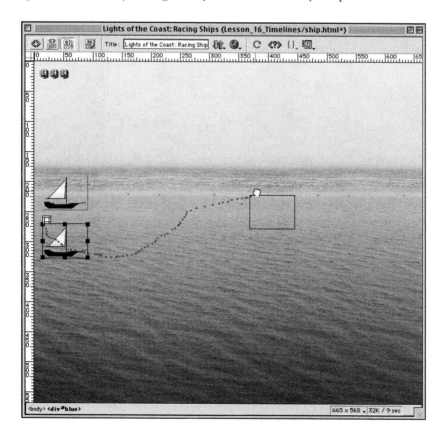

495

When you stop dragging and release, the dotted line is converted to the animation line. Dreamweaver adds the layer to the timeline with the necessary keyframes to control the layer's movement.

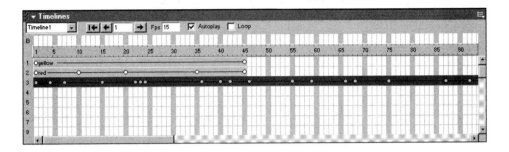

4) Scroll toward the right in the Timelines panel until you reach the end of the blue animation bar. Drag the last keyframe of the blue animation bar toward the left, placing it at frame 60 to shorten the time for the animation.

Depending upon the amount of time that you took to drag the animation bar while recording the path of the layer, this new animation may be very long. The longer the path you create, the longer the animation will be. Keep in mind that long, complicated animations and pages with many different animation channels will take much longer to load and increase the possibility of crashing the visitor's browser.

As you shorten the animation bar, all the keyframes in the animation shift, so their relative positions remain constant. The keyframes will stay in the same positions relative to other keyframes and the beginning and end of the animation bar.

TIP *To prevent the other keyframes from moving, press Ctrl (Windows) or Command (Macintosh) while dragging the keyframe at the end of the animation bar. If you drag the keyframe without the modifier keys, all the other keyframes in the animation move proportionally. The modifier keys restrain the movement to only the last keyframe. This is useful if you have a short animation bar and need to extend it without the keyframes moving to other frames.*

5) Save the ship.html file and test it in the browser.

You can also preview the path of the layer in Dreamweaver by clicking and holding down the Play button.

NOTE *To shift the location of an entire animation path, select the animation bar on the timeline and then drag the layer on the page. Dreamweaver adjusts the position of all keyframes. Making any change when an entire bar is selected changes all the keyframes in the bar.*

CHANGING IMAGE PROPERTIES

Timelines allow you to change the source properties of an image.

1) Place the insertion point in the document window. Insert spacer.gif from the Lesson_16_Timelines/Images folder and with the image still selected use the Property inspector to change the size to 437 for width and 40 for height. Click the Align Center button and name the image title by using the image-name text box on the upper left corner of the Property inspector.

When you insert an image, it is automatically selected when Dreamweaver inserts it into the page. If you have inserted a spacer image, it is easiest to immediately change the width and height to the necessary values before clicking anywhere else in the document window, which would cause the image to be deselected.

2) Click the first frame in the Timelines panel by clicking the 1 in the row of frame numbers. Select the spacer image in the document window and choose Modify > Timeline > Add Object to Timeline.

The image is added to the timeline; the title animation bar appears.

NOTE *If you do not name your images, they will appear in the Timelines panel with their default names: Image1, Image2, and so on. You named images when you worked with Behaviors in Lesson 5.*

3) Click the last keyframe on the title animation bar and move it to frame 60.

Frame 60 is the ending frame of the animation. In this exercise, the image source should change at that point. If you wanted the image to change at a different point you would need to add a keyframe to the title animation bar at the desired frame.

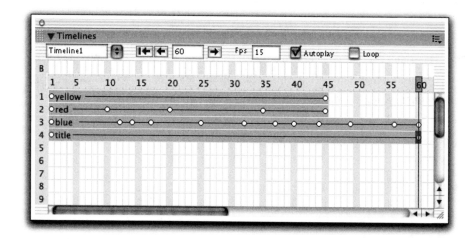

497

4) On the Property inspector, click the folder icon to the right of the Src text field to browse for a new image source. Select the ship_header.gif image located in the Lesson_16_Timelines/Images folder.

With the last keyframe in the title animation bar still selected at frame 60, you should see the ship_header.gif image appear in the document window. Using a spacer image as the initial image as you have done in this exercise is one way to make the image appear. You can also achieve this effect by changing the visibility of a layer, which you will do in the following exercises.

5) Command-click (Macintosh) or Ctrl-click (Windows) on the title animation bar at frame 15. On the Property inspector, click the folder icon to the right of the Src text field to browse for a new image source. Select the ship_title.gif image located in the Lesson_16_Timelines/Images folder.

You can save and preview the document. When you are done, close the ship.html file.

CREATING THE ANIMATION LAYERS

You can easily create more complex animations in Dreamweaver. The remaining exercises in this lesson take you through the process of creating a more complicated animation. You'll start off by creating all the layers that will be used in the animation.

1) Create a new page and save it as navigate.html in the Lesson_16_Timelines folder. Title the page *Lights of the Coast: Coastal Navigation*. Set the background of the page to white and the text to black. Draw one large layer on the page, name the layer cliffs in the Layers panel, insert the cliffs.jpg image from the Lesson_16_Timelines folder into the layer, and give the image a 1-pixel border.

The cliffs image depicts a fictitious environment. This mock coastline will serve as the background for an animation that you will create to serve as an illustrative example of how lighthouses aid navigation.

2) Draw three small layers along the edge of the coast. Name the topmost layer white and insert LHW_off.gif into it; name the middle layer red and insert LHR_off.gif into it; and name the bottommost layer black, inserting LHB_off.gif into it.

All images are in the Lesson_16_Timelines/Images folder. These layers now contain the graphics that each change during the animation.

TIP *While a layer is selected, you can use the arrow keys to get that layer into the exact location you want.*

498

3) Draw a small layer in the lower right corner of the cliffs image. Name the layer ship and insert ship_Y.gif into it.

In the finished animation, the ship layer will move and cause changes to occur to the white, red, and black layers.

Your document should now look similar to the example shown here.

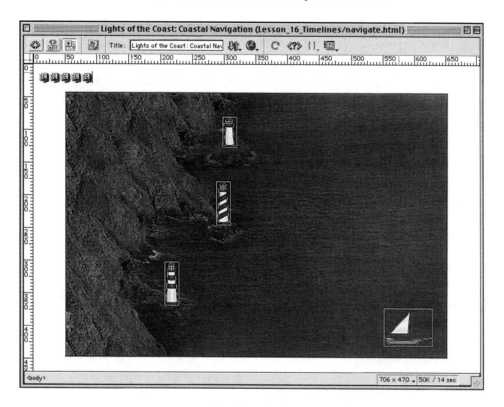

4) Draw a layer to the left of the black layer and name it blackText. Insert a table into the layer with 1 row, 1 column, cell padding of 1, cell spacing of 0, width of 150 pixels, and a 0 border. Set the background of the table to black. Click inside the table and insert a table with 1 row, 1 column, cell padding of 2, cell spacing of 0, width of 100 percent, and a 0 border. Set the background of this nested table to white. Type Captain sees Black Stripe Lighthouse and knows he needs to head northeast. into the nested table and format it as Verdana, –2.

You have just inserted a table with a second table nested inside of it in order to create a border like you did in Lesson 4. You may need to adjust the position of this new layer so it does not overlap the black layer containing the lighthouse icon.

499

5) Repeat step 4 to add a layer called redText **next to the red layer with the text** Captain recognizes through the fog the flashing pattern of the Red Stripe Lighthouse and knows he needs to head north. **Repeat step 4 again to add a layer called** whiteText **next to the white layer with the text** Captain sees the White Lighthouse and drops anchor at the final destination.

TIP *To speed up the process, you can copy the outer table inside the blackText layer and paste it into the new layers you create in this step. Then simply replace the text in the table with the corresponding text for that layer.*

These text layers will be hidden at the beginning of the animation. They will appear individually over the course of the animation.

6) Add the black, blackText, red, redText, and ship layers to the timeline. Place each layer in its own animation channel, starting each one in frame 1. Check the Autoplay box.

The timeline now contains five animation channels: black, blackText, red, redText, and ship. The animation is set to begin when the page loads. The white, whiteText, and cliffs layers should not be added to the timeline.

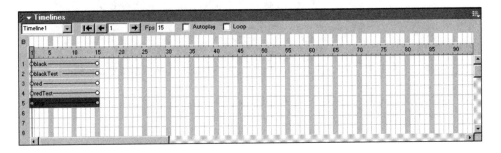

ADJUSTING THE KEYFRAMES

Keyframes give you precise control over the movements of your layers. In this exercise, you will use them to make the ship image go through a series of movements and pauses.

1) Drag the last keyframe of the ship animation bar to frame 40. Hold down Command (Macintosh) or Ctrl (Windows) and move the pointer over the animation bar until it changes to a circle and click the ship animation bar to add new keyframes at frames 10, 15, 20, 25, 30, and 35.

These keyframes are points of change in the movement of the ship layer.

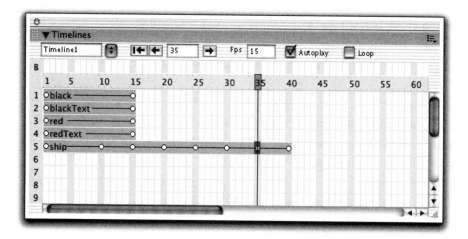

2) Select the last keyframe in the ship animation bar at frame 40. Drag the ship layer in the document window near the coastline just above the white layer.

This is the ending position of the ship layer.

Your document window should now look similar to the example shown here.

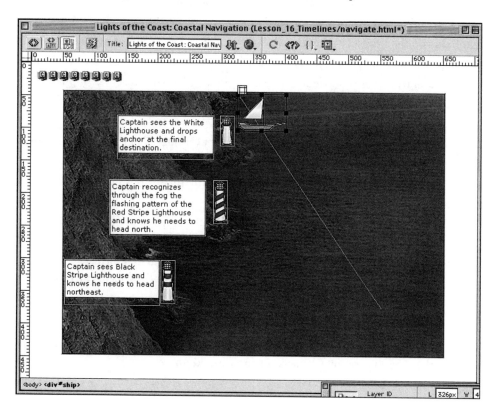

3) Select the keyframe on the ship animation bar at frame 35 in the Timelines panel and drag the ship layer in the document window just to the right of the white layer. Look at the Property inspector and make a note of the resulting value in the L and T text fields.

This is the fourth position (the seventh keyframe) of the ship layer.

4) Select the keyframe on the ship animation bar at frame 30 in the Timelines panel, select the ship layer in the document window and change the value in the L and T text fields on the Property inspector to match the value you made a note of in step 3 for the position of the ship layer at frame 35.

The block of five frames between frame 30 and frame 35 will cause the ship layer to pause in the fourth position (the sixth and seventh keyframes).

5) Select the keyframe on the ship animation bar at frame 25 in the Timelines panel and drag the ship layer in the document window just to the right of the red layer. Look at the Property inspector and make a note of the resulting value in the L and T text fields.

This is the third position (the fifth keyframe) of the ship layer.

6) Select the keyframe on the ship animation bar at frame 20 in the Timelines panel, select the ship layer in the document window and change the value in the L and T text fields on the Property inspector to match the value you made a note of in step 5 for the position of the ship layer at frame 25.

The block of five frames between frame 20 and frame 25 will cause the ship layer to pause in the third position (the fourth and fifth keyframes).

7) Select the keyframe on the ship animation bar at frame 15 in the Timelines panel and drag the ship layer in the document window just to the right of the black layer. Look at the Property inspector and make a note of the resulting value in the L and T text fields.

This is the second position (the third keyframe) of the ship layer.

8) Select the keyframe on the ship animation bar at frame 10 in the Timelines panel, select the ship layer in the document window and change the value in the L and T text fields on the Property inspector to match the value you made a note of in step 7 for the position of the ship layer at frame 15.

The block of five frames between frame 10 and frame 15 will cause the ship layer to pause in the second position (the second and third keyframes).

NOTE *You may want to create a smoother animation, in which the ship does not move in such an angular fashion. To do so, you would need to create more keyframes and adjust the position of the ship layer at each keyframe, as you did when you made the red ship move in a more freeform line earlier in this lesson.*

CHANGING THE VISIBILITY OF LAYERS

Timelines allow you to do more than simply moving layers. You can also use timelines to change the visibility of a layer over time. For example, you might want a layer to be displayed only after another layer animates across the screen. The initial state of the second layer would be hidden and would then become visible at a certain frame.

1) Select the last keyframe of the black layer and move it to frame 10.

The default length of an animation bar is 15 frames, so you need to adjust the black animation bar to match up with the second position of the ship you set at frame 10 in the previous exercise.

TIP *You can also use the eye icons on the Layers panel to change visibility. This was covered in Lesson 15.*

2) Select the first keyframe of the blackText layer and use the Vis drop-down menu on the Property inspector to change the visibility of the layer to hidden. Select the last keyframe of the blackText layer at frame 10, and use the Vis drop-down menu to change the visibility to visible.

In this step, you have changed the visibility of the blackText layer so it will be hidden when the page loads initially. This layer will appear when the ship moves to its second position in frame 10.

NOTE *You have not changed the visibility of the black layer; the Black Stripe Lighthouse will remain visible throughout the animation.*

3) Select the first keyframe of the red layer and change the visibility of the layer to hidden. Select the last keyframe of the red layer, drag it to frame 20, and change the visibility of the layer to visible.

The visibility of the red layer is changed to visible when the last keyframe is selected, because the layer should only appear at that point. Frame 20 is the third position of the ship layer.

4) Repeat step 3 for the redText layer.

You have changed the visibility of both the Red Stripe Lighthouse and its corresponding text. Both layers will be hidden initially and become visible at the same time the ship layer moves near them in frame 20.

Your Timelines panel should now look like the example shown here.

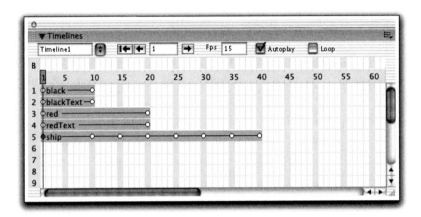

5) Save the navigate.html file and test it in the browser.

NOTE *If the animation doesn't play, make sure Autoplay is selected in the Timelines panel.*

The ship moves from its first position in the lower right corner of the image of cliffs and water, and it stops at the second position. The Black Stripe Lighthouse is set to be visible throughout the animation, but the blackText layer was set to hidden in the first frame and now appears when the ship reaches the lighthouse. As the ship moves up and stops at the third position, the hidden red and redText layers become visible. The ship continues upward to the fourth position, reaching the last layer, white, which has been visible during the entire animation. The ship then moves slightly to its ending position.

NOTE *In addition to changing the visibility of a layer, you can also change the size of a layer. The process is the same as the techniques you used to change the visibility during the animation: To change the size of a layer, you would select the keyframe at which you want the change to occur on the animation bar for the layer you wish to affect, then change the W and H text fields on the Property inspector or use the resize handles in the document window. Keep in mind, browsers have varying capabilities and not all will display properly—test your pages to be sure.*

Leave the navigate.html file open for the next exercise.

ADDING BEHAVIORS TO THE TIMELINE

Adding a behavior to the timeline is similar to adding a behavior to any other object, except that you attach the behavior to a single frame in the timeline and not to the entire animation bar. The behavior is added to the Behaviors channel, and a dash in the Behaviors channel indicates which frame the behavior was applied to.

In the previous exercise, the layers that appeared when the ship layer moved near them were added to the timeline. In this exercise, you will make the whiteText layer stay hidden and appear when the ship layer moves near the white layer without adding the whiteText layer to the timeline. You will use behaviors to display the layer at a specific point in the timeline.

1) Select the whiteText layer and use the Layers panel to change the visibility to hidden by clicking in the visibility column until the closed eye icon appears to the left of the whiteText layer.

The whiteText layer disappears; the white layer is still visible.

2) Select the keyframe at frame 30 on the ship animation bar in the Timelines panel.

The ship layer is in the fourth position (the sixth keyframe), to the right of the white layer.

3) Click frame 30 in the Behaviors channel above the playback head.

The frame in the Behaviors channel above the playback head turns black to indicate that it is selected.

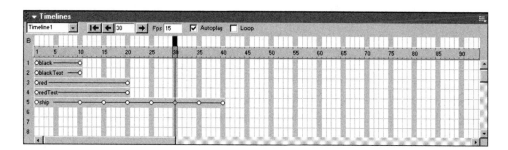

4) Choose Windows > Behaviors to open the Behaviors panel. Click the plus sign (+) button to add a behavior and choose Show-Hide Layers from the pop-up menu.

The Show-Hide Layers dialog box appears with a list of the layers on the page.

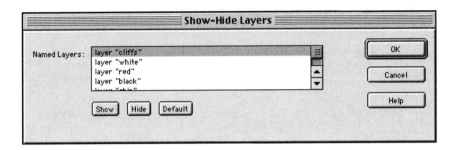

5) Select the whiteText layer from the Named Layers list and click the Show button. Then click OK.

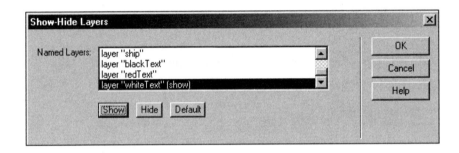

When you click the Show button, "(show)" displays next to the whiteText layer in the list box on the Show-Hide Layers dialog box. This behavior will be triggered when the ship layer reaches frame 30, causing the whiteText layer to become visible.

NOTE *You can make multiple layers appear and disappear at once by selecting other layers in the Named Layers list and clicking the Show or Hide buttons. Default will restore the layer's default visibility. Layers do not have to be in the Timelines panel in order for you to show or hide them with this behavior.*

6) Save the navigate.html file and test it in the browser.

Leave this file open for the next exercise.

MAKING THE TIMELINE PLAY

In the previous exercises, the timeline automatically played in the browser because you selected the Autoplay option. At times you might want the user to control the playback of the timeline. You can add a Start Timeline button to play the animation when the user rolls over a button or clicks an image.

1) In the navigate.html document, deselect Autoplay on the Timelines panel. Select the first frame in the Timelines panel by clicking the 1 in the row of frame numbers.

The playback head moves to frame 1 when you select the first frame. When you deselect Autoplay, the JavaScript Play Timeline action, which used an onLoad event to start the animation once the page loaded, is removed from the **<body>** tag.

2) Draw a layer on the page just below the lower right corner of the cliffs layer. Name the layer start and insert the play.gif image from the Lesson_16_Timelines/ Images folder into the new layer.

This is the graphic to which you will attach the Play Timeline behavior in the next step.

NOTE *The object you attach the Play Timeline behavior to does not have to be contained in a layer. It can be any text, graphic, or object on the page. In this exercise, using a layer is an easy way to control the placement of the graphic.*

3) Select the play.gif image. In the Behaviors panel, click the plus sign (+) button to add a behavior and choose the Timeline > Play Timeline behavior.

TIP *Be sure that frame 1 is selected in the Timelines panel.*

The Play Timeline dialog box appears. Click OK.

4) With the play.gif image still selected, select the Play Timeline behavior in the behaviors panel. Click the down arrow to the right of onLoad to open the event drop-down menu and choose (onClick).

You may need to choose the Show Events For option at the bottom of the actions drop-down menu and select 4.0 and Later Browsers.

5) Click OK. Save the navigate.html file and test it in the browser.

When you click Play, the animation should begin.

You can close this file.

ON YOUR OWN: INTERACTIVE NAVIGATION

You could make the navigation animation that you have created in this lesson a more interactive experience for the visitor by splitting it up into three different timelines. The first timeline would be the movement of the ship to the Black Stripe Lighthouse, and the appearance of the blackText layer. At this point, you would make an additional layer appear that the visitor could click to begin the second leg of the ship's journey that would start the second timeline. You can add a timeline by choosing Modify > Timeline > Add Timeline. Use the Timeline drop-down menu on the Timelines panel to select a timeline if you have multiple timelines for a document. You would need to apply the same Play Timeline behavior that you used in this exercise to start the animation to an object in the additional layer. You might also make the blackText layer disappear at the start of the second timeline. The second timeline would be the movement of the ship to the location of the Red Stripe Lighthouse, and the appearance of the red and redText layers. At this point, you would make an additional layer appear that the visitor could click to begin the third leg of the ship's journey that would start the third timeline. You might also make the redText layer disappear at the start of the third timeline. The third timeline would be the movement of the ship to the location of the White Lighthouse and the appearance of the whiteText layer.

NOTE *Versions of the lighthouse icons with the light on are included in the Lesson_16_Timelines/Images folder with the suffix _on. You can use them to experiment with the animation you've created in this lesson.*

WHAT YOU HAVE LEARNED

In this lesson, you have:

- Added layers to the Timelines panel to create animations that would add more dynamic action to your pages (pages 482–485)

- Made layers move around the page in straight lines and in freeform curves (pages 485–494)

- Altered the timeline with keyframes to create points in the animation when a layer's properties, such as direction and visibility, changed (pages 485–498)

- Changed the speed and duration of the animation by shortening or extending the animation bar on the Timelines panel (pages 489–490)

- Recorded the path of a layer as you moved it around the page so keyframes would automatically be created (pages 494–496)

- Controlled when the animation started by using Autoplay to begin the animation once the page finished loading in the browser (page 500)

- Used keyframes on the Timelines panel to control when layers were visible and when they were hidden (pages 500–504)

- Added behaviors to the timeline to control when layers were visible or hidden (pages 505–506)

- Made it possible for the viewer to start the animation by attaching a behavior to a graphic that would play the timeline when it was clicked (pages 507–508)

extending Dreamweaver

LESSON 17

You can expand Dreamweaver's capabilities with the use of extensions. Dreamweaver was designed to be extensible, allowing users of the program to expand functionality. An **extension** is a piece of software you can add to Dreamweaver to enhance Dreamweaver's capabilities. There are several different kinds of extensions, from simple HTML that you can add to the Insert bar and the Insert and Commands menus, to JavaScript commands you can add to the Command menu or Behaviors panel.

In this project, you will customize Dreamweaver with extensions that will enable you to insert elements like QuickTime movies and breadcrumbs.

Advanced users who are proficient in JavaScript can create new behaviors and insert them into Dreamweaver. Even with only a basic understanding of HTML, you can create simple objects or commands for use within Dreamweaver. You can also use extensions created by others using the Dreamweaver Extension Manager to download and install extensions from the Dreamweaver Exchange Web site. In this lesson, you will use extensions that have been provided for you on the CD that accompanies this book. There is a wide range of extensions available, ranging from ones that you can buy to freeware-style scripts. Extensions on Macromedia's Dreamweaver Exchange are free. Many are created by developers who offer both free and paid scripts.

To see examples of the finished pages for this lesson, open lighthouse.html and cabrillo_qtvr.html from the Lesson_17_Customize/Completed folder.

WHAT YOU WILL LEARN

In this lesson, you will:

- Add extensions using the Extension Manager
- Use new extensions
- Create your own objects

APPROXIMATE TIME

This lesson should take about one hour to complete.

LESSON FILES

Media Files:
Lesson_17_Customize/Images/…(all files)

Starting Files:
Lesson_17_Customize/Objects/…(all files)

Extensions:
Lesson_17_Customize/MacExtensions/… (all files)
Lesson_17_Customize/WinExtensions/… (all files)

Completed Project:
Lesson_17_Customize/Completed/…(all files)

INSTALLING EXTENSIONS

Extensions are installed into Dreamweaver using the Extension Manager. In this exercise, you will install several extensions that have been provided for you on the CD-ROM that accompanies this book

1) Quit Dreamweaver. Find and open the Macromedia Extension Manager.

The Macromedia Extension Manager folder is usually installed in the same folder as the Macromedia Dreamweaver MX folder. Look in your Applications or Programs folders.

TIP *Double-click or open the extension file from the Finder (Macintosh) or Windows Explorer (Windows) to launch the Extension Manager automatically.*

The Extension Manager enables you to install extensions, remove extensions, find out more information about an installed extension, and write a review of an installed extension. It also provides a convenient way to bring up the Dreamweaver Exchange Web site, which will help you find more extensions.

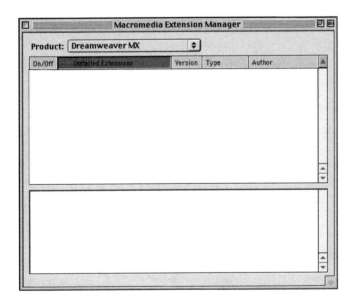

TIP *You can launch the Extension Manager from within Dreamweaver by choosing Commands > Manage Extensions. You can install extensions while Dreamweaver is open, but you need to restart for the changes to take effect.*

2) Choose File > Install Extension in the Extension Manager.

TIP *Windows users can also click Install New Extension.*

The Install Extension (Macintosh) or Select Extension to Install (Windows) dialog box opens.

3) Locate and open the MacExtensions folder (Macintosh) or the WinExtensions folder (Windows) in the Lesson_17_Customize folder. Choose MX324944_m_ superscript2.mxp from the list of extensions, and then click Open (Macintosh) or Install (Windows).

NOTE *Extensions from the Dreamweaver Exchange Web site will begin with "MX" followed by a number and the extension name.*

Dreamweaver will begin to install the extension.

4) Read any legal information about the extension that the author has provided.

To continue with the installation, click Accept.

If you click Decline, the extension will not be installed.

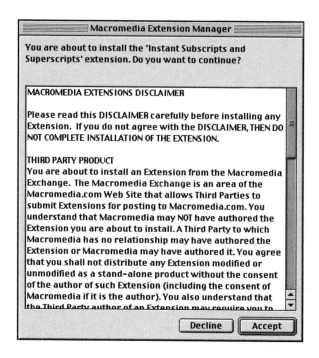

NOTE *If you already have another version of the extension installed—or another extension with the same name—the Installer asks whether to remove the one already installed. If you click Yes, the previously installed extension is removed and the new extension is installed. If you click No, the installation is cancelled, leaving the existing extension in place.*

If the installer doesn't encounter any problems, it displays a message to inform you that the extension has been successfully installed.

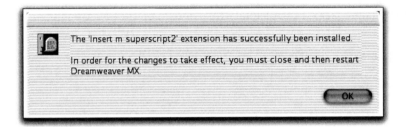

5) Click OK.

The Macromedia Extension Manager displays the extension name, version number, type, and author. The Type column tells you where the extension is installed: commands indicates the extension was installed in the Command menu, objects indicates the extension was installed in the Insert bar, and so on.

6) Repeat steps 2 through 5 to install the following extensions:

- breadCrumbs.mxp

- MX282845_fiXMovie.mxp

- MX323286_advRandImage.mxp

The Macromedia Extension Manager will now display a list of the extensions you have installed.

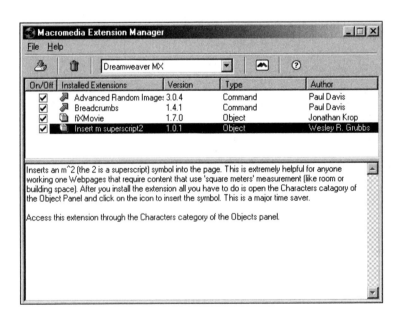

NOTE *To find more extensions, open the Macromedia Extension Manager. Choose File > Go to Macromedia Exchange to open the Macromedia Exchange for Dreamweaver Web page in your browser. You must be a member of macromedia.com to download, submit, or review extensions. This is a free membership. You can sign up and log in at the Dreamweaver Exchange home page. Macromedia provides the Dreamweaver Exchange Web site as a repository for all kinds of extensions. When you find an extension you're interested in on that site, you can download it via your Web browser and then install it in Dreamweaver by using the Extension Manager as you have done in this exercise. Macromedia creates some extensions, while others are created by third parties. Those extensions that are created or authorized by Macromedia are marked on the Dreamweaver Exchange Web site with a small Macromedia icon in the Approval column.*

If you find an extension you want, the file you download is an extension package file and its name ends with .mxp. When you click an extension's name to download it, some Web browsers provide the option of opening the package file directly from its location on the Web instead of simply downloading the file. If you download the package file and save it on your hard disk, you'll have it handy in case you need to reinstall it later, but you'll have to open it explicitly (by double-clicking the file's icon on your desktop, for example) to install it. If you choose to open the package file from its current location, the Macromedia Extension Manager automatically launches to enable you to install the extension, but you won't retain a copy of the package file for later use. It's up to you which approach you prefer.

7) Choose File > Quit (Macintosh OS 9), Extension Manager > Quit Extension Manager (Macintosh OS X), or File > Exit (Windows) to close the Extension Manager. Restart Dreamweaver.

When you restart Dreamweaver, you will be able to use the new extensions.

Dreamweaver MX has changed dramatically from Dreamweaver 4. While many of the extensions that were used in Dreamweaver 4 will still work in Dreamweaver MX, not every extension will. Some extensions may cause errors in Dreamweaver MX. If you find this to be the case, just remove the problematic extension. The Extension Manager allows you to temporarily turn off extensions. If you run into a problem, you can test your extensions by turning them off.

NOTE *To remove an extension, choose File > Remove Extension from the Extension Manager. Select an extension from the list of installed extensions and confirm that you want to remove the extension by clicking Yes in the confirmation dialog box. Only extensions that appear in the list can be removed with the Extension Manager. If you manually installed an extension, you will need to manually remove it. Restart Dreamweaver for the changes to take effect.*

USING THE M SUPERSCRIPT 2 EXTENSION

The M Superscript 2 extension inserts m^2 on your page. This example refers to the square meter unit of measurement, often used to indicate an amount of space in a building. You can replace the "m" and the "2" with letters or numbers of your own choosing, to easily achieve the superscript affect for dates, footnotes, mathematical expressions, and so on.

Dreamweaver Exchange Category: Text
Extension Developer: Wesley R. Grubbs

1) Open a new basic HTML document and save it as lighthouse.html in the Lesson_17_Customize folder. Set the background to white, the text to black and type Lights of the Coast for the title.

You'll use superscript text on this page in the following step.

2) Type June 1 at the top of the page. Click the m^2 icon on the Characters tab of the Insert bar to insert the square meter symbol. Change the m to 3 and change the superscript 2 to th.

Your page should now display "June 13th." This is an easy way to get a superscript into your document.

NOTE *Another extension available on the Dreamweaver Exchange Web site is Instant Subscripts and Superscripts, which allows you to insert both subscripts and superscripts.*

Leave this file open for the next exercise.

USING THE ADVANCED RANDOM IMAGES EXTENSION

This extension will enable you to place a script on your page that displays a random image each time the page is reloaded.

Dreamweaver Exchange Category: Scripting
Extension Developer: Paul Davis
Developer URL: http://www.kaosweaver.com

1) Place the insertion point on a new paragraph line below the date you typed in the last exercise.

You'll place the random image here.

2) Choose Commands > Random Images.

The Random Images dialog box opens.

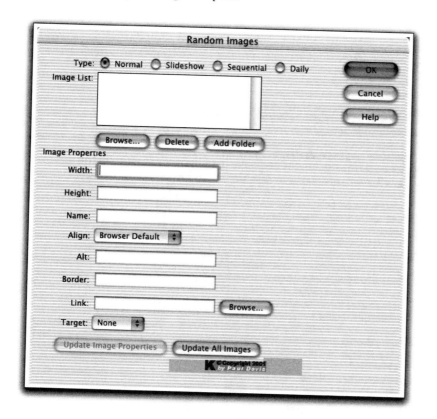

3) From the Type options, verify that Normal is selected. Click the Add Folder button beneath the Image List box. Browse to find the Lesson_17_Customize/Images folder. For Macintosh users, select the folder but do not open it; click Choose. For Windows users, open the folder and click Select.

NOTE *You may not see any of the images in the folder while you are selecting the folder.*

All four images from the Images folder are added to the list.

4) Select the first image in the list, cabrillo.jpg. In the Width text field, type 250 and in the Height text field, type 167. In the Name text field, type lights. Leave the Align drop-down menu set to Browser Default and type Lighthouse Images in the Alt text field. Type 1 in the Border text field. Leave the Link text field blank and leave the Target drop-down menu set to None.

These are the Image Properties. You can set properties for individual images or for an entire list.

5) Click Update All Images.

All four images are displayed with an asterisk indicating that the Image Properties have been applied to them. Using Update All Images will apply the same settings to all the images listed. If you want to adjust the settings for an individual image, you can select the desired image, make changes to the Image Properties and click the Update Image Properties button.

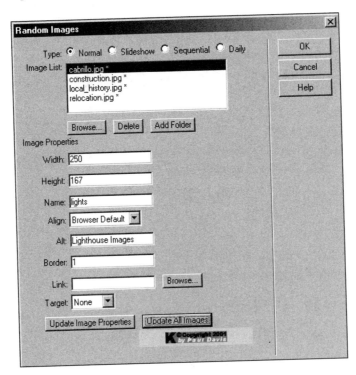

6) Click OK.

The script is inserted into your page. An alert box may appear to inform you that you will not see the script marker unless you have visual aids turned on. Preview the page in a browser in order to see the Random Images script in action.

You can save and close the lighthouse.html document.

TIP *Click the Reload or Refresh browser button to see images change.*

USING THE FIXMOVIE EXTENSION

You can insert QuickTime movies with the fiXMovie as easily as you can insert Flash movies. This particular extension creates pages with embedded QuickTime movies that work cross-platform in both Netscape and Explorer, fixing an issue with QuickTime movies in Explorer. This extension is a great choice for quickly and efficiently inserting movies into your Web pages. In this exercise, you will use the fiXMovie extension to insert a QTVR movie: a 360-degree panorama of Point Cabrillo Lighthouse.

Dreamweaver Exchange Category: Rich Media
Extension Developer: Jonathan Krop
Developer URL: http://www.atomicpopmonkey.com

1) Create a new, basic HTML page and save it as cabrillo_qtvr.html in the Lesson_17_Customize folder. Set the background to white and the text to black. At the top of the page, insert the pt_cabrillo_header.gif image from the Lesson_17_Customize/QTVR_Media folder.

In the following steps, you'll embed the QuickTime movie into this page.

2) Select the Special tab on the Insert bar. Click the fiXMovie icon.

> **TIP** *You can also access this object by choosing Insert > fiXMovie.*

The Special tab was created when you installed the extensions earlier in this lesson.

The Select File dialog box opens.

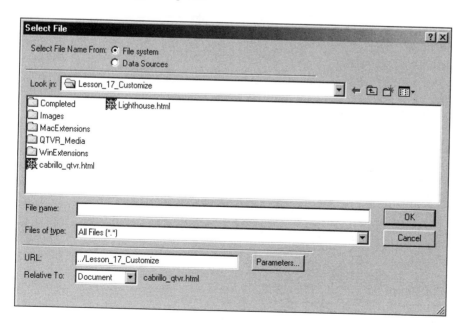

3) Browse to find the cabrillo.mov file in the Lesson_17_Customize/QTVR_Media folder and click Open (Macintosh OS 9), Choose (Macinstosh OS X), or OK (Windows).

This is a fairly large file—it is approximately 1.47MB. When you include files as large as this on your Web site, it is best to give your visitors an idea of what they are getting into before they get to the page. One way of doing this is to provide a thumbnail or a still image on a separate page, with a link to a page with the movie file, and information about the type of file as well as the size.

4) In the Property inspector, set the Width to 320 and the Height to 256. Leave all other options on their default settings.

You won't see the movie in the document window unless you click Play. You will probably have to wait for a few moments for the QuickTime movie to appear, since it is a fairly large file. The document window may appear to be empty while you wait for the movie to appear. When it does appear, you will be able to click inside the image and drag across the image to move it up, down, right, or left. Use your Shift key to zoom in and the Control key to zoom out.

The Parameters button, located beneath the Play/Stop button, will open a small dialog box in which you can make a couple of additional choices. Autoplay determines whether or not the movie will begin playing immediately after the page loads; True will turn on Autoplay while False will turn it off. The Controller is the bar below the image with buttons and information for your visitor; True will place the Controller on the page while False will leave it off.

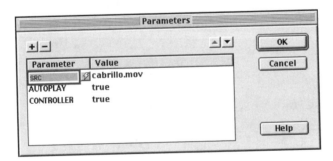

TIP *Sometimes when you insert movies, they may appear cropped, or the controller bar may seem to be missing. In these cases, try enlarging the amount of space allotted to the movie by increasing the width and height. The controller generally requires approximately 16 pixels of additional height, on top of the dimensions of the movie itself.*

5) On a blank paragraph line below the embedded movie, type Click in the image and drag to see the panoramic view. **Format the text as Verdana, –2, #666666. Press return twice and type** © 2002 Lights of the Coast. **Format the text as Verdana, –2, #333333. Select everything on the page and center it.**

TIP *To insert the copyright symbol, choose Insert > Special Characters > Copyright or press Option+G (Macintosh).*

It is always a good idea to let your visitors know how to use the materials you include on your Web site.

You can save this file and leave it open for the next exercise.

USING THE BREADCRUMBS EXTENSION

You learned a bit about the breadcrumb navigational tool in Lesson 6 when you used the Site Window navigation text to look at a subset of your site. **Breadcrumbs** are a very easy-to-use method of navigation that many of your visitors will be familiar with. It shows the structure of the Web site, helping users to understand where they are. This extension works by following the trail from the root directory to the individual files, eliminating the need to manually insert breadcrumbs from page to page and allowing you to make use of breadcrumbs on your site quickly and easily.

Dreamweaver Exchange Category: Navigation
Name: Breadcrumbs
Extension Developer: Paul Davis
Developer URL: http://www.kaosweaver.com

A folder on a Web site is known as a directory. The default file in any given directory, generally index.html or some variation thereof, will usually be displayed to the viewer if no specific file is called for. For example, the URL http://www.macromedia.com will take the visitor to the index or default page of the root directory for Macromedia's Web site, whereas http://www.macromedia.com/software/dreamweaver/ will take the visitor to the index.html file that is inside of the Macromedia Dreamweaver MX folder. These base files are commonly placed in each directory on a Web site, in order to create a default page for their respective folders.

For the breadcrumbs extension to work properly, your site needs to be set up in an organized structure of folders and you need to have one of these base files, such as index.html, in each of those directories.

1) Place the insertion point at the top of the cabrillo_qtvr.html document window, directly to the left of the header image. Press Return (Macintosh) or Enter (windows) to create a new paragraph line above the header image, and align that paragraph block to the left. Choose Commands > Kaosweaver.com > Breadcrumbs.

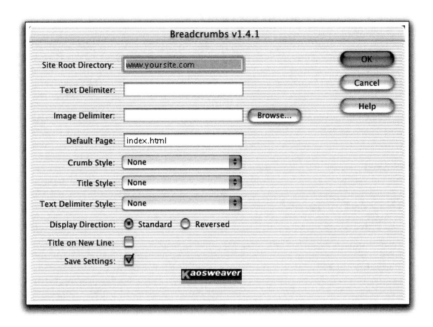

The Breadcrumbs dialog box opens. You can create CSS styles (covered in Lesson 13) to control the display of the breadcrumb elements: Crumb Style, Title Style, and Text Delimiter Style. Once you have attached a style sheet or created internal styles, you can choose from those styles with the drop-down menus. The drop-down menus will display None if there are no available internal or external styles.

NOTE *The delimiters, which are the objects or characters between the filenames such as ">", can also be images. To use an image, click the Browse button next to the Image Delimiter text field.*

2) Leave the default settings as they are and click OK.

You will see "{Kaosweaver Breadcrumbs Trail}" displayed in the document window where you have inserted the script. You will need to upload the file to a remote Web site in order to see the actual breadcrumbs.

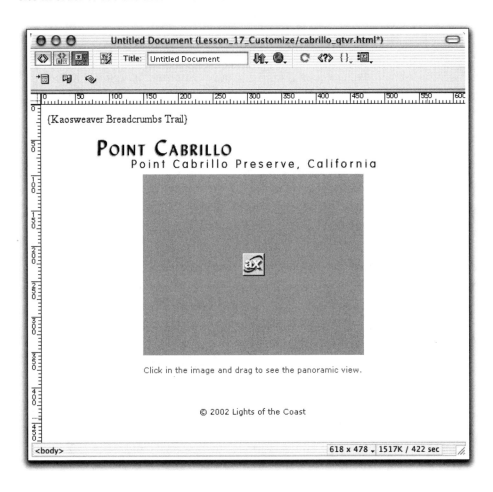

To remove the breadcrumbs on a page, choose Commands > Kaosweaver.com > Breadcrumbs and click the Remove button. A message box will inform you that the breadcrumbs command has been removed from the page. The script will be deleted from the head of the document, but you will still need to select and delete the {Kaosweaver Breadcrumbs Trail} object displayed on the page.

TIP *The Breadcrumb Associative Array modification at http://www.kaosweaver.com/ Extensions/Breadcrumbs/ is an addition to the script created by the Breadcrumbs extension that allows you to replace the names of your directories for more control over your breadcrumbs.*

523

CREATING A SIMPLE OBJECT

The Insert bar is divided into tabs, each of which corresponds to a folder within the Dreamweaver Program Folder. Use the Finder (Macintosh), My Computer (Windows) or Windows Explorer (Windows), to locate the Macromedia > Dreamweaver MX >, Configuration > Objects folder. If you look in the Common folder that is in the Objects folder, you'll see an HTML file and a GIF image file for each of the objects in the Common tab. For example, an image.htm file and an image.gif file correspond to the Image object. Some objects also have a JavaScript file ending with the .js extension. Earlier in this lesson, you installed the fiXMovie extension, which placed the fiXMovie object into a new tab called Special on the Insert bar.

The Insert bar is an easy way to insert HTML elements that you use regularly into your pages. All the objects included in the Insert bar can be modified to suit your needs. Using only some basic HTML, you can create an object for use in all your documents.

NOTE *The example in this exercise is a simple copyright line that could also be created as either a library item (covered in Lesson 8) or as a snippet (covered in Lesson 12) to serve similar, although not identical, function. Some items will work better as library items, while others will work best as snippets, and still others will be most useful as objects in the Insert bar. It depends on the purpose of the object or code you are creating and how you want to access it.*

1) Create a new, basic HTML document. Save it as LC_copyright.html in the Lesson_17_Customize folder. Do not give the document a title.

In the following steps, you will create a copyright tag line for the "Lights of the Coast" Web site and convert it into an object.

2) Choose Insert > Horizontal rule to insert a line across your document, set the width to 300 pixels and the height to 1 pixel. Uncheck the Shading check box in the Property inspector to specify no shading. Change the Align drop-down menu from Default to Center. Click on the horizontal rule and arrow once to the right and type © 2002 Lights of the Coast.

You now have the copyright information in your document. The text will automatically drop down just beneath the horizontal rule. Don't use a line break (Shift+Return) or a regular paragraph (Return) in this exercise.

3) Create a line break by pressing Shift+Return (Macintosh) or Shift+Enter (Windows). On the next line, type modified:, and then choose Insert > Date.

The Insert Date dialog box appears.

4) In the Insert Date dialog box, choose Day Format: [No Day]; Date Format: March 7, 1974; and verify that the Time Format is set to the default [No Time]. Check the Update Automatically on Save box and click OK. Format all the text on the page as Verdana, –2, and use the Align Center button on the Property inspector to center the text.

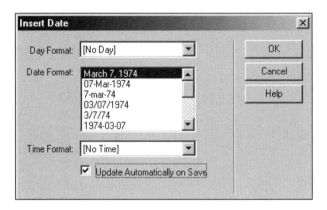

The current date is inserted into your document at the insertion point.

5) Click the Code View icon on the document toolbar to view the HTML. Delete everything in the document except for the following (your date line will show the current date):

```
<hr align="center" width="300" size="1" noshade>
<div align="center"><font size="-2" face="Verdana, Arial, Helvetica,
sans-serif">&copy; 2002 Lights of the Coast</font>
<font size="-2" face="Verdana, Arial, Helvetica, sans-serif">
<br>Modified: <!--#BeginDate format:Am1  -->June 13, 2002
<!--#EndDate  --></font> </div>
```

In Code View, your document will look like the example that follows.

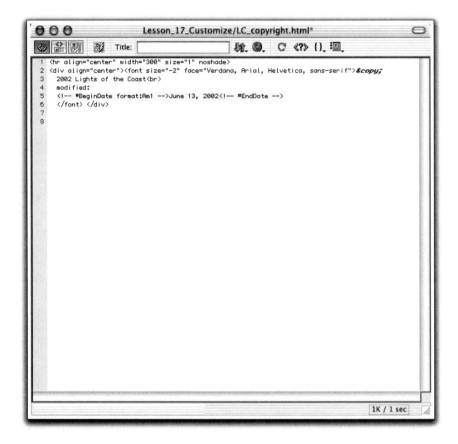

6) Click the Design View icon on the document toolbar to switch back to Design View and see your changes. Save your file and quit Dreamweaver.

After you have created the HTML file, you need an icon that represents the HTML. The icons used by Dreamweaver are GIF files. In this exercise, an icon has already been created for you and is provided on the CD-ROM. The icon and the HTML need the same name. In the following steps, you will add your object to the Dreamweaver application.

NOTE *To create your own icons for the Insert bar, create an 18×18–pixel GIF image in a program such as Macromedia Fireworks. Make sure the name of the GIF image is the same as that of your HTML file.*

7) Using the Finder (Macintosh), My Computer (Windows), or Windows Explorer (Windows), open the Lesson_17_Customize folder and locate the LC_copyright.html and LC_copyright.gif files.

These are the files you are going to use for the new object.

8) In the Dreamweaver application folder, open the Configuration > Objects > Special folder.

NOTE *If you are working in a multi-user environment (such as Macintosh OS X, Windows NT, Windows 2000, or Windows XP) then you will have your own Configuration folder, separate from any other users. This allows multiple users to have different set ups on the same computer. On Macintosh OS X for example, your Configuration folder will be located in the Hard Disk > Users > Username > Library > Application Support > Macromedia > Dreamweaver MX > Configuration folder. On Windows, your configuration folder will be located in the C:\Documents and Settings\user\Application Data\Macromedia\ Dreamweaver MX\Configuration folder.*

The Special tab was created when you installed extensions earlier in this lesson. At this point, the Special tab has only one object in it. That object is created by the three files you see for the fiXMovie extension in the Special folder. Since the Special tab already exists and has only one object in it, you'll place the Lights of the Coast copyright object there. The tabs on the Insert bar are specified in the insertbar.xml file, which contains information about the order of tabs and objects. Objects that are not listed in the insertbar.xml will be given lower priority, being displayed after those that are listed. Folders that are not specified in the insertbar.xml file are ignored; they will not display as tabs on the Insert bar.

NOTE *Please be aware that the files that are contained within the Configuration folders in the Dreamweaver application folder are essential files; these files are central to the Dreamweaver program. You should be very careful when modifying, deleting, or adding to these files and folder—do so only if you intend to customize Dreamweaver and are familiar with the code and file structures. If you plan to make changes to files such as the insertbar.xml file, make backup copies first. There is a Configuration_ReadMe.htm file in the Configuration folder of the Dreamweaver application folder with more information on the Configuration files. If you have installed multiple versions of Dreamweaver on your computer, you may see an older and unnecessary Configuration folder called Configuration-1 if you have not completely uninstalled or deleted the program.*

9) Select the LC_copyright.html and LC_copyright.gif files. Copy them both into the Special folder and restart Dreamweaver.

When Dreamweaver restarts, you will be able to see the LC_copyright icon on the Special tab of the Insert bar. The name of the HTML file is the name of the menu item.

10) Open a new, basic HTML document and click your new LC_copyright icon on the Special tab of the Insert bar.

The horizontal rule, copyright tag line, and modified date are all inserted in your page.

You can close this file without saving it.

ADVANCED CUSTOMIZATION

Up to this point in the lessons, you've worked with a wide variety of Dreamweaver's toolbars and panels. In Lesson 1, you learned how to arrange the toolbars and panels by rearranging their order within existing panel groups, moving them to different panel groups, creating new panel groups, as well as docking and undocking panel groups. You worked with the Dreamweaver Preferences throughout the book. In this lesson, you've learned how to install extensions as well as create your own objects.

There are many other things that you can do to customize Dreamweaver to suit your needs. Other possibilities include, but are not limited to: changing FTP Mappings to specify file extensions and file creators; customizing the Dreamweaver menus by adding, removing, changing, or moving menu items; changing the keyboard shortcuts; customizing default documents; customizing browser profiles; and creating your own extensions.

Use caution when making changes to any of the Dreamweaver program files; advanced customization is best done by those with a thorough understanding of HTML, JavaScript, and the structure of the Dreamweaver program.

ON YOUR OWN: IDEUM MEDIA PORFOLIO

The Ideum portfolio displays use of the Dreamweaver fiXMovie extension. Web developers must embed the movies into the code themselves or use an extension such as this one. Ideum found this particular version of the QuickTime extension very useful because it addresses a movie display issue in Internet Explorer. The Ideum Web site needed to showcase their work on QTVR cubic and standard panoramas.

http://www.ideum.com/mediafolio.html
Credits: Design and QTVR development by Ideum (www.ideum.com)
QuickTime VR Movies appear courtesy of Provincia Di Torino © 2002

"Having a library of extensions to choose from helps us with the variety of projects and tasks that we deal with. The FixMovie extension helps us embed QuickTime and change the necessary parameters. Our portfolio site has about a dozen QuickTimeVR movies in two formats, and having the ability to easily place them into HTML pages really saved us time."—Jim Spadaccini, Ideum

In this bonus activity, you will use the fiXMovie extension that you installed and worked with earlier in this lesson to insert the QuickTime VR movies into the appropriate Ideum portfolio pages on your own. The files you will need for this exercise are located in the Bonus/Lesson_17 folder. You can view the final files in the Bonus/Lesson_17/Completed folder. Examine the Completed file before you begin.

WHAT YOU HAVE LEARNED

In this lesson, you have:

- Added extensions to expand Dreamweaver's capabilities using the Macromedia Extension Manager (pages 512–515)
- Learned where to find more extensions (page 515)
- Used new extensions to create superscript text, insert random images, and work with a QuickTime movie (pages 516–521)
- Learned about breadcrumb navigation (pages 521–523)
- Created a new object and placed it into the Insert bar (pages 524–528)

regular expressions

The following table lists special characters in regular expressions and their meanings.

Type	Description	Example
^	Beginning of input or line	**^T** matches "T" in "This good earth" but not in "Uncle Tom."
$	End of input or line	**h$** matches "h" in "teach" but not in "teacher."
*	The preceding character zero or more times	**um*** matches "um" in "rum," "umm" in "yummy," and "u" in "huge."
+	The preceding character one or more times	**um+** matches "um" in "rum" and "umm" in "yummy."
?	The preceding character at most once	**st?on** matches "son" in "Johnson" and "ston" in "Johnston."
.	Any single character except newline	**.an** matches "ran" and "can."
x|y	Either x or y	**FF0000|0000FF** matches **"FF0000"** in **BGCOLOR="#FF0000"** and **"0000FF"** in **FONT COLOR="#0000FF"**.
{n}	Exactly n occurrences of the preceding character	**o{2}** matches "oo" in "loom" and the first two o's in "mooooo."
{n,m}	At least n and at most m occurrences of the preceding character	**F{2,4}** matches **"FF"** in **"#FF0000"** and the first four Fs in **"#FFFFFF"**.

Type	Description	Example
[abc]	Any one of the characters enclosed in the brackets	**[aeiou]** initially matches "a" in "apple," "e" in "egg," and "i" in "pig." Specify a range of characters with a hyphen (for example, **[a-f]** is equivalent to **[abcdef]**).
[^abc]	Any character not enclosed in the brackets	**[^aeiou]** initially matches "r" in "orange," "b" in "book," and "k" in "eek!". Specify a range of characters with a hyphen (for example, **[^a-f]** is equivalent to **[^abcdef]**).
\b	A word boundary (such as a space or carriage return)	**\bb** matches "b" in "book" but nothing in "goober" or "snob."
\B	A nonword boundary	**\Bb** matches "b" in "goober" but nothing in "book."
\d	Any digit character. Equivalent to **[0-9]**.	**\d** matches "3" in "C3PO" and "2" in "apartment 2G."
\D	Any nondigit character. Equivalent to **[^0-9]**.	**\D** matches "S" in "900S" and "Q" in "Q45."
\f	Form feed	
\n	Line feed	
\r	Carriage return	
\s	Any single whitespace character, including space, tab, form feed, or line feed	**\sbook** matches "book" in "blue book."
\t	A tab	
\w	Any alphanumeric character, including underscore. Equivalent to **[A-Za-z0-9_]**.	**b\w*** matches "barking" in "the barking dog" and both "big" and "black" in "the big black dog."
\W	Any nonalphanumeric character. Equivalent to **[^A-Za-z0-9_]**.	**\W** matches "&" in "Jake & Mattie" and "%" in "100%".

macintosh shortcuts

You can add, remove, or modify Dreamweaver's keyboard shortcuts by choosing Edit > Keyboard Shortcuts to open the Keyboard Shortcuts dialog box.

MENU SHORTCUTS

FILE MENU	
Command	**Shortcut**
New...	Command+N
Open...	Command+O
Open in Frame	Command+Shift+O
Close	Command+W
Save	Command+S
Save As...	Command+Shift+S
Print Code	Command+P
Preview in Primary Browser	F12
Preview in Secondary Browser	Command+F12
Debug in Primary Browser	Option+F12
Debug in Secondary Browser	Command+Option+F12
Check Links	Shift+F8
Validate Markup...	Shift+F6
Quit	Command+Q

Command	Shortcut
Undo	Command+Z or Option+Delete
Redo	Command+Y or Command+Shift+Z
Cut	Command+X or Shift+Del
Copy	Command+C
Paste	Command+V
Clear	Delete
Copy HTML	Command+Shift+C
Paste HTML	Command+Shift+V
Select All	Command+A
Select Parent Tag	Command+[
Select Child	Command+]
Find and Replace	Command+F
Find Again	Command+G
Go to Line	Command+,
Show Code Hints	Control+Space
Indent Code	Command+›
Outdent Code	Control+‹
Balance Braces	Command+'
Set Breakpoint	Command+Option+B
Preferences	Command+U

Command	Shortcut
Switch Views	Command+`
Refresh Design View	F5
Live Data	Command+Shift+R
Head Content	Command+Shift+W
Table View › Standard View	Command+Shift+F6
Table View › Layout View	Command+F6
Visual Aids › Hide All	Command+Shift+I
Rulers › Show	Command+Option+R
Grid › Show	Command+Option+G
Grid › Snap to Grid	Command+Shift+Option+G
Plugins › Play	Command+Option+P
Plugins › Stop	Command+Option+X
Plugins › Play All	Command+Shift+Option+P
Plugins › Stop All	Command+Shift+Option+X
Hide Panels/Show Panels	F4

Command	Shortcut
Tag...	Command+E
Image	Command+Option+I
Media › Flash	Command+Option+F
Media › Shockwave	Command+Option+D
Table	Command+Option+T
Template Objects	Command+Option+V
Named Anchor	Command+Option+A
Special Characters › Line Break	Shift+Return
Special Characters › Non-Breaking Space	Command+Shift+Space

MODIFY MENU

Command	Shortcut
Page Properties	Command+J
Selection Properties	Command+Shift+J
Quick Tag Editor	Command+T
Make Link	Command+L
Remove Link	Command+Shift+L
Table > Select Table	Command+A
Move to the Next Cell*	Tab
Move to the Previous Cell*	Shift+Tab
Table > Merge Cells	Command+Option+M
Table > Split Cell	Command+Option+S
Table > Insert Row	Command+M
Table > Insert Column	Command+Shift+A
Table > Delete Row	Command+Shift+M
Table > Delete Column	Command+Shift+-
Table > Increase Column Span	Command+Shift+]
Table > Decrease Column Span	Command+Shift+[
Library > Add Object to Library	Command+Shift+B

*Command is not included in the Modify Menu.

TEXT MENU

Command	Shortcut
Indent	Command+Option+]
Outdent	Command+Option+[
Paragraph Format > None	Command+0
Paragraph Format > Paragraph	Command+Shift+P
Paragraph Format > Heading 1	Command+1
Paragraph Format > Heading 2	Command+2
Paragraph Format > Heading 3	Command+3
Paragraph Format > Heading 4	Command+4
Paragraph Format > Heading 5	Command+5
Paragraph Format > Heading 6	Command+6

TEXT MENU (continued)

Command	Shortcut
Align > Left	Command+Shift+Option+L
Align > Center	Command+Shift+Option+C
Align > Right	Command+Shift+Option+R
Align > Justify	Command+Shift+Option+J
Style > Bold	Command+B
Style > Italic	Command+I
CSS Styles > Edit Style Sheet	Command+Shift+E
Check Spelling	Shift+F7

COMMANDS MENU

Command	Shortcut
Start Recording	Command+Shift+X

SITE MENU

Command	Shortcut
Site Files	F8
Site Map	Option+F8
Refresh	F5
Site Files View > New File	Command+Shift+N
Site Files View > New Folder	Command+Shift+Option+N
Site Files View > Refresh Local	Shift+F5
Site Files View > Refresh Remote	Option+F5
Site Map View > View as Root	Command+Shift+R
Site Map View > Link to New File	Command+Shift+N
Site Map View > Link to Existing File	Command+Shift+K
Site Map View > Change Link	Command+L
Site Map View > Remove Link	Command+Shift+L
Site Map View > Show/Hide Link	Command+Shift+Y
Site Map View > Show Page Titles	Command+Shift+T
Get	Command+Shift+D
Check Out	Command+Shift+Option+D
Put	Command+Shift+U
Check In	Command+Shift+Option+U
Open	Command+Shift+Option+O
Check Links Sitewide	Command+F8

WINDOW MENU

Command	Shortcut
Insert	Command+F2
Properties	Command+F3
Answers	Option+F1
CSS Styles	Shift+F11
HTML Styles	Command+F11
Behaviors	Shift+F3
Tag Inspector	F9
Snippets	Shift+F9
Reference	Shift+F1
Databases	Command+Shift+F10
Bindings	Command+F10
Server Behaviors	Command+F7
Site	F8
Assets	F11
Results › Search	Command+Shift+F
Results › Validation	Command+Shift+F7
Results › Target Browser Check	Command+Shift+F8
Results › Link Checker	Command+Shift+F9
Results › Site Reports	Command+Shift+F11
Results › FTP Log	Command+Shift+F12
Others › Code Inspector	F10
Others › Frames	Shift+F2
Others › History	Shift+F10
Others › Layers	F2
Others › Sitespring	F7
Others › Timelines	Option+F9
Show Panels	F4
Next Document	Control+Tab
Previous Document	Control+Shift+Tab

HELP MENU

Command	Shortcut
Using Dreamweaver	F1
Using ColdFusion	Command+F1
Reference	Shift+F1

CODE EDITING SHORTCUTS

Command	Shortcut
Select Parent Tag	Command+[
Select Child	Command+]
Balance Braces	Command+'
Select All	Command+A
Bold	Command+B
Italic	Command+I
Copy	Command+C
Find and Replace	Command+F
Find Next	Command+G
Paste	Command+V
Cut	Command+X
Redo	Command+Y
Undo	Command+Z
Toggle Breakpoint	Command+Option+B
Print Code	Command+P
Delete Word Left	Command+Delete
Delete Word Right	Command+Del
Select Line Up	Shift+Up
Select Line Down	Shift+Down
Character Select Left	Shift+Left
Character Select Right	Shift+Right
Select to Page Up	Shift+PgUp
Select to Page Down	Shift+PgDn
Move Word Left	Command+Left
Move Word Right	Command+Right
Select Word Left	Command+Shift+Left
Select Word Right	Command+Shift+Right
Move to Start of Line	Home
Move to End of Line	End
Select to Start of Line	Shift+Home
Select to End of Line	Shift+End
Move to Top of File	Command+Home
Move to End of File	Command+End
Select to Start of File	Command+Shift+Home
Select to Start of File	Command+Shift+End
Snippets	Shift+F9

windows shortcuts

You can add, remove, or modify Dreamweaver's keyboard shortcuts by choosing Edit > Keyboard Shortcuts to open the Keyboard Shortcuts dialog box.

MENU SHORTCUTS

FILE MENU	
Command	**Shortcut**
New…	Ctrl+N
Open…	Ctrl+O
Open in Frame…	Ctrl+Shift+O
Close	Ctrl+W
Save	Ctrl+S
Save As	Ctrl+Shift+S
Print Code	Ctrl+P
Preview in Primary Browser	F12
Preview in Secondary Browser	Ctrl+F12
Debug in Primary Browser	Alt+F12
Debug in Secondary Browser	Ctrl+Alt+F12
Check Links	Shift+F8
Validate Markup	Shift+F6
Quit	Ctrl+Q

EDIT MENU

Command	Shortcut
Undo	Ctrl+Z
Redo	Ctrl+Y
Cut	Ctrl+X
Copy	Ctrl+C
Paste	Ctrl+V
Copy HTML	Ctrl+Shift+C
Paste HTML	Ctrl+Shift+V
Select All	Ctrl+A
Select Parent Tag	Ctrl+[
Select Child	Ctrl+]
Find and Replace	Ctrl+F
Find Next	F3
Go to Line	Ctrl+G
Show Code Hints	Ctrl+Space
Indent Code	Ctrl+Shift+›
Outdent Code	Ctrl+Shift+‹
Balance Braces	Ctrl+'
Toggle Breakpoint	Ctrl+Alt+B
Preferences	Ctrl+U

VIEW MENU

Command	Shortcut
Switch Views	Ctrl+`
Refresh Design View	F5
Server Debug	Ctrl+Shift+G
Live Data	Ctrl+Shift+R
Head Content	Ctrl+Shift+W
Table View › Standard View	Ctrl+Shift+F6
Table View › Layout View	Ctrl+F6
Hide All	Ctrl+Shift+I
Rulers › Show	Ctrl+Alt+R
Grid › Show Grid	Ctrl+Alt+G
Grid › Snap to Grid	Ctrl+Shift+Alt+G
Plugins › Play	Ctrl+Alt+P
Plugins › Stop	Ctrl+Alt+X
Plugins › Play All	Ctrl+Shift+Alt+P
Plugins › Stop All	Ctrl+Shift+Alt+X
Show Panels	F4

INSERT MENU

Command	Shortcut
Tag	Ctrl+E
Image	Ctrl+Alt+I
Table	Ctrl+Alt+T
Media › Flash	Ctrl+Alt+F
Media › Shockwave	Ctrl+Alt+D
Template Object › Editable Region	Crtl+Alt+V
Named Anchor	Ctrl+Alt+A
Special Characters › Line Break	Shift+Enter
Special Characters › Non-Breaking Space	Ctrl+Shift+Space

MODIFY MENU

Command	Shortcut
Page Properties	Ctrl+J
Selection Properties	Ctrl+Shift+J
Quick Tag Editor	Ctrl+T
Make Link	Ctrl+L
Remove Link	Ctrl+Shift+L
Table > Select Table	Ctrl+A
Move to the Next Cell*	Tab
Move to the Previous Cell*	Shift+Tab
Table > Merge Cells	Ctrl+Alt+M
Table > Split Cell	Ctrl+Alt+S
Table > Insert Row	Ctrl+M
Table > Insert Column	Ctrl+Shift+A
Table > Delete Row	Ctrl+Shift+M
Table > Delete Column	Ctrl+Shift+-
Table > Increase Column Span	Ctrl+Shift+]
Table > Decrease Column Span	Ctrl+Shift+[
Timeline > Add Object to Timeline	Ctrl+Alt+Shift+T

*Command is not included in the Modify Menu.

TEXT MENU

Command	Shortcut
Indent	Ctrl+Alt+]
Outdent	Ctrl+Alt+[
Paragraph Format > None	Ctrl+0
Paragraph Format > Paragraph	Ctrl+Shift+P
Paragraph Format > Heading 1	Ctrl+1
Paragraph Format > Heading 2	Ctrl+2
Paragraph Format > Heading 3	Ctrl+3
Paragraph Format > Heading 4	Ctrl+4
Paragraph Format > Heading 5	Ctrl+5
Paragraph Format > Heading 6	Ctrl+6
Align > Left	Ctrl+Shift+Alt+L
Align > Center	Ctrl+Shift+Alt+C
Align > Right	Ctrl+Shift+Alt+R
Align > Justify	Crt+Shit+J
Bold	Ctrl+B
Italic	Ctrl+I
CSS > Styles > Edit Style Sheet	Ctrl+Shift+E
Check Spelling	Shift+F7

COMMANDS MENU

Command	Shortcut
Start Recording	Ctrl+Shift+X

SITE MENU

Command	Shortcut
Site Files	F8
Site Map	Alt+F8
Get	Ctrl+Shift+D
Check Out	Ctrl+Shift+Alt+D
Put	Ctrl+Shift+U
Check In	Ctrl+Shift+Alt+U

WINDOW MENU

Command	Shortcut
Inserts	Ctrl+F2
Properties	Ctrl+F3
Answers	Alt+F1
CSS Styles	Shift+F11
HTML Styles	Ctrl+F11
Behaviors	Shift+F3
Snippets	Shift+F9
Reference	Shift+F1
Databases	Ctrl+Shift+F10
Bindings	Ctrl+F10
Served Behaviors	Ctrl+F9
Components	Ctrl+F7
Site	F8
Assets	F11
Hide/Show Panels	F4
Results > Search	Ctrl+Shift+F
Results > Validation	Ctrl+Shift+F7
Results > Target Browser Check	Ctrl+Shift+F8
Results > Link Checker	Ctrl+Shift+F9
Results > Site Reports	Ctrl+Shift+F11
Results > FTP Log	Ctrl+Shift+F12
Results > Server Debug	Ctrl+Shift+F5
Others > Server Debug	F10
Others > Frames	Shift+F2
Others > History	Shift+F10
Others > Layers	F2
Others > Sitespring	F7
Others > Timelines	Alt+F9

HELP MENU

Command	Shortcut
Using Dreamweaver	F1
Using ColdFusion	Ctrl+F1
Reference	Shift+F1

SITE PANEL FILE MENU

Command	Shortcut
New File	Ctrl+Shift+N
New Folder	Ctrl+Shift+Alt+N
Rename	F2
Delete	Del
Check Links	Shift+F8
Exit	Ctrl+Q

SITE PANEL EDIT MENU

Command	Shortcut
Cut	Ctrl+X
Copy	Ctrl+C
Paste	Ctrl+V
Duplicate	Ctrl+D
Select All	Ctrl+A

SITE WINDOW VIEW MENU

Command	Shortcut
Refresh	F5
Show/Hide Link	Ctrl+Shift+Y
View as Root	Ctrl+Shift+R
Show Page Titles	Ctrl+Shift+T
Site Files	F8
Site Map	Alt+F8

SITE WINDOW SITE MENU

Command	Shortcut
Connect/Disconnect	Ctrl+Shift+Alt+F5
Get	Ctrl+Shift+D
Checkout	Ctrl+Shift+Alt+D
Put	Ctrl+Shift+U
Check In	Ctrl+Shift+Alt+U
Check Links Sitewide	Ctrl+F8
Link to New File	Ctrl+Shift+N
Link to Existing File	Ctrl+Shift+K
Change Link	Ctrl+L
Remove Link	Ctrl+Shift+L

CODE EDITING SHORTCUTS

Command	Shortcut
Select Parent Tag	Ctrl+Shift+[
Select Child	Ctrl+Shift+]
Balance Braces	Ctrl+'
Select All	Ctrl+A
Bold	Ctrl+B
Italic	Ctrl+I
Copy	Ctrl+C
Find and Replace	Ctrl+F
Find Next	F3
Paste	Ctrl+V
Cut	Ctrl+X
Redo	Ctrl+Y
Undo	Ctrl+Z
Switch to Document	Ctrl+`
Toggle Breakpoint	Ctrl+Alt+B
Character Select Left	Shift+Left
Character Select Right	Shift+Right
Delete Word Left	Ctrl+Backspace
Delete Word Right	Ctrl+Del
Select Line Up	Shift+Up
Select Line Down	Shift+Down
Move to Page Up	Page Up
Move to Page Down	Page Down
Select to Page Up	Shift+Page Up
Select to Page Down	Shift+Page Down
Move Word Left	Ctrl+Left
Move Word Right	Ctrl+Right
Select Word Left	Ctrl+Shift+Left
Select Word Right	Ctrl+Shift+Right
Move to Start of Line	Home
Move to End of Line	End
Select to Start of Line	Shift+Home
Select to End of Line	Shift+End
Move to Top of File	Ctrl+Home
Move to End of File	Ctrl+End
Select to Start of File	Ctrl+Shift+Home
Select to End of File	Ctrl+Shift+End
Snippets	Shift+F9

540

index

purpose of, 450–451
  recording path of, 494–496
  resizing, 458–459, 463, 488, 504
  setting background color for, 462
  using grids/rulers to place, 469–472
Layout group, 11
Layout View, 108–109, 111, 116
.lbi extension, 256
leading, 422
left parameter, 374
lesson files
  accessibility and testing, 235
  adding user interactivity, 162
  animating with timelines, 481
  creating forms, 335
  creating frames, 308
  creating layers, 451
  creating links, 89
  Dreamweaver MX basics, 7
  editing code, 365
  elements of page design, 107
  extending Dreamweaver, 511
  managing site, 191
  using Find and Replace, 427
  using libraries, 251
  using style sheets, 399
  using templates, 276
  working with graphics, 61
lessons, 1–5
  content/organization of, 1–2
  goals/objectives for, 4
  knowledge/skills required for, 3
  minimum system requirements, 4–5
LF option, 35
Library folder, 256, 262
library items, 250–273
  creating, 252–257
  modifying, 262–263, 268–272
  naming, 257
  placing on page, 257–260
  purpose of, 250–251
  recreating, 260–261
  setting properties for, 259
  updating references to, 264–265
  using behaviors in, 265–272
Library panel, 252, 258, 268
Life Along the Faultline Web site,
  231–232
lighthouse icons, 508
"Lights of the Coast" project, 2, 6, 16
line breaks, 36, 37, 66, 135
line-feed character, 34
Link text field, Property inspector, 92, 165

links, 88–105
  components of, 88
  controlling frame content with,
    328–329
  creating/inserting, 91–104, 385–387
  displaying status-bar message for,
    176–177
  how they work, 88–89
  setting states for, 413
  specifying colors for, 90–91, 93
  targeting, 95–96, 328–329
  testing, 242–243
  using styles to change appearance of,
    412–414
List/Menu icon/command, 351
List Properties dialog box, 38–40
List Values dialog box, 352, 353
lists, 38–42
  creating, 38–41
  nesting, 41–42
  types of, 38
  using in forms, 351–353
Load Query icon, 441, 442
Local Files pane, 192, 194
Local/Network option, 213, 216
local root folder, 15–16
local site, 15–22, 216–220
Location Toolbar attributes, 181
log, file transfer, 218
looping, 487
low-source images, 65

M

M Superscript 2 extension, 516
Macintosh
  and ASCII text files, 34
  changing orientation of Insert bar on,
    12
  and font sizes, 43
  keyboard shortcuts, 532–535
  and layer dimensions, 488
  system requirements, 4–5
  workspace options, 8
Macintosh Runtime for Java, 5
Macromedia
  Dreamweaver MX (*See* Dreamweaver
    MX)
  Extension Manager, 514–515
  Training from the Source series, 3
mailto: links, 92, 358–359, 387
Make Document XHTML Compliant
  option, 26
management tools, 190. *See also*
  Site window

map icon, 101
Map View, 203, 206
maps. *See* image maps; site maps
margins, 150
Match Case option, 429, 434, 447
MDAC, 5
memory issues, 5, 96
Menu Bar attributes, 181
menu commands. *See* commands
menus. *See also* specific menus
  creating jump, 360–362
  creating pop-up, 182–188
  using in forms, 351–353, 360–362
Merge Cells command, 133
meta tags, 178, 376–378
Microsoft
  Data Access Components, 5
  Excel, 121
  Windows (*See* Windows)
  Word, 34, 121, 394–395
Middle alignment, 78
minus sign (–) button, 168, 184
Modify menu, 534
monitors, 4, 5, 147
movies. *See* QuickTime movies
MRJ, 5
.mxp extension, 515
My Computer, 192, 196

N

name variations, finding/replacing,
  446–447
named anchors, 96–100
naming
  anchors, 97, 98, 99
  browser windows, 182
  buttons, 80, 355
  files, 27
  folders, 16, 27, 198
  forms, 337
  frames, 316, 317
  image maps, 100–101
  images, 67, 164, 167, 497
  layers, 456–457
  library items, 257
  panel groups, 13
  rollovers, 164, 167
  sites, 17
  templates, 277
navigation, breadcrumb, 205, 521
navigation bars, 322–326
Navigation Toolbar attributes, 181
Navigator. *See* Netscape Navigator

Macromedia Tech Support: http://www.macromedia.com/support

LICENSING AGREEMENT

The information in this book is for informational use only and is subject to change without notice. Macromedia, Inc., and Macromedia Press assume no responsibility for errors or inaccuracies that may appear in this book. The software described in the book is furnished under license and may be used or copied only in accordance with terms of the license.

The software files on the CD-ROM included here are copyrighted by Macromedia, Inc. You have the non-exclusive right to use these programs and files. You may use them on one computer at a time. You may not transfer the files from one computer to another over a network. You may transfer the files onto a single hard disk so long as you can prove ownership of the original CD-ROM.

You may not reverse engineer, decompile, or disassemble the software. You may not modify or translate the software or distribute copies of the software without the written consent of Macromedia, Inc.

Opening the disc package means you accept the licensing agreement. For installation instructions, see the ReadMe file on the CD-ROM.